*Literary Uses of Typology*

EARL MINER, *EDITOR*

# LITERARY USES OF TYPOLOGY

from the Late Middle Ages
to the Present

PRINCETON UNIVERSITY
PRESS

Published by Princeton University Press, Princeton, New Jersey
In the United Kingdom: Princeton University Press, Guildford, Surrey

Library of Congress Cataloging in Publication Data will be
found on the last printed page of this book

Publication of this book has been aided by a grant from the
Paul Mellon Fund of Princeton University Press

Printed in the United States of America
by Princeton University Press, Princeton, New Jersey

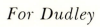

*For Dudley*

# Contents

# CONTENTS

# PREFACE

CHRISTIAN typology originated in the belief that Jesus Christ fulfilled certain Jewish prophecies, especially those of a Messiah. It therefore provided Christians from the beginning with a means of accommodating to Christian belief the Scriptures of the Jews. An "Old Testament" was related to a "New Testament" by virtue of "old" types, shadows, and figures that the Christian believer found fulfilled in Christ and other "new" elements in Christianity. Christians believed that the Jewish prophets had instructed the Jews in the Christian message, "informing them," as Milton said, "by types / And shadows." To early Christians, typological interpretation was involved in prophecy, moral allegory, and eschatology. It has never proved easy to keep these matters wholly separate (as the epistle to the Hebrews shows), and theologians have long quarreled over the use of typological and other interpretations of the Bible. The example of Milton shows that Christian artists have also drawn on these interpretive systems in numerous ways to embody the verities of Christian belief in their art. Typology and moral allegory are not everywhere to be found in the writings by authors from Prudentius to the present, but they are often enough found to make it necessary for literary interpreters to be able to recognize and distinguish them. For obvious reasons, students of literature have lagged behind theologians in their attention to such matters.

In an effort to examine the literary uses of typology, the Department of English at Princeton sponsored a two-day seminar in April, 1974. The major emphases fell on literary practice, especially such practice in England and America. The results of that effort appear in this book, the chapters of which represent revised versions of the papers presented to the seminar. Such was the discussion at our gathering that it was felt that the papers should be revised to reflect the exchange of information and then be edited with a Preface and an Afterword for a wider audience. We felt that no study existed that dealt with figuralism and typology over such a considerable period. We could well use, in the first place, a very detailed survey of the whole subject in the European literatures from late classical times to the present. And we also require authoritative studies of principal kinds of typological uses by major writers (not to mention also a survey of the vicissitudes of tropology in literary usage). It will be clear that this book seeks to meet the second need rather than the first. Long as it is, this study has some omissions, and given any recognition of practical concerns the gaps will be seen to be inevitable. This book rests instead on its representative character—its range of opinion, its choice of periods and literatures, and its selection of authors. We hope that it will be judged for what it has done rather than for what it has not done, and that its example will be both spur and rein for others in the same course.

The chapters included vary greatly in method as well as subject. Yet they show two repeated concerns. One amounts almost to a compulsion to clarify what typology, in its "strict sense," may mean. The other holds that, like theological exegesis itself, literary practice commonly adapts the strict sense to freer ends. The nature of the adaptation involves a response by a writer to the literary as well as religious understanding possible to a given age. It would be a pleasure to follow these two emphases in a summary of each chapter, but such enjoyment more properly belongs to the reader than to the editor of this book. It may not be over-officious, however, to refer to issues that might be overlooked in three of the essays appearing here.

In the third chapter Thomas P. Roche is concerned to show that renaissance epic, and particularly Tasso's *Gerusalemma liberata*, is rich in transactions between what St. Paul termed letter and spirit (2 Corinthians 3: 6). Clearly the critic of Tasso faces an interpretive problem. Much concern has been devoted to the two versions of the poem, and problems have been found in the poet's own allegorical interpretation. There is also the story of the mad poet. Roche seeks to make his way through these matters by showing that the poem concerns "the many ways in which human life participates in the divine, either directly or by analogy." He shows that critics have come to difficult ends on "the horns of the dilemma of Tasso's apparent schizophrenia between sensuousness and religious faith." In order to demonstrate "how the sensuous detail of the poem enables us to come to the Christian meanings," Roche pays close attention to "the ancient Christian metaphors and schemes of thought that inform the narrative." In other words, he is concerned to give a Christian interpretation of a Christian poem by using the allegory provided by the poet.

It might be said that such an interpretation does not involve typology in the sense of Old Testament types fulfilled in New Testament antitypes, as of the unburnt bush seen by Moses as a type of the Virgin Mary, and Roche himself has something to say about that. Moreover, as the chapters of this book show, the realm of religious figuralism and of typology itself is larger than such standard instances as that bush. Perhaps what Roche is getting at can be approached with evidence of another kind, a source familiar to Roman Catholics, the marriage service and nuptial mass. After the blessing in the service, there is the following prayer.

> In nomine Patris, et Filii, et Spiritus Sancti. Amen.
> Confirma hoc, Deus, quod operatus es in nobis.
> A templo sancto Tuo quod est in Jerusalem.

> (In the name of the Father and of the Son and of
>     the Holy Ghost. Amen.
> Confirm, O God, that which Thou hast wrought in
>     us.
> From Thy holy temple, which is in Jerusalem.)

The nuptial mass begins with the Deus Israel, and the Tract is Psalm 127: 4–6, which is often echoed elsewhere in the mass.

Ecce sic benedicetur omnis homo, qui timet Dominum. benedicat tibi Dominus ex Sion: et videas bona Jerusalem omnibus diebus vitae tuae. et videas filios filiorum tuorum: pax super Israel.

(Behold, thus shall the man be blessed that feareth the Lord. May the Lord bless thee out of Sion: and mayest thou see good things of Jerusalem all the days of thy life. And mayest thou see thy children's children: peace upon Israel.) [F. X. Lasance, *The New Roman Missal* (New York, 1937), pp. 14466 ff.]

In these passages from divine service we discover the Christian Zion, the Christian Jerusalem, and the Christian Israel, for the Psalm gives us the words of Christ: "David is both a prophet and a type of Jesus Christ, and the 'prayer of David' is therefore also the *Prayer of Jesus Christ*" (*ibid.*, p. 9). The Jerusalem for which Roche argues is and is not this Jerusalem. In Tasso's poem it is not to him exactly the Christian Jerusalem, because it there exists in a fiction. At the same time, it is the Christian Jerusalem—and this is Roche's chief point—in the sense that it and much else in the poem can be read tropologically, as moral allegory applied to the lives of believers. The various Jerusalems of divine service and of literature may be read at times literally or fictionally, typologically or tropologically. We may read these excerpts, then, to tell us what we should do (tropologically) or to tell us what we should believe (typologically). For although none of the Old Testament detail in the marriage service and mass makes sense without a typological presumption, it is also possible to read it as tropology with the lesson that we should fear God and learn to enjoy the fruits of his holy city. In other words, Roche is arguing for the relatively greater importance of tropology over typology in interpreting Tasso. The attentive Christian reader is expected to apply figurally or spiritually the numerous sites and episodes of the poem.

In theory at least there should be no need to argue the relative merits of tropology or typology when both are operative, as in the nuptial mass. In practice, however, it may make a difference if prophecy is involved and if we think that this rather than that symbolic system affords us the central meaning of a poem, as we can see in the old debates as to the relative importance of moral as against historical allegory in *The Faerie Queene*. (This general issue is one I discuss again in the Afterword.)

The connections between symbolic systems are as common in literature as in divinity, but they need not involve typology and tropology. In the fifth chapter Steven N. Zwicker addresses himself to a quite distinct set of issues that requires elucidation in the generations "from Marvell to Pope." Zwicker well shows the frequent human tendency to associate two or more major human concerns in the pursuit of yet another. The principle is simple enough: things thought sufficiently important tend to become associated, compared, or exchanged with each other. So it is that a "political typology" can emerge from "an understanding of history as prophecy" when people believe in the "continuous revelation of God's power and providence." In times of real crisis such as during the overturns of state in the middle of the sixteenth century and again of the seventeenth century, people would naturally turn to a source of religious assurance like the Bible for hopeful understanding of political stress. They would read "Scripture in public and civic terms." Such accommodation naturally enough would become a concern of poets as well, so that literature took on a politicized typology or a figural politics.

The wonder would be if such things did not occur, and not much is to be gained by our complaining that people in another age sullied the pure exegetical cloth of typology. Values have always merged in the same way. It may be granted, however, that once it becomes too easy to relate typology to non-religious matters some crisis will occur. Either there will be some reaction to extended applications in favor of stricter uses, or what Zwicker terms "the figural mode" will be in some danger. In fact he shows that signs of serious strain became evident toward the end of the seventeenth century in England. He concedes that perfectly orthodox handling of typology could continue with divines for many decades. And he certainly shows that a poet of Pope's stature could use a secularized version of typology with great effect. But Zwicker manages to emphasize a shift from the growth of typological usage to a decline from overuse. Most of the essays that follow his are concerned with the increasingly adaptive nature of typology, and his essay therefore marks a crucial stage in the history of English usage.

American practice differed somewhat in timing, and in its early stages it illuminates certain matters particularly clearly. For such reason Emory Elliott's chapter deserves a few words of comment. His previous work on such English authors as Donne and Milton insures that he does not think in narrowly colonial terms. Yet only he and Karlfried Froehlich among the authors of these chapters are involved with writings by divines. The writers with whom Elliott is concerned are New England preachers, not poets and novelists. Those preachers were very much Protestants in their devotion to the Word of God, and they were very much committed to using "typology in expressing the continuity between contemporary affairs and biblical precedents." The situation resembles that described by Steven Zwicker but really is quite different. Zwicker describes the use by poets of typology to adapted and secularized ends. Elliott's preachers certainly meddled in politics and other aspects of the daily lives of their congregations. But when they did so they presumed that religion determined all, that without it life was meaningless. For this reason the very nature of God as revealed to successive generations, as to that earlier chosen people, Israel, involved an interpretation of contemporary events that was equally an interpretation of the Bible. People from other countries often remark, and not always admiringly, on the way in which such absorbed zeal has continued in American life. Much of what is enduring in American assumptions begins with Elliott's Puritan preachers—even if the chapters that follow his show how radical the changes were to be in other respects.

In fact, Elliott is equally concerned to emphasize change

"from Father to Son." As he points out, there was from the outset a serious tension between official Puritan hermeneutics, which "insisted upon the strict and literal interpretation of the Old Testament," and a strong inclination "to interpret modern historical events as fulfillments of the scriptural prophecies." Such a tension led to the shifts Elliott recounts, and these involve nothing less than moments of near despair and other moments bright with hope. In either instance divines committed to "strict and literal interpretation" found prophecy and proof in the Bible and so communicated a changing revelation to their flocks. Such shifts within what is sometimes called a theocratic society are quite remarkable for the speed with which they occur. Their quickness implies a potential for yet more radical changes, in attitude as well as in writing, expressive of religious views. By focusing on a fairly short period of New England divinity, Elliott isolates a special case. As the next two chapters well show, that special case cast a long shadow on American literature.

These three chapters discuss many more topics than I have isolated, and their analysis of individual examples gives them much more life than my hasty description allows. Some stress is owed to both the rich detail and the importance of the issues I have abstracted from complex and consecutive discussions. The aim of a preface can be only a modest one at best, and it is enough if this one has suggested that in the rich variety of evidence included in the chapters are issues of importance to our understanding of writers over the centuries. It is a long journey in time and experience from Hollander's discussion of Prudentius in the first chapter to Ziolkowski's of modern writers in the eleventh. We may be inclined to think that the parodic use of typology by contemporary writers such as Vonnegut is the last tribute payable to orthodox typology before it expires. We students of typology in literature must, however, eschew prophecy—particularly in prefaces and conclusions.

November, 1974                                          E. M.

# CONTRIBUTORS

EMORY ELLIOTT is Assistant Professor of English at Princeton. He is the author of studies of seventeenth-century English poets and of colonial American writers. His *Power and the Pulpit in Puritan New England* has recently been published by Princeton University Press.

KARLFRIED FROEHLICH is Professor of the History of the Early and Medieval Church at Princeton Theological Seminary. Among his studies are *Formen der Auslegung von Matth. 16, 13–18 im lateinischen Mittelalter* (1963) and an edition, *Oscar Cullman: Vorträge und Aufsätze, 1925–1962* (1966). He is also co-author of *Understanding the New Testament* (3rd ed., 1973).

ROBERT HOLLANDER is Professor in European Literature at Princeton and the author of *Allegory in Dante's Commedia* (1969) as well as other studies of Dante. He has recently completed a monograph on Boccaccio's *Opere minori in volgare* and a study of Dante's relation to the Trecento argument concerning the truthfulness of poetry.

KARL KELLER is Professor of American Literature at San Diego State University. He has written many studies of Puritan and later American literature. His *Example of Edward Taylor* (1975), is being followed by another book on Emily Dickinson.

PAUL J. KORSHIN, Associate Professor of English at the University of Pennsylvania, has written studies of seventeenth- and eighteenth-century literature. He has edited *Studies in Change and Revolution, 1640-1800* (1972), has written *From Concord to Dissent: Major Themes in English Poetic Theory, 1640–1700* (1973), and is now completing a study entitled *Eighteenth-Century Typologies: Studies in the Figural Tradition*.

BARBARA KIEFER LEWALSKI is Professor of English at Brown University. Her books include *Milton's Brief Epic: The*

*Genre, Meaning and Art of Paradise Regained* (1966) and *Donne's Anniversaries and the Poetry of Praise* (1973). She has also written on other Renaissance topics and has edited, with Andrew Sabol, a collection of seventeenth-century poetry.

GEORGE P. LANDOW is Associate Professor of English at Brown. Among a number of studies expressing his interests in art, literature, and aesthetics is his book, *Aesthetic and Critical Theories of John Ruskin* (1971). He is completing another book on William Holman Hunt and pre-Raphaelite symbolism.

MASON I. LOWANCE is Associate Professor of English at the University of Massachusetts, Amherst. He has edited Samuel Mather's *Figures or Types of the Old Testament Opened and Explained* (1969) and has written *Increase Mather: A Critical Biography* (1974). At present he is bringing to completion a book, with Jesper Rosenmeier, *The Language of Canaan: Metaphor in American Literature from 1620 to 1776.*

THOMAS P. ROCHE, JR., Professor of English at Princeton, is author of *The Kindly Flame: A Study of the Third and Fourth Books of Spenser's Faerie Queene* (1964) in addition to studies of Renaissance sonnet sequences. He has also edited two books of essays by Rosemond Tuve: *Allegorical Imagery* (1966) and *Spenser, Herbert, Milton* (1970). He has finished an annotated edition of *The Faerie Queene* (Penguin) and is completing a study of Petrarch and English sonnet sequences.

THEODORE ZIOLKOWSKI is Class of 1900 Professor of Modern Languages and Chairman of Germanics at Princeton. Among his studies written in English and German there are the following: *Hermann Broch* (1964); *The Novels of Hermann Hesse* (1965); *Hermann Hesse* (1966); *Dimensions of the Modern Novel* (1969); and *Fictional Transformations of Jesus* (1972).

*xviii*

STEVEN N. ZWICKER is Associate Professor of English at Washington University, St. Louis. In addition to shorter studies of Dryden and Marvell, he has published *Dryden's Political Poetry: The Typology of King and Nation* (1972). He is presently engaged in study of literary and artistic iconography.

The editor, EARL MINER, is Townsend Martin Class of 1917 Professor of English and Comparative Literature at Princeton and also teaches classical Japanese literature. He recently completed a three-volume study of seventeenth-century English poetry and has in hand a book on classical Japanese literature.

# ACKNOWLEDGMENTS

Both as convener of our conference and as editor of the results I must thank above all the authors of the following chapters. They have entered into the spirit of things by making many changes based on our discussions, and they have put up with a good deal of editorial annoying. In editing the chapters, I have added some cross references in square brackets and an Afterword by way of a more general setting.

We whose names appear here in print owe much to the other participants. D. W. Robertson, Jr., led the medieval section. Sacvan Bercovitch led the session of Americanists, and Horton W. Davies that of the modernists. The last-named and Karlfried Froehlich were the two divines present. D. W. Robertson hardly needs any characterization for his interest in matters such as those involved in this book. Nor does Sacvan Bercovitch, except to say that the invaluable bibliography he compiled for his *Typology and Early American Literature* (Amherst, 1972) ranges so widely as to serve in effect for this book as well. I chaired the session on the Renaissance and seventeenth century and have taken the liberty of reordering some of the papers to make a more coherent succession for a book.

I wish to thank E.D.H. Johnson for his active support of our conference. For important suggestions about possible participants I am grateful to Sacvan Bercovitch, John V. Fleming, Barbara K. Lewalski, A. Walton Litz, and Thomas P. Roche. We have been extremely fortunate in the two readers of our manuscript, Florence Sandler and Joseph A. Wittreich, Jr. Both combined warm sympathy with cogent criticism. Both have sustained us in the last stage of readying the manuscript for press. For her work at a somewhat prior stage and in seeing this into decent order for print, Mrs. Arthur Sherwood deserves the admiration and gratitude of us all. As she should know better than anyone else, this book is much the better for her intelligent care.

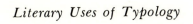

*Literary Uses of Typology*

# TYPOLOGY AND SECULAR LITERATURE:
## SOME MEDIEVAL PROBLEMS AND EXAMPLES

CRITICS of medieval literature have recently been increasingly involved in the importation of biblical typology to the study of secular literature. Although I am not in the best position to admit my own discomfort with some of the resulting critical procedures, I am glad to see that others are beginning to make their discomfort heard.[1] Put in the simplest terms, the problem has evolved from a total or at least near-total neglect of the typological aspects of secular works to a current situation in which the temptation to claim typology as a meaningful critical lens has perhaps, though not exhausting or even fulfilling the possibilities of such investigation, on occasion resulted in meaningless claims of the "typological" nature, or structure, or meaning of secular works. Those of us who work in the "typological mode" are probably increasingly eager to put our investigations into a more ordered form—witness our conference. At the least, we should like to be able to identify sure and certain cases of secular borrowing of this single aspect of biblical exegesis, to assert with at least a minimum of confidence that a given literary phenomenon is "typological" rather than anything else. The wish, it seems to me, is more readily fulfilled than the deed.

At the outset we should be willing to admit that two basic problems will always bedevil us. First, our authors were not always mindful of the sorts of distinctions we claim for them. To lodge this difficulty where it most likely belongs, we must say that writers are not always or even very often as literarily self-conscious as we their critics would like

---

[1] E.g., Hartmut Hoefer, *Typologie im Mittelalter* (Göppingen, 1971), which perhaps goes too far in denying the applicability of exegetical techniques derived from biblical typology to secular writings.

them to be. Further, though critics are often extremely imprecise, it is also true that writers are subject to the same failing. If we can say with reasonable certainty that some medieval writers "used typology" in secular works, we should also admit that they did not all understand literary adaptations of typology in more than approximately similar ways. Second, and even more damaging, is our own imprecision. At the very least we bring to distant phenomena inevitable distortions of perspective; at the worst we import sloppiness and confusion. Problems of this kind assault all critical enterprises, but perhaps it is worth being reminded of them—even if schematically—now that we have a new machine in which to jumble our inheritance of the past.

# I

*A tentative morphology of secular*
*medieval literary adaptations of typology*

A. NATURAL TYPOLOGY

Let me begin with a remark made some years ago by Gerhard von Rad, which steps back from scriptural exegesis to consider typology as a natural form of all human thought:

> What we are accustomed to understand under the heading of typology is, in a broad sense, by no means a specifically theological concern or, indeed, a peculiarity of ancient Oriental thought. Rather, typological thinking is an elementary function of all human thought and interpretation. . . . And, above all, without this interpretive, analogical sort of thinking there would be no poetry. The poet goes ceaselessly to and fro; he sees the often insignificant, obvious things and recognizes in them ultimate value. In the movements of the elements, the passing of the years and the days, in the most elementary relationships of man with man, in simple mechanical performances—in everything regularity reveals itself, in which the smallest as well as the greatest things participate.[2]

[2] "Typological Interpretation of the Old Testament," tr. John Bright, in *Essays in Old Testament Hermeneutics*, ed. Claus Westermann (Richmond, Va., 1963), pp. 17–39.

One thing seems clear here. Whatever the merit of this way of thinking about the roots of what we might call "the typological consciousness," it tends to make a conscious and highly developed system of thinking, like Christian typology, a sub-category of an independent kind of human awareness. The human perception of events that seem to occur in a pattern in time has given rise to various theories or doctrines of recurrence. We live—all of us do—with some kind of awareness of recurrence. However, it does little good to confound such theories of recurrence with Christian typology. They may in fact "explain" the "deeper structure" of typological thought. However, to thinkers like Paul, to Augustine, or even to Erasmus, von Rad's formulation would have seemed valueless because it fails to account for the unique and unparalleled nature of Christian exegesis. In the critical deliberations of literary students of Christian typology, natural typology should be kept as clearly as possible to one side. Not because its tenets are wrong, but because they are inapplicable.

B. HISTORICAL RECURRENCE

Both life and literature afford us examples of attempts to create artificial and elaborate correspondences between a past person or event and a present one. These may be undertaken by (among others) rulers, or painters, or priests, or poets, and are undertaken in order to guarantee the authority or desirability either of themselves or of those they portray. (They may also be undertaken in order to undermine authority or to cause distaste.) In all cases a fairly elaborate demonstration is brought to bear in order to establish the credentials of the newcomer. It is not enough to compare him (or it) to notable precursors. For, though topographical differences may exist, what is asserted is that $y$ is the continuation of, the direct inheritor of the essential characteristics of, $x$. This kind of comparing is clearly separable from "natural typology" in a number of respects. The most important of these is that both $x$ and $y$ are highly charged with some kind of significance, different from all others, and the focus of a unique historical process. If $y$ fulfills or continues $x$, it does so not as the sun comes back in the morning or the leaves come back in the spring, but as a valued and unique person or event establishes itself (or is said to be established) as that which was promised or prophesied by a unique person or event in the past. Christian typology, it seems clear to me, developed as a particular and more highly articulated application of historical recurrence. But before turning to our ostensible subject I should like to spend a moment with Vergil.

D.L.M. Drew, in *The Allegory of the Aeneid*, was, I believe, the first modern Virgilian to appreciate what might seem to us a "typological" structure in *The Aeneid*. He did so without benefit of clergy: "It is one of [Virgil's] methods to blend together events and scenes of different dates . . . , historical facts which, if separated in their actual occurrence by time, are still the steps of one progression."[3] Drew understood that a good deal of Virgilian effort went into the creation of an Aeneas who would clearly serve as a worthy "prefiguration" (the word is mine, not Drew's) of the great Augustus. In short, it would not be a dreadful breach of our post-Auerbachian literary language to say that for Drew *Aeneas Augusti figura est*. After Drew, many modern Virgilians do in fact understand that many of the scenes and actions of *The Aeneid* are handled in such a way as to show foreshadowings of Augustan history. It seems to me that if natural typology has little relevance to our deliberations, historical recurrence, at least as it is employed by Virgil, has a great deal in common with Christian typology. Virgil's operative technique is to create a "historical" Aeneas whose very deeds look forward to and sacramentalize the current deeds of Augustus. In this sense Augustans read of Aeneas' "defeat" of Dido as the promise of Augustus' defeat of Cleopatra at Actium. The process is very like that by which Christians found a *mysterium* that revealed the eventual coming of Jesus in such Old Testament scenes as Isaac's ascent of a hill encumbered by the wood which was to serve

---

[3] Drew, *The Allegory of the Aeneid* (Oxford, 1927), p. 4.

as the agency of his sacrifice, or Jonah's extraordinary three days and nights in the belly of the great fish. Historical recurrence thus closely approximates Christian typology. Before I say something about the latter, let me try to make our task more difficult and our morphology more complete.

## C. DECORATIVE TYPOLOGY

If, as no doubt occurred thousands of times in the recent past, enthusiasts for the New York Yankees (the very name of their city conforms to some kind of "typological" awareness) debated whether or not Mickey Mantle was the new Joe DiMaggio, we should not, it seems to me, either credit or blame them for being typologists.[4] The example is chosen lightly, but the intent is serious. Let me continue with two medieval examples that pose a similar problem. In an early passage of his Letter to Cangrande, Dante praises his former protector in the following double simile: "As the Queen of the South made for Jerusalem, as Pallas Athena made for Helicon, so sought I Verona." To the modern reader innocent of the ways of typology the passage may seem merely otiose.[5] To one versed in the types, then the praise may seem fulsome, the passage's source (in Matthew 12: 41-42, where Jonah is understood to have been a type of Christ) and language are unmistakably typological. It presents, indeed, a small and perfect example of secular use of typological procedures drawn from the Bible. Further, it is especially Dantesque in that it joins a moment from biblical history with one from pagan myth, and treats the two together as "historical" precedents of the current situation. But if this is typology, it is surely a forced and

[4] However, when J.-J. Rousseau, in the second book of his *Confessions*, refers to a clerk (whom he suspects of secretly coveting the married woman he himself covets) as "this new Aegisthus," the situation is less clear. Does the remark pertain to natural typology? I think not. But is it a refraction of historical recurrence, decorative typology, or Christian typology (*or* a conflation of some of these?)? It is difficult to say.

[5] So much so to Allen Gilbert that he cites this text as another indication that the Letter is ingenuine—"Did Dante Dedicate the *Paradiso* to Can Grande della Scala?," *Italica*, 43 (1966), 100–124.

perhaps even playful adaptation of the method, and may even depend for its effect upon Cangrande's recognition of the technique as well as of its exaggerated, even strained, employment.

Let me add a second and similar example. In a letter to Niccola Acciaiuoli in 1341, Boccaccio, like Dante intending to flatter, has this to say: "Niccola, if any trust may be placed in those who are miserable, I swear to you by my suffering soul that the departure of Trojan Aeneas was not a deeper sorrow to Carthaginian Dido than was yours to me . . . nor did Penelope long for Ulysses' return more than I longed for yours." Boccaccio's typological equation, whether it is heartfelt or playful, is perhaps more arresting than Dante's. For his referentiality is entirely pagan. Although it is possible to argue that no specifically Christian typological consideration lies behind Boccaccio's piece of business, I think the argument that what one observes here is the Christian method turned into decorative literary convention is the better one. For it is probably correct to assert that in many medieval secular writers typology is, if not a *forma mentis*, at least a minor habit of mind. Yet that does not require that the modern critic, coming upon such passages as these, should argue from them that the works containing them are therefore to be considered typological in nature. In short, I would argue that in both cases (and in many others) decorative typology is merely a trope, one that may or may not indicate a larger typological interest in a given work, but that in itself confers no typological status on anything outside itself.

D. CHRISTIAN TYPOLOGY

Again let me begin with an example—this time from modern literature.

> "Your excellency," [Lebedyev speaks] "have you read in the papers of the murder of the Zhemarin family?"
> "Yes," answered Myshkin.
> "Well, that's [pointing to his nephew, Doktorenko] the actual murderer of the Zhemarin family, there he is."

"What do you mean," said Myshkin.

"That is, allegorically speaking, the future second mur- derer of a future Zhemarin family, if such there be. He is preparing himself for it. . . ."

Everybody laughed.[6]

Here we have a pure and certain example of a literary use of Christian typology. Lebedyev, who likes to interpret the Apocalypse, is obviously an adept in typological thought. Until recently, it could be argued, not many literary critics understood exactly what Lebedyev meant by the word "al- legorically." But now that we do, can we say that *The Idiot* as a whole is in the typological mode?[7] Or must we say only that this particular passage and others like it in the novel are instances of decorative typology? I leave this question unanswered to return to our medievals.

The current assault on secular medieval literature comes far short of asserting that all medieval literary works are significantly typological. Among the individual works that have recently been discussed as being typological, whether in whole or in part, are the following: Prudentius' *Psychomachia*, Ambrose's hymns, the Old English *Advent*, Dante's *Vita Nuova* and *Commedia*, *The Pearl*, and *Piers Plowman*. In all these works, as well as in some others, what has come to be perceived is that typological exegesis corresponds only to the typological procedures of the work itself—at least that is the claim that is made. The work may "mean" roughly what we always thought it meant, but what we have now is a clearer sense of its precise mode of signifying—if not in its entirety, at least in its parts. And some of our sense of its meaning is as a result greatly changed. Perhaps one fault of typological criticism is that it tends to fail to point out the changing and even idiosyn- cratic quality of a given author's use of the technique. For instance, I would argue that this mode stands importantly

6 *The Idiot*, pt. 2, ch. 2 (tr. Constance Garnett, Modern Library).

7 I may mention my recent study. "The Apocalyptic Framework of Dostoevsky's *The Idiot*," *Mosaic*, 7 (1974), 123–139, which takes up, if indirectly, the problem of Myshkin as antitype of Christ.

behind Dante's *Vita Nuova*, is almost entirely absent from
the *Convivio*, and is importantly present in the text of the
*Commedia*. Further, I would want to distinguish Dante's
involvement with typology from that of his two great near-
contemporaries, Boccaccio and Petrarch, who hardly ever
evince typological concerns in their literary productions.
Some further thoughts along these lines will occupy the
concluding part of these remarks.

### E. "IMPROPER" CHRISTIAN TYPOLOGY

Here I do *not* join forces with those theologians who wish
to consider such figures as the priest Melchizedek or Abraham's three hundred eighteen servants as the forced (and
false) typological inventions of over-enthusiastic early
Fathers, reserving the status of "true types" only to those
Old Testament personages or events explicitly referred to
in the New Testament. I wish instead to deal with, or at
least indicate, some kinds of "improper" typology we find
in medieval secular literary texts. For, as I suggested at
the outset, writers are not bound to use a convention in
ways that we their critics would call logical or orthodox.
Two major cases in point occur whenever individuals or
events are said to be, or are treated as, types of an abstract
virtue or vice, or else to be significative of an allegorical
meaning that is similar to that found in interpretations of
parable. I offer examples from Dante.

In *Paradiso* 25, 31–33, Beatrice addresses St. James:
"Make hope resound unto this height; thou art able, who
didst figure it [*che . . . la figuri*] as many times as Christ
showed greatest favor to the three." The three are Peter,
James, and John, who were alone with Jesus at the Transfiguration, in Gethsemane, and at the raising of Jairus'
daughter. James, a historical (indeed biblical) character, is
said to have "figured hope." This is not "proper" typology.
But that it was practiced by Christian exegetes as well as
secular writers is made plain by Migne's "Index Alle-
goriarum."[8] In short, it is "orthodox improper typology."

[8] *Patrologia Latina*, 219.

An example of the second kind of "improper" typology referred to above may also be found in Dante, and also relates to the Transfiguration, which, according to *Convivio*, 2, 1, 5, signifies in its moral sense *not* that we should be transfigured within (I mean only to suggest an acceptable "orthodox" third sense), but that "in the most secret things we should have little company." Here a sacred text is being treated as though it were a fable that yields an allegorical meaning to the scrutinizer—not as historical event that looks back to a previous historical event (the transfiguration of Moses) and forward to its presence in the heart and mind of the contemporary Christian, and to its final validity in the Last Things or in the fulfillment of Eternity. Here again Dante is the child of the theologians of the Middle Ages, who were often tempted—especially in sermons—to use the third sense loosely rather than strictly, and as an occasion for fairly free moralizing. Of the four senses of medieval exegesis the third was the most fluid, probably because the other three were so evidently rooted in a particular time (the Old Testament, the Gospels, Eternity), and the moral or tropological sense, though it referred to the present, tended to ride upon a freer interpretive axis, the embattled soul of the believer.

There is another kind of "improper" typology; it is even more widespread among men of letters and is, for obvious reasons, peculiar to them. Here a fictional being or event is taken as prefigurative or postfigurative of an actual being or event.[9] We may think of Dante's use of mythical or fictional characters as "types" of himself—e.g., Theseus in *Inferno* 9, or Glaucus in *Paradiso* 1. Here the question involves not so much a logically "improper" manipulation of a technique of exegesis, one shared by theologians as well, but a literary importation of the technique. The critic is embarrassed by riches and the difficulty of distinguishing among them. We may think of cases as varied as that of

[9] Cf., for example, Robert Burlin's discussion of the at least approximate figuralism of the *Advent* poet's treatment of the Phoenix in *The Old English Advent* (New Haven, 1968).

Ulysses tied to the mast (who, for the wilder set of Ovid's interpreters, prefigured Christ on the Cross) and Boccaccio's Fiammetta (who, in several scenes of the *Elegia di Madonna Fiammetta*, "postfigures" Seneca's Phaedra). This varied form of literary adaptation of typology is probably the one that has widest currency in the Middle Ages.

This brief and surely incomplete morphology may serve to indicate the sort of distinctions we probably ought to be ready to entertain before setting to work on typological exegesis of medieval secular texts. If the morphology indicates some of our problems, I propose now to examine some examples of what seem to me clear cases of secular uses of Christian typology.

## II

*Typology in medieval secular literature:
some examples*

### A. PRUDENTIUS

Until recently Prudentius' *Psychomachia* was considered the very model of a kind of allegorizing that generally is understood to have little in common with typology. Such distinguished critics as C. S. Lewis have helped to keep hidden the typological element in Prudentius' most influential work.[10] Even Erich Auerbach, who did more to revive awareness of typology than any other literary critic, explicitly denies the presence of typological techniques in the *Psychomachia*.[11] Recently H. R. Jauss has established a better way of seeing the basic modes of signifying in that work.[12] And presently a young scholar, Macklin Smith, is revising for publication what I consider to be the finest treatment of Prudentius yet achieved. Let me briefly in-

[10] In *The Allegory of Love* (Oxford, 1936).

[11] Cf. "Figura," in *Scenes from the Drama of European Literature* (New York, 1959), p. 234n.

[12] Beginning with his "Form und Auffassung der Allegorie in der Tradition der *Psychomachia*," in *Medium Aevum Vivum: Festschrift für Walther Bulst*, ed. H. R. Jauss and D. Schaller (Heidelberg, 1960), pp. 179–206, and continuing in his more recent studies of medieval allegoresis.

dicate a small measure of the importance of typology in the *Psychomachia*. And let us admit that a poem which represents the war in the mind, replete with ladies doing battle, seems an unlikely place to find an entirely figural structure. The first line of the work should long ago have helped us to see what Prudentius was up to. It describes Abraham (when he was still Abram) as "Senex fidelis prima credendi via." The whole of Prudentius' *praefatio* is in fact an exercise in figural interpretation of Gen. 14–18. But let us examine that first line: Abram is the *first* "way of believing" which will be fulfilled in Christ. At the risk of sounding dogmatic, I would assert that any reading of the line which does not understand this typological inference has missed its most salient point. Summarizing the events of Genesis recounted in his *praefatio*, Prudentius says (lines 50–51): "Haec ad figuram praenotata est linea, / quam nostra recto vita resculpat pede" (translation in full below). Here he reveals the basic allegorical stance of the entire work: We move from the Old Testament *figurae* through Christ to a tropological sense in our present lives—which is where the "action" of this great conversionary poem takes place. If I am not believed, perhaps Prudentius may be:

This picture has been drawn beforehand to be a model for our life to trace out again with true measure, showing that we must watch in the armour of faithful hearts, and that every part of our body which is in captivity and enslaved to foul desire must be set free by gathering our forces at home; that we are abundantly rich in servants born in the house if we know through the mystic symbol [*figura . . . mystica*] what is the power of three hundred with eighteen more. Then Christ himself, who is the true priest, born of a Father unutterable and one, bringing food for the blessed victors, will enter the humble abode of the pure heart and give it the privilege of entertaining the Trinity; and then the Spirit, embracing in holy marriage the soul that has long been childless, will make her fertile by the seed eternal, and the dowered bride will become a mother late in life and give the Father's household a worthy heir.[13]

Just this much presentation and discussion of the *praefatio* should, it seems to me, make Prudentius' typological design clear. In the body of the poem we find that in each of the seven battle scenes that follow there is a historical (i.e., biblical) counterpart to the abstract virtues or vices:

FAITH: one thousand martyrs (Scripture and Church history)
CHASTITY: Judith, Mary; LIBIDO: Holofernes
PATIENCE: Job
PRIDE: Adam, Goliath; HOPE: David
SOBRIETY: Hebrews in the desert, David, Samuel, Jonathan
AVARICE: Judas, Achar
DISCORD: Belial

These characters do not function as "types" of Virtues and Vices (cf. the first kind of "improper" typology discussed above) so much as types of the Christian caught in the battle of conversion to whom Prudentius' poem is addressed. That is, in his susceptibility to pride, for instance, he is momentarily a new Adam or Goliath. This typological structure continues through the concluding "peace" episodes of the poem as well, until in the final moment of the work Christ, as Sapientia, comes to sit enthroned in the temple of the holy heart.[14] Although this is brief indeed as a discussion of typology in the *Psychomachia*, it will perhaps suffice to indicate the kind of restoration that is possible when we see this work in its typological perspective.

As a result of recent studies in typology, we now find our-

[13] Lines 50–68, tr. H. J. Thomson, Loeb Classical Library (Cambridge, Mass., 1949).
[14] Cf. Rev. 21. As in his *Dittochaeon*, Prudentius places this work also on the frame of universal history, beginning with Genesis and ending with Revelation. The study by Macklin Smith is now published: *Prudentius' Psychomachia–A Reexamination* (Princeton, 1976).

selves with two kinds of students of medieval allegory: the newer typologists alongside the older "wheat and chaff boys." (I need hardly point out that Professor D. W. Robertson, Jr., is probably the world's greatest practitioner in the second school.) What is the relationship between these two kinds of allegory? In the *Psychomachia* we find them both—typology and personification—in a blend that has not been even approximately understood until very recently. And let us admit that there is a problem in distinguishing not only two kinds of allegory (Dante's "allegory of the poets" and "allegory of the theologians" are labels that are as good as any), but two kinds of modes of detail: iconography and typology. If we find a lady tempting us in a garden in a medieval poem, when is she to be considered an antitype of Eve, and when are we merely to perceive that she should remind us of the moral significance of the Fall?[15] I think that there is no generally applicable answer to that question. On some occasions we shall be able to judge from the context that certain objects or actions in a scene seem iconographic without any figural intent or overtone (cf. the hilarious replay of the Edenic seduction in Boccaccio's First Tale of the Third Day, in which Masetto da Lamporecchio plays the willing Adam to a convent full of Eves). On others we may sense from the context that we are to see before us the new Eve—as when Dante shows us Matelda in the "actual" Garden of Eden as Eve before the Fall. Iconography plays a major role in both scenes. In one it reminds us of what Eve "means" morally. In another it insists—or so I would maintain—that we identify the literary character in such a way that her very existence seems dependent upon that of her model. The distinction is neither easily made nor easily agreed upon.

Let me pursue it a bit further. What I take to be the Robertsonian model for the structuring of significance in medieval texts is the threefold process presented by Hugh

15 [On the problems of distinguishing between "these two kinds of allegory," see Roche in chapter 3, concerning Tasso, and the reference to it in the Preface. Ed.]

of St. Victor in the *Didascalion*: We move from *letter* (the grammatical understanding of the words) to *sense* (the surface meaning of these words) to *sententia* (the doctrinal content of the words). In such an understanding of how texts mean there is no attempt to distinguish among differing kinds of literal senses. That is, the letter may be "historical" or "parabolic"—it does not matter, nor is the question considered. Now let me add that I think this Victorine process is frequently all that is needed in order to elucidate the significance of a given passage, or even of entire works. My own current study of the "minor" works of Boccaccio basically involves, in matters of interpretation, nothing more than this strategy. And it seems to be yielding interesting results, results that are in fact altogether Robertsonian. However, it is my contention that some medieval works, though they "make sense" when studied this way, make better sense when we see that they are organized with a further distinction in mind. In Dante we confront a poet who in fact promulgated such distinctions (in *Convivio* and the Letter to Cangrande).

B. DANTE

One of the reasons that the study of Dante is especially fruitful for this discussion, or argument, is that we can observe him working in both traditions. Let us examine his treatment of Marcia and Cato in his *Convivio*, a work which cares little or nothing for typology. In *Convivio* 4, 28, Dante discusses *lo senio* (which I have here gracelessly translated as "senility"), by which term he refers to the end of life, when one looks back gratefully down the road he has come. This is given expression by Lucan, in the second book of the *Pharsalia*:

> When he says that Marcia returned to Cato and besought him to take her back in her old age; for by Marcia is understood the noble soul. And we may comprehend this figure of speech in the following way: Marcia was a virgin, and in this state adolescence is signified; then she married Cato, and in this state youth is signified; then

she had children, by which are signified the virtues which are discussed above as being fitting to youth; and then she left Cato and married Hortensius, by which is signified that youth departs in favor of old age; she had children by Hortensius as well, by which are signified the virtues which are discussed above as being fitting to old age. Hortensius died, by which is signified the end of old age; and having become a widow—by which widowhood is signified senility—Marcia returned at the beginning of her widowhood to Cato, by which is signified that the noble soul at the beginning of its senility returns to God. And what earthly man was more worthy of signifying God than Cato? Surely none.

What Dante understands by the verb "to signify"[16] is exactly what Hugh of St. Victor and Professor Robertson understand—the result is *sententia*, and it does not in fact matter whether we start with historical or fictional persons or events. Indeed, here the historical Cato and Marcia are used to make an allegorical point; they could as well have been created by Guillaume de Lorris.

When we meet Cato in the first canto of *Purgatorio*, however, a great deal is changed. He is there presented, if only recently understood, as *figura Christi* (among other things, he has given up his life for the cause of liberty and is seen as one transfigured in words that are reminiscent of the Gospel account in Matthew 17). If in Dante's earlier discussion Cato was "worthy of signifying God," he in fact "signified God" because of his philological relationship to Marcia—she "signified" the noble soul, and since *that* in its "senility" returns to God, Cato "signified" God. But where is Marcia in *Purgatorio* 1? She is not there—she is in Limbo. It is not through her or through philological allegoresis that Cato is saved by Dante. Rather, he is perceived by the poet as having been, improbable as it may seem to us, *figura*

16 The next time Dante will use this verb, in *Purgatorio* 24, it will point to an entirely different kind of signification, one inspired (Dante's claim is oblique but clear enough) by the Holy Spirit.

*Christi* (in the *Pharsalia* of Lucan, which work he describes in the Letter to Cangrande as *scriptura paganorum*, Dante heard Cato say, "And let my blood ransom the people").[17] The difference, it seems to me, is enormous. I would go further. Until typological principles of interpretation were applied to Cato, Dante's exaltation of him left his readers baffled.[18]

In *Purgatorio* 2 Dante meets the freshly arrived soul of Casella, a musician whom he knew in Italy. Casella sings the second of Dante's Convivial Odes to the rapt pilgrims, Dante and Virgil. The vast majority of Dante's commentators find the song either "neutral" or positive in its moral implications. It helps, however, to examine it against Exodus 32: 18. There, when Moses comes down the mountain only to find the Israelites worshipping the golden calf and singing, he destroys the vain idol. That scene is the model for what Cato does in *Purgatorio* 2 when he scatters the pilgrims and sends them on up the mountain to better things.[19] The form of reference is best understood, it seems to me, as being a literary adaptation of biblical typology.[20]

[17] *Pharsalia*, 2, 312: "Hic redimat sanguis populos."

[18] This discussion is truncated, and I have not even referred to the first figural dimension of Cato in Canto 1, which is that of Moses. Cf. Robert Hollander, *Allegory in Dante's Commedia* (Princeton, 1969), pp. 124–126; Giuseppe Mazzotta, "Dante's Theology of History" (dissertation, Cornell University, 1969), ch. 1; Carol V. Kaske, "Mount Sinai and Dante's Mount Purgatory," *Dante Studies*, 89 (1971), 1–18.

[19] See my article, "*Purgatorio* 2: Cato's Rebuke and Dante's *scoglio*," *Italica*, 52 (1975), 348–63.

[20] Not all will agree with this estimate. Why not be content to call the technique "literary reference" and be done with it? Or even "iconography," and go no further? In the *Psychomachia* we can clearly see in Prudentius' text the very words and concepts of typology. In Dante the matter is only slightly less susceptible of "proof," and depends more upon the typological atmosphere and conception of the entire poem (and not only upon the testimony of the Letter to Cangrande—though that is imposing evidence). The whole matter is the subject for a book, not a footnote. It has been the subject of several studies. Most recently, there is the excellent survey of the problem by Jean Pépin, *Dante et la tradition de l'allégorie* (Montreal, 1970). And cf. the interesting discussion in J. A. Scott's review article in *Romance Philology*, 26 (1973), 558–591.

In these very few examples I hope I have given support to the notion that typological investigation of certain works does make a difference. Without it we have done poorly by the *Psychomachia* and the *Commedia*, two medieval works that are, by anyone's estimate, of some importance. The difference between allegory of event and allegory of words, which St. Augustine, in Paul's footsteps, established so long ago in *De trinitate* (15, 9, 15), is still a useful distinction with which to analyze at least some secular literature of the Middle Ages. The task confronting all students of allegoresis in the secular works of the period involves the initial recognition that there are in fact two rival traditions of allegoresis,[21] and then to try to determine to what degree each is applicable to a given work.

## A Note of Explanation

When I was invited to participate in the conference on typology and literature, I agreed on the condition that an over-burdened schedule allowed me to present an informal talk rather than a paper. The provision was accepted, and the reader now finds reproduced here the result of my deciphering of the notes for that talk.

[21] It is true that the predominant medieval position was to keep, or at least attempt to keep, the two separate. It is a position that was not always honored—and certainly not, in my opinion, by Dante. For a welcome addition to the printed texts that help study the debate, cf. the Appendix ("Selections from the Commentary of Bernardus Silvestris on Martianus Capella") of Winthrop Wetherbee's *Platonism and Poetry in the Twelfth Century* (Princeton, 1972), p. 267. Bernardus, who in his commentary on *The Aeneid* (or the six books he chose to attend to) only described what Dante called the "allegory of the poets," here distinguishes *integumentum* from *allegoria* (Dante's allegory of the theologians). For him *allegoria* is what St. Paul called "allegory of event" ("oratio sub historica narratione"), and pertains to Scripture, while *integumentum* ("oratio sub fabulosa narratione") pertains to poetry and "philosophy." (His fitting examples are, respectively, Jacob and Orpheus.)

## "ALWAYS TO KEEP THE LITERAL SENSE IN HOLY SCRIPTURE MEANS TO KILL ONE'S SOUL": THE STATE OF BIBLICAL HERMENEUTICS AT THE BEGINNING OF THE FIFTEENTH CENTURY

THE interpretation of Scripture has presented a problem to Christians since the earliest generation. Their Bible was Jewish Scripture in Greek guise reflecting a much older culture and state of consciousness. First-century Christians therefore shared the hermeneutic problems of Hellenistic Jews and of other interpreters of ancient religious literature. A recent book by Hans von Campenhausen has suggested that what made early Christians hold on to the Septuagint despite the interpretive problems was the fact that the advantages far outweighed the problems.[1] Once proper methods were found to lay claim to the Jewish Scriptures as Christian books, to tie them together as the "Old Testament" with their continuation in the "New Testament," the Septuagint proved a most successful ally in the apologetic and missionary enterprise. One does not easily discard a helpful tool, even if its handling presents problems. The proper methods, of course, included allegorization, a method practiced for centuries in hellenistic scholarship, as well as a deliberate shift of the interpretive center of the Old Testament canon from the *Torah* (Law) to the *Nebiim* (the Prophets). This shift is at the root of the specifically Christian form of allegory, "typological" exegesis, by which events, persons, or institutions of the old dispensa-

[1] von Campenhausen, *The Formation of the Christian Bible* (Philadelphia 1972).

tion were read as "types," "figures," "shadows" of things to
come or to be fulfilled in the time of Jesus and his Church:
the sacrifice of Isaac, Jonah in the whale's belly, Daniel in
the lions' den—all were seen as prefigurations of Christ's
life, death, and resurrection. Rudolf Bultmann has shown
that both early Christian allegory and typology are based
on the same assumptions about time and history and that
they therefore cannot be sharply distinguished one from the
other.[2]

# I

The language of both allegory and typology was present
in the letters of St. Paul who became a model for later generations of Christian exegetes. He developed the story of
Hagar/Ishmael and Sara/Isaac in Galatians 4: 22 ff. by his
own admission "allegorically," and described the wanderings of the people of Israel in the wilderness as a "type" for
his own generation (1 Corinthians 10: 1 ff.). But Paul was
less concerned with methodology than with conversion—
with the interpretation of his own conversion and the
resulting plea for the conversion of his fellow Jews and
Gentiles. In a passage in 2 Corinthians 3 that is fraught with
allegorical and typological terminology, he combined the
two conversions by interpreting the veil on Moses' face
(Exodus 34: 33–35) as a veil which still covers the Jewish
understanding of Scripture but is removed in the Christian
experience and by the Christian ministry of the "new covenant." The same text is being read, but this text, as Paul
himself experienced, can and does function in two diamet-
rically opposed ways: "The letter killeth, but the Spirit
quickeneth." (2 Corinthians 3: 6).

The pauline dialectic of letter and spirit, itself indebted
to hellenistic hermeneutical theory, remained a basic paradigm for Christian hermeneutics. Samuel Preus has used it
successfully as the *Leitmotiv* for a recent survey of the his-

2 Bultmann, "Ursprung und Sinn der Typologie als hermeneutischer
Methode," *Theologische Literaturzeitung*, 75–76 (1950–1951), 205–212.

tory of biblical hermeneutics through the Middle Ages,[3] and it will be convenient for our purpose to follow his precedent.

Origen of Alexandria, the most influential theologian of the pre-Nicene period, developed his biblical hermeneutics on the basis of a strict inspirational theory encompassing both the Old Testament and the emerging canon of Christian apostolic writings.[4] Since God through his Spirit is the author of Scripture, *all* Scripture must be expected to have a spiritual sense, though not everything in it has also a bodily sense. Incongruities in the text point to the deeper mysteries and spur the desire of the reader toward developing his skills in uncovering the intended higher level of understanding. Theology lives upon speculation. For Origen, the "hermeneutical divide" between letter and spirit has to be seen in terms of the anthropological hierarchy of body and soul or mind and applies equally to the Old and New Testaments: the exegesis of both has as its goal to leave the bodily, fleshly sense as quickly as possible and to arrive at the spiritual, mysterious sense to which the holy language is everywhere pointing.

Augustine, to whom the Western tradition must look as its main teacher, continued to stress the skills necessary for unlocking the mysteries of Scripture. In his hermeneutical handbook, *De doctrina christiana*, he not only included seven rules for figurative interpretation formulated by the Donatist Tyconius, but encouraged study of the biblical languages and of the liberal arts as a help in finding the figurative meaning of biblical words and "things." Adapting his theory of words as signs to the Christian typological method, he could regard both biblical words and the things they signified as figures of that higher level of spiritual reality which had to be sought beneath the surface of the

---

[3] J. S. Preus, *From Shadow to Promise: Old Testament Interpretation from Augustine to the Young Luther* (Cambridge, Mass., 1969).

[4] See particularly book IV of his *Peri Archōn* (*De principiis*); English translation by F. W. Butterworth: *Origen. On First Principles* (New York, 1966), pp. 256 ff.

literal reality. But since for Augustine this higher reality was identical with the theological virtues, faith, hope, and charity—charity being foremost[5]—and since this goal was plainly expressed in many passages, there was room for a "normative literal sense" beside the spiritual, a sense which in turn could assist the reader to find the true meaning of dark passages. The hermeneutical divide between spirit and letter was no longer just that of spiritual versus literal sense. Preus has correctly noted that in his later anti-Pelagian writings (especially *De spiritu et littera*), Augustine identified the "letter" with the theological function of the law which "kills" by demanding righteousness and manifesting sin without giving the spirit or the grace by which sin may be overcome.[6] This notion is much closer to St. Paul, but it is also closer to locating the hermeneutical divide squarely in the difference between the Old Testament and the New. Such locating is the procedure followed in much of medieval hermeneutics where the "mere letter," the "surface of the literal sense," or the "carnal sense," is frequently equated with the "sense of the Jews," and where the New Testament does not seem to need as thorough a treatment according to the spiritual senses as the Old.

The standard medieval theory of the four senses of Scripture only expands the literal-spiritual division by naming three specific modes of the spiritual goal (allegory or typology = *credenda*; tropology or *moralitas* = *agenda*; anagogy or eschatology = *speranda*). This theory seems to appear first with John Cassian and Eucher of Lyons, roughly contemporaries of Augustine.[7] Similar schemes, based on various numbers, had flourished and continued to be mentioned elsewhere. Already Philo Judaeus had read the mystery of the *merkabā*, the four-wheeled chariot in the prophet Ezekiel's vision (Ezekiel 1 and 10), as suggesting a fourfold sense of Scriptures. Moreover, another passage, Proverbs

---

5 *De doctrina christiana* 3. 10. 15.

6 Preus, p. 11 f.

7 Cassian, *Collationes* 14. 8. See H. de Lubac, *Exégèse Médiévale: Les quatre sens de l'Ecriture*, vol. I (Paris, 1959), 187 ff.

20: 22 ("portray them threefold in counsel and knowledge," as in the Septuagint), presented a biblical warrant for the convenient splitting of the spiritual sense into three. In practice, the theory did not mean that every scriptural passage had to be interpreted according to several senses. What was done depended on the convention concerning a particular text and on the intention of the exegete. Tropology as the sense closest to the literal was often the main focus, as in Gregory the Great's influential *Moralia in Job*; the Song of Songs had a long tradition of allegorical interpretation; and even the school theologians of the high middle ages in their biblical lectures rarely went beyond a sustained treatment of a biblical book according to *two* senses.

## II

As a field of special investigation, the development of biblical hermeneutics during the middle ages did not find much attention until after the Second World War. The major reason was the inaccessibility of exegetical materials. They are still buried, to a large extent, in immense tomes of manuscript commentaries and inadequate older editions of the materials. The first pioneer study, written in 1944 by Père Ceslas Spicq, a biblical scholar, had to be mostly a list of names and materials with only tentative generalizations.[8] Today we have the eight volumes of Friedrich Stegmüller's *Repertorium Biblicum Medii Aevi* as an indispensable inventory. With greater knowledge of the sources came the task of sorting out the exegetical production and its underlying hermeneutical principles. The advance in the historical understanding of medieval hermeneutics during the past few decades has been primarily connected with three names: Henri de Lubac, a prominent French Jesuit; Beryl Smalley of St. Hilda's College, Oxford; and Gerhard Ebeling, a theologian of the Protestant faculty of the University of Zürich, Switzerland.

Henri de Lubac had already shown considerable interest

[8] Spicq. *Esquisse d'une histoire de l'exégèse latine au moyen-âge* (Paris, 1944).

in the hermeneutical theory of Origen when he published his four volumes entitled *Exégèse Médiévale: Les quatre sens de l'Ecriture* in 1959–63.[9] It is not surprising that his love is for the spiritual senses and that his work, apart from its immense erudition, makes a strong case for a necessary return to the breadth of spiritual exegesis from the modern more or less sterile scientific exegesis. During the 1930's, Beryl Smalley went into the materials as a historian, studying Stephen Langton. Her *Study of the Bible in the Middle Ages*, though touching on the whole scene up to the fourteenth century, centered on the discovery, at the school of St. Victor in the twelfth century, of a trend that later became more pronounced in the biblical commentaries of the friar Nicholas of Lyra, a trend that Miss Smalley regarded as a move toward a more honest, scientific exegesis.[10] Not only was the investigation of the literal sense taken with utmost seriousness but, perhaps more importantly, the rich tradition of recent Jewish exegesis was studied and used. For Miss Smalley this latter tendency was a particularly hopeful sign because it could have led to a new, even more realistic scholarly era in biblical exegesis, an era which would be able, for example, to take the Jewishness of the Old Testament seriously and consider the various biblical books in their proper historical context. Miss Smalley has given credit to Père de Lubac for his "warm, persuasive plea" on behalf of the spiritual senses, but her hope was concentrated on the potential breakthrough toward the *hebraica veritas* and thus, as she would call it, toward sober biblical scholarship.[11]

Gerhard Ebeling has approached the field from his interest in Luther studies. Ever since his early book, *Evangelische Evangelienauslegung*, he has been concerned with

[9] See his *Histoire et Esprit: L'intelligence de l'Ecriture d'après Origène* (Paris, 1950).

[10] Smalley, *The Study of the Bible in the Middle Ages* (Oxford, 1952 [first ed., 1941]; repr. Notre Dame, 1964).

[11] Smalley, "The Bible in the Middle Ages," *The Church's Use of the Bible, Past and Present*, ed. D. E. Nineham (London, 1963), pp. 59 f.; 67 f.

the connection of the theological beginnings of Luther's reform with the shift in hermeneutical principles.[12] Interpreters had pointed to Luther's increasing rejection of all allegory and to his collapsing of all the spiritual senses into the one sense *de Christo* which he called the literal. Ebeling recognized that this tendency was not in itself an advance of that type of biblical scholarship Miss Smalley had stressed, although Luther made ample use of humanist philology. Luther's "literal sense" contained for the Old Testament a prophetic one and was dependent for its validation on the Holy Spirit and on faith, though in a peculiar dialectic with the written word. In a series of articles Ebeling tried to trace the hermeneutical aspects of Luther's reform in the earliest exegetical writings, particularly the *Dictata* on the Psalter.[13] He found that the young Luther was aware that letter and spirit were not simply synonymous with literal and mystical exegesis, but rather that, regardless of the technical sense aimed for by the interpreter, the interpreted text *always* functioned either as killing letter or as vivifying spirit in the theological conscience. Although Ebeling admitted that the picture is complicated, he and his students have traced similar trends elsewhere, particularly in late medieval Psalms commentaries such as those by Perez de Valencia, or Faber Stapulensis. It seems that, following the lead of Nicholas of Lyra, these writers recognized a christological sense of some, or even all, psalms as a second literal sense. The younger school of Heiko Oberman has since widened the scope, describing a thoroughly late-

[12] Ebeling, *Evangelische Evangelienauslegung. Eine Untersuchung zu Luthers Hermeneutik* (Munich, 1942; repr. 1962).

[13] "Die Anfänge von Luthers Hermeneutik," *Zeitschrift für Theologie und Kirche*, 48 (1951), 172–230; "Luthers Psalterdruck vom Jahre 1513," *ibid.*, 50 (1953), 43–99; "Luthers Auslegung des 14. (15.) Psalms in der ersten Psalmenvorlesung im Vergleich mit der exegetischen Tradition," *ibid.*, 50 (1953), 280–339. "Luthers Auslegung des 44. (45.) Psalms," in *Lutherforschung Heute*, ed. V. Vajta (Berlin, 1958), 32–48. All of these are reprinted in his *Lutherstudien. Band I* (Tübingen, 1971). See also his English summary, "The New Hermeneutics and the Young Luther," *Theology Today*, 21 (1964), 34–46.

medieval Luther. In terms of exegetical theory, the book by Preus belongs in this context.[14]

This brief survey highlights the importance of the early fifteenth century for our present understanding of the history of biblical hermeneutics. Working on a continuation of her earlier book (though with a different and for us less pertinent outcome than expected), Beryl Smalley so far has seen this period as a time of regression, a "blind alley," a time of the unfulfilled promise of a new style of biblical scholarship centering in the literal sense.[15] For Luther scholars it is a time of the probable creation of an exegetical climate that finally led to the overthrow of the fourfold sense in favor of a new blend of biblical philology and christocentric piety in Luther's one "literal sense." Everyone says that we know very little about exegesis and hermeneutics in that period, a time also crucial for the development of literature in the widest sense.

### III

The statement in the title of this chapter comes from this transitional period. "Semper tenere litteralem sensum in sacra scriptura est occidere animam suam." The sentence has no claim to special attention on account of its *content*, which, after all the talk about allegory and spiritual senses, seems rather trivial. Compared with the tradition it is a truism—an Augustinian truism, to be precise—since it paraphrases Augustine's warning in Book III of *De doctrina christiana*: "At the outset you must be very careful lest you take figurative expressions literally. What the Apostle says pertains to this problem: 'For the letter killeth, but the spirit quickeneth.' That is, when that which is said figuratively is taken as though it were literal, it is understood carnally. Nor can anything more appropriately be called the death of the soul than that condition in which the thing

---

14 It was written as doctoral dissertation under Professor Oberman at Harvard.

15 Smalley, *English Friars and Antiquity in the Early Fourteenth Century* (Oxford, 1960).

which distinguishes us from beasts, which is understanding, is subjected to the flesh in the pursuit of the letter."[16] The *content* is not new. But the *context* is most surprising and must give us pause.

The statement was proposed for nothing less than dogmatic *condemnation* at a General Council of the Church, the Council of Constance (1414-18). Though the attempt failed in the end, the very fact of a controversy in this official setting raises some hard questions. What had happened to the hegemony of the spiritual senses in hermeneutical theory if Augustine's traditional position could come under suspicion of heresy? Was biblical allegory already losing ground, at least in theory? Was there really a movement afoot to reverse the old order and go all out for the *literal* sense?

The proposition belongs in the context of the so-called French "tyrannicide" of 1407 when the Duke of Orleans, the king's brother, was assassinated at the order of Duke John of Burgundy. The special feature of the case was the outrageous public justification of the murder before king and court by Jean Petit, a Parisian master in theology. Petit declared the murder "licit tyrannicide" in the interest of protecting the king from a vassal plotting his destruction—i.e., from a person self-condemned as a "tyrant" by Petit's definition. Significantly, his main proofs were biblical: a host of biblical examples of praiseworthy tyrannicides, and the contention that the deed was not in conflict with the commandment "Thou shalt not kill." On the contrary, Petit said, laws always have to be adjusted to circumstances—here he drew on the aristotelian principle of *epikeia* ("equity"), the "rectification of the law when it fails because of the particular"[17]—and this tyrannicide was fully within the spirit of the law, i.e., the scope of charity, if not within its letter. In this connection, he quoted 2 Corinthians 3: 6: "The letter kills, but charity makes alive," and then con-

[16] *De doctrina christiana* 3. 5. 9, tr. D. W. Robertson (Indianapolis etc., 1958), 83 f.
[17] Aristotle, *Nicomachean Ethics*, V. 10 (1137b. 27).

tinued: "c'est-à-dire que tenir le sens litéral en la Sainte Ecriture est occîre son âme."[18]

It was only years later, with a shift in the political constellation, that the Orléanist party at the university under the leadership of the formidable Jean Gerson was able to challenge this "doctrine." A Paris council called by the bishop condemned nine "Assertions" Gerson had extracted from Petit's speech, and, when John of Burgundy appealed to the pope, the matter ended up in the commission *De Fide* of the Council of Constance. In the fall of 1415 the Commission asked for *opiniones* from council members posing the question whether or not the Nine Assertions should be condemned. The eighth Assertion was the one quoted in our title.

Seventy-five of these written opinions have come down to us, fifty-one against and twenty-four for the condemnation. Most of them contain detailed comments on the eighth Assertion. The texts make fascinating reading, even though the names of the writers are suppressed in the official deposition, and although the result seems to reflect more the political realities than an honest wrestling with the issues.[19] Even so, the comments on our problem from churchmen all over Europe cannot be lightly dismissed when we discuss the problem of scriptural hermeneutics at the beginning of the fifteenth century. They should at least be helpful in gaining an impression of the general state of the matter, of the mood of the time, and of at least some elements of the most common attitudes.

## IV

"Always to keep the literal sense in Holy Scripture means to kill one's soul." Most of the pro-Burgundy defenders of

18 The French text of the entire speech may be found in *Chroniques d'Enguerrand de Monstrelet*, ed. Buchon, vol. I (Paris, 1826), 241 ff.; the quotation here on p. 285.

19 I have used the version printed in L. E. Du Pin, *Joannis Gersonii . . . Opera Omnia*, vol. V, 2nd ed. (Den Haag, 1728), cols. 719–1010. Unfortunately, I was unable at this time to compare the text with the manuscripts, particularly Paris nat. lat. 1485–1487, which may have helped in amending the rather unreliable printed version.

this Assertion take a common-sense approach that must have appealed to wider circles not particularly interested in the intricacies of hermeneutical theory. The Assertion for them says no more than that the literal sense is insufficient in reading the Bible; other senses, according to the accepted tradition, have to be used. In proof of this contention they quote a variety of figurative expressions, ranging in scope from the parable of Judges 9: 8 ff. ("The trees went forth to anoint a king over them") to Jesus' word in Matthew 10: 34: "I am not come to send peace but a sword." The full list shows that this group tends to understand literal sense in a rather narrow way, often to the exclusion of even the most obvious figures of speech.[20] A quotation from Duns Scotus, found repeatedly, stresses that the context often decides whether a phrase is figurative or not.[21] Jesus' words of institution, "This is my body," are not, because they are followed by a clear literal "for you"; but John 15: 1, "I am the vine," is a figure because the continuation calls the disciples "branches."

Many Old Testament commandments cannot, or can no longer, be literally understood, particularly when they have been replaced by more perfect commandments in the New Testament, or when they seem to imply *aliquid turpe* (an immoral act): Genesis 17: 14, the command to circumcise every male, is often adduced, or (in one case) Hosea 1: 2, the command to the prophet to marry a harlot— which must mean, as Jerome had suggested, that such an action was for the purpose of converting her. Lyra is

[20] Matt. 5: 2–3 (Du Pin, V, 806A); Matt. 11: 5 (V, 801C); Matt. 18: 6 (V, 758C); Acts 7: 49 (V, 809C); Heb. 12: 23 (V, 891C).

[21] "Unde Doctor Subtilis in IV° suo ad ostendendum quod Christus non intellexerit corpus suum tantum esse figurativum in sacramento altaris cum dicit 1 Cor. 11: 24 *Hoc est corpus meum*, probat per verba sequentia cum ait: *quod pro vobis tradetur*; sicut etiam exemplificat per oppositum quando intelligit de figurativis locutionibus ut ibi Jo. 15: 5 *Ego sum vitis vera, vos palmites*, ubi clare patet quod quia Apostoli non erant palmites nisi figurative nec Christus vitis. Similiter 1 Cor. 10: 4 *Petra erat Christus* apparet ex praecedentibus. . . ." Du Pin, V, 810C. See 765CD.

quoted as expressing the view that even if such a commandment *once* was literally true, it no longer is.[22]

The New Testament has similar commands: "If your eye bothers you, tear it out" (Matthew 5: 29); "there are eunuchs who have made themselves eunuchs for the kingdom's sake" (Matthew 19: 12). To take them literally would mean to offend against other commands. All these examples say merely that the spiritual or mystical senses are necessary; otherwise many errors would occur.

The array of fathers quoted in support of this position is not extensive, yet some standard texts are common fare. Augustine's text from *De doctrina* 3.5.9 appears, as does his sequence of four senses from *De utilitate credendi* 3, and his interpretation of 2 Corinthians 3: 6 from *De Spiritu et littera* c. 6, where letter and spirit are interpreted in the terms of "literal" and "spiritual" sense before the theological interpretation of law and grace is introduced as "another sense." The crown witness in almost all *opiniones* is Gregory the Great, whose dedicatory letter attached to the *Moralia* (1.3) says clearly that statements of Scripture "sometimes cannot be understood *iuxta litteram* because, when they are accepted according to their surface, they cause not instruction but error in the reader." Another statement from Gregory's *Homilia 1 in Ezechielem* is equated with Petit's Assertion: "Si omnia ad litteram sentiamus ( = always to keep the literal sense), virtutem discretionis amittimus ( = is to kill one's soul)." In the common understanding of the time, Greg-

---

22 "Et quantum est de materia, super isto passu dicit Magister Nicolaus de Lyra quod per *litteram* intelligitur Vetus Testamentum, et per *spiritum* Novum. Qui ergo nunc reciperet litteram, hoc est legalia quae post promulgationem Evangelii mortifera sunt, occideret animam suam." Du Pin, V, 805D. This argument is criticized by the other side: "Vel si exponitur Apostolus ut exponit ipsum Magister Nicolaus de Lyra quem adversarii adducunt, intelligendo per litteram Vetus Testamentum, specialiter quoad caeremonialia, et per spiritum Novum Testamentum: non tamen propter hoc non (*fortasse del.*) habent intentum. Quia licet talis littera modo occideret observantem caeremonialia, non tamen ejus sensus litteralis occideret quemque: quia non est idem littera et sensus litteralis." Du Pin, V, 987BC.

ory seems to be used as the clearest witness against the sufficiency of the literal sense. Reference to him is almost completely absent on the Gersonist side. Listed with somewhat less frequency is a passage from Bonaventure's *Sentences* commentary (III, dist. 40 q. 2 concl.), which is paraphrased as: "The old law kills if it is taken according to the literal sense, but not if it is taken according to the spiritual sense." One *opinio* reads this statement to mean that, the true literal sense always being true, the grammatical sense may sometimes be false.[23] However, Bonaventure himself speaks only of the Old Testament, where the literal sense was the carnal sense of the majority, while some (prophets, seers) were already privileged to understand the law "spiritually." Among the authors less frequently quoted were Hugh of St. Victor, Alexander of Hales, and Nicholas of Lyra.

For the supporters of the eighth Assertion, then, the literal sense had at best a preparatory function. With much of the tradition, they in fact relegated it to an inferior position of *"superficies."* And like much of the tradition they read 2 Corinthians 3: 6, "the *letter* killeth," mainly as a hermeneutical rule about the *literal sense* of scripture.

The identification of "letter" with "literal sense" was indeed one of the crucial points in their argument, because the eighth Assertion rested on it. Letter is "mere letter," *"superficies litterae,"* "literal simplicity," "carnal sense." Since *littera* (Greek: *gramma*) by any textbook definition[24]

[23] "hic [the grammatical sense] non est sensus Scripturae a Spiritu Sancto principaliter intentus quem semper necesse sit esse verum, sed quem frequenter contingit esse falsum ut expresse dicit S. Bonaventura, III Sent. Dist. ult." Du Pin, V, 782BC. See also 766A; 786C; 809B; 814D; 860B.

[24] "Tenet consequentia per locum a nominis interpretatione ad interpretatum: *Grammaticale* enim dicitur a *gramma*, Graece, quod est *littera*, Latine. Ergo grammaticale per interpretationem idem est quod litterale." Du Pin, V, 734D–735A. "in Libro *De expositione vocabulorum Theologorum* 'Littera' ait 'proprie carta est vel Epistola. Unde legitur quod Urias tulit secum litteras mortis suae. *Littera* historia est secundum quod soliti sumus dicere: *Istud exponitur ad litteram*, id est historice. *Littera* litteralis intelligentia est: unde *Littera occidit, Spiritus autem vivificat*. Et quia idem est litteralis intelligentia et

is literal understanding, and "literal" is the translation of
"grammatical," it follows that the "killing letter" must be
the grammatical surface sense. *"Sensus"* had been absorbed
into *littera* in the threefold scheme of *littera, sensus, sententia* Hugh of St. Victor had expounded.[25] This identity was
everywhere doggedly defended. Part of the defense was the
interpretation of "killing one's soul" as "falling into heresy."
Indeed, literalism can and does lead to heresy. Examples
are provided by the Jews, by the "Anthropomorphites" of
Isidore's catalogue of heretical movements,[26] and, finally,
by people who draw from 2 Corinthians 9: 9 ("Does God
care for the oxen?") the thesis that God is not ruling the entire universe.

The evidence in favor of the eighth Assertion seemed
overwhelming and the need for "spiritual" understanding
easy to demonstrate. Yet in most cases an obvious un-
easiness remained. The theologians of the Constance generation, whatever the reasons, were no longer satisfied with
the traditional exaltation of the "spiritual" interpretation at
the expense of the literal. Even among the defenders of
Petit no one indicated a special fervor for the spiritual
senses. For none of them was the hermeneutical divide between letter and spirit that between "false" and "true." As
a matter of fact, the playing down of the literal sense, which
seemed to be needed for the procedure of *epikeiare*, of
adjusting the letter of the law, left too little room for the
"truth" of the letter of Scripture of which they all were very
much convinced. Sensitivity to the "truth" of the letter,
despite all the disparaging comments, is a phenomenon
common to the *opiniones* on both sides. Of course, after
Origen and Augustine, the praise of spiritual exegesis was
rarely connected with an open neglect of the literal sense,

litteralis sensus: ideo quando hoc legimus: *Littera occidit* exponitur
per hanc propositionem.' " Du Pin, V, 915D.

[25] Hugh of St. Victor, *Didascalicon* 3. 8.

[26] Quoted from Gratian's *Decretum*, C. XXIV, q. 3 c. 39 (ed. Fried-
berg, I, p. 1003): Du Pin, V, 785C.

though the theories of both had elements that encouraged
"jumping" the literal level. The procedural sequence was
briefly expressed by Gregory: "*First*, we lay the foundation
of history." For the theory of the later Middle Ages this
aspect seems to have received its major encouragement by
the systematic treatment of the literal sense in the first
Question of Thomas Aquinas' *Summa Theologiae* (Ia q. 1
a. 10). Thomas declared there that the historical or literal
sense is the foundation and presupposition of the multiple
spiritual senses, which he restricted to the multiple meaning of the *things* rather than the *words* of Scripture according to God's intention, thus defining the literal sense as falling in the province of the investigation of words. It is
certainly true that Thomas' authority was not widely accepted outside his own order. It is also true that his
hermeneutic theory in its components said nothing new but
rather systematized and slightly modified elements from
various sources, especially Augustine. However, in a correc-
tive move he used the *fundamentum* language to emphasize,
again with explicit reference to Augustine, that no theological argument was possible on the basis of the spiritual
senses—the meaning of "things" in the intention of God—
but only on the basis of the literal sense, the meaning of
words.[27] Moreover, this meaning was, if the interpreter included rhetorical figuration, unambiguous. "Holy Scripture
sets up no confusion, since all meanings are based on one,
namely the literal sense. From this alone can arguments be
drawn and not, as St. Augustine remarks in his letter to
Vincent the Donatist from the things said by allegory. Nor
does Holy Scripture lose anything by this, for nothing
necessary for faith is contained under the spiritual sense
that is not openly conveyed through the literal sense elsewhere."[28] I disagree with the opinion that Aquinas has

[27] The reference is to Augustine's *Epistola* 93. 8 (Migne, *Patrologia
Latina*, Paris, vol. 33, 1865, col. 334A): "Quis autem non impudentissime
nitatur aliquid in allegoria positum pro se interpretari nisi habeat et
manifesta testimonia quorum lumine illustrentur obscura?" It appears
repeatedly in our texts.
[28] Thomas Aquinas, *Summa Theologiae* Ia q. 1 a. 10 ad 1.

thereby decisively clarified the hermeneutical rules, because the non-ambiguity of biblical words is still closely tied to the inspirational theory of God as the author of Scripture, i.e., to a "reading of the mind of God" rather than a reading of the mind of the human author. Preus sees here a major "loophole" in the theory. However, Aquinas in fact was widely understood as calling exegetes back to the foundational "truth" of the literal sense as the proper place of their endeavor. The text of Q. 1 a. 10 was quoted more often in the later Middle Ages than many of his presumedly more important or original doctrines.

It seems to have been this support, strengthened by the work of men like Nicholas of Lyra, that forced the defenders of the spiritual senses and of Jean Petit's Assertion into splitting Aquinas' "unambiguous" nature of the biblical words into a lower and a higher level—a lower level which could draw to itself all the negative consequences of an "insufficiency" theory of words, including their sometimes being "false"; and a higher level that would do justice to the positive consequences of affirming that the literal sense, inasmuch as it expresses what God as the author intends, must always be true. Thus we find in almost all the supporters of the eighth Assertion the use of a doctrine of a double literal sense, *duplex sensus literalis*. Its advocates were convinced that it is a common doctrine "which all the doctors teach." Most implied that Petit of course was speaking about the lower level, or that he used the term, literal sense, "confusedly" and therefore could not be condemned, his statement making perfect sense when applied to the negative literal sense.

The terminology explaining this double literal sense is most interesting. It seems to take its start from the point where Aquinas had allowed the "parabolic" sense (and that means figuration) to be part of the one, unambiguous literal sense of words. Words, he said, can signify something "properly" and "figuratively." This pair naturally appeared in the *opiniones*. But there were others that tended to qualify the neutral thomistic description in terms of a two-

value system: good and less good (sometimes even bad).
Thus, Thomas' "true literal sense," defined as the one intended by the author, was contrasted with a low-value "mere
grammatical sense" of which Thomas had not spoken because it would have been precisely the one "from which
alone argument can be drawn." Thomas' theory stressed the
unity of the literal sense by referring it to the mind of the
*author*. Now, however, the split into two levels was justified
by a recurring argument which added another dimension,
the effect of words upon the mind of the hearer: words can
differ in the sense "quem faciunt," "quem repraesentant in-
tellectui," from the sense "in quo fiunt," in the intention of
the author.[29] Since in the interest of truth the latter must
prevail in case of conflict, the first may be a "deception,"
and therefore "false." This possibility of deception now also
dominated the distinction of the "exterior" from the "interior," of the "surface" from the "underlying truth." Even
the venerable distinctions of husk and kernel, rind and core,
shell and nut were used for this purpose: "Take the example of a nut. It presents to the sense of sight one color
when seen in its bark and shell, another when seen in its
marrow; the shell presents to the sense of taste a taste different from that of the hidden kernel."[30] But while the in-

[29] ". . . habent duplicem sensum litteralem, unum quem faciunt,
alium in quo fiunt, necessario enim verba litterae generant aliquem
sensum superficialem, alium ab illo quem loquens intendit." Du Pin,
V, 809C. Similarly numerous other texts: "Nec est dubitandum ali-
quando verba Sacrae Scripturae in sensu quem faciunt esse minus
congrua, quae tamen in sensu in quo sunt [*lege*=fiunt] veritate plena
sunt." Du Pin, V, 801C; "penultima assertio . . . intelligitur de sensu
litterali quem littera primo facit ex grammaticali vocum significatione,
et non est sensus quem Auctor litterae primo intendit." Du Pin, V,
834B; see also 766A; 782BC; 786B; 812D; 824C; 825C; 839A; 860B.
[30] ". . . patet exemplo de nuce quae alium colorem ingerit sensui
visus in cortice et in testa et alium in medulla: alium etiam saporem
sensui gustûs cortex ingerit el alium nucleus latens." Du Pin, V, 766A.
See also 900A: "Pro cujus adversariorum dictorum elucidatione ponitur
distinctio talis vulgata apud Theologos, Doctores et Philosophos natu-
rales, morales et sermoniales, videlicet quod sensus alicujus Proposi-
tionis litteralis dupliciter potest capi: Unus dicitur sensus in quo fit
Propositio alius [*lege pro*: alicujus] quem ipsum facit et ingerit sensibus prima fronte. Unus vocatur sensus interior, alius exterior; unus
superficialis, alius medullarum."

terior sense, the core, or the sweet nut used to be the
spiritual understanding, it is here the true literal, the sense
of the *intentio Spiritus sancti.* Exterior, bark, and rind are
metaphors for the possibly deceptive wrapping of words,
the false literal sense. We may dislike the nominalist scepticism about words. It is clear, however, that such scepticism did not hinder the defense of the spiritual sense, of
creativity in interpretation. On the contrary, it probably
even enhanced it.

The application of the double literal sense to the case under discussion was easy enough: If the true literal sense of
the commandment, "Thou shalt not kill," lay in the intention of the law-giver, *not* in its possibly deceptive wording,
who then could charge Jean Petit or Burgundy with having
read this intention wrongly in their attempt to adjust the
letter of the law to the circumstances? Certainly not the
people who offered no other, more objective criteria in
demonstrating that *their* reading was right!

## V

This was precisely the dilemma in which the advocates
of the other side found themselves. On the one hand, they
of course held to the same definition of the true literal sense
of the Bible as the one which God, or the Spirit, intended.
They also shared, almost without exception, the nominalist
tendency to distrust words. Gerson himself could say that
"the words of Scripture are equivocal," as the bishop of
Arras reminded him.[31] On the other hand, they were convinced that Petit's entire "Justification" was a piece of
sophistry, a monumental fraud,[32] intended to cover up the
immoral motives behind the murder. To do this by appealing to Scripture was a monstrosity, a blasphemous attack not

[31] "Scripturae verba saepius sunt ambigua, et in uno loco aliter
capiuntur quam in alio aut quam communis Grammaticus acciperet."
Sermo *Vivat Rex*, Du Pin, IV, 599A. Martin Porré quotes this passage
in a slightly different form: "Verba sacrae Scripturae sunt saepe aequi-
voca et capiuntur aliter in uno loco quam in alio vel aliter quam in
communi Grammatica." Du Pin, V, 735A.
[32] "Facit fraudem," Du Pin, V, 239A, in a text by the abbot of St.
Denis used during the Paris Council's inquiry.

only on the whole moral fiber of the Bible but on the integrity of God himself, who wrote it. What the Gersonists objected to in this debate was the total divorce of the intended sense from the words, the "free-for-any-guess" attitude, the reversal of Aquinas' *trust* in biblical words into such radical *mistrust* that even the meaning of the commandment could be anyone's choice. We have here the key to their desperate fight for the integrity and unity of the literal sense against its doubling; we have the explanation of their posing as "literalists"—the last thing we would expect of a man like Gerson, who had his own problems with the biblical literalism of a Wyclif or Hus.[33] Despite the ambiguity of words, suspicion and scepticism have to stop at the threshold of the Bible. The strange and sometimes almost grotesque logic of this position must be seen against the background of its defenders' moral cause.

Time and again they repeated that the literal sense in Holy Scripture is *always* true. They said that, in fact, the essence of Scripture *is* its literal sense—the sound of its words and the ink with which they are written included, inasmuch as these express nothing but the intention of the Holy Spirit, even though of themselves they pass away.[34] To admit that the literal sense could sometimes be false, or must sometimes be adjusted, invites disastrous consequences. Three such consequences were mentioned with some regularity. 1. To admit a deficient literal sense would

[33] "Si forsan inveniatur quod per Ecclesiam vel Praelatos vel Doctores aliquos reprobati sint quidam haeretici dicentes quod Scriptura sacra semper est vera ad litteram vel sensum grammaticalem vel ad litteram secundum intellectum Judaeorum; haec utique reprobatio stare potest cum reprobatione seu reprobationis modo hujus octavae Assertionis juxta diversas acceptationes terminorum et varias dicendi causas." Du Pin, V, 928D. For the connection with Wyclif and Hus see 930C; 996B.

[34] This must be the sense of the somewhat unclear passage: "Constat quod vox nec atramentum non est sacra scriptura nisi in respectu ad sensum litteralem, cum secundum Beatum Augustinum: *Non est efficax argumentum in theologia nisi sit super sensum litteralem fundatum.* Etiam quia vox cito transit et Scriptura comburitur, et Sacra Scriptura quoad suas veritates semper manet juxta illud Salvatoris, Lucae XXI. 33." Du Pin, V, 966A.

invalidate all theological proof from Scripture, which (as Thomas and Augustine had said) must proceed from the literal sense. This basis must be reliable. If it is not, if theological words, words of the Bible, are treated with the same suspicion as other words are, theology would become impossible. 2. To admit a deficient literal sense would weaken the authority of Scripture. Augustine had made the point in his controversy with Jerome that, if one "lie" was found in Scripture, the whole Scripture would become suspect, and Aquinas had repeated it.[35] Scripture would become, as one *opinio* puts it: "a plumbline unfit to straighten out the crooked," and one would need at every point the guide of special revelation to know an intended truth from an intended lie. 3. To admit a deficient literal sense would also deny the *need* to seek out the intention of the Holy Spirit. Behind this curious charge appears the ideal of a holy, contemplative life as the veritable measure of truth in one's exegetical statements. Here again, moral outrage dictated the argument. The Gersonists could not imagine how a sincere, prayerful exegesis of the commandment could yield Petit's result.

But if it is not an "open-to-any-choice" affair, how *does* one seek out the intention of the Holy Spirit? How does one determine the true literal sense of Scripture? It is here that Gerson and his friends tried *their* common-sense approach, implying that it was not only in full accord with tradition, but also up-to-date. At the one place where Gerson's own *opinio* formulated the actual rules of this search, he drew conspicuously upon a "modern" theologian: Henry Totting of Oyta (d. 1397), a Parisian master of the preceding generation: "This subject Master Henry of Oyta explained beautifully in his Prologue to the Sentences."[36] Henry's three basic rules as repeated by Gerson are: 1. considera-

[35] See Augustine, *Epistolae* 82. 1; Thomas Aquinas, *Summa Theologiae* Ia q. 1 a. 8 ad 2.

[36] "Hanc materiam de sensu litterali sacrae Scripturae declaravit pulchre Magister H. de Henca (*lege*: Henricus de Hoita) in suo prologo *super Sententias*. Videatur illic si habeatur." Du Pin, V, 928A.

tion of the context; 2. consideration of figures, tropes, and rhetorical conventions; 3. consideration of the exegetical tradition of the fathers and exegetes. These or similar rules appear elsewhere in our materials; the one about context often as a quotation from Nicholas of Lyra's First Prologue.[37] They seem to say that the finding of the true literal sense is a matter of hard work, of painstaking professional exegesis ("professional" here including a pious life and moral character) in conformity with the best of the Church's tradition. It is fitting that the main textbook recommended for every professional exegete in this connection is Augustine's *De doctrina christiana*.

At any rate, the literal sense cannot be split into "sometimes true" and "sometimes false" by the whim of the exegete. It is *only* and *always* true. And it is therefore not identical with Paul's "letter that killeth." Every *opinio* against Petit seeks to make this point. "Letter" is not "literal sense." Yet it is interesting to notice that in many cases the temptation of the double literal sense was too great. Precisely those who declare that the "letter that killeth" is not a *sense* at all but something less than a *sensus* (thus moving the *sensus* of the *littera-sensus-sententia* triad over into *sententia*) go on to identify it with the "mere words," the "exterior impression of words upon our mind," the "cortex grammaticalis." The following quotation shows all the features of this slip: "Paul does not say: the *literal sense* kills, but significantly: the *letter* kills. The letter, i.e., the grammatical sense which the terms used in the text seem to convey is frequently false and kills the soul. For example (Luke 9: 62): 'No one who puts his hand to the plow and looks back is fit for the kingdom of heaven.' For if the grammatical sense which these words at the first impression seem to convey would come true, then the poor plowmen

---

[37] "Unde Lyra in primo Prol. suae Postillae: 'Sensus litteralis S. Scripturae est sensus qui concluditur ex circumstantia litterae esse primarius et principalis intellectus ejus.'" Du Pin, V, 950A. See the same quotation in the beginning of Gerson's second *Cedula*, Du Pin, V, 927D f.

(*pauperes rustici arantes*) would be in greatest danger concerning their souls. For the literal sense of Holy Scripture which the Holy Spirit as its author principally intends, is never false and does not leave room for calumny. Therefore, he who wants to avoid error must make a difference between letter and literal sense in Holy Scripture as was said before."[38]

To make this statement means to refute one's own point about the unity of the literal sense. It means that, under the guise of pushing out the "lower level" from the discussion of the senses altogether, one is embracing the same theory of a double literal sense which the other party held. Martin Porré, the most eloquent advocate of the Burgundian position, saw this inconsistency clearly and suggested that Gerson himself really endorsed the thesis, "always to keep the literal, i.e., the *mere grammatical sense*, means to kill one's soul."[39] He may have been right with regard to most Gersonists. But he was not right with regard to Gerson himself.

## VI

As far as I can see, Gerson speaks in our materials only once of a *sensus litteralis duplex*. Answering the question what the literal sense of Genesis 17: 14 was ("Any non-circumcised male shall be cut off from my people"), he distinguished a figurative literal sense pointing to baptism, and

---

[38] "Unde amplius non dicit: Sensus litteralis occidit, sed notanter dicit: littera occidit. Littera, id est sensus grammaticalis quam termini in textu positi videntur importare, saepius est falsa seu falsus, et occidit animam . . . Luc. 9. 62, 'Nemo mittens manum ad aratrum et aspiciens retro aptus est regno celorum.' Si enim littera, id est sensus grammaticalis quem haec verba prima fronte videntur sonasse verificaretur, tunc pauperes rustici arantes essent in periculo maximo animarum; sensus enim litteralis sacrae scripturae quem author Spiritus sanctus principaliter intendit numquam est falsus nec alicubi patitur calumniam. Qui ergo errare [adde: non] vult in sacra Scriptura ponere debet differentiam inter litteram et sensum litteralem ut jam dictum est." Du Pin, V, 945C.

[39] Cf. the entire line of argument in Du Pin, V, 734–735. The text has been identified as coming from the pen of Martin Porré, bishop of Arras, by H. Finke, *Acta Concilii Constantiensis*, vol. IV (Münster, 1928), p. 246.

a preceptive literal sense which had been superseded by the advent of the perfect order.[40] This is not at all the "double literal sense" of the Burgundian party. Rather, it closely parallels what Ebeling and Preus have described as a double literal sense in the Psalms commentaries of Lyra, Perez, Faber, and the young Luther.

Gerson is careful not to say that the Old Testament law was "mere letter" or belonged to a lower level of literal sense. He quotes Jesus' words in Matthew 5: 18 ("not an iota, not a dot, will pass from the law") to the effect that the law is still true in Jesus' figurative literal sense.[41] The letter killeth—this does not mean that the letter itself is bad; without the spirit it kills, just as knowledge, which is not in itself bad, puffs up without charity (1 Corinthians 8: 1).

Yet if the double literal sense of Gerson's opponents, and its variant of *letter* as against *literal sense* in his own camp, expressed the hermeneutical mind of the time, he had his own way of drawing the line between "true" and "false" sense in biblical interpretation. "Holy Scripture must not be expounded according to the method of logic or dialectic which serves the speculative sciences; by doing this the sophists deceive themselves terribly. But Holy Scripture has its own proper logic and grammar just as the moral sciences have rhetoric for their logic."[42] I have not fully investigated

---

40 "Respondetur quod ipsa locutio considerata de Antiqua Lege habet duplicem sensum litteralem, videlicet unum ad erudiendum intellectum, inquantum erat figurativa; alium ad excitandum affectum in quantum praeceptiva. Nunc vero ipsa considerata sub Nova lege non habet nisi unum sensum litteralem, videlicet in quantum figurativa; quia per ipsam plus intendit Spiritus sanctus exercere affectum humanum, eo quod per Baptisma multo perfectius exercetur et gratiam suscipit. Unde adveniente quod perfectum est evacuatur quod imperfectum est." Du Pin, V, 927C (doublet *ibid.*, 899D f.).

41 "Apparet praeterea quod Vetus Lex est vera ad sensum litteralem sicut expresse tradit Christus, Matt. 5. 18 ubi dicit quod *Unum jota et unus apex non transibit de Lege*, etc. Verum est quod Judaei daeviant a sensu litterali quem Christus docuit esse verum litteralem." Du Pin, V, 928B.

42 "Apparet denique quod Sacra Scriptura non est exponenda secundum vim Logicae seu Dialecticae quae deservit scientiis speculativis; sic facientes Sophistae se turpiter decipiunt; sed habet Scriptura sacra

this statement, which sounds very much like Reformation hermeneutics. But this much seems clear to me. If for Gerson there was something like an "inferior" literal sense in the exposition of Scripture, it was not to be found in the Scriptures themselves which can never be wrong, but rather in the sophistry of dialecticians and logicians whose "art," often introduced so irresponsibly into the explanation of Scripture, easily becomes the "killing letter" which leads into error. Obviously, Petit and his defenders belonged to this category. Theology has its own rules of speaking. If one reads the Spirit's intention, the literal sense, *theologically*, he will always uncover what is true, what is good, what is moral, what is edifying, because God never deceives. A frivolous, immoral reading of the Spirit's intention only reveals the use of a non-theological sense, a *sensus logicalis*. And if such a statement is analyzed for its own true literal sense, for the intention of its author, the result is clear enough: immorality, the will to deceive. To seek and discover the *intentio auctoris* in Scripture unfailingly brings out the best; to do the same with *human* words and writings is bound to bring out the worst. Wyclif's and Hus's statements may sound at first quite biblical, but they come from heretical intentions. The *sensus logicalis* of Petit's Assertion may sound correct and admissible, but it is never the *sensus theologicus litteralis*.[43]

For Gerson, the hermeneutical divide between letter and spirit seems to fall between *sensus logicalis* and *sensus theologicus*, between human sciences and theology, between the possibly deceptive intention of men and the eternally good intention of God. It comes as no surprise that other contemporary literature, separated from the biblical citadel of truth, had a hard time overcoming the suspicion of this critic. His distrust of words was a distrust of human motiva-

suam propriam Logicam et Grammaticam, quemadmodum scientiae morales habent pro Logica Rhetoricam." Du Pin, V, 928B.

[43] Preus, op. cit., p. 80 f., reads this statement in *De Sensu litterali*, propositio 2, without reference to this context and therefore misses the point.

tion. In his nominalist tendency toward separating the Bible from all other literature, Gerson was against extending to any other writing the positive privilege of biblical "truthfulness," in which not only words but also things signified by words reveal the good intention of the author: he was against extending to Holy Scripture the negative privilege of universal doubtfulness or equivocation so freely used to cover up dubious moral intentions of human authors. It might be interesting to take another look at his criticism of the *Roman de la Rose* in this respect. Gerson's "theological literal sense" of the Bible was the attempt of a sophisticated fundamentalist to keep the unity and uniqueness of the Bible and, while still deriving its meaning from a set of personal standards, to stay within the orbit of Scripture itself where, regardless of the employment of other sciences, theology still reigned as queen.

## VII

What can we say, on the basis of our material, about the "state of biblical hermeneutics at the beginning of the fifteenth century?" I would like to present no more than some preliminary observations.

It can be said that, on the whole, the theory of biblical interpretation was still highly traditionalist, i.e., highly dependent on stimuli immediately connected with some facet of traditional hermeneutics. Challenged by a question of biblical hermeneutics, theologians would look for the most widely acceptable *consensus patrum et doctorum.* Hermeneutics does not seem to be a field of speculative innovation. We have observed Augustine's omnipresence: his *De doctrina christiana* not only stood behind the eighth Assertion and was often quoted on the Burgundian side; it was, together with the quotation from the *Epistola contra Vincentium* and *De Spiritu et Littera,* the main authority invoked by the Gersonists as well, and the model textbook for Gerson's ideal professional exegete. But the accents in the broad Augustinian framework fall differently.

*44*

1. There was considerably more talk about "literal" sense than in either Augustine or in authors from intervening centuries. One almost discovers a reluctance to speak of spiritual senses. Beryl Smalley has suggested that the spiritual senses had "worn so threadbare," and that the subsequent "extension of spiritual interpretation from the Bible to profane texts of recent invention must have lowered it in men's eyes."[44] I have problems with the second part of her remark. In whose eyes? Those of theologians? I think that the analysis of our materials hardly allows this conclusion. The men of letters? The general public? I have to leave the judgment to others. However, the revival of *talk* about the importance of the literal sense in our period is a fact. In the traditionalist atmosphere of biblical hermeneutics, I would trace this trend to the effect of Aquinas' restatement of the fundamental role of the literal sense which seems to have functioned as a turning-point without being intended as such. To concern oneself with the glory of the literal sense was *en vogue*. Burgos' *Additiones* to Lyra's *Postilla*, written in 1430, and widely circulated thereafter, could place the entire hermeneutical section under the heading: "Utrum sensus litteralis ceteris sensibus sacrae Scripturae sit dignior."

2. In the definition of the literal sense, the older line of tying it to the human words and thus to the surface meaning of a text was being abandoned. The definitional key was now the ancient formula of God (or the Holy Spirit) as the principal author. His intention defined the literal sense. It is possible that here again Aquinas' restatement of the theory fostered the change. This definition was used in a side argument of his article.[45] However, the wording in our

[44] Smalley, "The Bible in the Middle Ages," p. 69.

[45] Thomas Aquinas, *Summa Theologiae*, I a q. 1 a. 10 corp.: "Quia vero sensus litteralis est quem auctor intendit, auctor autem sacrae scripturae Deus est qui omnia simul suo intellectu comprehendit, non est inconveniens, ut Augustinus dicit XII *Confess.* si etiam secundum litteralem sensum in una littera Scripturae plures sint sensus."

texts may also have been influenced by a current formula of general hermeneutics. I have not been able to pursue this question sufficiently. Very rarely is any consideration given to a biblical writer as a "secondary author."

3. The emphasis on God's intention as the definition of the literal sense was frequently coupled with a nominalist and decidedly anti-thomist distrust of words. On one side in our controversy this emphasis led to the re-assertion of the insufficiency of the literal sense in an attempt to gain greater freedom and creativity in interpreting words in the Bible and elsewhere. Because words were no longer regarded as invested with some kind of unambiguous truth but rather can be deceptive, they might be related to truth in different ways, and biblical words were no exception. On the other side, it led to a strong assertion of the absolute sufficiency of the literal sense in the *Bible* in distinction from all other books and sciences. As *biblical* words become ever more invested with truth, all other literature must lose out. Distrust of words has indeed its full force here. It renders *all* literature suspect on account of a potentially deceptive literal sense hiding the suspicious motives of a human author; but it has no place in truly theological literature.

4. Another common feature was the surprisingly widespread doctrine of a "double literal sense"—rarely in connection with a special prophetic sense in Old Testament writings, but more regularly as a distinction between a lower, or outright "false," literal sense, the "mere grammatical signification of the words," and the true literal sense, the one the Spirit intended. Since the two sides disagreed about the latter, it was already an *interpreted* sense, its criterion lying outside the Bible in whatever one regards as guarantee for a "right" reading of the Spirit's intention.

This highly subjective character of the discussion about the literal sense shows that the new terminology did not really imply a change in the basic hermeneutical structure which, ever since Origen and Augustine, gave the primacy

Père de Lubac's eloquent statement is not an exaggeration, and it is this symbolic city that Tasso chose to liberate in the minds of his readers. Tasso intended the action of his poem to be both literal narrative and spiritual enlightenment.

I would now like to turn my attention to the major episodes in Cantos 4 and 5. Tasso informs us in one of his letters that all the episodes of the poem derive from Canto 4, in which the enchantress Armida arrives and divides the Christian army. For many critics, who in addition to their other faults are apparently believers in male superiority, this means that all the episodes derive simply from the appearance of Armida. Now it is true that Armida is both beautiful and wily, as any enchantress should be who has been schooled by Homer's Circe, Virgil's Dido, and Ariosto's Alcina. I would be the last in the world to deny her seductive appeal, but Canto 4 contains other events of importance equal to Armida's arrival at the Christian camp. Canto 4 begins with a formidable tribunal in Hell in which Pluto and his comrades consecrate themselves to the defeat of Godfrey's crusade at precisely the moment when Godfrey is about to construct those wooden machines to scale the walls of Jerusalem, a point to which I shall return later. Pluto's harangue is as insidious as that of Milton's Great Consult in the second book of *Paradise Lost*, and to the same purpose—to seduce man from God, not only for his destruction but out of malice for God. It may be argued that Tasso devoted only nineteen stanzas of the canto to the devils, but they are powerful stanzas and cannot be dismissed as simple *meraviglie*. Tasso, like Milton, believed in a literal devil or Satanic force, and we are wrong in our false sophistication to dismiss this part of the poem as if it were similar to the machinery of the sylphs in Pope's *Rape of the Lock*.

The insidious force of the devils against Godfrey provides the spiritual foundation for Armida's emergence into the poem. Her wicked uncle, as the poem tells us, convinces

her to pervert the work of the Christians by presenting herself as a damsel in distress, which she does.[7] She arrives at
Godfrey's camp, escorted by Godfrey's younger brother,
Eustace, who immediately falls in love with her. Armida's
deceit is superb; she tells her plaintive story of being
deprived of her kingdom; she tempts Godfrey's chivalry to
place her distress and that of her false kingdom before that
of God's citadel, Jerusalem. At issue is what Rosemond
Tuve has called the higher and lower chivalry,[8] allegiance
to the Lord God or to the lady in distress; Godfrey replies
that he cannot help her before Jerusalem is taken, a decision that we as readers must accept as right because we
have already seen the forces of evil gathering to test Godfrey's virtue even before we are given the full picture of
Armida's deceit. Nevertheless, Eustace from love persuades
his brother to send ten knights, chosen by lot, to help
Armida. Tasso is very clear about the foolishness of the
venture:

> Così conclude; e con sì adorno inganno
> cerca di ricoprir la mente accesa
> sotto altro zelo: e gli altri anco d'onore
> fingon desìo quel ch'è desìo d'amore.      (5.7)

Fairfax, Tasso's Elizabethan translator, is even more explicit:

> Thus devis'd the knight,
> To make men think the sun of honor shone
> There where the lamp of Cupid gave the light.
> The rest perceive his guile, and it approve,
> And call that knighthood which was childish love.

The narrative of Canto 5 continues, completing the story
of the election of the ten knights to help Armida, but it con-

[7] The anonymous commentator of the Venice, 1593 edition reads the
triumvirate of wicked uncle, Armida, and Pluto as the world, the
flesh, and the devil.

[8] Rosemond Tuve, *Allegorical Imagery: Some Medieval Books and
their Posterity* (Princeton, 1966), pp. 51 ff.

trives to combine with this story another election that Tasso brilliantly weaves into the emerging development of the Armida story. In Canto 3, Dudone, one of the most powerful of the Christian warriors, is killed and the command of his troops must be filled. Eustace urges Rinaldo to seek the honor. Another warrior, Gernando, who covets the honor, insults Rinaldo publicly, and in fury Rinaldo kills him in sight of the whole army. On Tancredi's advice, in order to avoid the wrath of Godfrey Rinaldo flees. Godfrey consents to help Armida; the lots are chosen and Eustace, who was not among the ten selected, also flees. Once more we are faced with an incredible amount of narrative detail that looks like pure romance filigree work.

Once more I think that this is not the case. There is a symmetry in Canto 5 that amounts to a double election: the election to replace Dudone's command in the Christian army and the election of the ten knights to help Armida. In both elections there is an error brought about by the appearance of Armida. Eustace originally suggests Rinaldo for Dudone's post so that Rinaldo will not be among the ten selected to help Armida. Gernando is equally jealous that Rinaldo may be given Dudone's honor; thus Rinaldo is caught by another knight's erroneous desire for love or power. Rinaldo deserts the army because of his angry murder of Gernando. Eustace leaves the army because of his love of Armida. Both have defected from their proper task of freeing Jerusalem. Neither one has been elected to his desired post.

Tasso's comment on the episode is instructive and shows that he had a firm idea in combining the two episodes in this canto. In true Renaissance fashion Tasso treats the army as a single body, with Godfrey as the head, or Reason, and the other princes as the lesser powers of the soul.[9] Rinaldo, Eustace, and Tancredi are all made to appear less than perfect in their commitment to the liberation of Jerusalem. Rinaldo and Eustace desert in Canto 5. Because

[9] This common metaphor has its biblical source in 1 Cor. 12.

*57*

of his love of Clorinda, Tancredi does not respond to Ar-
gante's challenge as he should in Canto 6. Thus Tasso is
commenting with accuracy and profundity when he writes:
"But coming to the inward impediments, love, which
maketh Tancredie and the other woorthies to dote and
disioine them from Godfrey, and the disdaine which
entiseth Rinaldo from the enterprise, doe signifie the conflict and rebellion which the concupiscent and Irefull
powers, doe make with the Reasonable." That is, Rinaldo,
Eustace, and Tancredi—for anger and for love—have
deserted Godfrey and the pursuit of Jerusalem; and Godfrey, who is at all times reasonable, figures Reason in the
poem. These younger knights have shown less than total
moral awareness in their actions.

An allegorical reading of the narrative specifies their
moral defection precisely. The Middle Ages and the Renaissance knew well Plato's allegory of the charioteer drawn by
horses which had to be controlled, and they read the allegory as the reason commanding the concupiscent and
the irascible passions, both necessary for the human condition, both needing the control of the reason.[10] Canto 5, far
from being merely prosaic, as my Italian school text calls
it, brilliantly and with complete artistic control shows us
that Godfrey, threatened by malice and deceit from without, must suffer the further threat of desire and wrath from
within his own forces. It is for this reason that Tasso treats
Godfrey and his army as one body. In reading the narrative
of Canto 5 we see clearly that through no fault of his own
Godfrey has lost control of both Eustace and Rinaldo and
that their defection will have consequences for the taking
of Jerusalem.

In reading these same events allegorically as the rebellion
of the concupiscent and irascible passions against reason,
we are not merely naming the specific defects described in
the narrative but adding a new dimension to our understanding of the narrative, a new dimension that humanizes

[10] See *Phaedrus* 246.

this heroic struggle and relates it instructively to the reader's own struggle to control his own passions. The allegorical reading narrows the gap between the vast heroism of the narrative and the daily moral struggle of the individual reader. It makes the reader, as it were, participate in the action in ways that he could not if he were reading the narrative simply as a series of individual acts. To see the ancient division of the passions into the concupiscent and irascible as the informing structural device of Canto 5 is to enrich our reading in the same way that a knowledge of the rivalry between Turnus and Aeneas in the *Aeneid,* or the part that anger plays in the character of Achilles, enables us to understand the actions of Tancredi and Rinaldo as we could not if we did not have this knowledge. To interpret the action so is not to impose new schemes or additional facts on the narrative but to see structural forms that the narrative is trying to declare as part of its meaning. For this reason it is imperative to be aware of the ancient Christian metaphors and schemes of thought that inform the narrative. To amplify the richness that allegorical reading brings to the poem I should now like to consider the role of Rinaldo in the poem, in particular his disenchantment of the enchanted woods. In doing so I shall also be trying to show how the sensuous detail of the poem enables us to come to the Christian meanings.

It will be recalled that when the Christian army comes in sight of Jerusalem, Godfrey's main effort is to find some way to scale the walls of the city. At the end of Canto 3 men are dispatched to cut down a forest to make machines for that purpose, but once constructed the machines are burned, all but one, and this one Clorinda burns in a fit of pique at the beginning of Canto 12. In Canto 13 the devilish Ismeno enchants the forest to prevent any further manufacture of machines. As the poem progresses, more and more Christian heroes go out to disenchant the forest but are rebuffed by the fierce enchantment. When Tancredi attempts the forest, he too is defeated because every time he tries to cut down a tree he finds in it the figure of Clorinda mocking him for killing her. The moment is psychologically poignant and totally practical, for the Christians are prevented from getting the wood needed to scale the walls of the city. Godfrey is told in a dream that he will not take Jerusalem until he recalls Rinaldo, who, since his departure from the Christian camp, has fallen prey to Armida. In the most famous passage of the poem the three knights, sent to fetch the errant Rinaldo, succeed in freeing from the embraces of Armida this obviously reluctant Achilles, without whose aid neither Troy nor Jerusalem will be taken. Rinaldo returns, and is chosen to attempt the enchanted forest. In Canto 18 we see his triumph and, more important for the purposes of this chapter, the meaning of Tasso's enchanted woods.

Rinaldo returned is Rinaldo repentant. He subjects himself to Godfrey. He tells his story to his friends, is told by Peter the Hermit the meaning of what he has done, has his confession heard, and prepares himself to assault the woods. This is nothing more than the normal process of Christian reconciliation, repentance, and resolution. He sets off in the morning, alone and afraid, until he comes to the edge of the enchanted forest, enters the *locus amoenus*, crosses the miraculous bridge of gold, gazes upon the burgeoning myrtle, listens to the nymphs, resists the blandishments of Armida, and cuts down the myrtle. The spell disappears. The woods can now be cut down and Jerusalem be won. Rinaldo's disenchantment of the woods is the climactic moment of the poem, although many critics feel that as an episode it does not have sufficiently heroic stature to sustain the weight that Tasso places on it.

They are right, of course, if we read the episode as just another romance convention, but they should be reminded that epic poems can have as their climactic moments subjects as unheroic as the delinquency of eating an apple. This episode is not just another romance convention; it is an allegory, whose meaning Tasso goes to great lengths to explain in quasi-Aristotelian categories:

The inchantments of *Ismen* in the wood, deceiuing with illusions, signifie no other thing than the falsitie of the reasons and perswasions which are ingendred in the wood; that is, in the varietie and multitude of opinions and discourses of men. And since that man followeth vice and flieth vertue, either thinking that trauels and dangers are euils most greeuous and insupportable, or judging (as did the Epicure and his followers) that in pleasure and idlenesse consisted chiefest felicitie; by this, double is the inchantment and illusion.

Tasso continues by showing that the horrors of the woods are "honest travails and honorable danger" shown as evil, and that the beauties of the woods are the delights of the senses shown as good. He concludes: "So let it suffice to have saide thus much of the impediments which a man findes as well within as without himself: yet if the Allegorie of anything be not well expressed, with these beginnings everie man by himselfe may easily finde it out."

With such a generous invitation from his author what critic could resist pushing the allegory a little bit further? I shall do this in the manner of a medieval allegorical commentary. The woods, as is most notably shown in the beginning of Dante, is the world, held in the power of the devil, who uses the world to tempt each man with his own particular weakness, for man will be kept from using the world properly either through fear of harm or unpleasantness that might come to him or through too great delight in the things of the senses which he sees as the only good. Not until man has reconciled himself to God and accepted his grace, can he overcome the false enchantments of the woods and use them, as God ordained he must, to gain eternal salvation within the walls of the holy city of Jerusalem. This, I take it, is the spiritual meaning of this episode of the poem. Far from merely relying on romance convention, Tasso is manipulating radical metaphor in wondrous ways. He takes the very simple metaphor of the world as a woods and literalizes it into a mechanical requirement for the action of the narrative. We as readers first see these woods as a beautiful landscape outside Jerusalem. We then see them as the material requirements for those machines. We are drawn into the literalization of the metaphor and do not see beyond the noses of the characters so busily engaged in cutting wood and building machines. The brilliance and ease with which Tasso makes us see only what he wants us to see at any particular point in the poem are positively cinematographic. We are made to fret and worry about the destruction of those machines—only one left—and now that one is burned, and Ismeno has enchanted the woods. . . .

Until this point in the poem Tasso does not give us time to think beyond the senses back to metaphor, but with Tancredi's defeat in Canto 13 and Rinaldo's success in Canto 18 those woods begin to shimmer with meaning beyond that "required for narrative." For a brief moment in the poem, while Rinaldo is enduring his temptation and agony, Tasso gives us the stasis necessary to ponder the meaning of those woods and to see that they are indeed metaphor as they have been throughout, without our having realized it. Immediately after Rinaldo's disenchantment of the woods (and this is the most brilliant stroke Tasso ever achieved) he sends us back to our everyday concern about constructing those machines, but with this difference: we have learned that those woods are not merely what they are in the narrative and therefore we cannot merely literalize the metaphor any more. Here Tasso sees most profoundly into the Christian mysteries which impel us to believe in such "romance conventions" as that a virgin gave birth and that a god became man. Only when belief comes in question do we torment convention, and Tasso is a believer, a believer who in his poem insists on the most incarnational aspects of Christianity, that the world must be used if we are to gain Jerusalem and that only through this trial and constant temptation will we be worthy to dwell within the walls of the holy city. His radical and literalized metaphor insists that we read his epic in this way.

Now, let me begin to show how any reader as well as the poet in his allegorization of the poem can arrive at this conclusion, and how this reading will get the critic off the horns of the dilemma of Tasso's apparent schizophrenia between sensuousness and religious faith. One might call this the disenchantment of the bedeviled critic.

Rinaldo is prepared for his test in the woods by a brief interlude of prayer (Canto 18. 11–16):

> e tutto solo e tacito e pedone
> lascia i compagni, e lascia il padiglione.    (18.11)

> And on his way, sole, silent, forth he went
> Alone, and left his friends, and left his tent.

Unlike Achilles, Rinaldo leaving his tent is silent. He first comes to Mount Olivet, that range of hills above Jerusalem which encloses at its foot the Garden of Gethsemane where Christ was betrayed after His agony of prayer. We cannot read this simply as just another locale in a poem, or even in this poem. Rinaldo-Achilles is not a Christ figure (of which there was only one for the Renaissance), but Tasso is insisting that his Rinaldo participate in the meaning of another episode in the same garden in which that other and greater human being accepted his divine mission: "Not my will but thy will be done."[11] The descriptive detail of the passage is meant to emphasize this conscious choice:

> con gli occhi alzati contemplando intorno
> quinci notturne e quindi mattutine
> bellezze incorruttibili e divine.    (18.12)

[11] Matt. 26: 39; Mark 14: 36; Luke 22: 42. This is not an example of typological imagery, which is, strictly speaking, the prefiguration in the Old Testament of some event in the life of Christ, e.g., Abraham's sacrifice of Isaac as a type of the Crucifixion. To suggest that Rinaldo figures Christ here or that he is a Christ figure (to use the more popular critical idiom) is to verge on blasphemy. This is tropology, the moral sense, in which Rinaldo like all Christians must suffer his hour in the Garden in imitation of Christ. For an excellent discussion of tropology and typology see D. W. Robertson, Jr., "The Question of 'Typology' and the Wakefield *Mactatio Abel,*" *American Benedictine Review*, 25 (1974), 157–173.

And saw (as round about his eyes he twined)
Night's shadows hence, from thence the morning's
    shine;
This bright, that dark; that earthly, this divine.

Rinaldo is turning away from his earthly understanding of
things to that deeper understanding of human experience
that is the center of Christian life. His prayer invokes the
same meaning:

Padre e Signor, e in me tua grazia piovi,
sì che il mio vecchio Adam purghi e rinovi.     (18.14)

Father and Lord, pour into me your grace
So that my old Adam is purged and renewed.
                                          (my translation)

His prayer is answered in the rain of dew that falls upon
him and transfigures his garment:

. . . e tal di vaga gioventù ritorna
lieto il serpento, e di nov'òr s'adorna.     (18.16)

The heav'nly dew was on his garments spread,
    To which compar'd his clothes pale ashes seem;
And sprinkled so that all the paleness fled,
    And thence of purest white bright rays out-stream.
So cheered are the flow'rs, late withered,
    With the sweet comfort of the morning beam;
And so, return's to youth, a serpent old
Adorns herself in new and native gold.

I do not see how one can read this episode without hearing echoes of St. Paul's injunction to kill the old Adam and
to put on the new man, with its powerful insistence on
repentance, rejection, and renewal.[12] But that, it may be
said, is not the critical point; the description of this small
episode on Mount Olivet may be thought to pale in comparison with the immediately following sensuous detail
lavished on the enchanted woods. I would not deny it, but

---

[12] 1 Cor. 15: 22, 45–50.

the words in this earlier episode are so laden with meaning that a poet needed only to speak them in order to evoke in his readers a whole flood of associations.

In this transfigured state Rinaldo can enter the lush enchantment of the woods, fortified beyond the descriptive powers of any poet. I am well aware that the fortification of grace has not kept many critics from feeling somewhat squeamish about Rinaldo's hacking up the trees, but this is really not a matter of ecology. The episode is brilliant as psychology, but that I think was also not Tasso's point. The hero has been prepared, and he will be tested through the senses, which is why Tasso is so elaborate in his sensuous detail. But those details have iconographical histories almost as elaborate as that of Jerusalem. The golden bridge that leads us across the flood only to leave us stranded, the myrtle that all the mythographers tell us is sacred to Venus, the chorus of worldly nymphs leaping from that ancient oak, the traditional symbol of despair—all these recapitulate in figurative language Rinaldo's former enchantment by the world in the person of Armida. The lushness of the detail is not meant to show that Tasso was really of the devil's party, seduced by his sensual desires and giving the victory to Rinaldo only because of his worries about the Council of Trent. If that were the case, we would have few or no Italian saints. The defeat of the enchanted woods is accomplished by Rinaldo's willing cooperation with divine grace, and it is accomplished with perfect artistic decorum.

But still, I am sure, there will be a cry about the incivility of my interpretation of the person of Armida. Virgil can give Dido her regal silence in Book 6 and Ariosto can just drop Alcina as his fictive world will allow, but poor old Tasso has to violate Armida by dragging her back into the last canto of the poem, only to be converted and married off to that lout Rinaldo. Now, as readers will no doubt have come to expect, I do not agree with this reading of Armida's conversion. Tasso uses fully the prototypes of Circe, Dido, and Alcina, but he has further uses for his enchantress. She begins as a witch and ends as a bride. Here again Tasso has been accused of not knowing what he was about, and once more I disagree with received critical opinion.

That Tasso had different plans for his enchantress is clear from the amount of space devoted to her lament when Rinaldo abandons her, in Canto 16. She outdoes her prototype Dido in eloquent fury, and Rinaldo, unlike Aeneas, has the misfortune to be present. Heroes, like Aeneas and Rinaldo, do not come off well when they have been shown the error of their ways and try to do the gentlemanly thing. Virgil finesses the situation by showing us only Aeneas' shock and hurt when Dido turns away from him without a word in Book 6, but Tasso leaps in to supply this gap with words on both sides:

> Poi le risponde:—Armida, assai mi pesa
> di te; si potess'io, come il farei,
> del mal concetto ardor l'anima accesa
> sgombrarti; odii non son, né sdegni i miei;
> né vuo' vendetta, né rammento offesa;
> né serva tu, né tu nemica sei.
> Errasti, è vero, e trapassasti i modi
> ora gli amori essercitando, or gli odi.
>
> ma che? son colpe umane, e colpe usate:
> scuso la natìa legge, il sesso e gli anni.
> Anch' io parte fallii: s'a me pietate
> negar non vuo', non fia ch'io te condanni.
> Fra le care memorie ed onorate
> mi sarai ne le gioie e ne gli affanni;
> sarò tuo cavalier, quanto concede
> la guerra d'Asia e con l'onor la fede.     (16. 53–54)

Madam (quoth he) for your distress I grieve,
   And would amend it if I might or could;
From your wise heart that fond affection drive;
   I cannot hate nor scorn you, though I would;
I seek no vengeance, wrongs I all forgive,
   Nor you my servant nor my foe I hold;
Truth is, you err'd, and your estate forgot;
Too great your hate was, and your love too hot:

But these are common faults, and faults of kind
    Excus'd by nature, by your sex, and years:
I erred likewise; if I pardon find,
    None can condemn you that our trespass hears,
Your dear remembrance will I keep in mind,
    In joys, in woes, in comforts, hopes and fears;
Call me your soldier and your knight, as far
As Christian faith permits and Asia's war.

Human comfort is impossible when the higher and the lower chivalry clash, and words only make the pain worse, as the passage I have just quoted shows. Rinaldo is absolutely right and totally wrong. The reader does not know to whom to give his sympathies—an uncertainty that might appear as an error on Tasso's part. But I have come to believe that it is a purposeful irresolution in order to keep the Rinaldo-Armida relationship a workable possibility which Tasso insures by making Armida vow vengeance on Rinaldo, with the help of the Egyptian army. Remorse and vengeance do not make good conclusions.

Thus we are prepared for that staggering moment in Canto 20 when—Jerusalem won—Rinaldo once more comes upon Armida. She is passionate, she is resentful, she is about to commit suicide but is prevented by that most rapturous and flamboyant rescue. She ends her long lament:

Felice me, se nel morir non reco
questa mia pèste ad infettar l'inferno!
Restine amor; venga sol sdegno or meco,
e sia de l'ombra mia compagno eterno:
o ritorni con lui dal regno cieco
a colui che di me fe' l'empio scherno,
e se gli mostri tal, che 'n fere notti
abbia riposi orribili e 'nterrotti.

Qui tacque: e, stabilito il suo pensiero,
strale sceqlieva il più pungent e forte;
quando giunse e mirolla il cavaliero
tanto vicina a l'estrema sua sorte;

già compostasi in atto atroce e fèro,
già tinta in viso di pallor di morte.
Da tergo ei se le avventa, e 'l braccio prende
che già la fèra punta al petto stende.

Si volse Armida, e 'l rimirò improviso;
ché nol sentì quando da prima ei venne.
Alzò le strida, e da l'amato viso
tòrse le luci disdegnosa, e svenne.
Ella cadea, quasi fior mezzo inciso,
piegando il lento collo; ei la sostenne:
le fe' d'un braccio al bel fianco colonna;
e 'n tanto al sen le rallentò la gonna.

E 'l bel vòlto e 'l bel seno a la meschina
bagnò d'alcuna lagrima pietosa.
Qual a pioggia d'argento e matutina
si rabbellisce scolorita rosa;
tal ella, rivenendo, alzò la china
faccia, del non suo pianto or lagrimosa.
Tre volte alzò le luci, e tre chinolle
dal caro oggetto; e rimirar no 'l; volle.

E con man languidetta il forte braccio,
ch'era sostegno suo, schiva respinse:
tentò più volte, e non uscì d'impaccio;
ché via più stretta ei rilegolla e cinse.
Al fin raccolta entro quel caro laccio,
che le fu caro forse, e se n'infinse,
parlando incominciò di spander fiumi,
senza mai dirizzargli al vólto i lumi.   (20. 126–130)

And tell him, when twixt life and death I strove,
My last wish was revenge, last word was love.

And with that word half-mad, half-dead, she seems;
    An arrow, poignant, strong, and sharp she took:
When her dear knight found her in these extremes,
    Now fit to die and pass the Stygian brook,
Now prest to quench her own and beauty's beams,
    Now death sat on her eyes, death in her look;

When to her back he stepp'd, and stay'd her arm,
Stretch'd forth to do that service last, last harm.

She turns, and, ere she knows, her lord she spies,
  Whose coming was unwish't, unthought, unknown;
She shrieks, and twines away her 'sdeignful eyes
  From his sweet face; she falls dead in a swoon;
Falls as a flow'er half cut that bending lies:
  He held her up, and, lest she tumble down,
Under her tender side his arm he plac'd,
His hand her girdle loos'd, her gown unlac'd;

And her fair face, fair bosom, he bedews
  With tears, tears of remorse, of ruth, of sorrow.
As the pale rose her color lost renews
  With the fresh drops fall'n from the silver
    morrow;
So she revives, and cheeks empurpled shows,
  Moist with their own tears, and with tears
    they borrow;
Thrice she look'd up, her eyes thrice closed she,
As who say, let me die ere look on thee.

And his strong arm, with weak and feeble hand,
  She would have thrust away, loos'd and untwin'd:
Oft strove she, but in vain, to break that band,
  For he the hold he got not yet resign'd;
Herself fast bound in those dear knots she fand,
  Dear, though she feigned scorn, strove, and
    repin'd,
At last she speaks, she weeps, complains, and cries,
Yet durst not, did not, would not see his eyes.

She tearfully states her case, and Rinaldo offers to return
her kingdom and her wealth and to make her his lady if
the veil of paganism is removed. His passionate request,
which Tasso likens to the sun that melts the snow, recapitulates Rinaldo's own transfiguration by grace on
Mount Olivet and elicits from Armida that surrender that
has made my friend A. Bartlett Giamatti wince:

Ecco l'ancilla tua: d'essa a tuo senno
dispon, gli disse, e le fia legge il cenno.    (20. 136)

Behold your handmaid, and of those things [her worldly
possessions] dispose yourself, she said, and let the sign
be a law to her [that is, to your handmaid]. (my translation)

Professor Giamatti's embarrassment comes from the fact
that Armida is using here the words of Mary to Gabriel at
the moment of the Annunciation: *Ecce ancilla tua.*[13]

I think that we should not feel embarrassment, because
Tasso is not trying to make an equation between Mary and
Armida, which *would* be in bad taste. The phrase is spoken
by Mary in humble submission to that sudden and unexpected intrusion of grace, which changed all life with her
acceptance. Tasso needed a phrase to indicate submission
and not defeat, a phrase that would make the sudden conversion believable, that would imply the future promise
of the submission; in all these ways the words of Mary work
here simply and profoundly. We have not been accustomed for several centuries to deal so boldly and so fa-
miliarly with Scripture in our poetry, but I cannot help
thinking of Spenser's sonnet on the resurrection which
ends: "So let us love, dear love, like as we ought / Love is
the lesson which the Lord us taught."[14] We are so used to
making an opposition between human and divine love that
we find it hard to accept the many ways in which human
life participates in the divine, either directly or by analogy,
as here.

I cannot help worrying about the contorted economy of
Armida's two-line reply. There is the dramatic simplicity

[13] Luke 1: 38; A. Bartlett Giamatti, *The Earthly Paradise and the
Renaissance Epic* (Princeton, 1966), p. 209. A more sympathetic treatment of Tasso's problem with Armida is Robert M. Durling's *The
Figure of the Poet in Renaissance Epic* (Harvard, 1965), pp. 184–185.
[14] *Amoretti* 68. The twentieth-century reader is more inclined to
see the two loves as totally separate, nurtured as we were by statements
such as Eliot's "We only live, only suspire, / Sustained by either fire
or fire."

of the first half-line, which releases so many associations that we tend to forget the complicated ambiguities of the rest. The second half-line begins with that "d'essa" to which Armida reduces her kingdom, her crown and herself, but what is "il cenno" (the sign) that will become law to her?[15] Is the sign her submission to Rinaldo or is the sign the phrase "Ecco l'ancilla tua," which she now understands and extends to Rinaldo as the pledge of her acceptance of the law of love? I cannot say for certain, but to make the point in a different way I would like to quote these lines in Fairfax's translation:

Behold (she says) your handmail and your thrall
My life, my crown, my wealth, use at your pleasure.
Thus death her life became, loss prov'd her treasure.

Fairfax is a careful translator, and his translation makes explicit the Christian content of the original. The death which is life is the new life of Christianity and her loss, or disposal of her worldly goods, gains her a treasure, by which Fairfax surely had in mind the pearl of great price, or salvation. No matter how much or how little we see in Tasso's lines, and whether or not we approve of them, for Tasso Armida's submission to Rinaldo and her acceptance of Christianity are simultaneous and identical, which is why his use of Mary's reply to the angel seems so brilliant to me, and why I brought in Spenser's couplet, with its insistence on the essential identity of human and divine love.

In conclusion, let us turn back to the instruction of Tasso's narrative. Like all Christians, Armida has moved from being a pawn of the devil in Canto 4 to being the submissive handmaid in Canto 20. Like the enchanted woods she is the same but different. Armida, and the enchanted woods, were once a peril to Rinaldo because he understood

15 My colleague Professor Charles Klopp may be quite right in suggesting that I am overreading or mistranslating here since "essa" in older Italian can refer to a person. If so, the translation should read: "Behold your handmaid; dispose of her according to your wisdom and let your sign be her law."

them only in a worldly sense. Having conquered the woods through grace and gained Jerusalem, he once more encounters Armida—now at the point of death—and can be united with her because of that sudden, imperious, and humbling demand of grace we call conversion. It does not matter that Tasso cut this passage from the final version of the poem. That is a different country. Tasso tells us in the *Allegoria del poema* that Armida and Ismeno who enchanted the woods are "servants of the devil": "Ismeno doth signifie that temptation, which seeketh to deceive with false beliefe the vertue (as a man may call it) Opinative: Armida is that temptation which laieth siege to the power of our desires, so from that proceed the errors of Opinion; from this, those of the appetite." Ismeno and his errors of the intellect can be dismissed with the disenchantment of the woods, but the errors of the senses, of the appetite, Tasso will not dismiss so easily, either because he knew them better or knew better how they might be redeemed, so that in a sense Armida's conversion is the triumph of human and divine love. With grace Rinaldo can undo Ismeno's mischief, and the Christian army can win Jerusalem, that "Politicke Blessedness." But Tasso knows of another blessedness, neither anterior nor superior to civil felicity, but of such importance that Tasso feels he must make Rinaldo win another victory that would not depend on strength of arm or mind but on the cooperation of grace and human love, and so we have this final meeting of Rinaldo and Armida and the redemption of the sensual passions. Far from being a conflict of sense and religion, Tasso's poem should persuade us that it is only through enchantresses and enchanted woods that we gain the felicity of any Jerusalem and that Tasso's Jerusalem can even include, in her newly transfigured state, the peril that was Armida.

My interpretation of Tasso's enchanted woods may appear strange in a volume devoted primarily to typological imagery in English and American literature, stranger still in that I have studiously avoided the use of the word

72

*typology.* My treatment of Rinaldo's agony in the Garden of Gethsemane may require some theoretical explanation in view of the popularity of recent studies of medieval drama and early American literature, through which *typology* has become a specialized branch of literary interpretation.[16]

Typology, strictly defined as the prefiguration of events in the life of Christ by events or figures in the Old Testament, is deeply embedded in Christian thought. It has the authority of Christ himself: "And as Moses lifted up the serpent in the wilderness, even so must the son of man be lifted up" (John 3: 14). Typological reading of the Old Testament was the principal means available to the early Church to prove the divinity of Christ and at the same time to proclaim itself as the true continuation of the Providential history of Israel. The central purpose of biblical typology is the assertion of historical continuity between the Old and New Testaments, in order to document God's providential plan of redemption in time. This basic historicity of biblical typology separates it from merely verbal symbolism in very important ways. Typological figures are *true* in ways that purely literary figures cannot be. As Rosemond Tuve has written: "Types properly precede the figure that fulfills them, Moses before Christ. Only a divine Author can so write history that the types foreshadow the revelation of pure truth in another historical occurrence, and the serious use of this figurative relation requires a religious conception of man's reason for being."[17] Typological figures are *true* in ways that human imitations even of divine providential history cannot be; they are created by God and are *fact*, i.e., Moses' raising of the brazen serpent (Numbers 21: 9) is a historical fact. Therefore, typological figures are part of the literal sense of

[16] Rosemary Woolf, *The English Mystery Plays* (London, 1972); V. A. Kolve, *The Play Called Corpus Christi* (Stanford, 1966); *Typology and Early American Literature*, ed. Sacvan Bercovitch (Amherst, Mass., 1972).

[17] Rosemond Tuve, *Allegorical Imagery* (Princeton, 1966), p. 47.

Scripture. They are prior to the verbal act of Scripture and partake of Incarnational theology: the Word become flesh. They record and witness.

Biblical commentators of whatever period must treat these typological facts as they are received in the words of Scripture, thus becoming part of the exegetical tradition of handing on the Word to later ages. Within the so-called "fourfold" reading of Scripture typological figures are accommodated by the allegorical sense (*quid credas*), the sense that teaches the faithful what to believe as truth. The particular form that this exegetical teaching takes has been best described by D. W. Robertson, Jr.:

> The Old Testament "types" are more than foreshadowings of the Gospels; they are historical manifestations of principles set forth in the New Law. Isaac bore a bundle of faggots to his own sacrifice. In Christ's burden of the Cross we may discern the philosophical meaning of this event. But Isaac was an historical figure, a man like ourselves, and we, too, it is suggested, bear a burden which in one way or another leads to sacrifice. Isaac, in other words, is an historical exemplar whose action suggests something about the inner life and obligation of the observer. In technical language, typology employs allegory to imply tropology, which is its ultimate aim. "Typology" requires careful and systematic organization, it is instructive in an exemplary fashion, and at the same time, it contains that element of the enigmatic necessary to what the medieval mind considered to be aesthetic appeal. The relationship between the two elements, old and new, is implied rather than stated, but the spiritual meaning for the individual which arises from their combination is something which can result only from the intellectual effort of the observer.[18]

18 D. W. Robertson, Jr., *A Preface to Chaucer* (Princeton, 1962), pp. 189–190. [For other views of these matters, relating to minds after "the medieval mind," see the ensuing chapters. See also my speculations in Lewalski's chapter, n. 40, and Zwicker's, n. 39. The basic point is that by concerning ourselves exclusively with either typology or

Robertson's discussion of the typological figure, as it is used in Christian art (whether pictorial or verbal), quite properly places the emphasis on the renewal of the Word in the hearts and actions of believers, in which *quid credas* becomes *quid agas*, the moral sense of "fourfold" allegory, or (to use its technical name) tropology.[19] *Typology employs allegory to imply tropology, which is its ultimate end.* That end is the perfecting of God's Providential plan, salvation for mankind, for individuals, for readers, by making them knowing and willing partakers in the continuing history begun in Genesis. That miracle occurs because, as Robertson states in a later essay: "Tropology releases Scriptural events from the limits of space and time and makes them perennial."[20] Without denying the primacy of Old Testament historicity, the literary use of biblical typology conflates the times of Moses, of Christ, and of readers into a universal *imitatio Christi.* This is not to say that Moses will become Christ, or that we will. Our sense of time and our discriminations about historical and personal identities will not allow such identification.

A similar point is made by Rosemond Tuve in the passage preceding the one already quoted:

> The present ease with which the relation of type is claimed argues a verbal rather than profound understanding. Nevertheless, it seems to me that these long centuries of practice—very common practice—and acceptance of Christian allegorical interpretation left a mark on the ordinary understanding of allegory. The more so because careful theory, New Testament sanction and doctrinally necessary safeguards kept the religious definitions of allegory incredibly pure, moving and deep

tropology we may fail to see that both undergo vicissitudes, change, and reappearance.—Ed.]

[19] D. W. Robertson, Jr., "The Question of 'Typology' and the Wakefield *Mactatio Abel*," *American Benedictine Review,* 25 (1974), p. 160.

[20] *Ibid.,* p. 160.

(considering that we deal with the wide breadth of Christendom and at least twelve loquacious mediaeval centuries).

We should not lose sight of the fact that certain commonplaces of Christian doctrine have much to do with the current overeasy detection of types (usually of Christ) in some secular writings, often Shakespeare's or Spenser's. It is a doctrinal commonplace to think of the faithful Christian who tries to "imitate" Christ as attempting an image of Christ, as restoring through grace the relation to God which man held before the Fall—when he was truly and recognizably "in His image." Typology is not needed to understand the most important way in which Red Crosse "becomes" or "takes on" Christ; the Pauline terms describe what is supposed to happen constantly in the life of any Christian, and it is a misuse of a word needed for its own meaning to find types in all these.

"Christ figures," as Ziolkowski's essay suggests, are the invention of the twentieth century, a century not noted for its knowledge of, nor its devotion to, ancient Christian commonplaces.

For these reasons I have eschewed the use of the term *typology* in relation to the experiences of Rinaldo and Armida in Tasso's poem. The "strict constructionist" definition I am trying to enforce is important for critics and readers of Christian poetry of the Middle Ages and Renaissance. Tasso, who chose as his poetic figures names and places that figure prominently in Christian history, knew that poetry could serve the purposes of Christian history. His unstated but implied marriage of Rinaldo and the converted Armida, who will produce the Este of Ferrara, links that family to the conquest of Jerusalem by Godfrey, an historical fact, and brings it into the unfolding of Christian history. Neither Rinaldo nor Armida is typological in any sense of the word. Each exists only as a creation of Tasso. They exist after the life of Christ on earth. They work, however, as fictions within the scheme of this Christian epic because of the nature of their actions, which can be interpreted tropologically.

Rinaldo cannot function as a typological figure, first because of his nature as a poetic fiction, and second because Tasso chose to place him in the Garden of Gethsemane, the garden of Christ's agony, an incident that proclaims his humanity just as his transfiguration on Mount Tabor proclaimed his divinity (Matt. 17; Mark 9). Tasso's use of the garden to test Rinaldo's humanity is almost an affront—unless we understand in what sense Rinaldo is "imitating" Christ. His presence in *this* garden must be read tropologically. Rinaldo does not figure Christ; he is particpating in that event as we all participate in all the events of Christ's life—through the grace of God and willed human endeavor. His transformation in the garden renews the meaning of Christ's agony, not the event. Similarly, Rinaldo's transfiguration deals not with the event on Mount Tabor but with its meaning of divine grace inspiriting humanity. Rinaldo, if he figures anything at all, figures the Christian knight cooperating with divine Providence and grace to bring about the winning of Jerusalem, which is the subject of the poem and the goal of every Christian.

The scholars whose essays follow mine in this volume treat poetry from later periods when allegory as a language was slowly being forgotten in favor of newer modes of symbolism. Theology and art were finding new ways to teach the Good News. As these new ways, explicated in the later essays, gained ascendancy, the old language failed. Nineteenth- and twentieth-century critics of the arts may trace this stylistic change back to the rise of capitalism, Protestantism, skepticism, or science, but the epic writers of the sixteenth and seventeenth centuries were steeped in the language of the old ways of expressing belief and of inculcating faith. Later theologians and poets tried the newer ways, but Tasso, Spenser, and Milton created their poems in the full knowledge of what that inherited language could do. The loss of the distinction between typology and tropology is an important part of the vast stylistic shift that occurs in Christian literature between the sixteenth and twentieth centuries. What I consider confusion about these literary terms may be treated by others as prevailing custom. My historical bias in criticism allows such divergence from the poet and the century about which I am writing. We, as literary critics, are faced with the difficult task of trying to explain how these precise terms were absorbed, altered, and applied in literary art. For Tasso, however, such confusion was unthinkable.

# TYPOLOGICAL SYMBOLISM AND
# THE "PROGRESS OF THE SOUL"
# IN SEVENTEENTH-CENTURY LITERATURE

THIS inquiry—at once historical and critical—seeks to explore just how the ancient mode of Christian symbolism we call typology was understood in seventeenth-century England, and how it informs some of the most important literary works of that period. These works, drawn from several genres, include the prose meditations of Donne and Traherne, the religious lyrics of Herbert, Vaughan, and Traherne, the *Anniversary* poems of Donne, Milton's epics, Bunyan's *Pilgrim's Progress*—all concerned in some fundamental way with that favorite seventeenth-century theme, the progress of the soul. Any reader of Luther on Romans, Calvin on Hebrews and Corinthians, the annotations to the Geneva Bible, William Whitaker's *Disputation on Holy Scripture*, Thomas Taylor's *Christ Revealed: or the Old Testament Explained*, George Wither's *Preparation to the Psalter*, or a host of similar exegetical works,[1] will have no doubt that the typological mode of interpretation was alive and well after the Reformation, and that it flourished in sixteenth- and seventeenth-century England. Moreover, any reader of Rosemond Tuve on George Herbert, William Madsen on Milton, Richard Jordan on Traherne, Joseph A.

---

[1] Martin Luther, "Lectures on Romans," *Works*, ed. Jaroslav J. Pelikan and Helmut T. Lehmann, vols. 1– (St. Louis, Mo., 1955–), p. 25; Jean Calvin, *A Commentarie on the Whole Epistle to the Hebrewes*, trans. C. Cotton (London, 1605); Calvin, *A Commentarie upon S. Paules Epistles to the Corinthians*, trans. Thomas Tymme (London, 1577); *The Bible and Holy Scriptures* (Geneva, 1560; London, 1599); William Whitaker, *A Disputation on Holy Scripture against the Papists*, ed. and trans. William Fitzgerald (Parker Society, Cambridge, 1847); Thomas Taylor, *Christ Revealed: or the Old Testament Explained* (London, 1635); George Wither, *A Preparation to the Psalter* (London, 1619).

Mazzeo on Marvell, or, conceivably, myself on Milton and Donne,[2] will not doubt that typological symbolism in some understanding of the term was an important element in the literature of the era.

Despite all this, the inquiry must anticipate skepticism in some quarters. The theologian may insist that typology in a strict sense—God's design of history wherein Old Testament personages and events are recognized as types, recapitulated and fulfilled in Christ and his Church—pertains only to sacred Scripture, not to art or literature. The literary scholar is apt to assume a general discrediting or attenuation of all modes of biblical allegoresis, including typology, after the Reformation, and so to doubt the usefulness of literary study conducted in these terms. And the ordinary reader of seventeenth-century literature may well complain about being asked to deal with yet another specialized vocabulary.

We may ask, then: Why not make do with general literary terms such as biblical allusion, or analogy, or even allegory to describe the patterns of reference these texts present? The answer is in part historical: the prevalence of the language and strategies of typological symbolism in much seventeenth-century literature imposes upon the literary historian a responsibility to reclaim and use as precisely as possible the contemporary symbolic vocabulary. To do so, I submit, will produce important critical dividends as we become better able to assess, for particular works and authors, the precise symbolic meanings, the special symbolic

[2] Rosemond Tuve, *A Reading of George Herbert* (Chicago, 1952); William G. Madsen, *From Shadowy Types to Truth: Studies in Milton's Symbolism* (New Haven, 1968); Richard D. Jordan, *The Temple of Eternity: Thomas Traherne's Philosophy of Time* (Port Washington, N.Y. and London, 1972); Joseph A. Mazzeo, "Cromwell as Davidic King," in *Renaissance and Seventeenth-Century Studies*, ed. Mazzeo (New York, 1961); Barbara K. Lewalski, *Milton's Brief Epic* (Providence, R.I. and London, 1966); Lewalski, *Donne's Anniversaries and the Poetry of Praise: The Creation of a Symbolic Mode* (Princeton, 1973).

charge, adumbrated through the language of typological reference.[3]

My suggestion is that typological symbolism became in the earlier seventeenth century an important literary means to explore the personal spiritual life with profundity and psychological complexity, and that certain characteristic Protestant alterations in the traditional typological formulae facilitated this exploration. These alterations, together with the prominence of the theme of the progress of the soul, arise from the same cause—the new Protestant emphasis upon the application of Scripture to the self, that is, the discovery of scriptural paradigms and of the workings of Divine Providence, in one's own life.[4] Medieval four-level exegesis had of course provided for the personal application of the Scripture text as the third or tropological level of meaning—*quid agas*, moral allegory, in the familiar formula. But this formula was discredited by the Reformation clarion call of the "one sense of Scripture," the literal meaning. As William Perkins put it, "There is but one full and intire sense of every place of scripture, and that is also the literal sense. . . . To make many senses of scripture, is to overturne all sense, and to make nothing certen." However, Protestant exegetes found typological symbolism to be an inseparable part or dimension of the literal sense: in Perkins' words, "not onely the bare historie, but also that which is therby signified, is the full sense of the h[oly] G[host]."[5] Or as Whitaker put it, explicating Gal. 4: 24:

---

[3] For a discussion of some of these issues see, e.g., Helen Gardner, *The Business of Criticism* (Oxford, 1959); Victor Harris, "Allegory to Analogy in the Interpretation of Scripture," *PQ*, 45 (1966), 1–23; H. R. MacCallum, "Milton and the Figurative Interpretation of the Bible," *UTQ* 31 (1962), 397–415; U. Milo Kaufmann, *The Pilgrim's Progress and Traditions in Puritan Meditation* (New Haven, 1966).

[4] For discussion of this point see William R. Haller, *The Rise of Puritanism* (New York, 1938); William H. Halewood, *The Poetry of Grace* (New Haven and London, 1970). Cf. Richard Bernard, *The Faithfull Shepheard* (London, 1607); William Perkins, *The Arte of Prophesying*, trans. Thomas Tuke, *Workes*, vol. 2 (London, 1613).

[5] Perkins, *A Commentarie . . . upon . . . Galatians* (Cambridge, 1604), p. 346.

A type is a different thing from an allegory. The sense, therefore, of that scripture is one only, namely, the literal or grammatical. However, the whole entire sense is not in the words taken strictly, but part in the type, part in the transaction itself . . . and by both taken together the full and perfect meaning is completed. . . . When we proceed from the sign to the thing signified we bring no new sense, but only bring out into the light what was before concealed in the sign.[6]

Along with this legitimation of typological symbolism, the shift in emphasis in reformation theology from *quid agas* to God's activity in us made it possible to assimilate our lives to the typological design, recognizing the biblical stories and events, salvation history, not merely as exemplary to us but as actually recapitulated in our lives. These various impulses led to a new, primary focus upon the individual Christian, whose life is incorporated within, and in whom may be located, God's vast typological patterns of recapitulations and fulfillments operating throughout history. This new focus upon the individual does not deny the traditional identification of the incarnate Christ as the antitype who fulfills all the types, *forma perfectior*, but it does promote new emphases and new formulations in typology, and does permit the use of such formulations in literary treatments of individuals presumed to be assimilated into God's typological design.

Evidence of these new emphases in typological interpretation might be adduced from Joseph Hall, William Perkins, Thomas Goodwin, William Guild, or a number of other seventeenth-century English preachers and exegetes,[7] but for our literary purposes it may be most useful to illustrate from Donne's sermons. Again and again Donne fo-

[6] Whitaker, *Disputation on Holy Scripture*, pp. 404–405.

[7] Joseph Hall, *Contemplations upon the Principall Passages of the Holie Storie* (London, 1642); Perkins, *The Arte of Prophesying*; Thomas Goodwin, *Moses and Aaron. Civil and Ecclesiastical Rites, used by the ancient Hebrews: observed, and at large opened* (London, 1625); William Guild, *Moses Unveiled: or, Those Figures which Served unto the Patterne and Shaddow of Heavenly Things* (London, 1620).

cuses his typological allusions directly upon the Christian individuals who constitute his auditory—us. Often he explains Old Testament texts in terms of their recapitulation in himself and his hearers—"a repeating againe in us, of that which God had done before to Israel"[8]—thereby presenting the Christian auditory as what I term a correlative type with Israel, undergoing much the same kind and quality of spiritual experience. This formulation builds upon the Calvinist sense that the Old and New Covenants are related, not as shadow and substance, but as less and more perfect embodiments of the same salvation history.[9] More often, Donne invites his listeners to consider themselves direct antitypes of the Old Testament types, enjoying through and in Christ all the privileges of the New Dispensation. Commenting on the Psalms, he declares: "*David* was not onely a cleare Prophet of Christ himselfe, but a Prophet of every particular Christian; He foretels what I, what any shall doe, and suffer, and say."[10] Or again, and perhaps most typically Donnean, is the assertion that the entire nexus of typological relationships pointed to in his biblical text is located in, embodied in, the particular Christian auditory he addresses. The Psalms must, he declares, be considered,

> historically, and literally . . . of *David*. And secondly, in their *retrospect*, as they look back upon the first *Adam*, and so concern *Mankind collectively*, and so *you* and *I*, and all have our portion in these calamities; And thirdly, we shall consider them in their *prospect*, in their future relation to the *second Adam*, in *Christ Jesus*, in whom

8 Donne, *Sermons*, ed. George K. Potter and Evelyn Simpson, 10 vols. (Berkeley and Los Angeles, 1953–1963) 3, 313. Sermon on Psalm 2: 12.

9 See, e.g., Calvin, *Commentarie upon . . . Corinthians*, fols. 116v–117. For some discussion of the idea of correlative types see my articles, "*Samson Agonistes* and the 'Tragedy' of the Apocalypse," *PMLA*, 85 (1970), 1050–1062; and "Typology and Poetry: A Consideration of Herbert, Vaughan, and Marvell," in *Illustrious Evidence: Approaches to English Literature of the Early Seventeenth Century*, ed. Earl Miner (Berkeley and Los Angeles, 1975), ch. 3. See also Steven Zwicker, *Dryden's Political Poetry* (Providence, R.I., 1972), pp. 3–27.

10 *Sermons*, VII, 41. Sermon on Psalm 63: 7.

also all mankinde was collected. . . . In all *David's* confessions and lamentations, though they be always literally
true of himself . . . yet *David* speaks *prophetically* . . . and
to us. . . . That which *David* relates to have been his own
case, he foresees will be ours too, in a higher degree.[11]

Remarkably, Donne can also take an occasion, an event
in the order of nature, as itself a type (within the ordinance
of God's providence) of certain antitypes, or fulfillments, in
the orders of grace and glory. These are the categories with
which Donne constantly works—nature, grace, glory—and
he sees them to be related typologically, even as Luther
did.[12] At the marriage of Margaret Washington, Donne set
as his sermon text Hosea 2: 10, "And I will marry thee unto
me for ever," uncovering in it all the typological associations between the marriages of Adam and Eve, of Christ
and the soul, and of the Lamb and his Bride. Moreover, he
saw in the particular human marriage he was celebrating
(an event in the order of nature) an adumbration of the entire course of salvation history and anagogical fulfillment
projected through these typological relationships:

> The first mariage that was made, God made, and he made
> it in Paradise. . . . The last mariage which shall be made,
> God shall make too, and in Paradise too; in the Kingdome
> of heaven. . . . The mariage in this Text hath relation to
> both these mariages; It is it self the spirituall and mys-
> ticall mariage of Christ Jesus to the Church, and to every
> mariageable soule in the Church: And then it hath a
> prospect to the last mariage. . . . Bless these thy servants,
> with making this secular mariage a type of the spirituall,
> and the spirituall an earnest of that eternall, which they
> and we, by thy mercy, shall have in the Kingdome which
> thy Son our Saviour hath purchased.[13]

[11] *Sermons*, II, 75, 99.
[12] For discussion of this see J. S. Preus, *From Shadow to Promise:
Old Testament Interpretation from Augustine to the Young Luther*
(Cambridge, Mass., 1969).
[13] *Sermons*, III, 241–255.

The literary texts with which we are concerned present the speaker, or a historical personage, or a contemporary Christian, as one who is related, in one or another of these characteristic Protestant ways, to the typological patterns of recapitulation and fulfillment ordered by Divine Providence.

Typological symbolism is not central to Donne's divine poems as a whole, but he uses it with some frequency in various works to embody in the self, or in a particular human individual, the entire network of typological relationships pointed to in God's word, and through that symbolism to explore our human condition. Moreover, he presents the individual as a participant in a particular event in the order of nature, designated in God's Providence as a type which shadows forth its antitypes in the orders of grace and glory. This symbolism serves as a means of self-definition and analysis in the *Devotions upon Emergent Occasions* and in the "Hymne to God my God, in my Sicknesse," and as a vehicle of praise in the *Anniversary* poems.

Donne's book of meditations, the *Devotions upon Emergent Occasions*, both sets forth explicitly Donne's view of God's typological method, and is itself devised in imitation of that method. In his striking description of God as poet, Donne presents God's symbolism as an all-encompassing system—which unites typology and anagogy as together constituting the figural dimension of Scripture, and assimilates to this mode his divine manifestations in nature:

> Neither art thou thus a *figurative*, a *metaphoricall God* in thy *word* only, but in thy *workes* too. The *stile* of thy *works*, the *phrase* of thine *actions*, is *metaphoricall*. The institution of thy whole *worship* in the *old Law*, was a continuall *Allegory*; *types* and *figures* overspread all; and *figures* flowed into *figures*, and powred themselves out into *farther figures*; *Circumcision* carried a *figure* of *Baptisme*, and *Baptisme* carries a *figure* of that *purity*, which we shall have in *perfection* in the *new Jerusalem*.[14]

14 *Devotions upon Emergent Occasions*, ed. John Sparrow (Cambridge, 1923), p. 114.

In the *Devotions* Donne finds that his own illness, a providential event in the order of nature, is ordained by God
to embody, and (as Donne meditates upon it) to reveal,
God's vast typological design. Accordingly, he orders each
section of his work into three parts—"Meditation," "Expostulation," and "Prayer"—to display that design and also to
display his own "progress of the soul" toward comprehending it. In the "Meditation" he analyzes his illness, the emergent occasions arising from it, and his eventual but perhaps
only temporary recovery, as manifestations of the distresses
and the mortality our humanity cannot escape in the order
of nature. In the "Expostulations" he understands these
physical conditions to result from and to point to the sicknesses of soul which, however alleviated by grace, cannot be
totally cured in this life. In the "Prayers" the prospect is forward, to final things, with the former sicknesses seen as types
of the eternal suffering and death which Donne hopes to
escape completely through resurrection to eternal life. This
movement may be illustrated from Section 1, entitled, "The
first alteration, The first grudging of the sicknesse." The
"Meditation" expatiates upon the "Variable, and therefore
miserable condition of Man," and upon the great miseries
which sickness introduces into his little world—"these
*earthquakes* in him selfe, sodaine shakings; these *lightnings*,
sodaine flashes; these *thunders*, sodaine noises; these
*Eclypses*, sodain offuscations and darknings of his senses."[15]
The "Expostulation" asks in reference to these symptoms,
"Why hath not my *soule* these apprehensions, these pres-
ages, these changes. . . Why are there not always *waters* in
mine eyes, to testifie to my spiritual sicknes?" And the
"Prayer" begs for the grace to "looke forward to mine end,"
to recognize God's grace in all these changes.[16]

The "Hymne to God my God, in my Sicknesse" is a poetic
treatment of the same kind of event, embodying the web
of typological relationships even more daringly in a particular individual. Imagining himself on his deathbed, Donne

[15] *Ibid.*, pp. 1–2.　　　　[16] *Ibid.*, pp. 3–4.

explores his situation in generic, geographical, and finally
typological terms, as he finds himself experiencing at one
and the same moment the mortal agony Adam's sin has
brought us to by nature, the redemption achieved by
Christ's crucifixion, and the anticipations of heaven glory—
"Where, with thy Quire of Saints for evermore, / I shall be
made thy Musique."[17] But his full comprehension of the
human situation comes as he perceives that he is himself the
true locus of "*Christs* Crosse, and *Adams* tree," related
typologically and geographically in medieval legend. In his
death throes he encompasses the first and second Adam, as
well as the three states of nature, grace, and glory:

> Looke Lord, and finde both *Adams* met in me;
>     As the first *Adams* sweat surrounds my face,
>     May the last *Adams* blood my soule embrace.
>
> So, in his purple wrapp'd receive mee Lord,
>     By these his thornes give me his other Crowne.
>
> (23–27)

Donne's *Anniversary* poems present the same typological
relationships, again embodied in a particular individual—
though in this case the individual is Elizabeth Drury, not
the speaker. This real individual, fifteen-year-old Elizabeth
Drury, is vital to the poems in that her untimely/religious
death (like Donne's own illness in the *Devotions*) is ordered
in God's Providence to incorporate and manifest the course
of salvation history. However, she is made the locus for
Donne's typological symbolism not because of her personal
virtues, but rather because, in Protestant theological terms,
she is assumed to be a regenerate Christian in whom the
image of God has been restored through Christ's justifying
grace.[18] On that understanding, Donne presents the girl as
both recapitulating and foreshadowing other conditions of
human goodness past and to come. She recapitulates in

17 *The Divine Poems*, ed. Helen Gardner (Oxford, 1959), p. 50.
18 I have argued this point at length in *Donne's Anniversaries and
the Poetry of Praise*, pp. 109–173.

some sense that image of God in the order of nature which we had in the created perfection of our first innocence; she bears that image robed with Christ's perfections in the order of grace; and both these conditions prefigure what the image of God in us will be in the condition of glory.

In the *First Anniversary (An Anatomy of the World)* Elizabeth Drury's regenerate status recapitulates and manifests the created perfection of man and nature, the innocence and goodness man first enjoyed when made in the image of God. In her, Beauty's ingredients grew "As in an unvext Paradise" (*1 Ann.* 363); in whatever she did "Some Figure of the Golden times, was hid" (*2 Ann.* 70).[19] The "untimely death" of a virgin in the first blush of youth is both an effect, and a particularly apt recapitulation, of the great mortal loss the young world suffered by original sin. Elizabeth has been dead "Some moneths," but the primal goodness she recapitulates has of course been "long" gone (*1 Ann.* 39–41). That goodness was "The Cyment which did faithfully compact / And glue all vertues," the world's "ntrinsique [sic] Balme, and . . . preservative" which never can be renewed (*1 Ann.* 49–50, 57–58).

In the *Second Anniversarie (Of the Progres of the Soule)* Elizabeth symbolizes the perfection of the order of grace on earth and its translation into the condition of heavenly glory. As Donne often explained in his sermons, the Christian through grace becomes "an abridgement of *Christ* himselfe"; his inchoate sanctification is viewed by God as if it were perfected, and his regenerate life presents a type of what he will be in heavenly glory.[20] So it is with Elizabeth Drury: she was "here / Bethrothed to God, and now is married there" (*2 Ann.* 461–462). Accordingly, the focus of this poem directs us to "Looke upward; that's towards her, whose happy state / We now lament not, but congratulate" (*2 Ann.* 65–66). However, the heavenly state is not itself the primary subject, but rather the way in which her

---

19 All quotations from the *Anniversary* poems are from Frank Manley's edition, *John Donne: The Anniversaries* (Baltimore, 1963).
20 Donne, *Sermons*, II, 289–290; III, 363; IV, 76–77, 340–341.

perfections on earth foreshadowed that heavenly condition: we are invited to consider her as she manifested in life the height of human goodness. And in this context some Christic allusions in the poem (e.g., to Psalm 85: 10, the union of opposites associated with Christ's nativity) present her as recapitulating in her own sphere certain aspects of Christ's life and role—crucifixion, pardon, redemptive power:

> And shee made peace, for no peace is like this,
> That beauty and chastity together kisse:
> Shee did high justice; for shee crucified
> Every first motion of rebellious pride:
> And shee gave pardons, and was liberall,
> For, onely herselfe except, she pardond all.
>
> (2 *Ann.* 363–368)

In the course of the poem, moreover, by an extension of the typological patterns enacted in Elizabeth Drury, the speaker relates himself and his audience to Elizabeth's progress. The speaker's own renunciation of the world is a figure of her "religious death." Her actual ascension to heaven in an instant was a type (recapitulation) of Christ's ascension, and the imagined flight of the speaker's own soul is a *figura* of hers. Moreover, the projected spiritual progress of the fit audience of the poems, the "new world" the speaker directly instructs and exhorts, will recapitulate both her progress and his.

Though typological symbolism is more nearly central to Herbert's poetic vision than to Donne's, and is couched in somewhat more traditional terms, Herbert also finds typological paradigms embodied in a particular individual—the poetic speaker of the volume entitled *The Temple*. The two poets do, however, employ quite different typological symbols to present quite different versions of the spiritual life. Donne, as we have seen, characteristically treats the two Adams and the three states of nature, grace, and glory as they are located in a single individual, and thereby probes the vast dislocations and disjunctions among those states. In his book of lyrics from *The Temple*, "The Church," Herbert characteristically presents his speaker's uneven, anxious, vicissitude-filled progress from an identification with the various Old Testament types he finds himself recapitulating, to a comprehension and incorporation of the Christic fulfillment of those types. Moreover, whereas Donne explores the movement from innocence to regeneration, from Law to Grace, sequentially in his two *Anniversary* poems, Herbert normally compresses this progress within the compass of an individual poem.

The poem "The Bunch of Grapes" affords the most explicit statement of Herbert's conception of typology as God's symbolism. As Rosemond Tuve has noted,[21] the poem depends for its meaning upon our recognition of the traditional typological relationship between the grapes hanging from the pole carried by the spies, and Christ on the cross, the true vine pressed in the winepress of the Passion (Isa. 63: 3) to become the wine of the New Covenant. What is most significant and characteristic, however, is the location of the entire typological relationship in the heart of the speaker. The poem is about the speaker's loss of spiritual joy and content: as he explores that loss he first sees himself recapitulating the wanderings of the Israelities in the desert, as a correlative type with them:

> For as the Jews of old by Gods command
> Travell'd, and saw no town;
> So now each Christian hath his journeys spann'd:
> Their storie pennes and sets us down.
> A single deed is small renown,
> Gods works are wide, and let in future times;
> His ancient justice overflows our crimes.[22]    (8–14)

Unlike the Israelites, however, he is given no cluster of grapes, no tangible earnest or assurance of the Promised Land. The resolution comes as the speaker recognizes the antitype, Christ's redemptive sacrifice, as a yet more basic

[21] Tuve, *A Reading of George Herbert*, pp. 112–117.

[22] All quotations from Herbert's poetry are from the edition of F. E. Hutchinson, *The Works of George Herbert* (Oxford, 1959).

part of his spiritual experience: "But can he want the grape, who hath the wine?" (22). Tracing a progress within himself from type to antitype, he is at length able to affirm that this earnest of Christ's sacrifice affords him a less tangible but far more certain and all-embracing guarantee of spiritual joy.

The first poem in "The Church" sets forth the terms for this progress from type to antitype, and also begins to establish the primary typological symbol which unifies the collection, the temple in the heart. In the emblematic poem "The Altar," the speaker's heart, the stage for all his spiritual experience, is first presented as recapitulation of that altar of unhewn stones divinely prescribed in the Old Testament ("thou shalt not built it of hewn stone: for if thou lift up thy tool upon it, thou hast polluted it," Exod. 20: 25):

> A broken ALTAR, Lord, thy servant reares,
> Made of a heart, and cemented with teares:
> Whose parts are as thy hand did frame;
> No workmans tool hath touch'd the same.
>> A  H E A R T  alone
>> Is    such    a    stone,
>> As    nothing    but
>> Thy  pow'r  doth  cut.
>> Wherefore each part
>> Of  my  hard  heart
>> Meets in this frame,
>> To praise thy Name:
> That,  if  I  chance  to  hold  my  peace,
> These stones to praise thee may not cease.
> O let thy blessed S A C R I F I C E be mine,
> And sanctifie this A L T A R to be thine.

But since the new altar is not simply stone, but a heart, it is also the antitype to the Old Testament altar, pointed to in that medley of texts customarily associated with the Exodus passage by the commentators: God's promise (Jeremiah 31: 33) of a new covenant written in the heart of man, "I will put my law in their inward parts, and write it in their hearts"; his declaration (Ezekiel 11: 19), "I will take the stony heart out of their flesh, and will give them a heart of flesh"; and his assertion (Isaiah 66: 1–2) that he does not dwell in houses built by men's hands but (alluding to Psalm 51) with the man "that is poor and of a contrite spirit." The fundamental problem for the speaker is posed in typological terms in this first poem: the need for his Old Testament stony heart to be hewn by God's power and wholly transformed into its New Testament antitype, so that it may accept, appropriate, and properly praise the sacrifice of the New Covenant, Christ.

This poem also identifies the typological symbol which unifies the entire collection of lyrics, that of the individual Christian as temple of God, the antitype to the Old Testament temple. This typology is derived from the familiar biblical texts: "Ye are God's husbandry, ye are God's building . . . / Know ye not that ye are the temple of God, and that the Spirit of God dwelleth in you?" (1 Corinthians 3: 9, 16); and, "Ye also, as lively stones, are built up a spiritual house, a holy priesthood, to offer up spiritual sacrifices, acceptable to God by Jesus Christ" (1 Peter 2: 5). Joseph Hall's comment on these texts offers an analogue for Herbert's radical personalizing of these theological ideas:

> Every renewed man [is] the individual temple of God. . . . What is the Altar whereon our sacrifices of prayer and praises are offered to the Almighty, but a contrite heart? . . . Behold, if Solomon built a Temple unto thee, thou hast built a Temple unto thy selfe in us. We are not only through thy grace living stones in thy Temple, but living Temples in thy Sion. . . . Let the Altars of our cleane hearts send up ever to thee the sweetest perfumed smoake of our holy meditations, and faithfull prayers, and cheerfull thanks-givings.[23]

Working out such terms, Herbert's speaker presents himself as the church of the New Covenant which must be built

[23] Joseph Hall, *Contemplations*, pp. 1158–1159.

by God. The first set of poems presents the theological basis for the speaker's formation as the new Church—his acceptance of, and relation to, Christ's sacrifice. Then, though not sequentially, various aspects of church architecture, church liturgy, the historical experience of the people of God, and the emotional and psychological experience assumed to be rendered in David's Psalms are shown to be recapitulated in this speaker—who is a Christian everyman who to be sure, but also a particular Christian priest and poet.

Several poems throughout the collection, like "The Bunch of Grapes," trace the speaker's spiritual anxieties and spiritual progress in terms of his relation, first to the Old Testament type, and then to the Christic antitype. In "The Collar" the speaker rebels because he experiences the spiritual life entirely in terms of duties, obligations, and Old Testament legal servitude; his problem is resolved as the Lord's call, "*Child,*" reminds him that his New Covenant status (Galatians 4: 3–7) is that not of a bond-slave but of a child and son, heir to the promises and the kingdom. In "Aaron" he begins by recognizing his need as priest to clothe himself with Aaron's priestly garments and ornaments, but yet his utter inability to put on the holiness they symbolize—and demand. He then comes to understand that this responsibility is not his, that Christ is now his head, breast, music, dress. At length, exhibiting the characteristic Protestant emphasis upon the individual Christian as antitype, he perceives that as a priest of the New Covenant he is himself (through Christ) the antitype and fulfillment of the Old Testament Aaron:

> So holy in my head,
> Perfect and light in my deare breast,
> My doctrine tun'd by Christ, (who is not dead,
> But lives in me while I do rest)
> Come people; Aaron's drest.          (21–25)

In "Jordan II" he invokes the typological relationship between the Israelites' crossing Jordan to the Promised Land and Christian Baptism to explore the "baptism" of his verse.

He begins by adhering to a "law of works" in poetry, in which he seeks out "quaint words, and trim invention," curling his plain intention with metaphors. He then recognizes that worthy praises, like the renovation of the heart, must be essentially God's doing, and so adopts an appropriate New Covenant poetics—to copy out the sweetness that is "in love . . . [al]readie penn'd."

*The Temple* as a whole is also unified by typological symbolism, its three parts related in terms of a radically personalized and somewhat altered version of the traditional symbolism of the three parts of the Old Testament temple—the Porch typifying the external and visible aspect of the church; the Holy Place typifying the communion of the invisible church on earth; and the Holy of Holies typifying the highest heaven of the saints.[24] In "Church-Porch" the speaker sets forth a series of dry, didactic prescriptions regarding the externals of the Christian life and the moral behavior appropriate to a Christian profession, which constantly echo their sources in classical ethical philosophy and in the Proverbs of Solomon. The lyrics of "The Church" define the new Christian temple as the inner essence of the Christian experience, the relationship between Christ and the individual soul, and the distresses and joys attendant upon it. However, Herbert's "Church Militant" does not relate to the Holy of Holies or to its antitype, the heavenly kingdom: the soul's movement into that third realm is intimated at the end of "The Church" in a series of poems on the last things—"Death," "Dooms-day," "Judgment," "Heaven,"—followed by the final, exquisite lyric, "Love III," which suggests the soul's

[24] The traditional typological equations are set forth in Thomas Adams, "The Temple," *Works* (London, 1629), pp. 980–981; Andrew Willet, *Hexapla in Exodum* (London, 1608), p. 629; Daniel Featley, "The Arke under the Curtaines" (1613), in *Clavis Mystica* (London, 1636), p. 576. Herbert's *The Temple* is discussed in terms of this typology in John D. Walker, "The Architectonics of George Herbert's *The Temple*," *ELH*, 29 (1962), 289–305; and Mary Ellen Rickey, *Utmost Art: Complexity in the Verse of George Herbert* (Lexington, 1966).

gracious reception at the heavenly banquet. In "Church Militant" the significant typological allusions are to Noah's Ark, the wandering Ark of the Covenant, and the fleeing woman of the Apocalypse.[25] All these are recognized types of the Church Militant in its relation to the world and are used to develop Herbert's vision of the sin-plagued round traversed by the corporate Church, which can have no security or true progress here. The Old Testament temple, with its intimations of permanence, has its true antitype solely in that church which is in the hearts of the elect, who can progress toward, and at length achieve, individual salvation.

In *Silex Scintillans* Henry Vaughan seems at first not unlike Herbert in his use of typology to explore the spiritual condition of the speaker. In the poem "White Sunday" Vaughan's speaker finds himself and his contemporaries recapitulating the experience of the Old Testament types:

> Besides, thy method with thy own,
> Thy own dear people pens our times,
> Our stories are in theirs set down
> And Penalties spread to our Crimes.[26]    (29–32)

And in "Mans fall, and Recovery" he underscores the spiritual advantages which the New Covenant provides to him, so that he fulfills the types *forma perfectior*:

> This makes me span
> My fathers journeys, and in one faire step
> O're all their pilgrimage, and labours leap,
>     For God (made man,)
> Reduc'd th'Extent of works of faith; so made
> Of their *Red Sea*, a *Spring*; I wash, they wade. (27–32)

[25] See Daniel Featley, "The Embleme of the Church Militant," in *Clavis Mystica*, p. 300: "The Portable Arke in the Old Testament, and the flying woman in the New, are images of the militant Church in this World." Also, Robert Cawdray, *A Treasurie or Store-House of Similes* (London, 1600), pp. 93–94.

[26] All quotations from Vaughan's poetry are from the edition of L. C. Martin, *The Works of Henry Vaughan* (Oxford, 1957).

Yet typology is not the dominant symbolic mode for
Vaughan, as it clearly is for Herbert. Vaughan's collection
of lyrics finds its unity not in a typological symbol such as
the Temple in the heart but in the dominant metaphor of
the Christian pilgrimage.[27] Moreover, when he does see
himself recapitulating the biblical types, Vaughan's speaker
—unlike Herbert's—usually does not stress Christ's redemption or claim a privileged role as antitype grounded
upon that redemption. Rather, he perceives himself standing on much the same plane of experience with the Old
Testament figures—a correlative type with them, expecting
the great antitypical fulfillment of the gospel promises at
the end of time or in the next world. His posture, like theirs,
is one of anticipation and expectation rather than fulfillment.

Vaughan, however, does employ typological symbolism
to assist in the development of his pilgrimage metaphor: the
speaker often sees himself as a pilgrim wandering through
a natural or biblical landscape (usually a conflation of
both), recapitulating the wanderings of the Old Testament
patriarchs. In the poem "Religion" the pilgrim-speaker
finds himself walking about in the same groves where
Elijah, Gideon, Ishmael, Jacob, Abraham, and other Old
Testament personages encountered angels or else heard the
voice of God himself. Attributing the disruption of such
conference in modern times to the ever-increasing corruption in the once pure "spring" of religion, he calls upon
Christ to cleanse these waters anew, recapitulating the
sweetening of the waters at Marah, the bringing forth of
water from the rock by Moses' rod, the change of water to
wine at the wedding feast. In *Silex Scintillans*, the poem
following "Religion" is "The Search," in which the pilgrim
speaker searches for Christ in the New Testament biblical
landscape where the notable events of this life took place

[27] I have discussed this point, together with the proposition that
Vaughan relies heavily upon contemporary Protestant allegorical read-
ings of the Song of Songs in terms of the Christian Pilgrimage, in
"Typology and Poetry," *Illustrious Evidence*, pp. 58–61.

but discovers, surprisingly enough, that these historical events and places are in fact correlatives with the Old Testament types, that the true antitypes lie in the universe within the self or in the heavenly world to come: "Search well another world; who studies this, / Travels in Clouds, seeks *Manna*, where none is" (95–96).

One favorite type for the speaker is Israel wandering in the desert. In the opening lines of "The Mutinie"— "Weary of this same Clay, and straw"—he sees himself recapitulating the situation of Israel enslaved at the brick-kilns of Egypt, and later he too is wandering in the wilderness. He re-enacts also the Israelites' murmurs against God, especially since he seems not to be experiencing the New Testament privileges he supposedly ought to enjoy: he knows that God has "a shorter Cut / To bring me home, than through a wilderness, / A Sea, or Sands and Serpents" (29–31), yet still he wanders like Israel of old. The conclusion affirms his willingness, despite all this, to follow obediently whatever path God has devised for him.

Again, the speaker often identifies himself with Ishmael, the first-born of Abraham by the bond-maid Hagar, who was cast out with his mother onto the desert so that he might not inherit with Isaac, the chosen seed, and who was saved from dying of thirst when an angel directed his mother to a water fountain. Though medieval exegetes regarded Ishmael as a type of the reprobate, Vaughan seems rather to call upon Luther's interpretation of the story, in which Ishmael is a type of the gentiles who were to become heirs of the promise, and in which God's providential act in preserving him is a foreshadowing of that grace.[28] In such terms Vaughan's speaker finds himself recapitulating the situation of the weeping, thirst-racked Ishmael. In "The Timber" he prays that on his way through the desert his bottle may be filled with the tears of his repentance; in "Begging II" he complains of God's coldness to his cries, whereas of old "thou didst hear the *weeping*

[28] Luther, "Lectures on Genesis," *Works*, IV, 41–43. See also, *Geneva Bible*, Annotations on Gal. 4: 22–31.

*Lad"* (12); in "Providence" he cites the story of Ishmael's rescue as a type of the providential care he expects of God; and in "The Seed Growing Secretly" he cries out as a new Ishmael for the dew of grace from heaven: "O fill his bottle! thy childe weeps!" (16).

Alternatively, the speaker is often in the situation of Jacob, who set forth for Laban's country, "on foot, in poor estate" as Henry Ainsworth explains, with only his staff in his hand.[29] In "The Pilgrimage" he finds himself lodged like Jacob in some nameless place but dreaming of heaven; in "Religion" and "The Search" he finds himself at Jacob's Well but desires instead its antitypical fulfillment, Christ the fountain of living waters offered to the Samaritan woman (John 4: 1–14). However, when he associates himself with the situation of Jacob at Bethel, he moves beyond the type to indicate his enjoyment of its antitype, the Christian Church. In the poem "Regeneration" the speaker finds himself suddenly in a fresh field—"Some call'd it, *Jacobs Bed"* (28)—where Jacob slept on a stone and dreamed of a ladder reaching to heaven, and where he later anointed the stone as an altar to God. The speaker comes to understand that this place is now the garden of the Church watered by the living fountain which is Christ and his word. So also in "Jacobs Pillow, and Pillar" the speaker finds Jacob's simple stone pillow to be a type of the Church of the New Testament located in the hearts of the faithful, and he finds Jacob's struggles with his brother to be repeated in the turmoils of the English Civil War; but he perceives also that the comfort afforded by Jacob's stone pillow is far surpassed by its antitype which he enjoys, Christ.

A further range of typological allusion is supplied by biblical references to the end of time which predominate especially in Part 2 of *Silex Scintillans,* and through which the speaker presents the Apocalypse, as the great antitype fulfilling all the types. In "Ascension-day," the first poem of Part 2, the speaker finds that the biblical event of Christ's

---

[29] See commentary on Gen. 28: 5–22 and 32: 10, in Henry Ainsworth, *Annotations upon the Five Bookes of Moses* (London, 1627).

ascension is recapitulated in himself, raising him to a new plane of spiritual assurance above the worldly vicissitudes of Part 1. The angels' reference at Christ's ascension to his return in glory (Acts 1: 11) provides the basis for viewing that episode as a type of Christ's Second Coming, and that typology is invoked at the end of this poem as the speaker echoes the plea to Christ at the end of the book of Revelation to "come quickly." The apocalyptic leitmotif recurs in poem after poem—"They are all gone into the world of light," "The Bird," "Fair and yong light," "The Day of Judgement," "The Throne," "The Feast." In the final poem, "L'Envoy," the speaker imagines with great vividness and immediacy his participation in the Second Coming—"Arise, arise! / And like old cloaths fold up these skies, / This long worn veyl: then shine and spread / Thy own bright self over each head" (7–10)—yet the poem and the volume end with the speaker's affirmation of his willingness to wait here with patience until the number of the saints shall be completed.

Although his vision of man's capacity in this life to apprehend and enjoy eternal felicity seems in many respects unique, Thomas Traherne also found in typology an important symbolic framework for exploring the human condition.[30] Unlike Augustine, Aquinas, and most other Christian philosophers who see eternity as wholly apart from and outside our time, Traherne perceives it (as Richard Jordan has noted) as the infinite duration and succession of ages.[31] On this understanding, even as we live our lives now we can learn to experience all the ages before us, as well as eternity itself: life is lived in eternity. Progress toward such understanding is grounded upon typology, as Traherne finds the course of human history recapitulated in himself: Adam in Eden, Adam fallen, Christ incarnate, Christ in Glory are all figures for the stages of human existence—

[30] Traherne discusses the typology of the ceremonies of the Temple and Christian worship quite conventionally in *Christian Ethicks*, ed. Carol L. Marks and George R. Guffey (Ithaca, N.Y., 1968), pp. 129–130.

[31] *The Temple of Eternity*, pp. 58–73.

Innocence, Misery, Grace, Glory. These figures and these states are not merely moral exemplars or analogies for Traherne, but are said to be actually repeated in him. That incarnation of the states of human goodness and that progress of the soul which Donne explored in the dead Elizabeth Drury, Traherne locates even more radically and completely in the self of his speaker, as a present possession in this life.

In his book of meditations, the *Centuries*, Traherne's sense of himself as image of God leads him to perceive himself as a correlative type with Adam, repeating the edenic experience:

> Being to lead this Life within I was Placed in Paradice without with som Advantages which the Angels hav not. And being Designed to Immortality and an Endless Life, was to Abide with GOD from everlasting to everlasting in all His Ways. But I was Deceived by my Appetite, and fell into Sin. Ingratefully I despised Him that gav me my being. I offended in an Apple against Him that gave me the whole World. (1. 75)[32]

Again, at the beginning of the "Second Century" he records his experience as Adam, in that the entire world has been made for him and all the elements and creatures serve him; his praises of the things of the creation are from the point of view of Adam, to whom all the treasures of heaven and earth were given as his sole possession. In the "Third Century" the speaker records his ecstatic perceptions of nature's glories as a specific recapitulation of Adam's innocent state—"The Corn Was Orient and Immortal Wheat, which never should be reaped, nor was ever sown. I thought it had stood from everlasting to everlasting" (3. 3). He also finds the experience of the Fall and the resulting alienation from God repeated in his life, though he sees the effects of Original Sin to inhere in the evil customs of the

---

[32] All quotations from Traherne's works are from the edition of H. M. Margoliouth, *Centuries, Poems, and Thanksgivings*, 2 vols. (Oxford, 1958).

world more than in our inborn corruption (3. 8). "Being Swallowed up . . . in the Miserable Gulph of idle talk and worthless vanities, thenceforth I lived among Shadows, like a Prodigal Son feeding upon Husks with Swine" (3.14). Continuing his re-enactment of the history of the race, he begins to look for a book from heaven, a revelation of the ways of felicity, and then he perceives that God has in fact supplied him: "For He had sent the Book I wanted before I was Born" (3. 27). That book leads him to see himself as one with Christ, the Second Adam: "And by that Book I found that there was an eternal GOD, who loved me infinitly, that I was his Son, that I was to overcom Death, and to liv for ever, that He Created the World for me, that I was to Reign in His Throne and to inherit all Things" (3. 29). Through this identification he experiences in various ways the conditions of grace and glory, even to the assimilation and possession of God's infinite felicity.

The poems trace the same progress in terms of the same typological relationships. The Dobell manscript, in part a holograph, begins with a group of poems in which the speaker recapitulates the situation of Adam in Eden. In "The Salutation" he proclaims, "From Dust I rise, / And out of Nothing now awake, / . . . Into this Eden so Divine and fair, / So Wide and Bright, I com his Son and Heir" (25–36). In "Eden" he asserts, "Only what Adam in his first Estate, / Did I behold; . . . / Those Things which first his Eden did adorn, / My Infancy / Did crown" (29–37). In "Innocence" he claims, "I felt no Stain, nor Spot of Sin / . . . that Day / The ancient Light of Eden did convey / Into my Soul: I was an Adam there, / A little Adam in a Sphere" (4, 49–52). He then traces in several poems how sin disrupts this identification (e.g., "The Instruction," "The Approach"), and in others manifests his new sense of himself as embodying the states of grace and glory ("My Spirit," "The Designe," "Amendment," "The Anticipation," "Love," "Thoughts IV").

The manuscript revised by Philip Traherne after Thomas' death contains many of the same poems and several new ones, arranged in a rather more carefully ordered and sequential progression through the several states. Again the sequence begins with poems in which the speaker relives the adamic innocence, though for the most part the speaker of these poems looks back on that state as one who has known sin and now is enabled to return to Edenic innocence through Christ—"An Infant-Ey," "The Return," "Adam," "The World." In the last-mentioned poem the speaker asserts that he still possesses "all God's Works divine" (11) even as Adam did: "Sin spoil'd them; but my Savior's precious Blood / Sprinkled I see / On them to be, / Making them all both safe and good" (13–16). "The Apostacy" treats his Fall, and the next several poems evoke the misery ensuing from the Fall—"Solitude," "Poverty," "Dissatisfaction." Then, as in the *Centuries*, the coming of the Bible brings the speaker a new typological identification with Christ, and a new possession, Christendom. This new identification enables him to recognize his own portion of Christendom, his own city, as the New Jerusalem:

> The City, fill'd with Peeple, near me stood;
> A Fabrick like a Court divine,
> Of many Mansions bright and fair;
> Wherin I could repair
> To Blessings that were Common, Great, and Good:
> Yet all did shine
> As burnisht and as new
> As if before none ever did them view:
> They seem'd to me
> Environ'd with Eternity.[33]

The final poems lay claim to divine felicity and power:

> That All things in their proper place
> My Soul doth best embrace,
> Extends its Arms beyond the Seas
> Abov the Hevens its self can pleas,
> With God enthron'd may reign.[34]

[33] "The City," 11–20. See also, "Christendom."
[34] "Hosanna," 51–55.

Milton made extensive and various use of typology in the portrayal of hero and action in *Samson Agonistes* and *Paradise Regained*; in several scenes of *Paradise Lost* (the war in heaven, Michael's prophecy, Eden); in numerous prose tracts presenting England as the new Israel; and even in the structure of his metaphors, as several recent studies have made clear.[35] Milton also used classical myth typologically: in the *Nativity Ode* Pan and the infant Hercules are types of the infant Christ; and in *Lycidas* (profoundly figural in its entire scope) Apollo, Orpheus, and the entire pastoral world are at length subsumed, recapitulated, and fulfilled in the heavenly pastoral scene which Lycidas enjoys.[36] So vast a topic as Milton's typology cannot be addressed in general terms here, but I shall suggest how, even in his epics, Milton turned to brilliant dramatic account the characteristic Protestant use of typological reference to explore the psyche and to analyze the spiritual progress of a particular individual.

Michael's prophetic account of the course of human history in *Paradise Lost* is ordered, as he explains to Adam, to display mankind progressing from "shadowy Types" (Noah, Abraham, Moses, Joshua, David) "to Truth"—Christ and his redemptive mission (12. 303). But Adam, in good Protestant fashion, is to do more than simply learn this typological theory and the role of Christ as antitype: he is to internalize all of it within himself. Accordingly, he is not merely a passive observer and listener during Michael's

[35] See, e.g., F. Michael Krouse, *Milton's "Samson" and the Christian Tradition* (Princeton, 1949); Lewalski, "*Samson Agonistes* and the 'Tragedy' of the Apocalypse," and *Milton's Brief Epic*; Madsen, *From Shadowy Types to Truth*; Michael Fixler, *Milton and the Kingdoms of God* (Evanston, Ill., 1964); John C. Ulreich, Jr., "The Typological Structure of Milton's Imagery," *Milton Studies* 5, 67–85; Jonathan Goldberg, "*Virga Iesse*: Analogy, Typology, Anagogy in a Miltonic Simile," *Milton Studies* 5, 177–90.

[36] For a detailed treatment of typology in "Lycidas," see David Berkeley, *Inwrought with Figures Dim: A Reading of Milton's "Lycidas,"* (The Hague, 1974). In addition to the classical types, Michael, St. Peter, and finally Edward King himself are types of Christ in this poem.

account, but lives through, as it were, the experience of his progeny, exhibiting in himself their miseries, mistakes, and misapprehensions about the Promised Seed.[37] He weeps his own flood of tears over the Flood, exults as Noah did over the rainbow and the renewed covenant, glories with the Israelites in the Mosaic deliverance but laments as well the imperfections and rigor of the law, apprehends Messiah as Son of David but (with the contemporary Jews) expects him to reclaim his throne and conquer Satan by force. Adam, living history in prospect, with and through his progeny, must himself work, "From shadowy Types to Truth" until he experiences a union with the Second Adam in achieving a wholly spiritual victory over Sin, Death, Satan. He is also upon a progress of the soul which involves re-enacting and surpassing the shadowy types until at length he himself becomes, in some sense, the Second Adam:

> Henceforth I learn, that to obey is best,
> And love with fear the only God, to walk
> As in his presence, ever to observe
> His providence, and on him sole depend,
> Merciful over all his works, with good
> Still overcoming evil, and by small
> Accomplishing great things, by things deem'd weak
> Subverting worldly strong, and worldly wise
> By simply meek: that suffering for Truth's sake
> Is fortitude to highest victory.          (12. 561–570)

In *Paradise Regained* the typology would seem traditional enough: Christ enacts dramatically his appropriate typological role as antitype of the various Old Testament (and classical) types alluded to in the discourse between himself and Satan. Yet Milton's Christ must himself undergo a progress of the soul, in that he begins without a full sense of himself and his mission and then progresses, in

[37] I have discussed this interplay in some detail in "Structure and the Symbolism of Vision in Michael's Prophecy, *Paradise Lost*, XI–XII," *Philological Quarterly*, 42 (1963), 25–35.

large part through the debate with Satan over the types and his relation to them, to a full clarification of his role as Prophet, Priest, and King, and of himself as Second Adam and Son of God. As I have argued at length elsewhere,[38] Satan's strategy throughout the temptation is to present Christ with false, inadequate, or less perfect types of himself and his roles (the Greek oracles, Baalam, Judas Maccabaeus, Alexander the Great, Scipio) as substitutes for certain major types to whom Christ relates himself: Moses, Elijah, Gideon, David, Hercules, Socrates, Job. Then, much more subtly, Satan urges Christ to repeat the actions and experiences of these same major types, literally and exactly. Christ's hard intellectual task is to discriminate between greater and lesser types, and then to recognize that he must not only recapitulate the major types but must do so *forma perfectior*. He is not to be fed miraculously in the wilderness by God, as were Moses and the Israelites and Elijah, but is to hunger rather for God's Word and so become the new "Living Oracle" fulfilling the Law and the Prophets. He is not to reclaim the lost tribes and reunite the physical Israel as a new David, but is to fulfill the Davidic type by a spiritual kingdom, whereby he will become *"Israel's* true King" (3. 441). He is not even to rest in the Socratic wisdom (so useful to him for moral and ethical precepts) or in the Jobean patience, but is to surpass and fulfill these highest types by expounding the Divine Wisdom, and by his patient endurance of the crucifixion, prefigured here in the Storm and Tower scenes.[39] Not entirely facetiously, we might argue that Christ's progress to full self-knowledge in this poem depends upon his becoming a skilled typologist, able to internalize and to enact all the theory defining him as the one who is to recapitulate and fulfill all the types, *forma perfectior*.

Finally, typology plays a limited but important role in

---

[38] *Milton's Brief Epic*, Chapters 7–12.
[39] See the argument supporting this reading of the storm and tower scenes in *Milton's Brief Epic*, pp. 303–321.

Bunyan's allegorical narrative of the progress of the soul, *The Pilgrim's Progress*.[40] Unquestionably, the dominant mode of this work is allegory rather than typology: the biblical figures most often encountered—e.g., the Slough of Despond, the Strait Gate, the Valley of the Shadow of Death, Vanity Fair, Hill Difficulty, the battle with Apollyon, the heavy burden of sin, the key of promise—are embodiments of biblical metaphors rather than types. The characters are for the most part manifestations of a single character trait (Worldly Wiseman, Pliable, Hopeful, Faithful, Talkative, By-ends, and the incorrigible Ignorance); sometimes abstractions of specific functions (Evangelist, Interpreter); or occasionally fully allegorical personages standing for abstract qualities (Piety, Prudence, Charity, Giant Despair). But in addition to these varieties of metaphor and allegory, Bunyan's pilgrims sometimes encounter types and typological situations which carry the spiritual significances accorded them in the New Covenant: Christian fears that Mount Sinai (the type of the Law) will fall upon his head and is saved by Evangelist preaching the New Law of Grace; Faithful is tempted by Adam the First and then beaten by Moses (the embodiment of the Law) for inclining toward him. More important, however, is Christian's gradually developing perception that he is following a well-trodden path, repeating the adventures of many biblical personages who have preceded him: after losing his scroll he is forced to retrace his steps, like the Israelites in the desert; he journeys as David did through the Valley of the Shadow of Death repeating verses from his Psalms; he passes by the biblical Demas still enamored of his silver; he encounters the pillar of salt into which Lot's wife was turned. Moreover, in Book II, Christian's journey itself becomes a type for that of his wife and children, as they frequently encounter signposts and memorials record-

[40] John Bunyan, *The Pilgrim's Progress*, ed. Roger Sharrock (London, 1965). [The "limited" role of typology does suggest a greater role for tropology or moral allegory, as argued for Tasso in Roche's essay above: see his n. 18.—Ed.]

ing his experiences even as they in their own manner are recapitulating those experiences. In this way, by degrees, we are invited to understand that although this pilgrim's progress allegorizes the spiritual journey of all Christian pilgrims, yet any particular pilgrim's progress is itself an episode within God's all-encompassing typological scheme.

One related topic may be addressed briefly—the matter of biblical *figurae* for the Christian poet. The seventeenth-century English Protestant poet felt keenly the responsibility laid upon him to exercise his Muse in God's service, to treat sacred subjects and render fitting praise to God; but at the same time he had to confront the issue of his own unworthiness and human limitations. Not surprisingly, he often approached these issues by relating himself to one of the biblical poets who (inspired by God) had confronted and resolved the same problems. This is not quite Protestant typology, since the Christian poet chooses his biblical model, and understands the relationship to be of his making rather than a genuine recapitulation worked by God's providence, but the issue is not altogether clear-cut. Perhaps it would be truer to say that in these cases the poet presents himself as seeking, striving, praying to become a genuine correlative type with one of the biblical poets— Moses for the epic or the epideictic/denunciatory poet, David for the religious lyricist.

At the conclusion of the *First Anniversary* Donne's speaker presents himself as a latter-day Moses whose song has been an analogue of the Mosaic song in Deuteronomy 32: he declares that he has invaded the "great Office" God laid upon Moses to compose that song, which, as an epitome of the Old Testament, was said by the commentators to combine magnificent praises of God with pervasive denunciations of the iniquities and corruptions of the Israelites.[41]

[41] See, e.g., Calvin, *Commentaries on the Four Last Books of Moses*, trans. Charles W. Bingham, 4 vols. (Edinburgh, 1852–1855), 4, 328–338; *Geneva Bible* (1599), fol. 77v; Immanuel Tremellius and Franciscus Junius, *Testamenti Veteris Biblia Sacra* (London, 1581), fol. 209:

The poet, as Mosaic singer, praises the image of God in Elizabeth Drury, and denounces and curses the order of nature as utterly corrupt, lost in sin, given over to death, and abandoned to God's wrath and judgment. At the conclusion of the *Second Anniversary* the poet characterizes himself as a trumpet, referring to the two trumpets of silver with which the Old Testament priests were to summon the people—in Protestant exegesis glossed as a figure of the Christian minister preaching the Word:[42] More than this, as Raymond D. Waddington suggests,[43] he becomes by implication a *figura* of John of Patmos, the New Testament prophet who proclaims the resurrection of the dead:

> Since his [God's] will is, that to posteritee,
> Thou shouldest for life, and death, a patterne bee,
> And that the world should notice have of this,
> The purpose, and th'Autority is his;
> Thou art the Proclamation; and I ame
> The Trumpet, at whose voice the people came.
>
> (2 *Ann.* 523–528)

By adopting this new *figura* for himself, the poet signals his own progress from an essentially Old Testament role of denunciation and judgment to the New Covenant one of sounding, mediating as an instrument, the redemptive proclamation of God embodied in Elizabeth Drury.

---

John Donne, *Essays in Divinity*, ed. Evelyn M. Simpson (Oxford, 1952), p. 92; Luther, *Lectures on Deuteronomy*, ed. Pelikan, *Works*, 9, 290.

[42] Numbers 10: 2–3, 10. See, e.g. Calvin, *Four Last Books of Moses*, 2, 458; Donne, *Sermons*, II, 166–170.

[43] See Raymond D. Waddington, *The Mind's Empire: Myth and Form in George Chapman's Narrative Poems* (Baltimore, Md., 1974), pp. 11–17. For fuller discussion of Donne's personae in the *Anniversary* poems, see my *Donne's Anniversaries and the Poetry of Praise*, pp. 236–240, 277–280. It should be noted that Donne associates his speaker here with the specifically biblical role of Prophet rather than with the high humanistic conception of the poet as Maker, imitator of God's creativity, so ably reviewed by S. K. Heninger in *Touches of Sweet Harmony: Pythagorean Cosmology and Renaissance Poetics* (San Marino, California, 1974).

In *Paradise Lost* Milton also presents himself as a new Moses, imploring in his epic invocation the inspiration of the Heavenly Muse given long ago to "That Shepherd, who first taught the chosen Seed, / In the Beginning how the Heav'ns and Earth / Rose out of *Chaos*" (1. 8–10). This reference in Milton's epic context activates the "Biblical Poetics" theories which identified Moses as an epic-like writer of hexameter verse, treating the lofty and wondrous deeds of the Creation and the Exodus.[44] Milton's reference to Moses as the one who "first taught" the subject matter of Genesis implies that he is now treating the same materials himself and requires the same illumination to do it worthily. Moses the mediator, receiving the revelation from God enveloped by a thick cloud (Exodus 19: 9), and delivering it with his face concealed by a veil (Exodus 34: 33–35) is also a *figura* for Milton's epic bard. In the "Invocation to Light" he suggests by means of the Exodus imagery his own recapitulation of this Mosaic condition, surrounded by "cloud . . . and ever-during dark," and thereby separated, even as Moses was, from the "cheerful ways of men" (3. 45–46). As emblems of the poet, Moses' cloud and veil are on the one hand the signs of his chosenness and authority, and on the other, of the limitations upon his vision which must be removed by Christ (2 Corinthians 3: 12–18).[45]

For the Christian lyric poet the biblical *figura* was most often David the Psalmist. Discussion of the Psalms from Athanasius and Augustine, to Luther and Calvin, to George Wither (whose *Preparation to the Psalter* in 1619 provided an important contemporary compendium and synthesis of traditional theory)[46] had focused upon their

[44] See, e.g., E. R. Curtius, *European Literature and the Latin Middle Ages*, trans. W. R. Trask (New York, 1953), pp. 215–246, 446–467; Israel M. Baroway, "The Hebrew Hexameter: A Study in Renaissance Sources and Interpretation," *ELH*, 2 (1935), 66–91.

[45] This argument is developed by Jason Rosenblatt, "The Mosaic Voice in *Paradise Lost*," *Milton Studies*, 7 (1975), 207–32.

[46] See, e.g., "A Treatise Made by Athanasius the Great," in Thomas Sternhold and John Hopkins *et al.*, *The Whole Booke of Davids Psalmes* (London, 1582), sig. [A 7]; Augustine, *Expositions on the Book of Psalms*, trans. J. Tweed *et al.*, 6 vols. (Oxford, 1847); Luther,

"poetic" character: the beauty and abundance of their metaphors and images; David's personation of various characters; the many lyric kinds represented in the Psalter —psalms, likened by Wither to "our ordinary English Sonnets," songs, hymns, hallelujahs, antiphons, meditations, prayers, instructions, etc.[47] Most important for our purposes, perhaps, is the conventional belief, emphasized especially by the Protestant commentators, that the Psalms present the entire range of feelings, emotions, adversities, sorrows, joys, and exaltations pertaining to anyone's spiritual life. Calvin termed them "An Anatomy of all the Parts of the Soul; for there is not an emotion of which any one can be conscious that is not here represented as in a mirror." Luther concluded, "The Psalms . . . will present to thee a true picture of thyself."[48]

In this context Herbert's speaker can easily relate himself to David the Psalmist, as a poet undergoing the same kinds of spiritual experiences and confronting the same kinds of artistic problems. Many of Herbert's poems—"Miserie," "Affliction," "Man," "Giddinesse," "Confession," "The Pulley," "The Collar," "Mortification"—suggest the spectrum of personal emotions, sorrows, and joys the exegetes found in the Psalms; and the range of Herbert's lyric forms (sonnets and numerous sonnet-like poems, prayers, instructions, meditations, praises, songs, antiphons, hymns) bears a close relation to the forms Wither found represented in the Psalms. The first poem of "The Church," "The Altar," with its imagery of the "broken Altar . . . / Made of a

---

*A Manual of the Book of Psalms*, trans. Henry Cole (London, 1837), pp. 5, 10–11; Calvin, *Commentary on the Book of Psalms*, trans. James Anderson, 5 vols. (Edinburgh, 1845); Wither, *Preparation to the Psalter*. For discussion of psalm commentary and metrical versions of the Psalms, see Lily B. Campbell, *Divine Poetry and Drama in Sixteenth-Century England* (Cambridge, 1959); and Coburn Freer, *Music for a King: George Herbert's Style and the Metrical Psalms* (Baltimore and London, 1972).

[47] Wither, *Preparation to the Psalter*, p. 54.

[48] Calvin, *Commentary on . . . Psalms*, 1, Preface pp. xxxvi–xxxvii; Luther, *Manual of . . . Psalms*, *pp.* 10–11.

heart, and cemented with tears" alludes to Psalm 51: 17—
"The sacrifices of God are a broken spirit: a broken and a
contrite heart, O God, thou wilt not despise." It thereby
recognizes in David the Psalmist the type of the broken
and contrite heart which must be the altar of the New
Covenant Church. Moreover, David's perception in the
same Psalm that his praises are directly dependent upon
the action of God—"O Lord, open thou my lips; and my
mouth shall show forth thy praise" (v. 15)—provides Herbert's speaker with a model for resolving his central poetic
problem, the inadequacy of human poetry for God's
praises.

Throughout "The Church" Herbert often appropriates
the Psalmist's words or forms, so as to try to approximate
his role—or, perhaps more exactly, to enact a New Testament version of it. In "Jordan I" he explains his renunciation of the "fictions . . . and false hair" of secular love poetry
by echoing David's phrase, "My God, My King" (Ps. 145:
1), and he produces his own version of Psalm 23, as well as,
in "Providence," a very free reworking of that great paean
of praise, Psalm 104. In "Easter" he devises a New Testament version of Psalm 57: 7–11: "My heart is fixed, O God,
my heart is fixed: I will sing and give praise. / Awake up,
my glory; awake, psaltery and harp: I myself will awake
early." Herbert's version develops the poetics for the New
Covenant psalmist. "Rise heart; thy Lord is risen . . .": the
heart must first imitate Christ's rising. "Awake, my lute, and
struggle for thy part . . .": the lute must be taught by the
wood of his cross and his stretched sinews to resound his
name. Finally, God must send his Holy Spirit to "bear a
part," in order to produce a fitting hymn of New Covenant
praise—which then follows: "I Got me flowers to straw thy
way. . . ." And in the later, very moving poem, "The Forerunners," the poet confronts and then resolves the problem
of age and waning poetic powers by repeating as a refrain
Psalm 31: 4 as his only necessary poetic statement—*"Thou
art still my God"*—in final, full understanding that God's
power, not his own, is the source of the praises produced

by the New Covenant temple built in the heart, even as it is of that temple itself.

Though Vaughan produced poetic versions of Psalms 65, 104, and 121, he does not seem to have taken David as a *figura* for himself as Christian poet. Traherne however does —less centrally than Herbert in respect to his total *oeuvre*, but even more explicitly. In the "Third Century" he explains his discovery of this figural relationship. He first wonders (3. 66) that none before him had entertained such thoughts as he has of God's communication to us of felicity and splendor, but soon he finds such perceptions in scripture and especially in the Psalms of David. He celebrates this discovery in a poem (3. 69) praising David as shepherd, soldier, divine, judge, courtier, king, priest, prophet, oracle, but especially as philosopher and poet who heard and rendered heavenly melodies and exercised all his art in God's praise. At this point Traherne declares the figural relationship cemented:

> When I saw those Objects celebrated in His Psalmes which GOD and Nature had proposed to me, and which I thought chance only presented to my view: you cannot imagine how unspeakably I was delighted, to see so Glorious a Person, so Great a Prince, so Divine a Sage, that was a Man after Gods own Heart by the testimony of God Himself, rejoycing in the same things, meditating on the same and Praising GOD for the same. For by this I perceived we were led by one Spirit. (3. 70)

Now he undertakes (3. 71–94) a running commentary upon various psalms, at times identifying and explicating them, at other times incorporating long passages of quotation into his own prose without identification, so that his voice becomes one with that of the Psalmist. At the end of this "Century" (3. 95–100) he relinquishes David's voice: describing the Psalmist as one who saw by the light of faith what the Christian sees as prophecies fulfilled, he now creates his own ecstatic, New Covenant prose-psalms celebrating the realms of grace and glory.

*The Thanksgivings* constitute a poetic version of just this process: poem after poem incorporates biblical passages, most of them from the Psalms, and many times they are so fully blended with the poet's own language that there is no apparent distinction. One example among very many must suffice to indicate the method—from "Thanksgivings for the Glory of God's Works":

> Thy works, O Lord, are for ever to be remembred.
> The earth is full of thy riches. [Psalms 104: 24]
> The earth is the Lords, and the fullness thereof: the
> world and they that dwell therein. [Psalms 24: 1]
> The heavens are the Lords, but the earth hath he given
> to the children of men. [Psalms 115: 16]

> As we are visible Bodies,
> Conversing here beneath,
> He hath given us the Earth.
> To his Image. (21–30)

That *The Thanksgivings* are indeed conceived as a new version of the Psalms, with the speaker a new David, is made quite explicit in "Thanksgivings for the Body":

> O that I were as *David*, the sweet Singer of *Israel*!
> In meeter Psalms to set forth-thy-praises. (341–342)

Subsuming David's voice, and sometimes that of other biblical poets and prophets as well, Traherne sets forth the *Thanksgivings* as his own "meeter" psalms, celebrating the New Covenant.

From early Christian times through the Renaissance, the ancient system of biblical interpretation, typology, had contributed themes, motifs, and even structural patterns to art and literature. I have been suggesting the emergence in seventeenth-century Protestant England of some special uses of this time-honored symbol system—to examine personal experience and the human condition in relation to certain recognized typological paradigms; to trace the "progress of the soul" of a particular speaker, or contemporary Christian individual, or historical personage; to probe the question of how to write worthy Christian poetry. Typological symbolism worked no literary magic of itself, of course, but it offered a rich repository of meanings which seventeenth-century writers learned to use in new ways, in the creation of some of the most remarkable, complex, and powerful religious poetry and prose in English literature.

STEVEN N. ZWICKER

# POLITICS AND PANEGYRIC:
# THE FIGURAL MODE FROM MARVELL TO POPE

TYPOLOGY is a method of scriptural exegesis universally
practised by seventeenth-century Christians, a mode of prophetic thought derived from Scripture itself. Seventeenth-
century sermons and religious poems often extend types beyond Scripture to include the life of the individual or the
fate of the Church in the timeless drama of salvation. In
Reformation England, salvation entailed—besides timeless
spiritual history—national and intensely partisan politics.
Moreover, the language of types, a rhetoric of high spiritual
authority in the early part of the century, was insistently
used in Civil War, Commonwealth, and Restoration England to argue questions that seem to us exclusively political
in mature.*

In devotional texts, types can be fully glossed from medieval and Renaissance scriptural commentary.[1] But political
typology is not simply an extension of scriptural exegesis;

* (Donne, Marvell, Dryden, and Pope, unless otherwise noted, are
cited throughout from the following texts: *John Donne: The Anniversaries*, ed. Frank Manley [Baltimore, 1963]; *The Poems and Letters
of Andrew Marvell*, ed. H. M. Margoliouth, 3rd ed. rev. by Pierre
Legouis, 2 vols. [Oxford, 1971]; *The Poems of John Dryden*, ed. James
Kinsley, 4 vols. [Oxford, 1958]; Pope, *Epistles to Several Persons*, ed.
F. W. Bateson, rev. ed. [London, 1961].)

[1] Rosemond Tuve's *A Reading of George Herbert* (Chicago, 1952);
Frank Manley's edition of Donne's *Anniversaries*, and Winfried
Schleiner's *The Imagery of John Donne's Sermons* (Providence, 1970)
argue the indebtedness of figural images in Herbert and Donne to
patristic scriptural commentary. The use of typology in seventeenth-
century literature has recently been explored by Barbara K. Lewalski,
*Milton's Brief Epic* (Providence, 1966); William Madsen, *From Shad-
owy Types to Truth* (New Haven, 1968); Earl Miner, "Plundering the
Egyptians; or, What We Learn from Recent Books on Milton,"
*Eighteenth-Century Studies*, 3 (1969): 269–305; Paul J. Korshin, *From
Concord to Dissent* (London, 1973); and my own *Dryden's Political
Poetry: The Typology of King and Nation* (Providence, 1972).

*115*

it is an understanding of history as prophecy, as a continuous revelation of God's power and providence. Scriptural exegesis identifies David with Christ, but the equation of David with Cromwell or David with Charles II assumes that Scripture contains not only types completed in Christ's life and recapitulated in the earthly pilgrimage of the individual soul, but also narrative and prophecy that would continue to apply to God's plan for his covenanted people until the millennium. The king as *typus christi*, the eschatological expectations of England as elect nation, the redemptive power of parliament[2]—such figural themes were proclaimed by men who believed that contemporary events formed part of salvation history, that the writings of the Old Testament and the promises of Revelation spoke directly to those who struggled to reform the elect and defeat a historical antichrist.[3]

The application of Scripture to the progress of God's elect as a political body is based on the theology of federal grace. The idea of corporate election developed in Reformation theology through a reinterpretation of the relationship between the Old Testament faithful and the present-day elect. Luther correlated prophecy and contemporary event to defend the Reformation against Roman Catholic objection;[4] Wyclif, Bale, and Bullinger saw in Rev-

[2] These figural themes were not of course invented by Civil War, Protectorate, or Restoration divines and poets; the king as *typus christi* is prominent in medieval political theology, and very much part of the language of Jacobean politics: see Francis Oakley, "Jacobean Political Theology: The Absolute and Ordinary Powers of the King," *Journal of the History of Ideas*, 29 (1968), 323–346.

[3] Prophecy as a mode of historical thought is not, of course, exclusive to radical Puritans; see, for example, the millenarian identification between Oceana and the Bride of Christ in Harrington's *Oceana, Works*, ed. Toland (London, 1771) p. 188; or, among Royalists, John Gadbury's *Natura prodigiorum* (London, 1660) with its assertions that the mark of the beast is the Scottish Covenant and that Charles II is the redeemer David, p. 21.

[4] See Sacvan Bercovitch, "Horologicals to Chronometricals: The Rhetoric of the Jeremiad," *Literary Monographs*, 3 (Madison, 1970), ed. Eric Rothstein, especially pp. 8–9.

elation the destruction of a specifically Roman antichrist.[5]
But for seventeenth-century Englishmen, federal grace and
elect nation were more than religious apologetics; they
were concepts that allowed the Protestant majority, and
then all manner of dissenters, to invoke for the nation or the
sect a covenant relationship with God, often against the
claims of human government.[6]

There is, of course, ancient precedent for reading Scripture in public and civic terms. Scripture as satire and
polemic is common in medieval literature, and Scripture as
politics, often as specifically political allegory, is found in
twelfth-century defenses of the Church, Joachimist writings
of the later Middle Ages, and Savonarola's fifteenth-century
Florentine prophecies.[7] The Tudor court also used Scripture as royal panegyric in progresses and triumphal entries,[8] but the fully politicized use of typology in England
dates from the identification of England as an elect nation
developed late in Elizabeth's reign.[9] It is this use of typology as a political language that shapes an important element in the later history of literary figuralism: the applica-

[5] William Lamont, *Godly Rule: Politics and Religion, 1603–1660*
(London, 1969), p. 23.

[6] J.G.A. Pocock in "Obligation and Authority in Two English Revolutions," *The Dr. W. E. Collins Lecture* (The Victoria University of
Wellington, 1973) analyzes the political implications of seventeenth-
century covenant theology.

[7] See Beryl Smalley, *The Becket Conflict and the Schools: A Study
of Intellectuals in Politics* (Totowa, New Jersey, 1973), "The Teaching
of the Schools," especially pp. 33–37; Marjorie Reeve, *The Influence
of Prophecy in the Later Middle Ages, A Study in Joachimism* (Oxford, 1969); and Donald Weinstein, *Savonarola and Florence, Prophecy
and Patriotism in the Renaissance* (Princeton, 1970), especially chs. 4
and 5.

[8] Examples can be found in Frances Yates, "Queen Elizabeth as
Astraea," *Journal of the Warburg and Courtauld Institutes*, 10 (1947),
27–82; Glynne Wickham, *Early English Stages* (London, 1959), I,
"Pageant Theatres of the Streets"; and Sydney Anglo, *Spectacle,
Pageantry, and Early Tudor Policy* (Oxford, 1969).

[9] William Haller, *The Rise of Puritanism* (New York, 1938) and
*Foxe's Book of Martyrs and the Elect Nation* (London, 1963) offer a
definitive account of the development of this theme in English political
life.

tion of Scripture to the public lives of individuals and institutions in the poetry of Dryden and his contemporaries.

But typology in the later seventeenth century is not solely political. Types are still found in devotional literature, in spiritual biography, and in the odes and epistles that celebrate the christic model in the persons and lives of private individuals.[10] Donne's *Anniversaries* brilliantly exemplify the personal mode. His achievement is echoed by Marvell, Dryden, and Pope, who could not, however, expand the significance of the individual in Donne's cosmic terms or assert with his boldness a claim for the private person as universal redeemer. Donne's *First Anniversary* anatomizes the world; in it the individual as type has profound public import:

> Shee, who if those great Doctors truely said
> That th'Arke to mans proportions was made,
> Had been a type for that, as that might be
> A type of her in this, that contrary
> Both elements, and passions liu'd at peace
> In her, who caus'd all Ciuill warre to cease. (317–322)

In the later seventeenth century, individuals so elegized are set in worlds that seem progressively narrowed; they perform acts of redemption in domesticated and embattled circumstance. From Marvell to Pope, the history of types is twofold: the wide proliferation, but final discrediting, of typology as a political language, and the related narrowing of typology as a vehicle for personal praise once the indi-

---

[10] On religious typology in *The Hind and the Panther* see Earl Miner, *Dryden's Poetry* (Bloomington and London, 1967), ch. 5; and Miner's extensive commentary on the poem in *The Works of John Dryden*, eds. H. T. Swedenberg, Jr. *et al.* (Los Angeles and Berkeley, 1956–), vol. 3. *Poems, 1685–92*, ed. Earl Miner (1969); typology in spiritual biography is discussed by U. Milo Kaufmann, *The Pilgrim's Progress and Traditions in Puritan Meditation* (New Haven, 1966), and J. Paul Hunter, *The Reluctant Pilgrim* (Baltimore, 1966); and the individual as type of Christ in earlier seventeenth-century poetry of praise is explored by Barbara K. Lewalski, "Donne's Poetry of Compliment: The Speaker's Stance and the Topoi of Praise," *Seventeenth-Century Imagery*, ed. Earl Miner (Berkeley, Los Angeles, and London, 1971), and Lewalski, *Donne's Anniversaries and the Poetry of Praise* (Princeton, 1973).

vidual as christic redeemer is separated from the life of the state.

Marvell's skeptical intelligence seems at odds with the eschatological fervor of mid-century England, yet Marvell takes the apocalyptic expectations of his contemporaries as serious poetic concerns in the 1650's. Typology and prophecy become for him ways of articulating the meaning of a sanctified family and the role of a godly leader in an elect nation. By the end of the century, poets no longer use redemptive terms to conflate private and political lives. But in the early 1650's and in such a poem as *Appleton House*, the figural mode is flexible and inclusive, allowing types to be at once public and private, straightforward and ironic.

*Appleton House* and *The First Anniversary* follow closely on the *Horatian Ode*, but the ode demonstrates no inclination toward personal or political figuralism. In the ode, Cromwell's role in history is accomplished fact; the source of his power is Providence, but Cromwell acts less as divine intelligence than as uncontrollable force of nature. History is predictive in the poem but only in the narrowest sense—one act will beget another; it is the record of inevitable forces controlled only by a physics of political morality: "Nature that hateth emptiness, / Allows of penetration less." Predictions, omens, and spirits are hedged with irony, "And for the last effect / Still keep thy Sword erect. . . . / The same *Arts* that did *gain* / A *Pow'r* must it *maintain*." The lines allude to Odysseus and Aeneas warding off the spirits of the dead, but for Cromwell the arts of war predict a future of grim vigilance.

In the *Horatian Ode*, Marvell declines the prophetic mode rendering Cromwell *de facto* rather than *de jure divino* political power, but in *Appleton House* typology and prophecy have become central to the poet's expression and design. Personal, familial, and national histories are conflated through biblical perspectives; the individual in retirement and in activity is set against scriptural models; the estate and the nation are imagined through scenes and narratives from the Old Testament that invite figural extension. Christ as savior is the overarching model, the anti-type of the Old Testament and contemporary figure, the regenerative pattern for active and contemplative lives.

The first lines of *Appleton House* echo Jonson's *Penshurst* in their rejection of envy and false praise and their emphasis on proportion and natural economy. But more insistently than Jonson, Marvell develops the image of the estate as sanctified ground, the house as dwelling separated from the world at large. Nun Appleton is the symbol of humility, the house itself, a *"Mark of Grace*; / . . . an *Inn* to entertain / Its *Lord* a while" (70–72). The ambiguities and scriptural overtones of the opening stanzas anticipate the redemptive role of the Fairfax family and point up the spiritual significance of individuals who reform religion, fight Protestant wars, and "promise some universal good."

The record of the estate as nunnery provides the first extended figural episode, alluding to the temptation in Eden (st. 22), Christ's defeat of satanic forces (sts. 26, 32–34), and his cleansing of the Temple (sts. 32, 35). William Fairfax rescuing the virgin Thwaites repeats the triumph of English Protestantism over papal superstition and authority, and the joining of bridegroom and bride is a figure of Christ and the Church, a redemptive promise: "Is not this he whose Offspring fierce / Shall fight through all the *Universe*; / . . . Yet, against Fate, his Spouse they kept; / And the great Race would intercept" (st. 31). Fairfax as christic figure is delineated in narrative and suggested through verbal allusion: "Ill-counsell'd Women, do you know / Whom you resist, or what you do?" (239–240; cf. Luke 23: 24). And his heroic descendant is imagined in fully apocalyptic terms: "Till one, as long since prophecy'd, / His Horse through conquer'd *Britain* ride" (245; cf. Rev. 6: 2).

Yet the tone of this episode is not solely heroic and apocalyptic. Fairfax does battle with wooden saints; his enemies are witches, perverse and comic nuns: "waving these aside like Flyes, / Young *Fairfax* through the Wall does rise" (257–258). The obvious disparity between defeating nuns and harrowing hell diminishes the figural image, yet the mock battle of divine with satanic forces is familiar epic material. Here, the comic qualifies but does not disallow the heroic; Marvell seems finely aware of both local wit and figural image, and the episode does not deny one for the other.

The poem's first history ends with the nunnery restored to true *"Religious House"* (280). Allusion and verbal echo pose moments of familial, national, and universal redemption against one another so that the experience of the individual might reflect and repeat the temptation in Eden and the English reformation. Contemporary and past event are combined, yet both retain full historicity. The narrative is not allegory, continuous or discontinuous, because one term does not replace another. Types are prophetic, and the prophesied person or event allows the full historical significance of the type, confirming the providential design of the history in which type and antitype participate.

The heroic action of William Fairfax anticipates the appearance of Thomas, Lord Fairfax: "From that blest Bed the *Heroe* came, / Whom *France* and *Poland* yet does fame" (281–282).[11] But the next scene takes as its subject retirement rather than reformation. The paradox of the Lord General's retreat in a moment of political crisis is felt throughout the passage. The garden as fort, tulips as Switzers, comment on a man obsessed with the arts of war— these are military images but they also allow for the spiritual vigilance of a figure whose Christian armor enables him to withdraw from the sensuous world to inward contemplation.[12] There is a familiar play of wit in Marvell's floral regi-

---

[11] I take the *Heroe* of line 281 to be the Lord General; there is no consensus as to the identity of this figure, some seeing a reference to Sir Thomas Fairfax, some to his son, the first Lord Fairfax, and others to the Lord General. The subject of the whole episode (sts. 36–46) seems to me to turn on the Lord General's difficult decision to retire from the military campaign against Scotland; see notes to *The Poems and Letters of Andrew Marvell*, 1. 284–285.

[12] On the theme of spiritual warfare and Christian armor see Baxter, *A Christian Directory* (London, 1673); Thomas Wall, *Spiritual Armour* (London, 1688); and Juan de Castanzia, *The Spiritual Combat: Or the Christian Pilgrim in his Spiritual Conflict and Conquest* (1698).

ments, but withdrawal and contemplation are the central meaning of this garden. "It is better for a man to live privately and to have regard to himself, than to neglect his soul, that he could work wonders in the World."[13] The refusal of earthly greatness conforms the individual to Christ, who abjured worldly honor and promotion. In Marvell's presentation, *imitatio Christi* might serve as a gloss on the Lord General's retirement:

> he preferr'd to the *Cinque Ports*
> These five imaginary Forts:
> And, in those half-dry Trenches, spann'd
> Pow'r which the Ocean might command. (st .44)[14]

The private garden, whether soul of the individual or country estate, flourishes with care and reflects paradise; England, the public garden, is fallen and wasted. Images of paradise, lost and restored, recall the full range of private and public experience: the seduction of the virgin Thwaites ("So through the mortal fruit we boyl / The Sugars uncorrupting Oyl" [172–174]), the "luckless Apple" of the Civil Wars (327), and the estate transformed through the regenerative presence of Mary Fairfax. Eden's prophetic meaning is felt in personal and national history, in

---

The image of garden as fort is fully annotated by Kitty Scoular, *Natural Magic* (Oxford, 1965), p. 131; Donald Friedman, *Marvell's Pastoral Poetry* (Berkeley and Los Angeles, 1969), p. 226; and Rosalie Colie, *My Ecchoing Song: Marvell's Poetry of Criticism* (Princeton, 1969), p. 240.

[13] Anon., *The Christian Pattern, or A Divine Treatise of the Imitation of Christ* (London, 1684), p. 53.

[14] The *imitatio Christi* is, of course, an ancient devotional theme. Translations and paraphrases of Thomas a Kempis, *De imitatione Christi* are numerous in the later seventeenth century; see, e.g., Ralph Robinson, *Christ the Perfect Pattern, or a Christian's Practice* (London, 1658); *The Following of Christ. In four books. Written in Latin by Thomas of Kempis. . . .* (n.p., 1685); *The following of Christ. Written in Latine by Thomas of Kempis. . . .* (London, 1686); *The Christian pattern paraphras'd; or, The book of the Imitation of Christ. . . .* (London, 1697); *The Christian's pattern: Or, a Treatise of the imitation of Jesus Christ* (London, 1699).

the restoration of a garden as in the political ordering of the nation.

The garden opens onto meadows and as Marvell enlarges the physical setting, the vista of scriptural history widens. Images in the meadow recall fragments of Jewish history from the Flood through the Exodus and transform tawny mowers into wandering Israelites; yet mowing and leveling have ambiguous political and spiritual meaning. The mowers' identity as Israelites discounts radical and dissenting claims of spiritual election (cf. Marvell, *The First Anniversary*, 289–320). Exodus in Scripture is marked by backsliding and ingratitude, and Marvell's adaptation of the desert episode depicts these Israelites in acts of ignorant destruction and careless victory. The poet's narrative leaves his Israelites wandering in exile. Here Scripture acts not as prophecy but as correction.

At the poem's close, Nun Appleton is redeemed through Mary Fairfax and universal restoration is cautiously prophesied through the extension of the Fairfax line. But before such resolution, Marvell poses a false messianic model, the narrator as *"Prelate of the Grove"* (592). The forest retreat recalls the first garden scene but reverses the earlier relationship between man and nature. If Fairfax errs in conforming the garden too explicitly to the image of man, the poet so loses identity that he merges with plant and flower. He becomes Christ to the woods (609–616), but his actions have no regenerative meaning. The only change that occurs is in the narrator's sense of self. Progressively confused by the delights and errors of the senses, he must await restoration in the awesome arrival of his young pupil.

The entrance of Mary Fairfax signals the "recollection of loose nature"—that elaborate celebration of the young virgin's power over the fallen world—and completes the figural movement of the poem. As the poem's first virgin recalls Eve, the second suggests the Virgin Mary, whose purity and innocence help restore the fallen world. And as Christ fulfills the prediction that the son of woman will bruise the head of the serpent and redeem the world, so the extension of the Fairfax line through this virgin Mary prophesies "some universal good" (741), recalling the earlier dream of universal heroes (214–218) and echoing the scriptural prophesies of redemption in Christ (Luke 1: 35; Gal. 4: 4; Rom. 16: 20). What Mary means to the estate, the Fairfax line promises to the world at large.

This family's history, their summing up of biblical narrative from the Fall to the prophecy of redemption, transforms the estate into *"Paradice's only Map"* (768). The metaphor suggests that Eden is recollected in the orderly world of Nun Appleton, and that this family demonstrates the meaning of God's image in man. The progress of figures through the poem, the movement from Isabell Thwaites to Mary Fairfax, echoes the progress from Old Testament type to antitype, partial foreshadowing to completion.

The figural mode of *Appleton House* is highly characteristic of Marvell: it bears the stamp of his verbal wit, philosophic seriousness, and historical moment. Written at the beginning of a momentous decade, it is the last of Marvell's poems in which the narrating voice can modulate gracefully from private to public utterance. Uniquely poised between the personal mode of Donne's *Anniversaries* and the political typology of Dryden's *Absalom and Achitophel*, it is a poem in which both the individual in the garden and the nation in civic disorder can be represented through figural image. After the failure of the puritan dream—an army of saints heralding the millennium, a union of political and spiritual election—the language of types begins a definitive separation into personal and political application.

The *Horatian Ode* is an unlikely prelude to *Appleton House*, but it is an even stranger precursor of *The First Anniversay*, which employs a figural language largely unqualified by the irony that touches so many passages in *Appleton House*. In the ode, Marvell scrupulously reserves judgment of the man and his acts. In *The First Anniversary* he unequivocally celebrates Cromwell's consolidation of power as Protector, turning contemporary political events, foreign policy, and biography into a Protestant apocalypse: a vision of Cromwell's solitary pursuit of the Roman beast and England's national destiny as herald of the Reformation. Together, godly prince and elect nation will hasten the advent of Christ's millennial rule. But in choosing Old Testament analogues, Marvell is denied the model of a divinely anointed king, not only by the obvious recollection of Charles I, but also by the widely held millennarian conviction that the execution of the monarch was a significant step in the defeat of antichrist.[15] For his godly leader, Marvell finds analogues in biblical patriarchs, prophets, and judges. Cromwell is David the psalmist, Elijah, Noah, and Gideon. The Old Testament figures are used with the force of prophetic type as well as of temporal analogy. Cromwell echoes and reembodies Old Testament figures, pointing to their eschatological completion in Christ. Gideon as Old Testament type and Cromwell as correlative of that figure invoke the model of Christ as judge destroying the wicked, defending the elect, and defeating antichrist at the end of time.[16]

At the beginning of the poem, Cromwell's office is carefully distinguished from kingship. Hereditary monarchy suggests mortality and defeat; Cromwell contracts time,

[15] On the millenarian interpretation of Charles' execution see Mary Cary, *The Little Horn's Doom and Downfall: or a scripture prophesie of King James, and King Charles, and of this present parliament unfolded* (London, 1651), sigs. B6–B7.

[16] See the readings of Judges in the following commentaries: Peter Martyr [Vermigli], *Most fruitfull and learned Commentaries (upon Judges)* (London, 1564); Richard Rogers, *A Commentary upon the whole booke of Judges* (London, 1615); Arthur Jackson, *A help for the understanding of the Holy Scripture* (Cambridge, 1643); John Diodati, *Pious and Learned Annotations upon the Holy Bible* (London, 1648); *Annotations upon all the Books of the Old and New Testament* [Assembly Annotations] (London, 1651); John Richardson, *Choice Observations and Explanations upon the Old Testament* (London, 1655); Christopher Ness, *A Compleat history and mystery of the Old and New Testament* (London, 1690). Barbara K. Lewalski, "*Samson Agonistes* and the 'Tragedy' of the Apocalypse," *PMLA*, 85 (1970), 1050–1062, discusses Protestant interpretations of the Book of Judges.

restores the day, ascends the heavens to learn the music of the spheres. The figure of David is invoked, but not as a kingly model. The image of the psalmist in the allusion to David (105–110), like the more obvious analogy with Gideon (249–256), is prophetic of Christ the judge who will conquer the Beast and destroy the wicked:

O would they rather by his Pattern won
Kiss the approaching, nor yet angry Son;
And in their numbred Footsteps humbly tread
The path where holy Oracles do lead;
How might they under such a Captain raise
The great Designes kept for the latter Dayes!

(105–110)

Cromwell's "Pattern," like David's, prophesies Christ's anger to all who oppose him. David and Cromwell are prophetic types in a history of national salvation; both figures anticipate the final captaincy of Christ. But England, like Old Testament Israel, is obstinate and backsliding: "Men alas, as if they nothing car'd, / Look on, all unconcern'd, or unprepar'd" (149–150). For them, as for the tawny mowers of *Appleton House*, the restoration of Israel is of little concern. The ambivalence of Israel as historical fact and prophetic type is a familiar theme in later decades. Here, as in *Absalom and Achitophel*, the figure has prophetic and satiric meaning.

But the typology of *The First Anniversary* is not restricted to Cromwell's roles in foreign affairs and domestic politics; biographical details are thrust into the same figural mode. At Cromwell's supposed death, earthquake and eclipse echo the distortion of nature at the Crucifixion, and his "ascent unto the Kingdom blest of Peace and Love" (218) suggests the Resurrection. Cromwell's power over nature, the prophesied miracle of his ascension, and other details in this christic biography attempt to strengthen Cromwell's image as redemptive leader, but the typology of this biographical digression falls uncomfortably between personal figuralism and the traditional typology of mon-

archical elegies in which the public life of king or prince
reflects the image of Christ as magisterial figure.[17]

Elijah, Noah, and Gideon extend the earlier pattern of
scriptural types and return the poem to the political and
figural meaning of Old Testament models. Like Gideon,
who followed war with peace, destroyed and then rebuilt,
Cromwell returns from war to redeem England. Gideon
and Cromwell are paralleled in their careers as in their
spiritual lives, so that humility before the Lord justifies
political action:

> No King might ever such a Force have done;
> Yet would not he be Lord, nor yet his Son.
>    Thou with the same strength, and an Heart as plain,
> Didst (like thine Olive) still refuse to Reign. (255–258)

The rejection of kingship is a crucial element in the narrative of both careers, an act that acknowledges God's govern-
ance of Israel.

The prophetic elements and apocalyptic schemes of *The
First Anniversary* establish its importance in the history
of political figuralism, but the poem is not a unique historical document. The restoration of Israel, the personal
reign of Christ, the role of Parliament and Protector in
establishing the millennium are commonplace themes in
the sermons, pamphlets, and verse propaganda of the 1640's
and 1650's.[18] The apocalyptic mode of *The First Anniversary* is doubtless a response to the language of Marvell's
audience.

---

17 See, for example, the use of scriptural typology in William
Leigh, *Queene Elizabeth, Paraleld in her Princely virtues, with David,
Josua, and Hezekia* (London, 1612), Donne's *Elegie upon the untimely
death of the incomparable Prince Henry* (London, 1613); or Dryden's
*Threnodia Augustalis* (London, 1685).

18 See, for example, Joseph Caryl, *The Saints Thankfull Acclamation
at Christs resumption of his great power and the initials of his king-
dome* (London, 1644); John Greene, *Nehemiahs teares and prayers for
Judahs affliction and the ruines and repair for Jerusalem* (London,
1644); William Bridge, *Christs Coming opened in a Sermon* (London,
1648); William Barton, *Hallelujah. Or certain hymns* (London, 1651);
Samuel Hunton, *His Highnesse the Lord Protector protected* (London, 1654).

Some students of the Restoration are surprised by the seamless continuity in the history of familiar political types. As Scripture had flawlessly prophesied the Puritan revolution to an army of saints, so the restoration of Israel, or Moses and David as redemptive leaders, seemed to Stuart apologists inevitable figures for the renewal of monarchy. Not only Dryden's Davidic parallels—familiar because they anticipate *Absalom and Achitophel*—but numerous sermons on the Restoration and its anniversaries invoke the same types that puritan divines had used a decade earlier.[19] David-Cromwell-Christ yields to David-Charles-Christ. With the Restoration, monarchy simply replaces republic, commonwealth, or Parliament as the correlative type which together with the Old Testament figure prophesied the return to Eden. England has been released from Egyptian darkness;[20] Jewish redemption realized in English restoration;[21] London's renewal prophesied by the rebuilding of

---

[19] See, for example, Thomas Pierce, *A Sermon preached . . . the 29th day of May* (London, 1661); John White, *The Parallel Between David, Christ, and K. Charls* (London, 1661); or the verse in *Domiduca Oxoniensis* (Oxford, 1662); J. W.'s *King Charles I. his imitation of Christ. Or the parallel lines of our Saviours and our kings sufferings; drawn through forty six texts of Scripture* (London, 1660); or the interesting "Heroick Poem" by Edward Howard, *Caroloiades, or, the Rebellion of Forty One* (London, 1689).

[20] John Locke's contribution to *Britannia Rediviva* includes that parallel, sig. Ff3ᵛ; or see *Regi Sacrum* (London, 1660), sig. A6, "We were lately under a Tyranny so sever, as transcends the Parallel of the preceding story; and our deliverance has been little less miraculous than that which *Israel* enjoyed, onely we have avoided the Red-sea, and Your Mercy denies the spoiling of our Egyptians. Our Church is believ'd the most beautiful upon the Earth, was languishing in its red ruines, and we are in some measure built again as the Temple of Old, without noise of Ax or Hammer." See also B. Bridgewater, *Domiduca Oxoniensis* (Oxford, 1662), sig. Ff2ᵛ, on the parallel between Charles and Moses as redeemers; and *The Regal Proto-Martyr; Or, The Memorial of the Martyrdom of Charles the First* (London, 1672), sig. C3ʳ.

[21] The parallel of Jewish and English restoration is a familiar theme in Restoration sermons and pamphlets; see, e.g., Edward Boteler, *Jus Poli et Fori: or, God and the King* (London, 1661); Thomas Pierce, *A Sermon preached . . . the 29th day of May* (London, 1661); and Henry King, *A Sermon preached . . . before the . . . House of Commons . . . upon the anniversary day of the King's and Kingdomes*

Jerusalem; and the attempt by Shaftesbury and Monmouth to usurp the crown foreshadowed by the seduction and betrayal in Eden and in David's Israel.[22]

That these schemes could not sustain indefinite political use, that the arbitrary and unscrupulously partisan appropriations of typology and prophetic history finally worked against their credibility, is an effect not wholly felt or acknowledged in the early years of the Restoration. But by the Revolution of 1688 both the language of public poetry and the whole vocabulary in which political obligation and power were debated has shifted definitively from covenantal to contractual. Dryden's career as typologist demonstrates the shift with schematic clarity. Like the nation, he begins by celebrating England's restoration with figural patterns, but political circumstance and the tides of his own belief force him to withdraw those schemes at the close of the 1680's. In the last decade of his life, types and prophecy express a Catholic's faith in the timeless Church and celebrate the pattern of exemplary private lives.

Dryden's poetry of the 1660's invokes standard scriptural types for obvious political ends. In *Astraea Redux, To His Sacred Majesty,* and *Annus Mirabilis* Dryden claims a pro-

---

*restauration* (London, 1661). Edward Bagshaw on the restoration of Charles is typical, "I am only able to liken it to the Inauguration of King *Solomon*; there were then such blowing of Trumpets, such piping with Flutes, such huge shouts of all the people, with God save King *Solomon*, that the earth rent with the sound of them; and there were such rejoycings in the City of Gihon, where he was anointed King, that the City rang for joy: so did the City of *London*, when our *Solomon* entered it on that day." See *The Rights of the Crown of England* (London, 1660), sig. A6–A6ᵛ.

22 The specific connection between the betrayal of David by Achitophel and the seduction of Eve is noted early in the century in *The Sermons of Maister Henrie Smith, gathered into one volume* (London, 1607), sig. V4ᵛ, "In Genesis 3. there is a Counsell of the Serpent: if you hearken to that you shall perish like *Eve*. In the 2. Samuel 18, there is a wisedome of *Achitophel*: if you hearken to that, you shall speede like *Absalon*." Of the spiritual meaning of political rebellion see John Allington, *The Grand Conspiracy of the Members against . . . their King* (London, 1653), p. 21.

phetic role, closing his sacred histories with signs of renewal and prosperity. Exile and return, suffering and
deliverance: the biblical patterns enacted by David as
type and Christ as antitype are renewed by Charles as correlative type. The analogy with David in *Astraea Redux*
is obvious, and the christic association emerges through the
accretion of detail: Charles suffers for the nation's sins
(49), inherits his Father's sorrows (52), lives "above his
Banishment" (60), confers Restoration as "Prince of Peace"
(149), and shares nativities with the Redeemer (288–289).
The figural identity of Charles as restorer and redeemer
allows for the multiple historical dimensions of the poem.
*To His Sacred Majesty* links restoration and coronation
with renewal after the Flood and the provision of manna in
the wilderness. Old Testament histories of redemption are
renewed in English political life while Charles' "Royal Oke,
like *Jove*'s of old" provides visions and destinies, "Propitious
Oracles" (129–131). The bounty of the land and future of
the nation will be assured through the continuity of the
Stuart line. The easy confidence of Dryden's prophetic
manner in these early poems partly reflects the political
serenity in the first years of the Restoration.

By 1666 the naval defeats in the Dutch Wars and the Fire
of London threw the court into a more obviously embattled
posture. The immense literature of prognostication antic-
ipating that year no doubt increased the Royalists' sense
that the prodigies would have to be accounted for,[23] and
Dryden responds to that challenge in *Annus Mirabilis*, in
part a Jeremiad that laments the nation's afflictions but affirms their meaning as part of God's plan for his people.

[23] Dryden's title itself, *Annus Mirabilis*, is also the title of widely
known Fifth Monarchist prophecies; the sense in which Dryden is
answering the court's opponents was argued by E. N. Hooker, "The
Purpose of Dryden's *Annus Mirabilis*," *Huntington Library Quarterly*,
10 (1946–1947), 49–67; and in his exhaustive study of the political
meaning and context of this poem, "Meanings of Dryden's *Annus
Mirabilis*" (Ph.D. dissertation, Columbia University, 1972), Michael
McKeon sets Dryden's prophetic efforts among those of his contemporaries; see "Meanings of Dryden's *Annus Mirabilis*," ch. 6.

Trial and redemption, suffering and restoration, the rhythm of sacred history is renewed in English political life; apostasy is answered by punishment, but God no more forsakes his people in the present than he did in the past. Like Old Testament prophets, Dryden predicts triumph and bounty. Charles is once again David and Christ: redeemer of the people, father of the nation, humble supplicant, sacrificial king. The narrator's final vision parallels the rebuilding of Jerusalem after the Babylonian exile with the renewal of London after the fire, and closes with a promise of material prosperity. Cleansed, in fact "deifi'd," London rises from her ashes: "Her widening streets on new foundations trust, / And, opening, into larger parts she flies" (1179–1180). Commercial elements in this prophecy recall Old Testament visions of agricultural prosperity in Isaiah and Ezekiel and resemble the apocalyptic vision in New England prophecies which assiduously link commercial gain with spiritual salvation.[24]

But the Stuart monarch enjoyed no future of serene prosperity. Beset with financial and political troubles, Charles entered into a secret French alliance in the 1670's, a decade of mounting public fears of foreign policy controlled by Catholic France and of papal slavery, when the Duke of York succeeded Charles. The fears culminated in the Exclusion Crisis, Dryden's subject for *Absalom and Achitophel*. The elaborate design of this poem, the linking of Scripture and politics, the davidic, christic, and jehovic roles of the king, and the identification of rebellion as primal disobedience transform political intrigue into prophetic history.

Familiar associations from the panegyrics of the 1660's form part of this mode, but the king's redemptive power can no longer be confidently asserted. Like other Stuart apologists in the 1680's, Dryden vigorously insists on the fallen nature of political rebellion, the satanic impulse in

[24] See Ernest Lee Tuveson, *Redeemer Nation: The Idea of America's Millennial Role* (Chicago, 1968).

individual and national politics.[25] No longer are the people simply victims of spiritual slavery; now they are "Adam-wits" "Whom debauched with ease / No King could govern nor no god could please." The satric expansion is not original with *Absalom and Achitophel*,[26] but the extended and simultaneous use of typology for panegyric and satiric ends reaches a new complexity with Dryden.

The typology of *Absalom and Achitophel* is striking yet subtle, at points ironic and throughout fully imagined. The centers of figural association are by now familiar—the king as *typus Christi*, the political opponent as Satan, and the English as elect nation, moody and rebellious—but each is established with new exuberance and wit. The poem begins with familiar claims. The tableau asserts the divine nature of kingship, but here fertility expresses the godhead, the king's sexual prodigality is evidence of God's bounty. The initial joke turns on the happy accident of David and Charles as vigorous patriarichs, but the patriarchal role itself, as Filmerites of the 1680's insisted, was no joke at all. Indeed Locke spent the first half of the *Two Treatises on Government* carefully dismantling Filmer's claims.[27] The

[25] See, for example, *A Satyr, by way of Dialogue between Lucifer and the ghosts of Shaftesbury and Russell* (London, 1683); *Sylla's Ghost: a satyr against ambition, and the last horrid plot* (London, 1683); *Algernon Sidney's Farewell* (London, 1687), or *No Protestant Plot, Or, The Whigs Loyalty: With the Doctor's New Discovery* (London, 1683).

[26] See in *The Poems of John Cleveland*, ed. Brian Morris and Eleanor Withington (Oxford, 1967), "The Kings Disguise" and "The Rebell Scot"; Henry King, "A Deepe Groane, fetch'd at the Funerall of that incomparable and Glorious Monarch" in *The Poems of Henry King*, ed. Margaret Crum (Oxford, 1965); *Chartae Scriptae: or a New game at cards* by Edmund Gayton (Oxford, 1645); or the interesting mock bibliography, *Bibliotheca Parliamenti, Libri Theologici, Politici, Historici . . . Done into English for the Assembly of Divines* (London, 1653), p. 7, "Whether our Saviours riding into *Jerusalem* upon an Asses sole, were any more than a Type of our deliverer *Cromwell's* riding into his Throne upon the backs of 120 Asses, to be elected out of the several Counties for that purpose."

[27] See Locke's attack on Filmer's use of Scripture to establish the political meaning of paternal and regal power, bk. 1, ch. 2 of *Two Treatises of Government* (London, 1698).

dual edge of this initial figure is then felt throughout the poem. Divine election for the nation means moodiness, rebellion, and ingratitude; but England as Israel is also the scene of repeated acts of political salvation. As divine monarch the king must govern a chosen people; without that half of the political metaphor, the king's redemptive power would have no scope or meaning. Isolated from the poem's central metaphor, the closing apocalypse—death defeated and the new order divinely proclaimed—would be as Johnson asserts, the destined knight blowing his horn. Read as part of the poem, it firmly connects hyperbolic fantasy with political prophecy.

The king as expression of the Godhead and the nation as moody Israelites form part of the typological drama, but the most obsessive figural identity is that of Achitophel with Satan. Political corruption is the seduction and disobedience in Eden, the betrayal of Christ, and finally the antichristian warfare of all disobedience and betrayal: father by son, king by ungrateful subject, God by rebellious creation. This inverted typology is not traditional in scriptural figuralism, but Protestant handbooks and prophetic histories of the later seventeenth century often explored the reversal of figural models. Egypt and Israel, Babylon and the captive Jews, Rome and England figure forth the continuous battle between Satan and Christ; Rome is foreshadowed by Sodom, Jericho, and Babylon,[28] and the efforts of the reformed church to realize Christ's kingdom are adumbrated in "Types of the appearance of the Kingdom of Christ and Types of that Kingdom Estopp'd."[29]

The association of Achitophel with Satan finally allows Dryden the completion of a metaphor he had often partly rendered. From the panegyrics to *Absalom and Achitophel* we have divine monarch and elect nation, but the deeply troubled relationship between the two can no longer

[28] Samuel Mather, *Figures or Types of the Old Testament* (London, 1695), p. 675.
[29] Beverly, *Prophetical History of the Reformation* (London, 1689), p. 19.

be fully stated without the Satanic figure. The power of evil as dramatic figure and abstract idea has such energy in this poem that it must be drawn from the Edenic myth. Coiled tightly as a spring of persuasion, Achitophel begins his seduction of the unfallen Absalom, "Auspicious prince, at whose nativity / Some Royal planet ruled the southern sky," and through the next seventy lines elaborates an image of the prince as prophesied savior, fulfillment of scriptural promise. Reversing the Christian understanding of Fortune and Providence, Achitophel constructs his own sacred history: Old Testament types have prophesied Absalom; vaunting ambition must be realized through usurpation; and Fortune's slow descent must be seized lest heaven's anointing oil go wasted. The inversion of Christian history is complete: divine plans here depend on human action.

As a prophecy of English political life, Jewish history was in the 1660's an occasion for narratives of redemption, in the 1680's for records of ingratitude.[30] *The Medall, Britannia Rediviva,* and *Threnodia Augustalis* may continue to assert the king's divinity and redemptive power, but they do so with steadily diminishing confidence. That political redemption could not long continue as a theme for Stuart apologetics seems in retrospect an obvious conclusion. It must have been more difficult for Dryden to discern, although the gradual narrowing and final withdrawal of the figural system from his political poetry is an admission that the English simply would not be redeemed.

Scriptural motifs appear, of course, in the Williamite panegyrics and in coronation odes and court elegies of the 1690's and beyond,[31] but there is no sustained effort by a

[30] See, for example, the scriptural material in such satires of the 1680's as *Algernon Sidney's Farewell* (London, 1687); *Ryot upon ryot: or, a chant upon the Arresting the Loyal L. Mayor & Sherrifs* (London, 1683); *A Satyr, by way of Dialogue between Lucifer and the ghosts of Shaftesbury and Russell* (London, 1683); *Sylla's Ghost: A Satyr Against ambition, and the last horrid plot* (London, 1683).

[31] In Edward Nicholas' "Ode" in *Vota Oxoniensia* (Oxford, 1689), William is a "second Moses, whose avenging Rod / Wav'd o're the

major writer to assert a biblical mythos for the new re-
gime.[32] Poems on the Treaty of Ryswick, for example,
analogize William almost exclusively with classical figures.[33] There is of course intermixture of classical with
scriptural heroism in political panegyrics throughout the
seventeenth century, but the triumphs and historical poems
on the occasion of the Treaty draw heroic images from
Homer, Greek mythology, and shepherd colloquies; the
entrance of the returning monarch is imagined "in the style
of a Roman emperor."[34] *Absalom and Achitophel* is the last
important poem to invoke the figural system in defense and
celebration of public figures and institutions. With its
delicate analogy between England and Eden and prophetic
vision of Pax Britannica, Pope's *Windsor Forest* resembles
Dryden's early efforts at sacred history, but Pope's youth-
ful vision of an English golden age is a momentary echo of
older themes, reflecting a personal as well as a national
optimism that is displaced in Pope and his circle by a pro-

---

Land does set it free / At Once from Pharoahs Gods slavery" (sig.
2Z); and in "A Poem on the Queen" (London, 1695) on Mary's death,
"*Faith* was her *Canaan* and Mount Pisgah too, / From whence She had
the Promis'd Land in view; / By which She Heaven in its Type
possest, / Drew its Celestial Landskip in her Breast." See Earl Miner's
essay on biblical and classical typology in *Poems on the Reign of
William III* (Los Angeles, 1974; Augustan Reprint Society, no. 166),
"Introduction."

[32] Matthew Prior's poem "Presented to the King, at his arrival in
Holland . . . 1696," *The Literary Works of Matthew Prior*, ed. H.
Bunker Wright and Monroe K. Spears, 2 vols. (Oxford, 1959), greets
William as King David, but Prior has no sustained biblical interpre-
tation of the monarch's role; the "Carmen Seculare, For the Year
1700, To the King" is a fully classical celebration of the monarch.

[33] In Thomas Baker's *Nassau: A Poem occasion'd by the Peace*
(London, 1698), William is Orpheus and Hercules; his reknown outdoes that of Agamemnon in John Phillips' *Augustus Britannicus: a
poem upon the conclusion of the peace of Europe* (London, 1697);
Ceres is William's bright attendant in John Hughes' *Triumph of
Peace* (London, 1698); and in the *Idyll on the Peace* (London, 1697)
the shepherd Thyrsis sings, "let every Muse be heard, / *Caesar* returns,
and in his smiles we see / His Mercy is triumphant o're his Rage, /
*Caesar* and Peace returns, to make us blest," p. 5.

[34] *Poems on Affairs of State*, ed. George deF. Lord (New Haven,
1965- ), vol. 6, 1697–1704, ed. Frank H. Ellis (1970), 12.

found distrust of politics and public life. For Defoe, spokesman of the new order, sacred history—indeed history itself—offers no special models, no sanctity. In *The True-Born Englishman*, Defoe ridicules attempts to derive nobility from ancient pedigree,[35] and in *The Mock Mourners* neatly articulates the presentist position of Whig apologetics: "If back to *Israel's* Tents I shou'd retire, / And of the *Hebrew* Heroes there enquire, / I find no Hand did Judah's Scepter wear, / Comes up to William's Modern Character" (343–346).

The Exclusion Crisis is the final moment when political intrigue could seriously be read as prophetic history. But if the king can no longer be celebrated as "type of him above,"[36] the individual might still be so imagined. The great odes and epistles of Dryden's last decade do not abandon the figural system, but it is seldom a language of political argument. *Eleonora, To my Honour'd Kinsman*, and the other poems of praise and lament argue perfection and redemption, but only for individuals within a severely restricted sphere: the home, the country estate, the rural village. Dryden's ode to the Duchess of Ormonde (1700) celebrates the individual as redemptive public figure, but the public redeemed is no longer the English nation. Among Catholics and in a foreign land, the duchess promises a renewal of God's covenant (70–79); at home she maintains a quiet domesticity, embroidering and holding the promise of children, but for England signifying no "Millenary Year" (82).

*Eleonora*, the first of the odes, elegies, and epistles Dryden wrote after his retirement from court, owes much of its complexity and interest to an active recollection of Donne's elegies on Elizabeth Drury. What animates the figural system of *Eleonora* is the idea that the individual life participates in the typological paradigm, takes shape and meaning from Old Testament prophetic types and from their anti-typical completion in Christ. Eleonora is the heavenly

---

[35] *Poems on Affairs of State*, 6, 265–309 and 374–397.
[36] *The Poems of John Dryden*, 1, 449.

manna, the Jewish sabbath, the healing touch, the second Eve, and the virgin church awaiting Christ. A perfect exemplar of virtue, she is translated to heaven like Enoch and Elijah as a reward for sinless perfection. The Old Testament figures prophesy Christ's acts of charity and devotion, and Dryden's saint's life conforms the individual to Christ. But the emphasis in the personal panegyric is on the earthly rather than triumphant Christ. Type and antitype as analogy and allusion point to Christ's earthly ministry: healing the sick, feeding the multitudes, clothing the needy. Eleonora enacts the truly Christian life: "cou'd there be / A copy near th' Original, 'twas she" (300). As in *To my Honour'd Kinsman* and Pope's *Epistle to Bathurst*, the contemporary figure becomes a type again in a recurrent history of personal, not political, salvation.

Redemption as domestic or rural activity sharply distinguishes the personal figuralism of these poems from the political typology of *The First Anniversary* or *Absalom and Achitophel*: "Want pass'd for Merit, at her open door, / Heav'n saw, he safely might increase his poor . . ." (32–33); "All, in the Compass of her Sphear, she drew . . ." (37); "Her Lord himself might come, for ought we know; / Since in a Servant's form he liv'd below: / Beneath her Roof, he might be pleas'd to stay" (54–56). The center of the poem is not king or protector leading the nation toward the millennium, not the individual as instrument of universal renewal, but the private person in acts of familial or rural piety and virtue. An eschatological perspective for the nation has all but disappeared, and the narrowed scope of salvation in the personal elegies and epistles is reflected in the poet's hostile public stance. The elaborate analogy that opens *Eleonora* tries to imagine her death in civic terms, "As, when some Great and Gracious Monarch dies / . . . The Nation felt it, in th'extremest parts." But Dryden's interests and belief are no longer in national redemption: "They say my Talent is Satyre; if it be so, 'tis a Fruitful Age; and there is an extraordinary Crop to gather. . . . They have sown the Dragons Teeth Themselves; and 'tis but just they

shou'd reap each other in Lampoons."[37] Prophecy has become implicitly satiric, and Dryden's praise of the individual is a satire on the nation and the times:

> Where ev'n to draw the Picture of thy Mind,
> Is Satyr on the most of Humane Kind:
> Take it, while yet 'tis Praise; before my rage
> Unsafely just, break loose on this bad Age;
> So bad, that thou thy self had'st no defense,
> From Vice, but barely by departing hence.   (365–370)

A familiar elegiac *topos*, the allusion in the last couplet
imagines Eleonora as Astraea fleeing a corrupt world, a
reversal of Christ's redemptive mission.

The *Ode on the Death of Purcell* poses the christic model,
through the example of Orpheus, not as redemptive figure
but as sacrifice to the gods. The christic significance of Orpheus is obvious in the language of Dryden's praise (10–
15, 21–22) as it was familiar through the long tradition of
Christian commentary on classical figures. The power of
music to tune the spheres and the virtues of the godlike
man take their full meaning from Christ, "the true Orpheus."[38] The individual is enlarged and celebrated
through the image of God in man; but on this elegiac occasion the typology is distinctly private. "Alas, too soon re-
tir'd, / As He too late began"; the force and mood of the
poem are regret rather than reformation. The christic and
orphic meaning of Purcell's death is completed in the
poem's final stanza, which imagines him as sacrifice to
the gods:

> Ye Brethren of the *Lyre*, and tunefull Voice,
> Lament his lott: but at your own rejoyce.
> Now live secure and linger out your days,
> The Gods are pleas'd alone with *Purcell's Layes*,
> Nor know to mind their Choice.        (27–31)

---

37 *The Poems of John Dryden*, 2, 584.
38 Alexander Ross, *Mystagogus Poeticus* (London, 1675), p. 338.

In political poems, contemporary figures are set in a typological perspective so that redemption can have prescriptive social meaning. In personal odes, funeral pieces, and in Horatian epistles, the ends of figural analogy are compliment, contemplation, and private action.

The Horatian epistle is one of the most interesting of the several modes essayed by both Dryden and Pope. The genre allowed for the praise of country life—a topic of special significance for the disenfranchised Catholics and one with obviously classical rather than hebraic meaning—but it also permitted both poets to combine georgic setting with figural imagery to represent the individual in retirement re-enacting Christ's life through charity and self-governance. Pope's commingling of pastoral with prophecy is familiar from *Messiah* and *Windsor Forest*, but it is the portrait of the Man of Ross that most explicitly complements Marvell, Dryden, and indeed the whole figural tradition in the private mode. In the epistles of Dryden and Pope, Eden is no longer England restored or restorable, but the private estate, that domain where the force of the *imitatio Christi* can still be felt.

The epistle to Driden of Chesterton falls into separate sections praising the subject in retirement and in public life. Although the first half of the poem anticipates the second, there are aspects of language and imagination that deny this coherence. Country life removes the individual from cares of state and domesticates acts of magistracy, judgment, charity, and physic. Rather than provide for England and heal the nation, the poet's cousin cares for his own;

> As Heav'n in Desarts rain'd the Bread of Dew,
> So free to Many, to Relations most,
> You feed with Manna your own *Israel*-Host. (47–49)

Israel is not England or a political party, but friends, relatives, and local community. The promised land as domestic circle is not the "little room" of Donne's lovers, but no

longer is it the expansive state of *Absalom and Achitophel.*
To Driden as judge and arbiter "contending Neighbors
come"; his wealth is dispensed to those who pass through
his door. In this poem Eden is attainable for the individual,
but only as a local paradise and only for the celibate. As
second Adam, patriarch to this Eden, Driden of Chesterton
contradicts the political meaning of patriarchalism. He will
"father" no community. The striking contrast is of course
the opeining of *Absalom and Achitophel* which takes
patriarchalism both wittily and seriously as sexual and
political metaphor. Driden's Eden at Chesterton denies the
basis of social continuity, but it is a logical choice as image
of paradise for Dryden. Now exiled from the court, he
celebrates the country estate as source of spiritual renewal.
The poem offers a redemptive model for the individual, not
for the nation.

To my Honour'd Kinsman also praises Driden as public
figure and patriot; but the figures are separate, and the distance between them is reflected in the imagery of compliment. As Dryden turns to public life, the language becomes
distinctly classical. Roman, not Jewish, history is, in the
1690's, the analogue for public affairs. As country gentleman Driden is Jacob, Adam, and by suggestion and analogy, Christ as healer and savior, *topoi* familiar from *Eleonora* and the *Epistle to Bathurst.* But as public man and sen-
ator he is a figure appropriate to Cicero's *de Republica*, not
to Scripture. For a moment, the classical and scriptural
models merge in the figure of the patriot, independently
wealthy, above temptation, preserving prerogative and
privilege, "When both are full, they feed our bless'd Abode;
/ Like those, that water'd once, the Paradise of God"
(178–179). But Driden of Chesterton is no millennial republican, and redemption in this poem is finally the immortal-
ity of verse rather than political action. The earthly and
heavenly destinies of the country gentleman are continuous
only through the power of verse. In *To my Honour'd Kinsman* political action is a form of good behavior, not an
apocalyptic necessity.

The poem is perhaps more interconnected than these remarks allow, but this schematization locates a striking tension in the later Dryden and in succeeding generations of poets between private and public life, individual grace and national politics, virtue and corruption.[39] In these familiar pairs the tension runs through the English renaissance and augustan literature and history; in the terms of my present subject, the shift from a prophetic to a secular interpretation of political life can be sharply felt within individual poems at the close of the seventeenth century. Prophecy assumes that national history and institutions are an expression of God's salvation plan; for the secular historian, politics is a way of managing civil affairs, not an instrument of redemption. Divine and secular models of personal and national behavior co-exist, as *To my Honour'd Kinsman* demonstrates, but there is an increasing distance between them; the private life might still be imagined in redemptive terms, but not national politics.

Pope's *Epistle to Bathurst* is heir to the political disintegration of the figural mode. In this poem, the redemptive figure is an endangered species, brittle and abstract, a figure that needs the protection of a rural environment to work those transformations of place and constituents that are so powerfully depicted, so energetically stated at the close of *Appleton House* or in the confident rhythms of *Absalom and Achitophel*. But of course individual redemption for Pope does not prophesy national restoration. The village of Ross may be "Paradice's only Map," but it is safely hidden in the forest, and it can be read by only a few: the weary traveler, Age, Want, the sick, the poor, the old, the orphaned. Those who experience redemption at Ross are hardly in a condition to restore the nation. In the design of

---

[39] For somewhat different views, see J. A. Levine, "John Dryden's Epistle to John Driden," *JEGP*, 63 (1964), 450–472; and Alan Roper's remarks on this poem in *Dryden's Poetic Kingdoms* (London, 1965), 124–135. [Also a rise in tropology, or moral allegory, in some of Dryden's late works, might be considered. See Roche's chapter, above, n. 18.—Ed.]

Pope's poem, politics and redemption are inimical to one another.

The portait of the Man of Ross, Robert Kyrle, is surrounded by figures of power and corruption; Kyrle is at the center of the poem, but he cannot struggle free, is not felt at any other moment in the poem. Public affairs belong "To Ward, to Waters, Chartres and the Devil" (20); paper credit bribes senates and buys kings (78). Poised against this corruption is the Man of Ross, but the figure is ineffectual, rural, and retired. Feeding the hungry, bringing solace to the weary, this redeemer is imagined in terms even more obviously figural than Dryden's in *To my Honour'd Kinsman*, but unlike Driden of Chesterton he is given no public life in secular politics. Like the patriarch of Chesterton, Kyrle is "clear" of wife and children; the redemptive figure is again celibate—a model for individual imitation, not political action. His deeds promise personal grace, salvation for a specific community; but that body is set apart, explicitly non-political. Pastoral description in the portrait of the village severs the edenic community from the nation. Echoing rivers, wooded mountains, and thick forests give a sense of physical enclosure, a separateness heightened by Kyrle's redemptive power. Like Mary Fairfax at the close of *Appleton House*, Kyrle orders the world around him, "Who hung with woods yon mountain's sultry brow? / From the dry rock who bade the waters flow?" (253–254). The images extend the heroic aspect of the figure, suggesting a world partly redeemed, responsive to the divine.[40] But unlike Mary Farifax who closes *Appleton House* with a meteoric brilliance, Pope's redemptive figure is imagined safely dead, "And what? no Monument, Inscription, Stone? / His Race, his Form, his Name almost unknown?" No virgin branch this, awaiting completion and fulfillment; Pope's portait closes with the Man of Ross disappearing into anonymity.

---

[40] Earl R. Wasserman, *Pope's Epistle to Bathurst* (Baltimore, 1960), pp. 41–43, offers an extensive and illuminating reading of biblical materials in the portrait of the Man of Ross.

But the poem does not end in pastoral harmony or individual renewal. In the dialectic of this poem, the Man of
Ross is answered by Sir Balaam, the type of Christ coun-
terbalanced by the satanic figure who "curses God and
dies." Not only are the virtues of the christic model inverted in Sir Balaam—charity, devotion, and humility become greed, hypocrisy, and social ambition—but the figural
system itself, which earlier conflated Moses, Christ, and
Kyrle, is so presented in this portrait that Job is subsumed
in and reversed by Balaam. The typology of Job repeats the
pattern of the fall in Eden and prophesies, in denial,
Christ's triumph over Satan. The meaning of Christ's refusal of worldly glory is renewed by the Man of Ross who
feeds the hungry and relieves the afflicted. Sir Balaam aims
only to redouble his wealth, a goal whose end is always the
same:

> Congenial souls! whose life one Av'rice joins,
> And one fate buries in th'Asturian Mines. (133–134)

> There, Victor of his health, of fortune, friends,
> And fame; this lord of useless thousands ends. (313–314)

> The Devil and the King divide the prize,
> And sad Sir Balaam curses God and dies. (401–402)

The poem closes in reversal and darkness. Pope recoils both
from the individual and an entire society: "There dwelt a
Citizen of sober fame . . ."; "Sir Balaam now, he lives like
other folks . . ."; "In Britain's senate he obtains a Seat." The
Man of Ross lives in obscure retirement; Balaam is part of
a large social world. The portrait is brilliantly particular,
the indictment sweepingly large. In the *Epistle to Bathurst*
the virtuous few provide no spiritual bulwark against the
wicked many; here greed and darkness are invincible
powers.

The history of types in the later seventeenth century can
be written from various materials, but the poetry of
Marvell, Dryden, and Pope reveals its distinctive nature.
Part of that history is the continuity of figuralism as per-

sonal praise from the earlier to the later seventeenth century. Despite obvious changes and attenuations, the individual as type of Christ is a powerful and continuously deployed trope for the celebration of the private person from Donne's *Anniversaries* to Pope's *Epistle to Bathurst*. But it is as a technique of political discourse that typology is most distinctively the product and expression of the half-century between the outbreak of the Civil Wars and the Glorious Revolution. Political typology is not of course unique to those years, but the intensity and the art with which typology was adapted to the needs of political statement are peculiar to that long and difficult moment between the two English Revolutions. That a technique of scriptural exegesis should have provided a significant element of a nation's political language results from the convergence of theology and politics. As historical event, the convergence can be identified with the English Civil Wars. A distinctly scriptural rhetoric developed in earlier decades for devotion and the interpretation of Scripture was, by mid-century, applied to questions of political authority.

Such a language, characteristic of England's most introspective and internecine decades, could not sustain indefinite political use. Typology as a method of scriptural exegesis and prophecy as a mode of historical thought came under increasing attack in the later seventeenth century.[41] The rise of Deism and natural religion, the concerted effort to undermine the mysteries of Scripture, gradually discredited the belief in Scripture as literal and predictive truth. The later seventeenth-century attacks on Enthusiasm,[42] the increasingly secular vocabulary of polit-

[41] Victor Harris considers this issue in "Allegory to Analogy in the Interpretation of Scriptures," *Philological Quarterly*, 45 (January, 1966), esp. 14–23. Leonard J. Trinterud's essay, "A.D. 1689: The End of the Clerical World," *Theology in Sixteenth- and Seventeenth-Century England*, William Andrews Clark Library (Los Angeles, 1971), offers an interesting analysis of the crisis of the Restoration church.

[42] See, for example, George Hickes, *The Spirit of Enthusiasm Exorcised* (London, 1680); Henry Wharton, *The Enthusiasm of the Church*

ical debate, and the presentist arguments of Whig apologetics are all important components of what has often been identified as the cooling intellectual temper of augustan England. In the history of literary expression, this change is seen in the decline of the heroic mode and concurrent rise of satire and burlesque at the close of the seventeenth century.

But the disintegration of typology as a political language can also be understood in ways that more closely integrate literary, political, and intellectual history. The language of millenarianism, of puritan and royalist apocalypse with its attendant types, prefigurations, and prophecies, had not simply worn down by the close of the seventeenth century; it had become a vocabulary inappropriate to the political facts and issues of a different age. England's commitment to the European wars, the financial revolution which supported those wars, and the management of parliament by the monied interest were new facts of national political life that Old Testament history and prophetic inspiration were ill-equipped to justify. The middle decades of the seventeenth century were a time when men sought salvation not only as an individual goal but also as a national destiny. For this merging of private and public lives the history of Israel provided an ideal narrative. But late in the century, as the distance widened between Jewish history and English politics, between the rhetoric of national election and the way men saw their own lives, another myth gained dominance. Rome, not Jerusalem, was the capital of secular empire.

Prophecy as a political language posits the active presence of God in history. The systematic demonstration of this presence in sacred history is typology; persons and events are predictive and the final design of these predic-

---

*of Rome* (London, 1688); Anthony Collins, *Scheme of Literal Prophesy considered* (London, 1727). Ronald A. Knox, *Enthusiasm, A Chapter in the History of Religion* (Oxford, 1950) is the standard account of enthusiasm; see also Susie I. Tucker, *Enthusiasm, A Study in Semantic Change* (Cambridge, 1972).

tions is the closure of time administered by a deity whose own design history obeys. Vicissitude itself, as in the Old Testament, can always be understood as the fluctuations of God's anger toward, and love for, his people; but cyclical and degenerative interpretations of history contradict typology. Without a belief in a divinely ordered and one-directional history, typology as a political language has no meaning. That Dryden himself should have come in 1700 to express a cyclical interpretation of history is an interesting document in our reading of the individual's beliefs. But we need not insist that the *Secular Masque* reflects Dryden's own weariness or disillusion to understand the famous lyric that closes the masque as the expression of a crucial shift in historical consciousness:

> All, all, of a piece throughout;
> Thy Chase had a Beast in View;
> Thy Wars brought nothing about;
> Thy Lovers were all untrue.
> 'Tis well an Old Age is out,
> And time to begin a New.

Read as political statement, Dryden's lyric suggests the Polybian anacyclosis: a perpetual system of the decay of different forms of government which rise and fall with what seems biological necessity. It is not surprising that the characters of Dryden's *Secular Masque* should be pagan deities; prophetic poets and Davidic kings belong to a world differently imagined.

PAUL J. KORSHIN

# THE DEVELOPMENT OF ABSTRACTED
# TYPOLOGY IN ENGLAND, 1650–1820

## I

EXEGETES have traditionally employed interpretative typology for prefigurative or postfigurative reasons, either to justify a certain reading of a text or event by alluding to a desired future circumstance, or to support a favorite interpretation by arguing that it fulfills something prophesied or predicted in the past. If we wish to interpret Graham Greene's whiskey priest in *The Power and the Glory* as a postfiguration of Jesus,[1] then this typological interpretation does not *predict* so much as it *completes* an unseen hermeneutic sequence started at some time in our distant cultural past. With another Christ figure, Richardson's Sir Charles Grandison, we would be justified in viewing this paragon as a prefiguration, a typical figure foreshadowing the greater perfections of some urbane, socialized, quintessentially gentleman Jesus. The behavior and situation of Greene's trapped priest dimly replay a few scenes from the New Testament: his humanity and the humaneness of his predicament impress many readers with the similarity of everyday life to the Christian situation everywhere. The cold typology of *Sir Charles Grandison*, on the other hand, is difficult for twentieth-century readers to relate to life, but for Richardson's audience, Sir Charles was the perfect Christian, a character plucked from the pages of a typological homily. The failure of *Grandison* with its original pub-

---

[1] See Theodore Ziolkowski, *Fictional Transformations of Jesus* (Princeton, 1972), pp. 221–223. Cf. John J. White, *Mythology in the Modern Novel: A Study of Prefigurative Techniques* (Princeton, 1971), pp. 11–14. Both Ziolkowski and White use the concept of prefiguration loosely, yet both emphasize the likelihood that a type or a prefigurative myth would evoke a familiar pattern for the reader. [See also Ziolkowski's chapter below.—Ed.]

*147*

lic is curious: sermons were popular in the eighteenth century.[2] Perhaps Sir Charles's perfections were unrealistic, making him appear too similar to that other frequently typologized Charles, the one whom the eighteenth-century public was accustomed to see prefigured and postfigured in annual martyrology.[3] Their popularity apart, the two novels cited give examples of a typological mode of reference considerably removed from *traditional* theological concerns. Neither Greene nor Richardson is writing homilies or works of Christian apologetics. Their typologies are therefore *abstracted*, drawn away from the theological field of action, although there may be religious significance in the way each is introduced. Literary historians of the last twenty years have shown how pervasive and acceptable typological imagery was in seventeenth-century English literature. What is responsible for the change which led to the development of abstracted typology? This is the question to which I hope to offer some answers in this essay.

## II

Four factors play a large role in the gradual rise of abstracted typology. The first is a seventeenth-century confusion of terminology which, in its narrowest range, caused typology to expand its area of reference. Pierre Legouis has protested against the "abuse" of typology in criticism of seventeenth-century literature: it should always, he argues, involve the study of types and antitypes.[4] So it should. But seventeenth-century writers themselves were often indistinct in their application of types: sometimes the word "type," in a theological context, describes an emblem, a

[2] On the reception of *Grandison*, see Alan Dugald McKillop, *Samuel Richardson, Printer and Novelist* (Chapel Hill, N.C., 1936), pp. 215–225.

[3] The annual Martyr's Day sermons still require more study, despite the helpful essay by Helen W. Randall, "The Rise and Fall of a Martyrology: Sermons on Charles I," *HLQ*, 10 (1947), 135–167.

[4] "Some Remarks on Seventeenth-Century Imagery: Definitions and Caveats," in *Seventeenth-Century Imagery: Essays on Uses of Figurative Language from Donne to Farquhar*, ed. Earl Miner (Berkeley and Los Angeles, 1971), pp. 192–193.

hieroglyphic, a heraldic device, a historical painting, a portion of a picture or portrait, an engraved title page, or a purely representative device like a symbol.[5] Our seventeenth-century forebears were torn between belief in the realities of messianic persons and the potentially prefigurative qualities of a welter of signs. It is well to remember that the period of this terminological confusion, the century from 1625 to about 1725, was not so exclusively an age of print as our own. The reading experience of the average literate person was augmented by a rich visual iconography, one far different from what the modern reader knows. The lists of objects in *A Tale of a Tub* and other works had visual, often prefigurative, life for Swift's audience. Books explaining visual devices, pictorial details, even the decorative qualities of architecture, were common. Some are sophisticated, like emblem books. Others, like Ripa's *Iconologia* (literally the *stories* of visual images), books of coins and medals, and antiquarian compilations like Gronovius and Graevius, vary in appeal.[6] Even such a keen observer as Johnson was affected by the confusion: one of his *Dictionary* definitions of "typical" is "figurative of something else" (the absence of a designation for *prefiguring* or foreshadowing is significant).[7]

Confusion over terminology can lead to difficulties. This, too, has happened with abstracted typology, as with that

[5] Francis Quarles, in the Preface to his *Emblemes* (London, 1635), provides a good example of the confusion, by using "Types" synonymously with *"Emblemes," "Parables,"* and "Hieroglyphicks." See Sig. A3[r].

[6] The first English edition of Cesare Ripa's *Iconologia: or Moral Emblems* did not appear until 1709; there was another edition in 1778. However, there were as many as a dozen Continental editions during the seventeenth century. Liselotte Dieckmann, *Hieroglyphics: The History of a Literary Symbol* (St. Louis, 1970), pp. 48–99, surveys a generous portion of the literary tradition surrounding these devices.

[7] Martin Kallich, "Swift and the Archetypes of Hate: *A Tale of a Tub,*" *Studies in Eighteenth-Century Culture,* 4 (1975), 43–67. Kallich boldly interprets "type" to mean "any symbol," which allows him uncommon latitude in interpreting Swift, since he assumes the corollary to be true ("any symbol" = "a type"); he seems unaware of Legouis' caveats (see above, note 4).

problem of historians called "the fallacy of prediction by analogy."[8] Seventeenth- and eighteenth-century historians, seeking analogies from the past to vindicate events and governmental policies in their own time, sometimes propose that ancient history may foreshadow the present. The Puritans in particular delighted in seeing their persecutions as a minority as the antitype of the persecutions of the Israelites in Egypt, or as an antitype of the persecutions carried on against the primitive Christians by pagan Rome.[9] Scholars in other branches of learning have found predictive analogy helpful; often it is evident that they are using a methodology derived from abstracted typology. Linguists, for example, at one time believed that the grammar and syntax of Indo-European languages could be taken as a type of the morphology of other, more primitive tongues.[10] This belief, highly speculative, caused linguists to "generate" grammatical structures for non-literary languages by constructing antitypes that were *predicted*, as it were, by Western languages.

There is nothing that the modern student of figuralism can do to prevent such enthusiasm; indeed, to a considerable extent, its very existence in the past makes our inquiries necessary. In seeking the *raisons d'être* for abstracted typology, however, we must bear in mind that the original meaning of "type" and "typology" includes a connotation that is more than verbal or literary. Types are always *signs* whose meanings would be known to those fortunate enough to "read" the code they embody and of which they are a part. The meaning of abstracted typology is conveyed through words with an imagistic, pictorial, visual, or

---

[8] The coinage, so far as I know, is David Hackett Fischer's; see his *Historians' Fallacies: Toward a Logic of Historical Thought* (New York, 1970), pp. 257–258.

[9] [See Lowance's chapter, below.—Ed.] Here is a twentieth-century example of this variety of abstracted typology: "Cortez's plight in Mexico foreshadowed Richard Nixon's plight in Washington" (Russell Baker, "Moods of Washington," *New York Times Magazine*, 24 March 1974, p. 72). This may be self-parody.

[10] See, for example, J. van Ginneken, *La réconstruction typologique des langues archaïques de l'humanité* (Amsterdam, 1939).

symbolic effect or by an author's introducing names, characters, places, or events which would induce an audience to regard them as prefigurations of something else. The English audience advised by Dryden that their restored monarch, Charles II, had been "forc'd to suffer for Himself and us," or that the King was like "banish'd *David*," or that he had been made "at his own cost like *Adam* wise" is being instructed that a typological code (a rather simple one, it happens) is in operation.[11]

In the 1730's, Pope acquaints his audience with his typological purposes, as in the *Epistle to Bathurst*, in a different manner. We become aware that the Man of Ross is a typological character because of his Moses-like actions in the text and because of the long footnote added in 1735. The reader was encouraged to see Sir Balaam as a type of sin (or as a negative type) because of the signals Pope scatters about his text to suggest that this is no ordinary sinner but one who postfigures and also prefigures a known pattern. The associations with the Judas-character are telling: he accepts a bribe from France to betray his country (or master), his friends at Court forsake him and he "hangs," and finally, "sad Sir Balaam curses God and dies" (396–402). Pope's situational details leave no doubt of the extra-verbal, typological qualities his figure possesses. Fielding, still differently, emphasizes the typological qualities of certain characters, like Joseph Andrews or Squire Allworthy, by events: Joseph is chaste under trying circumstances, Allworthy is forgiving. The figure surrounded with symbolic detail, then, is the special handiwork of an author using abstracted typology. A character or a situation which would otherwise lack prefigurative force is thus transformed into a typological sign.

This distinguishing stamp separates genuine abstracted types from narrative or logical devices like predictive analogy. For signs are not just words. In a literary medium, they are *expressed* through words, but they have special cogni-

11 Dryden, *Astræa Redux*, ll. 50, 79, 113.

tive status, like numbers. Susanne K. Langer comments,
"Numbers seem to have a special status; their symbolic expression by numerals, which every reader verbalizes according to his own language, shows that number concepts
are not ordinary elements of vocabulary, but may long have
been conceived and conveyed by non-linguistic symbols,
and perhaps had a history of their own in our cerebral evolution."[12] Signs, as they appear in literature, may also be
regarded as "non-linguistic symbols"; they have a life of
their own outside and beyond a text in which they may
appear.

A reader, for instance, who comes upon the figure of
Joshua in a poem about Cromwell could well expect that
Joshua's military qualities would suggest something about
Cromwell's martial skills. If the same reader, any time between 1650 and 1750, finds a pagan worthy like Hercules in
a text about an English sovereign, he might well remember
that Hercules was a pagan type of Christ. This identification would very likely cause him to predict certain qualities
of the sovereign in question. A reader in 1749 who picked
up a poem called *The Vanity of Human Wishes* might recall
that the character of Cardinal Wolsey had lately been used
to symbolize the faults of overweening political power; for
such a reader, then, "Wolsey's end" could prefigure the fall
of some more recent power-grabbing statesman.[13] These
figures would qualify semiotically as non-linguistic symbols,
which can be shifted about from one text to another, always
keeping the same approximate significance. True abstracted
types always retain something of the sign. Like numbers,
they are in a class by themselves, expressed through the

12 Susanne K. Langer, *Mind: An Essay on Human Feeling*, 2 vols.
(Baltimore, 1967–1972), 2, 349.
13 See *The Vanity of Human Wishes*, ll. 99–128; Wolsey was a character for Sir Robert Walpole. Since the historical details of Wolsey's
fall were well known to the contemporary reader, it seems likely that
the Wolsey-character functioned in a prefigurative manner for an
eighteenth-century audience, shadowing forth the fall of Walpole.
See Maynard Mack, *The Garden and the City: Retirement and Politics
in the Later Poetry of Pope, 1731–1743* (Toronto, 1969), pp. 133, 159,
205.

medium of language, but usually visual or semiological, working on a plane separate from language. They may be seen as a sort of non-visual iconography.

Not every word-picture, however, can be so classified. Typological events, persons, and places are distinct from other imagistic materials, for they are, as A. C. Charity puts it, events with an afterlife.[14] The circumstances of abstracted typology have an accepted and acknowledged history of their own; a writer who used an abstracted type could expect—or hope—that some of his audience would spot the connection. Those who believe that late seventeenth- and eighteenth-century writers drank deep from the Cup of Clarity may take issue with me here. How, it may be objected, could writers who strove to *narrow* the hermeneutic gap between author and reader possibly be guilty of hidden meanings?[15] My answer is that the cup must have contained some dregs, or that it somehow intoxicated—the constant interplay of allusions, complex wordplay, and deliberate political obscurities in the literature of this period suggest nothing else. Like the typological inscriptions in medieval and renaissance paintings, some of these types must have escaped the attention of many contemporary readers.[16]

Semioticists call the elements of a code "semantic enclaves." The abstracted types I am discussing here are such units, typological clusters which probably were not completely clear for every member of the audience. The mysterious youth of unknown genealogy who appears often as a character type in the gothic novel, later in the eighteenth century, may have seemed nothing more than a romantic hero to many middle-class readers. To the informed reader, however, the character of Theodore in *The Castle of*

[14] See Charity, *Events and their Afterlife: The Dialectics of Christian Typology in The Bible and Dante* (Cambridge, 1966), pp. 1–4.

[15] For discussion of the "hermeneutic gap," see my *From Concord to Dissent* (London, 1973), pp. 7, 72, 79, 196.

[16] For a particularly interesting treatment of this largely unnoticed aspect of typology, see Mieczsław Wallis, "Inscriptions in Paintings," *Semiotica*, 9 (1973), 1–28, especially 11–14, 16–17, 27.

*Otranto* (1764), with his sacrificial and redemptive qualities and his other christomimetic overtones, could have seemed a type of the suffering deity. The fact that the "semantic enclave" of such a character might pass unremarked by some readers does not negate its existence even if only the twentieth-century exegete reports on it. A code can lose its significance rapidly, as we can see from the heavy annotation Pope's editors gave his works only a few years after his death. Pope, as I have suggested, was good at using semantic enclaves. Less than twenty years after some of his best abstracted typology, which he had presented in the 1730's without any explanation, Warburton felt compelled to add much explanation to its occurrence in his 1751 edition of Pope's *Works*. The confusion in terminology I mentioned earlier, then, caused writers of the later seventeenth and eighteenth centuries to lose sight of the theological distinctions which governed typology as a system of biblical exegesis. Types, emblems, symbols, hieroglyphics—all come to be used synonymously. Thus, farther from the fount, the stream at random strayed.

The second important cause of abstracted typology, closely related to the terminological factor, was the politicizing of theological contexts, particularly in the last half of the seventeenth century. As early as the 1650's Harrington objected to typologizing kingship at every possible opportunity, but his complaints were little heeded.[17] Perhaps the decline of divine-right theories aided this secularizing process more than anything else. The Coronation of Charles II led to an outpouring of Old Testament and Messianic typology from poets and poetasters alike,[18] but as the divine-right susceptibilities of the Stuart house declined and as the king-making powers of Parliament rose, the picture

---

[17] See Harrington, *The Grounds and Reasons of Monarchy Consider'd* (c. 1655) in *The Oceana of James Harrington, and His Other Works* (London, 1700), pp. 5–6.

[18] Gerard Reedy, S.J., "Mystical Politics: The Imagery of Charles II's Coronation," *Studies in Change and Revolution*, ed. Paul J. Korshin (London, 1972), pp. 19–42, deals with many of the typological variations in detail.

changed. Later coronations called forth fewer biblical types
(Adam, Noah, Moses, Joshua, David) and more abstracted
typological figures from classical mythology (Hercules,
Amphion, Timotheus, Orpheus) and secular classical history
(Alexander, Caesar, Cato). There would be yet another
transformation in the eighteenth century to the types drawn
from English history: Alfred, Edward the Confessor, Edward III, and Henry V.[19]

It is interesting to note how the subjects or reference
points of typology change as it becomes less theological and
more abstract. The typology of the Old Testament figures
had been established by centuries of exegesis: it was based
on a strong Christian belief in the unity of the two Testaments. That drawn from classical mythology was no nov-
elty: the search for mysterious Christian meanings in pagan
texts during the late Middle Ages and Renaissance had succeeded in giving Christian citizenship to the heroes of ancient myth, even though they lacked the birth certificates
of natives.[20] An unfettered Christian holism led Samuel
Bochart to declare that the pagan gods were Old Testament
patriarchs by birthright. Less adventurous but dutiful antiquarians like Gerardus Vossius, Athanasius Kircher, and
Bishop Stillingfleet at least gave pagan myth an acceptable
rationale and genealogy. From the assumed unity of Christian and pagan myths, it was a short step to the belief that
secular history is predictive, and that the histories of an-

[19] The panegyric verse available from the Coronations of Charles II,
James II, William III, Anne, and George I reveals much fluctuation
and uncertainty in the use of Old Testament types and classical
figures. William III and the first two Georges are sometimes seen as
postfigurations of Roman or English rulers (not exclusively in favorable terms). In non-Coronation verses, we can note the introduction of historical typology at least as early as the 1630's. The memorial volume for Edward King, *Justa Edovardo King naufrago, ab
Amicis mœrentibus* (Cambridge, 1638), contains an untitled and un-
signed poem which compares King, by punning on his last name and
his first name, with "Edward the Confessour, or the Saint" (see pp.
8–9). [For another view, see Zwicker's chapter, above.–Ed.]

[20] Don Cameron Allen, *Mysteriously Meant* (Baltimore, 1971), chs.
8 and 9 (pp. 201–278), offers an account of the symbolic interpretations
of Renaissance mythographers unlikely to be surpassed.

cient Greece and Rome, of the great kings of the Middle
Ages and Renaissance, might hold forth some special lesson
to seventeenth- and eighteenth-century England. The maturing of English history in the first third of the eighteenth
century—the work of many writers from Temple to Rymer
and Rapin—established the characters of England's historical past as patterns for present emulation. Narrative history was *expected* to inform politics. When Sir William
Temple, in his *Introduction to the History of England*
(1695), stressed the similarities between William the Con-
queror and William III, his contemporaries noted the post-
figuration of the Prince of Orange with approval.[21]

The use of an abstracted typology came about as a result
of secular historians' efforts to parallel their subject with
sacred history. Church historians from the time of Eusebius
had done the same. There can be little doubt that historians
and early political scientists adopted typological practice
to their methods. Even titles are expressive: consider Henry
Nevile's *Plato Redivivus, or a Dialogue concerning Government* (1681), whose subtitle runs as follows—"Wherein, by
observations drawn from other Kingdoms and States, both
ancient and modern, an endeavour is used to discover the
present politic distemper of our own; with the causes and
remedies." Three speakers, a physician, a noble Venetian,
and an Englishman, hold a discussion on statecraft; their
talk turns (inevitably) to what's wrong with the state of affairs in seventeenth-century England:

> And you would have good store of practice in your for-
> mer capacity, if the wise custom of the ancient Greeks
> were not totally out of use. For they, when they found
> any craziness or indisposition in their several govern-

21 See Abel Boyer, *Memoirs of the Life and Negotiations of Sir
William Temple* (London, 1714), p. 413. It should be noted that there
is no "fallacy of predictive analogy" at work here or in similar situations; the eighteenth-century historian was not trying to show a cause-
and-effect relationship between past history and the present. Rather,
he would be trying to show that the actions of a modern ruler, like
James II or William III, were acceptable *postfigurations* of past times.

ments, before it broke out with a disease, did repair to the physicians of state . . . and obtain'd from the same good Recipes, to prevent those seeds of distemper from taking root, and destroying the publick peace. But in our days, these signs or forerunners of diseases in state are not foreseen, till the whole mass is corrupted; and that the patient is incurable, but by violent remedies.[22]

To understand Nevile's lament about the shortsightedness of the present, we have to bear in mind that seventeenth-century exegetes of the Pentateuch habitually insist that the ancient Hebrews were well enough informed to be able to interpret correctly the foreshadowings of the Messiah in their surroundings and situation. The patriarchs, in other words, understood the language of the types.

In these latter times, the argument runs, men have to be guided to a proper interpretation of prefigurative signs; the old vision has failed. Hence Nevile shows the ancient Greeks as informed readers of "signs," or "forerunners" of civil instability. Not only does his dialogue stress the uses of abstracted typology in running the state, but he also presents early historical events or circumstances as prefigurative desiderata. One of the purposes of Nevile's republican tract was to show that the vision of classical government had vanished from Stuart England. What he does for republican Greece others would do for ancient Rome, for the obsession with the success or failure of previous governments was a national concern. For example, Walter Moyle's "Essay on the Constitution of the Roman Government" (c. 1710) shows at some length "the Reasons of the Corruption and Ruin of the *Roman* Commonwealth." Moyle's "Reasons" have a bearing on Stuart England, for every one of them is predictive of flaws in the English monarchy.[23] Secular historians, then, contribute substantially to the spread of abstracted typology, principally by their willingness to

[22] Henry Nevile, *Plato Redivivus*, 4th ed. (London, 1763), p. 12.
[23] *The Works of Walter Moyle, Esq.*, 2 vols. (London, 1726), 2, 99–148, especially p. 132.

treat history as something parallel to Scripture, as something possessed of a unified purpose and a narrative consistency. The past is a series of chronicles scattered with *significant events and characters* which, if properly understood, would enable Englishmen to predict correct solutions for the present.

## III

A third factor in the movement toward abstracted typology is what I shall call the post-Restoration expansion of the number of genres using typology. During the first half of the seventeenth century, the most common locations of typological imagery are biblical exegesis, Christian apologetics, homilies, divine poetry, the pastoral, the epic, and ecclesiastical history. The last of these was already a form of abstracted typology, for the belief that the history of the Church in antiquity foreshadowed religious history in the Reformation and afterwards, held by more than a few church historians in the seventeenth century, is an innovative, non-canonical use of the device.[24] By the last half of the century, however, typology becomes attractive to the practitioners of other literary genres, especially to satirists, character writers, the authors of prose and verse fables, and, perhaps most important, the writers of prose narrative. None of these genres is new to the late seventeenth century, but all change enormously after about 1650. The increased sophistication of satire, for instance, particularly in cultivating new rhetorical strategies, naturally leads satirists to seek fresh methods of ridicule. Typology is susceptible to parody for, as we know from seventeenth-century Anglican,

[24] Church historians also sometimes regarded themselves as fulfilling a role that had been hinted at in former ages. See, for example, Paolo Sarpi, *The Historie of the Councel of Trent*, trans. Nathanael Brent, 2nd ed. (London, 1629), "Dedication," Sig. ¶6r-v. See also Laurence Echard, *A General Ecclesiastical History* (London, 1702), pp. 3, 32; Basnage's *History of the Jews, from Jesus to the Present Time*, trans. Thomas Taylor (London, 1708), p. vii; and cf. Benjamin Keach, *Antichrist Stormed: or, Mystery Babylon the Great Whore, and Great City, proved to be the present Church of Rome* (London, 1689), pp. 103–116, for a polemical use of historical typology.

Puritan, and Roman Catholic exegesis, it is capable of being abused by the exegete. Since much Restoration and early eighteenth-century satire has a theological basis, it is not surprising that satirists found the distortions of typology attractive as methods of ridicule.[25] Cleveland, Butler, and Swift all find distorted typology useful for attacking the excesses of Puritanism. The minor scribblers who swarm through the pages of *Poems on Affairs of State* afford other examples. In *The Dunciad,* Pope creates the most consistent distorted typologies of all, and his *First Epistle of the Second Book of Horace Imitated* is scarcely less successful.

We would be unlikely to turn to the Theophrastan characters of the early seventeenth century for abstracted typology, but this genre, too, becomes less moral and more satiric as the century progressed. The sobriety of Bishop Hall gives way to the wit and nastiness of Butler, and with Butler comes the distortion of accepted prefigurative forms for satiric purposes. The late seventeenth-century efflorescence of fables contributes to the growth of abstracted typology in interesting ways, as I shall show later. The prose or verse fable, whether Aesopic or modern, not only provides a stage for typological characters and beasts, but it revives the *glossa* and the *moralia.*[26] Typological readings often lurk in the *glossa ordinaria* to the vulgate Bible (a work which continued to be available in seventeenth-century England); so, too, do they crop up in the lengthy prose explanations which accompany many collections of fables.

[25] On typological satire, see my essay, "Swift and Typological Narrative in *A Tale of a Tub,*" *Harvard English Studies,* 1 (1970), 67–91.

[26] Animal symbolism was amazingly popular in the seventeenth century, as is demonstrated by the numerous editions of Wolfgang Frantz's *Historia Animalium Sacra* (1612). The first part of Frantz, "De Quadrupedis," was translated by "N.W." as *The History of Brutes* (London, 1670), and the work itself was gradually enlarged "cum Commentariis & Supplementis. Observationum ex recentiori Historia naturali, Similitudinem, Emblematum, Hierogylphicorum. . . ." into an enormous syntagma. There were at least ten editions by 1712. A helpful study of beast symbolism (and relevant typology) is Beryl Rowland, *Animals with Human Faces: A Guide to Animal Symbolism* (Knoxville, Tenn., 1973).

The commentaries may be even more important than the fables themselves and are frequently much longer than the texts they illustrate.

The genre that expands more than any other after 1660 is prose narrative or, more properly, prose fiction. With an early writer of fictive narrative like Bunyan, typological situations (as in *The Pilgrim's Progress* and *The Holy War*) may remind us more of the sermon than the novel. The contemporary sermon writer would use Old Testament types to demonstrate or underscore a certain Christian doctrine (such as the truth of the prophecies). But Bunyan is a leader in encouraging abstracted typology in fiction, and for one very persuasive reason: his complex typologies are highly appropriate to the requirements of the novel; they are invented scenes and little predictive dramas, Christian and biblical in their subject but original in their presentation.[27] His fictional types are structural units (cf. "semantic enclaves") which prefigure later plot developments. Nor are they accidental foreshadowings: Christian's sojourn at the House of the Interpreter and the death and instantaneous resurrection of Faithful play deliberate prefigurative roles. Bunyan is echoing Puritan homiletics, meditations, and confessional autobiography, but those who follow him are more concerned with the problems of the novel.

The eighteenth-century novel provides a field for a unique literary operation, the blending of two alien literary forms and methodologies, the character and the type. The *character*, if we think of it in Theophrastan terms, is Grecian, pagan; it portrays a single, representative specimen

[27] There are many typological promises vouchsafed to Christian which help the reader to predict the book's conclusion. The events and prophecies which take place at the House of the Interpreter are among the most vivid such scenes. See *Grace Abounding to the Chief of Sinners and The Pilgrim's Progress*, ed. Roger Sharrock (London, 1966), pp. 161–169. [And see Lewalski's chapter, above.—Ed.] This section ends with a typological Pisgah-sight. *The Holy War* is often typological in the scenes involving Emmanuel's mission and the promises regarding the paradisical future of Mansoul. See the ed. of James F. Forrest (New York, 1967), pp. 75, 131, 132 (for typological riddles), pp. 161–162, 169, 253, 280.

of a generalized class of individuals that are—and always will be—everywhere the same. The *type* is Christian, prefigurative, a structural unit relating closely to the great drama of the promise of Christian salvation. Both of these literary forms and methods, as I have suggested, are popular about 1700. In the expansion of prose fiction during the eighteenth century, there occurs a blending of these two elements, of pagan and Christian, character and type, into a new literary device, the *character type*. We use the term all the time, yet without adequate recognition of its origins or purpose. It is unrelated, I think, to the stock characters of renaissance drama; these personages are seldom prefigurative. The term, "character type," in fact, is a nineteenth-century invention: the first distinctions of the word "type" to refer to "a general class of individuals" date from the 1840's.[28]

However, though the formal literary term is relatively recent, the prefigurative phenomenon it expresses appears to be mainly a seventeenth- and eighteenth-century development. The early English novelists had the many character books, sketches, and political polemics of the previous century ready at hand; stock "characters" abound in the fiction of Defoe, Richardson, Fielding, Smollett, and a score of lesser novelists.[29] What we have hitherto ignored is that many, if not most, of these characters were immediately recognizable to an audience well-acquainted with character books, literary emblems, iconology, and other signs, predictive or non-predictive. As soon as a reader identified and classified a fictional person as a representation of a known "character," he or she would be able to *predict* the person's behavior. This was possible because the characters in the

---

[28] See *NED*, s.v. "Type," *sb.*,[1] 5a, 6, 7ab, quots.

[29] Benjamin Boyce, *The Theophrastan Character in England to 1642* (Cambridge, Mass., 1947), is the standard work on the early character; see also Boyce, *The Character Sketches in Pope's Poems* (Durham, N.C., 1962), pp. 44–59. La Bruyère's *Caractères*, translated as *The Characters, or Manners of the Age*, 2nd enlarged ed. (London, 1700), was widely used as a source for character sketches, augmenting Theophrastus and the English character books.

early English novel frequently are also abstracted types. Not every fictional person can be so identified, and the process of prediction is made difficult by variations in behavior. But Lady Booby and Lady Bellaston, Bliful and Ferdinand Count Fathom, Lovelace and Sir Hargrave Pollexfen, Roxana's fool husband, the misanthropic Sir Matthew Bramble, and dozens of others perform more or less as we would be likely to predict if we were acquainted with the contemporary *characters* each of them represents. They are not so much *prefigurative personages* as they are *predictive structures*, a knowledge of which serves to foreshadow information about the novel to its audience. The *character type*, then, becomes a standard eighteenth-century fictive entity whose behavior could be predicted, whose place in a work of fiction an audience would probably understand without special authorial commentary. Such developments in the novel are a principal reason why abstracted typology flourished after 1700.

## IV

The last of the four factors that influence abstracted typology involves the theological controversy of the early eighteenth century over the meaning of the Old Testament prophecies. This topic may seem distant from English literary history; it is still a matter primarily for discussion among theologians.[30] Yet it is a part of the intellectual tapestry that includes questions of prefiguration and character typing in imaginative literature. The controversy begins with Deist attacks upon the mysteries of religion in the 1690's. I cannot go into the intricacies of the debate in detail here, and to summarize the burden of a book like John Toland's *Christianity Not Mysterious* (1696) is beyond my powers of condensation. It may be said, however, that in questioning the mysteriousness of Christianity, Toland casts doubt on the importance of "figurative Words, Types and

---

[30] For a thorough (but poorly organized) study of the controversy, see James O'Higgins, S.J., *Anthony Collins: The Man and His Works* (The Hague, 1970), pp. 155–199.

Ceremonies" to modern believers.[31] They may have been mysterious in antiquity, but they were perfectly intelligible in the eighteenth century.[32] He strikes out broadly against figuralism:

> Every one knows how the Primitive *Christians,* in a ridiculous imitation of the Jews, turn'd all Scripture into Allegory; accommodating the Properties of those Animals mention'd in the *Old Testament* to Events that happen'd under the *New.* They took the same Liberty principally with Men, where they could discover the least Resemblance between their Names, Actions, or State of Life; and carry'd this Fancy at length to Numbers, Letters, Places, and what not. That which in the *Old Testament* therefore did, according to them, represent any thing in the *New,* they call'd the *Type* or *Mystery* of it. Thus *TYPE, SYMBOL, PARABLE, SHADOW, FIGURE, SIGN,* and *MYSTERY,* signify all the same thing in *Justin Martyr.*[33]

Seldom has the terminological confusion I mentioned above been more clearly stated.

The controversy was to go on for more than thirty years, aided by the annual Boyle lecturers, and by numerous theological publications. Discrepancies in biblical quotations and in scholarly methods would be exposed; the sound evidentiary methods of Father Simon would help cast considerable doubt on the accuracy of the Old Testament prophecies. Anthony Collins, the Deist whose *Discourse of the Grounds and Reasons of the Christian Religion* (1724) is probably the most significant work in the controversy, holds that a prophecy has one immediate literal fulfillment, and that the notion of a long-term fulfillment is nonsense. He argues that the child promised in Isaiah 7. 14 was Isaiah's

---

[31] See John Toland, *Christianity Not Mysterious: or, A Treatise shewing That there is Nothing in the Gospel Contrary to Reason, nor above it: and that no Christian Doctrine can be properly call'd A Mystery,* 2nd ed. (London, 1696), p. 66; cf. pp. 72–73.

[32] *Christianity Not Mysterious,* pp. 102–103.

[33] *Ibid.,* p. 115.

son, not the Messiah, and elsewhere he is scornful of vague
attempts to impose an artificial unity upon the two Testaments by inventive typologizing.[34] Yet Collins, paradoxically, is not out to destroy typology; he is eager to establish
its justifiable limits. The inventions of patristic writers like
St. Clement, who thought that the myth of the phoenix
could be taken as a type of the Resurrection, are unconvinc-
ing.[35] But Collins' defense of typology, one of the strongest
in the eighteenth century, has been unjustly neglected:

> It seems therefore most destructive of christianity to
> suppose; that *typical* or *allegorical arguing* is in any re-
> spect *weak and enthusiastical*; and that the Apostles al-
> ways argu'd in the matter of *prophesies* according to the
> literal sense of the *prophesies* and the way of reasoning
> used in the schools: since it is most apparent; that the
> whole Gospel is in every respect founded on *type* and
> *allegory*; that the Apostles in most, if not in all cases
> reason'd *typically* and *allegorically*; and that, if the
> Apostles be suppos'd to reason always after the *rules* used
> in the schools, and if their writings be brought to the test
> of those *rules*, the books of the Old and New Testament
> will be in an *irreconcileable state*, and the *difficulties*
> against christianity will be incapable of being solv'd.[36]

The "rules" to which Collins refers are the imaginative
methods of interpretation used by the ancient Jews and
early patristic writers. Collins, then, opposes figural extrav-

[34] See Anthony Collins, *A Discourse of the Grounds and Reasons of
the Christian Religion* (London, 1724), pp. 45-46, 51; cf. O'Higgins,
*Anthony Collins*, p. 166.

[35] *A Discourse of the Grounds and Reasons of the Christian Religion*, p. 231.

[36] *Ibid.*, pp. 269-270. Collins' entire ch. 10, entitled "Typical or
Allegorical Reasoning defended against Mr. WHISTON; wherein is
a digression that compares together the allegorical Scheme and Mr.
WHISTON's literal Scheme, and that proves his literal Scheme false
and absurd." William Whiston's *Essay towards restoring the true
Text of the Old Testament* (London, 1722) is strongly deistical.
O'Higgins, curiously, ignores this chapter completely in his study of
Collins.

agance, but typology, properly applied, is entirely acceptable to him.

The effect of his position, and of the Deist-inspired controversy, leads to a new movement to find rational bases for typology. Warburton's *Divine Legation of Moses Demonstrated* (1737-1741) and John Jortin's *Remarks on Ecclesiastical History* (1751-1753), respected works by members of the Church establishment, show how the controversy established abstracted typology more firmly than ever before. Warburton confuted and rejected the idolatrous animal worship of the ancient Egyptians, but argued that there was a rational basis for making the images of external nature prefigurative and predictive.[37] Jortin was dubious of excessive typologizing, but conceded that if the Prophets had accurately "foretold the things relating to Babylon, Tyre, etc.," then it was reasonable to accept their types and signs of the Messiah as well. "A Type," he said convincingly, "is a rough draft, a less accurate pattern or model, from which a more perfect image or work is made."[38] The basis for abstracted typology is as clear here as it had been in Anthony Collins' rhetorical question in 1724: "For what is a *Poetick Description* fulfill'd, but a Typical Prophesy *fulfill'd?*"[39] Neither statement has an entirely theological context; the figural transformation from typology as exegetical system to typology as imagistic technique is nearly complete. Let me turn now to an examination of several stages on which the scenes from abstracted typology are played.

## V

Among the most natural subjects for typology is kingship. In seventeenth-century England, when the destinies of Church and state were closely linked and when civil insta-

37 For a convenient summary of Warburton's position, see Burton Feldman and Robert D. Richardson, *The Rise of Modern Mythology, 1680-1860* (Bloomington, Ind., 1972), pp. 112-113.

38 See John Jortin, *Remarks on Ecclesiastical History*, 5 vols. (London, 1751-1753), 1, 183 and, in general, 1, 179-197.

39 *A Discourse of the Grounds and Reasons of the Christian Religion*, pp. 238-239.

bility constantly threatened, the urge to typologize the monarchy seems to have been greater than at any other time in English history since the Reformation. Poets were prepared, beginning with the Restoration, to write flattering verse panegyrics of the Stuart house, but, as I said earlier, Old Testament typology waned gradually as the fortunes of the Stuarts—and the century—petered out. Davidic typology remained popular long after Edenic and Noahic imagery had fallen into desuetude, perhaps because of the flawed nature of David himself. William and Mary, like Charles II before them, were seen as postfigurations of Moses when they arrived in England, and one of the elegists of Mary at her death in 1695 would recall the Mary-Moses comparison.[40] But the later Stuarts seldom inspired such lyricism. Classical, rather than Christian, mythology was deemed more suitable. John Willis, of New-Inn Hall at Oxford, greeting the birth of the Prince of Wales (the future Young Pretender) in 1688, saw the new arrival as a "Messenger of Peace," but his christomimesis is otherwise modest. Somehow, pagan typology seemed more appropriate:

> If a new Hydra dares our World molest
> This Prince shall crush the many headed Beast.
> Our Jove no more shall lead his Hosts to fight,
> The Son shall Conquer in the Fathers right.[41]

The analogy of the male infant to the infant Hercules, popular in visual iconography, was a standard typological allusion in poems about royal princes.[42]

[40] See Robert Smithies, "On the Late Happy Revolution: A Pindarique Ode," st. 9, in *Musae Cantabrigienses Serenissimus Principibus Wilhelmo et Mariae* (Cambridge, 1689), Sig. a3ᵛ; cf. *Lachrymae Cantabrigienses in Obitum Serenissimae Reginae Mariae* (Cambridge, 1695), Sig. Zzᵛ (untitled ode by Bart. Stote).

[41] See *Strenae Natalitiae Academiae Oxoniensis in Celsissimum Principem* (Oxford, 1688), Sig. T2ʳ⁻ᵛ.

[42] There are other examples, like the poem addressed to Anne, later Queen, on her marriage to George Prince of Denmark. See *Hymenaeus Cantabrigiensis* (Cambridge, 1693), Sig. R3ᵛ-4ʳ (untitled verses by William Ayloffe).

An alternative for the panegyrist eager to typologize without bringing up the touchy question of divine right was the abstracted type from classical history. One of the Cambridge versifiers on the landing of William and Mary remembered that Julius Caesar had landed in England, too (and forgot that Caesar's fortunes there had been indifferent):

> The Mighty *Julius* whose illustrious Name
> Till now stood first in the Records of Fame;
> Who by his Courage kept the World in awe,
> Was but a Type of the Divine *Nassau*.[43]

The funerary exercises at William III's death could not match this, but among the small number of poems written on the death of Anne (published, almost as an afterthought, in 1716) was a "Pindarique Ode" containing the following stanza:

> *Vespasian*, whose Imperial Name
> Triumphant rides upon the Wings of Fame
>    That measur'd Time's swift Hand,
>    Not by the Ebb and Flow of Sand,
> But the more reg'lar Motions of his Mind,
> Which ev'ry Beat, struck Blessings to Mankind,
>    No more Illustrious Shade shall mention'd be,
>       But as the Type of Thee.[44]

The straining for a typological association here suggests not so much the weakness of abstracted types as it does the enervation of the Stuart myth. The panegyric verse addressed in the next half-century to the Hanoverian kings was bland, lacking in the tumid enthusiasm of the seventeenth-century paean.

The typology of kingship did not die out quite yet, for

[43] *Musae Cantabrigienses*, Sig. c1ᵛ (untitled verses by Richard Stone). I owe this reference to Earl Miner.

[44] *The Loyal Mourner for the Best of Princes: Being a Collection of Poems Sacred to the Immortal Memory of her Late Majesty Queen Anne* [ed. John Oldisworth?] (London, 1716), p. 41. The verses are by W. Paul.

there remained a much more fertile field—the Martyr's Day sermon. Hundreds of them survive, including a great many for the first sixty years of the eighteenth century. Charles the Martyr had obvious Christological properties; for many of the homilists, he was both post-figuration and fore-shadow, both antitype and type.[45] Sometimes, as in Joseph Trapp's 1729 sermon, the typology is flawed;[46] at times of great national crisis, Charles' martyrdom would be seen as a prefiguration of all the nation's present troubles, as in Edward Banyer's 1747 sermon.[47] Throughout the 1740's and 1750's we continue to find sermons which see the king in terms of minor Old Testament types like Daniel and Jonah.[48]

One remarkable quality in eighteenth-century Regicide sermons, practically unknown during the last half of the seventeenth century, is the tendency for homilists to draw a "character" of Charles I, usually as the perfect Christian ("Christianus Perfectus"), less frequently as the picture of the good magistrate. Edward Young, for example, in his 1729 sermon, draws a "Character of a Good Prince," and, before his abstracted typology begins, compares Charles I to David, Aemilius Lepidus, Cato, Alcibiades, and Pericles. Clarendon's famous character of the King, in his *History of the Rebellion* (1702–1704), had been favorable, but it was not exactly a whitewash. Young's vision of the Good Prince is different:

[45] See, for example, Thomas Fothergill, *The Reasonableness and Uses of Commemorating King Charles's Martyrdom* (London, 1753), pp. 4–5. It is noteworthy that this kind of typology continued to be employed over a century after Charles's death.

[46] *A Sermon Preached . . . at the Cathedral Church of St. Paul on Friday, January 30, 1729* (London, 1729), p. 1.

[47] *A Sermon Preached Before the Right Honourable the Lord Mayor . . . Jan. 30, 1746–7* (London, 1747), p. 18. Banyer sees the 1745 troubles in Scotland as antitypes of the martyrdom.

[48] A good instance is Samuel Johnson, *A Sermon Preached in the Parish-Church of Great Torrington, on Sunday, the Thirtieth Day of January, 1742* (London, 1745), pp. 2–3, 6–7, 8–10. Johnson was the Vicar of Great Torrington.

He labours for the Good, wakes for the Care, feels for
the Wants, lives for the Glory, or sets Death at defiance
for the Preservation of the Whole. The good Prince is the
*Eye* of Government that never closes; the *Hand* of Government that is never weary; the *Heart* of Government
that never ceases pouring out the Vital Streams of Prudence and Good-will; to feed, and support the *Publick
Safety*, and the *Publick Peace*.[49]

The good prince is obviously a type, but in Young's context
he might almost be a character in a novel. Images of Christian perfection, inspired in part by Steele's *Christian Hero*
(1701), are important in English fiction; in Young's vivid
homily we may glimpse the vital link between the abstracted type in a quasi-theological situation and the same
figure in literature.

Young is not alone in seeing the martyred Charles as a
type whose chief significance has been abstracted to the
concerns of everyday life. One of the more reflective homilists, John Whalley, in his 1740 Martyr's Day sermon, meditates on the prefigurative qualities of his subject:

Indeed this is the most noble End, as well as the prop-
erest Use to be made of all History, to teach us that best
sort of Wisdom, a practical Wisdom, by transmitting
down to us the Actions of our Forefathers, that so by an
attentive Consideration of their bad and good Conduct,
together with the Causes and Consequences of both, we
may come to know by what most likely Means we are to
avoid the one, and imitate the other. . . . The Life and
Actions of the Divine Author of our Holy Religion are set
out to us in the Gospel History, as a Pattern for our
Imitation.[50]

[49] *An Apology for Princes, or the Reverence due to Government*
(London, 1739), pp. 48–50. Young's iconographical allusion to "the *Eye*
of Government" recalls Matt. 6: 22, Luke 11: 34, Eccles. 2: 14, and
Job 11: 4.
[50] *A Sermon Preached before the House of Commons . . . Jan. 30,
1739/40* (London, 1740), pp. 1–3.

Charles I, the homilist concludes, speaking to all of us through his sufferings, is both Christ's typical postfiguration and an abstracted type, presented to us as the perfect Christian. Characters of perfection appear in many other sermons, but their typological associations are seldom so obvious as when they relate to kingship. The typological "character" in the sermon now brings me to a consideration of the character books themselves.

## VI

Joseph Hall, the first English character-writer, recognizes the universal qualities of his art. In his "Premonition of the Title and Use of Characters," he describes the evolution of his form: "The Divines of the olde Heathen were their Morall Philosophers: These received the Acts of an inbred law, in the *Sinai* of Nature, and delivered them with manie expositions to the multitude: These were the Overseers of maners, Correctors of vices, Directors of lives, Doctors of vertue, which yet taught their people the body of their naturall Divinities, not after one maner."[51] The character was an acquired, highly specialized piece of knowledge, but, as Hall understands the genre, it is more than mere information. He says that the learned men who specialized in this branch of knowledge "bestowed their time in drawing out the true lineaments of every vertue and vice, so lively, that those who saw the medals, might know the face: which Art they significantly termed Charactery. . . ." The allusion to medals is doubtless inspired by the Greek origin of the word, meaning "to engrave." That Hall should mention medallic art is significant, since Renaissance numismatists were agreed that medals embodied a special sign language

[51] Joseph Hall, *Characters of Vertues and Vices in two Bookes* (London, 1608), Sig. A4$^r$. See the entire Preface, Sig. A4$^r$–6$^v$. Hall sees Theophrastus, the founder of his genre, as a kind of Moses figure, and the character writer as a dispenser of typological wisdom. Isaac Casaubon, whose *editio princeps* (Leyden, 1612) of Theophrastus inaugurated modern study of characters, makes no such claim; cf. his "Prolegomena," pp. 83–92.

of their own.[52] It is not necessary for us to inquire into the mysterious qualities of old coins. It is enough that Hall sees the prose character as a kind of sign, which would allow its viewers to "know the face," for this suggests that as early as 1600 characters were thought to be predictive. Hall's *Characters of Vertues and Vice* are, in fact, strongly prefigurative throughout. The characters of Vices are drawn in such a way that the reader, once acquainted with a certain kind of viciousness, would be able to anticipate its ramifications, predict its behavior. The characters of Virtue are more obviously typological and christomimetic.

Perhaps one brief example from Hall's collection will tell us how the predictive, typological character functions in the seventeenth century. Here is "The Characterism of the *Faithfull man*":

> Examples are his proofes; and Instances his demonstrations. What hath God given, which hee can not give? What have others suffered, which hee may not bee enabled to endure? is hee threatned banishment? There he sees the Deare Evangelist in Pathmos cutting in pieces; hee sees Esay under the saw. Drowning? hee sees Ionas diving into the living gulfe. Burning? he sees the three children in the hote walke of the furnace. Devouring? hee sees Daniel in the sealed den amids his terrible companions. Stoning? hee sees the first Martyr under his heape of many gravestones. Heading? loe there is the Baptists necke bleeding in Herodias platter. He emulates their paine, their strength, their glorie. . . . He is not so sure he shall die, as that he shall be restored; and outfaceth his death with his resurrection. . . . In common opinion miserable, but in true jugement more than a man.[53]

---

[52] On medallic symbolism, see Allen, *Mysteriously Meant*, pp. 256–262; and Ernst H. Kantorowicz, *The King's Two Bodies* (Princeton, 1957), including the illustrations.

[53] *Characters*, pp. 23–25. The characters of the humble man (pp. 27–31) and "Of the good Magistrate" (pp. 57–62) are also typological, even to the point of echoing biblical texts commonly linked with Christ.

Not only does Hall specifically compare the faithful man
with a number of traditional Old and New Testament types
and figures, he emphasizes that this character itself is typological, for the person he figures forth is only a shadow of
what he *shall* be. Hall's homiletic style, with its biblical
overtones, may seem stiff and unattractive to the reader of
imaginative literature. His characters of Vices are less rigid;
there is a compelling variety about evil. Here, too, his declared purpose of providing the *signs* which will acquaint
the reader with the entire character is central.[54] Just as
Hall's virtuous characters tend to foreshadow Christ-like
perfections, his vicious types prefigure full-blown, satanic
evils.

Typological characters are common homiletic devices.
One popular sermon writer, for instance, giving a character
of the cunning hunter, asserts that "The wicked oppressors
of the world are here Typed and Taxed." A character of the
plain-dealing man, which takes Jacob as its exemplar, suggests that his behavior foreshadows that of *all* plain-dealing
men ever since.[55] Sermon-characters, chiefly associated with
aspects of Christian behavior, are a standard rhetorical device well into the eighteenth century.[56]

Character books become progressively larger and more
elaborate during the course of the seventeenth century and,
though the popular appeal of this kind of literature tended
to preclude much theorizing about character types, we may
occasionally find a telling description. The Overburian
characters, often satirical and abusive, conclude with a

[54] See Hall's characters of "The Hypocrite" (pp. 71–77), "The *Profane*" (pp. 93–97), "The Flatterer" (pp. 113–118), and "The Envious"
(pp. 167–173).

[55] See *The Works of Thomas Adams. Being the Summe of His Sermons, Meditations, and Other Divine and Morall Discourses* (London,
1629), pp. 116, 131. Adams delivered a series of "character" sermons
in the second decade of the seventeenth century which seems to have
been much imitated.

[56] A case in point is Samuel Clarke who, like Thomas Adams, devoted many sermons to subjects like "The Character of a Good Man" or
"The Excellency of Moral Qualifications." See *The Works of Samuel
Clarke*, 4 vols. (London, 1738), 1, 147, 154–159, 237–242, 248–253, 266–
270.

brief apothegmic account, "What a Character is." This little theoretical coda emphasizes that the genre is meant to make a deep impression (the etymological sense of the word) on the reader and to function as a sign that will leave "a strong seale in our memories." One recalls the semiological terminology—"semantic enclaves." But the character is more: "Character is also taken for an Ægyptian Hieroglyphicke, for an imprese, or a short Embleme; in little comprehending much. To square out a Character by our English levell, it is a picture (reall or personall) quaintly drawne, in various colours, all of them heightened by one shadowing."[57] This is terminology we have come to recognize as prefigurative, as deliberately conceived for typological purposes. Sir Thomas Overbury, it might be noted, was not writing for ecclesiastical preferment or apologetic glories: his collection was intended to do nothing more than what most of these modest duodecimos and sextisimos aimed at—to entertain a literate but not necessarily pious audience.

Earle's *Micro-Cosmographie* (1650), often regarded as the best of the seventeenth-century collections (Butler's characters, which are without peer, did not appear until 1759), begins to show resemblances to actual individuals from the world of fiction. The sign-like, semiological qualities I have noted occur continually, but now the names of characters become more explicit. Earle's character of "The Worlds Wise Man" evokes Bunyan's Mr. Worldly Wiseman and Fielding's Jonathan Wild ("His conclusion is commonly one of these two; either a Great Man, or Hang'd.").[58] His contemplative man, his skeptic in religion, his "good old Man," and his "Prophane Man" are all exemplars of character types which were the common coin of the world of English fiction by the early eighteenth century. The religious

[57] Sir Thomas Overbury, *His Wife. With Additions of New Characters, and Many other Wittie Conceits*, 11th ed. (London, 1622), Sig. Q4^r.

[58] John Earle, *Micro-Cosmographie. Or, A Piece of the World Characteriz'd; In Essays and Characters* (London, 1650), pp. 69–71. See also Samuel Butler, *Characters*, ed. Charles W. Daves (Cleveland, 1970), pp. 5–12, for brief remarks on all the major character books.

aura in which Hall and homiletic authors like him were wont to enwrap their character sketches gradually diminishes, but its typological properties linger on.

In the development of abstracted typology whose course I have been attempting to chart, the elements of religious prefiguration, whether positive or negative ("positive" means Christic typology; "negative" refers to images which foreshadow Satan or satanic evils), are less important than the methodology of prefiguration itself. "A *Type* is a mould or a pattern of a thing," wrote Anthony Collins in support of "Typical Prophecys."[59] He then proceeds to give a theological context and application to this helpful definition, but we need not accompany him. For, in the imaginative literature of which character writing is an undoubted part, the definition of "character" is practically the same as what Collins gives for "type." And what the character writers present in their limited theorizings, they practice. My suggestion, then, is that the predictive qualities of the seventeenth-century character type sustain and inform later fictional creations. In eighteenth-century prose fiction, from the brief stories in the periodical essay (those of Addison and Johnson come to mind), to the longer, unstructured narratives of Defoe, to the carefully plotted craftsmanship of the century's major novelists, abstracted typology is a constant presence.

## VII

The distinguishing quality of abstracted types is that, unlike mere words, they embody *signs* recognizable to a literate audience; they have a life beyond the text in which they are incarcerated. It is easy to see how this rule applies with character types, for the character is a unit that, under certain circumstances, may establish semiological communication between the author and the reader. Yet another area of abstracted typology involves the *fable*. Here, at first glance, it might seem that typology of any kind would be impossible. Yet such was not the case in the eighteenth cen-

[59] *The Scheme of Literal Prophecy considered* (London, 1726), p. 345.

tury. The fable genre may have been more popular from 1690 to 1750 than at any other time in our literary history. Its many practitioners firmly believed that it possessed special semiological qualities that distinguished it from more recently developed genres. Virtually all commentators agreed that, in Addison's words, "Fables were the first Pieces of Wit that made their Appearance in the World, and have been still highly valued, not only in times of the greatest Simplicity, but among the most polite Ages of Mankind."[60]

The definition in Johnson's *Dictionary* emphasized the fictive nature of the fable, but also noted that it was a story or the "contexture of events" which constitutes the plot of a work of literature. It was further agreed that the fable gave a partial, figurative, frequently allegorical vision of the truth; it was similar to the parable, unprepossessingly simple, yet filled with latent meaning. Seeking to mitigate this apparent simplicity, one translator of Aesop, Edmund Arwaker, assured his readers that fables were not merely for children, but were a special vehicle for conveying truth, whether moral or satirical. For "few can contemplate Truth, in its full Splendour, but must have it convey'd to them by *Mediums*, and its Beam let gently in upon them, as it were through Chinks and Crannies."[61] Other versions of Aesop took a similar view, insisting that fables were eminently suited for the instruction of children but that they were inherently figural, profoundly laden with emblematic meaning. It was inevitable that writers in an age when figural interpretations were the rule rather than the exception would realize that fables were both condensed behavioral guides for all readers and typological, predictive, stories or plot-signs.

The most popular English version of Aesop was that of

[60] See *The Spectator*, ed. Donald Bond, 5 vols. (Oxford, 1965), 2, 219–220 (No. 183).

[61] *Truth in Fiction: or, Morality in Masquerade. A Collection of Two Hundred twenty five Select Fables of Aesop, and other Authors* (London, 1708), pp. ii, iv–v, vi. The entire Preface (pp. i–xvi) is relevant.

Sir Roger L'Estrange, which appeared in nearly a score of editions from the later seventeenth to the eighteenth century. The work snowballed as it passed from one edition to the next, accumulating materials from other fabulists, scholia, and a large body of moral reflections. L'Estrange saw his work as thoroughly symbolic:

> For there's Nothing makes a Deeper Impression upon the Minds of Men, or comes more Lively to their Understanding, than Those Instructive Notices that are Convey'd to them by Glances, Insinuations, and Surprize; and under the Cover of some *Allegory* or *Riddle*. But, What can be said more to the Honour of This *Symbolical* Way of Moralizing upon *Tales* and *Fables*, than that the Wisdom of the Ancients has been still Wrapt up in *Veils* and *Figures*; and their Precepts, Councels, and salutary Monitions for the Ordering of our Lives and Manners, Handed down to us from all Antiquity under *Innuendo's* and *Allusions?* For what are the *Ægyptian Hierogliphicks*, and the whole History of the *Pagan Gods*; The Hints, and Fiction of the Wise Men of Old, but in Effect, a kind of *Philosophical Mythology*: Which is, in truth, no other, than a more Agreeable Vehicle found out for Conveying to us the Truth and Reason of Things, through the *Medium* of *Images* and *Shadows*.[62]

Particularly important to L'Estrange, Dryden, and other English fabulists was the association of the fable with the biblical parable; if Jesus taught symbolically, might not the fables of antiquity do the same? L'Estrange's placid acceptance of the symbolical interpretations of the ancient gods sounds like a rich serving of Stillingfleet with a healthy dose of Alexander Ross. Yet his credulity need not be emphasized; the work of the scholarly antiquarians like Richard Bentley, who would demonstrate the inauthenticity of Aesop during the 1690's, had little effect upon those who

---

[62] *Fables of Aesop and other Eminent Mythologists: with Morals and Reflexions*, 2 vols. (London, 1694), 1, Sig. A2ᵛ.

wished to find figural readings in old books.[63] Nor would what Don Cameron Allen calls "the rationalization of myth" have such a widespread effect in the eighteenth century as one might expect. L'Estrange's *Aesop*, complete with this highly figural preface, would continue to be reprinted *in toto* for fifty years.

It is clear from his remarks just quoted that L'Estrange took advantage of the terminological confusion over typology current in the seventeenth century. He goes on to clarify matters substantially:

> How much are we Oblig'd then, to those Wise, Good Men, that have furnish'd the World with so sure, and so Pleasant an Expedient, for the Removing of All These Difficulties [of teaching moral precepts]! And to *Æsop* in the First Place, as the *Founder*, and *Original Author*, or *Inventer* of This Art of Schooling Mankind into Better Manners; by Minding Men of their Errors without Twitting them for what's Amiss, and by That Means Flashing the Light of their Own Consciences in their Own Faces. We are brought Naturally enough, by the Judgment we pass upon the Vices and Follies of our Neighbours, to the Sight and Sense of our Own; and Especially, when we are led to the Knowledge of the Truth of Matters by *Significant Types*, and *Proper Resemblances*.[64]

The fables, then, instruct prefiguratively, by presenting the reader with a situational type which, by thorough acquaintance, will enable him to interpret proper behavior under similar circumstances. L'Estrange's hundreds of fables (the two-volume collection contains nearly 500) are carefully planned to be interpretative in this way. Like all other versions of Aesop, they are obscure, but the moral reflections, which their author called "Emblems," re-

---

[63] On Bentley's role in the Phalaris controversy, see J. E. Sandys, *A History of Classical Scholarship*, 3 vols. (Cambridge, 1903–1905), 2, 403–405.

[64] *Fables of Aesop*, Sig. A3ʳ.

move all ambiguities. Sometimes the commentary runs on for ten pages, as in the fable called "A Horse and an Ass," where the proud and contemptuous behavior of the Horse, who scorns the humble Ass, becomes a type of the miserable behavior of all proud men.[65] We can go on to multiply examples by the score: fables of "A Cock and a Diamond" (an emblem of industry and moderation), of "A Dog and a Shadow" (a type of excessive desire), of "A Fowler and a Partridge" (the bird is a type of the guilty sinner), of "A Crow and a Dog" (on false religion), and many others.[66]

The *corpus* of Aesop's original fables was insufficient to satisfy eighteenth-century tastes for moral dicta. So the book was swelled with contemporary, Aesop-like tales, which differ mainly in that they are political in application. Perhaps the best of these is L'Estrange's "Kingdom of the Apes," where the reflection informs us that "It is the proper Business of *Mythology* to point out the Represent the Images of Good and Evil, and under those Shadows to Teach us what we ought to do, and what not."[67] Fables, in other words, contain both positive and negative types, either foreshadowing desirable, Christ-like behavior, or evil, Satanic traits. They are a kind of "social" typology. The fable can even become a vehicle for historical interpretations (Gay's verse fables are notable for their success in this sphere). Samuel Croxall's translation of Aesop, in the "Application" to the well-known Aesopic fable, "The Wind and the Sun," waxes ecclesiastical:

> Persecution has always fix'd and riveted those Opinions which it was intended to dispel; and some discerning Men have attributed the quick Growth of Christianity, in a great Measure, to the rough and barbarous Reception which its first Teachers met with in the World. I believe the same may have been observ'd of our Reforma-

[65] *Fables of Æsop*, 7th ed. (London, 1724), 1, 45–53 (Fable 38).
[66] *Ibid.*, 1, 1–2 (Fable 1); 1, 6–8 (Fable 6); 1, 148–149 (Fable 132); 1, 192–193 (Fable 179). The moral is frequently a christianizing of a pagan situation, almost always in explicitly typological terms.
[67] *Ibid.*, 1, 444, and see pp. 444–447.

tion: The Blood of the Martyrs was the Manure which
produc'd that great Protestant Crop on which the Church
of *England* has subsisted ever since.[68]

Croxall's genius was smaller than that of L'Estrange, who
was never so bald in attributing typological relationships.
Perhaps the lack of deftness in Croxall's touch suggests how
common abstracted typology had become by the 1720's, and
how traditional it was for the fable to be a vehicle for historical prediction and fictive prefiguration. The end of my
story is not an ending—typologies do not end, they only
*foreshadow* endings—but is another proposal. I propose
that the abstracted typology practiced by the fabulists helps
establish a prefigurative style that would be used freely and
with immense facility for the rest of the eighteenth century.

## VIII

The shape of the prefigurative style in later eighteenth-
and early nineteenth-century England is determined by
several important currents in intellectual history. The first
of these I have already mentioned: the debate over scriptural prophecy in the 1720's. As a result of this lengthy controversy biblical prophecy was established as an accepted
mode of rhetorical discourse. Solid antiquarian-historical
studies of Old Testament texts and languages, like Bishop
Lowth's *De Sacri Poesi Hebraeorum* (1753; Eng. trans.
1753), gave further historical justification for the prefigurative style of Hebrew poetry. Most influential of all, however, in giving abstracted typology a popular basis for
everyday usage was the controversial William Warburton.
*The Divine Legation of Moses Demonstrated* (1738–1741)
was Warburton's most popular theological work. Like his
other writings, it is primed for controversy—assertive,
authoritative, argumentative. Warburton wrote to confute
a generation of freethinkers and deists who had suggested
that, among many other heretical propositions, certain

---

[68] Samuel Croxall, *Fables of Aesop and Others. Newly done into
English, with an Application to each Fable* (London, 1722), pp. 76–77.

figural passages in the Old Testament could not be understood to refer typologically to Jesus or, in fact, to any
aspects of Christianity except in a secondary sense. In order
"to shew the Logical Truth and Propriety of *Types* in
*Action*," Warburton enters upon an unusual justification of
the intellectual bases of Biblical typology.[69] As other students of antiquity since Richard Bentley and William Wot-
ton had done, he attempts to supply a historical basis for
symbolic language. His presentation is actually an early
kind of structural anthropology:

> In the gradual Cultivation of Speech, the Expression by
> *Action* was improved and refined into an ALLEGORY or
> *Parable*; in which the Words carry a double Meaning;
> having, besides their obvious Sense that serves only for
> the Envelope, a more material and secret one. With this
> Figure of Speech all the moral Writings of Antiquity
> abound. But when it is transferred, from *civil* use into
> *religious*, and employed in the Writings of inspired Men,
> to convey Information of particular Circumstances, in
> two distinct Dispensations, to a People who had an equal
> Concern in both, it is then what we call a DOUBLE
> SENSE; and undergoes the very same Change of Nature
> with an *expressive Action* converted into a *Type*; that is,
> *both* the Meanings, in the *double Sense* are of *moral Im-
> port*; whereas in the *Allegory one* only is so: And *this*,
> which arises out of the very Nature of their Conversion,
> from *civil* to *religious* Matters, is the only Difference be-
> tween *expressive Actions* and *Types*, and between *Al-
> legories* and *double Senses*.[70]

If we follow Warburton's definition, allegory is a figural
equation in which the first term is clear but the second requires exegesis. Typology is a form of figural expression

[69] *The Divine Legation of Moses Demonstrated*, 3 vols. in 2 (London,
1738–1741), 2, 626–627.
[70] *Ibid.*, 2, 629–630. Warburton's entire chapter on figuralism, 2,
627–678. anticipates later eighteenth-century discussions of the rise and
progress of language and the purposes of symbolism in primitive cultures.

in which both terms of the equation have a double sense. Both type and antitype are obscure and require interpretation. Typology is an advanced form of figural expression, but it has arisen "in the gradual Cultivation of Speech." Thus the language of the types, for Warburton, arose *naturally*, as a result of the nature of discourse in primitive societies. Although Warburton, like other ecclesiastical historians, thought that typology was primarily employed in religious contexts, his justification is so sweeping that it provides a reliable basis for typological expression in *any* context.

If we accept Warburton's contention that there was a *"logical Propriety"* for the existence of typology—that predictive structures are somehow inherent in patterns of human thought and expression—then it is but a short step to arguing that typology is part of the design of primitive religions, Christianity, and, indeed, secular societies. Two years before the publication of the first volume of Warburton's *Divine Legation*, Bishop Butler had already argued that the structural basis for typological imagery in pre-Christian Judaism and early Christianity was substantial. Furthermore, the "Mythological" and the "Satyrical" kinds of writing were similar to Scriptural prophecy in the way they shadowed forth future events; civil history was clearly analogical to the historical continuum of the Bible.[71] Butler's *Analogy* was one of the most popular theological treatises of the eighteenth century.[72] The development of predictive structures in theories of secular history would continue for the rest of the century. The use of an argument from design as a justification for the existence of typology received even stronger impetus from David Hartley, whose *Observations on Man*, first published in 1749, was republished in 1791, and whose writings were especially influential for English Romantic writers.

71 *The Analogy of Religion, Natural and Revealed, to the Constitution and Course of Nature* (London, 1736), pp. 250–256.
72 The *Analogy* had more than a dozen full editions by the early nineteenth century.

Like other Christian apologists, Hartley begins with the certainty of the Old Testament types, but he insists that there is a hidden logic in such complex structures: the design of typology is so intricate that no serious, considerate person could fail to believe them. Hartley goes even further than his predecessors in his argument from design: if God's scriptures are orderly in a predictive, typological way, then one would naturally expect an analogical order in the external world.[73] Scriptural typology, then, becomes the basis for the existence of abstracted typology or for other, analogical, predictive structures, not only in various kinds of literature and learning but in the works of Nature herself. Hartley's sweep is so broad that he prepares the way for the predictive structures of Blake, Wordsworth, Shelley, and Byron by extending typology far beyond the narrow theological sphere:

> As in the body, so in the mind, great and lasting changes are seldom wrought in a short time; and this the history of association shows to be the necessary consequence of the connection between body and mind. And yet he who made the blind to see, the lame to walk, the deaf to hear, the lepers clean, and the maimed whole, by a word, can as easily perform the analogous things, the antitypes, in the mind.[74]

Hartley continues his quest for analogies, and finds that animals and the brute creation in general function as types (a circumstance which the sacred zoologist Wolfgang Frantze had proposed on different grounds a century earlier). Secular history, for Hartley, is most typological of all, for what he saw as the wickedness of contemporary England was surely to be regarded as a type of Christ's Second Coming. We can see why Hartley, whose political sensibilities were acute, was reprinted at the time of the French Revolution (1791). Hartley, it is worth mentioning,

---

[73] *Observations on Man, His Frame, His Duty, and His Expectations,* 3 vols. (London, 1791), 2, 160–161; cf. 2, 162–166.
[74] *Ibid.,* 2, 413.

theorized at great length on the typology of the Jews, whose restoration to their kingdom and conversion were widely regarded as a sure sign of the Second Coming.[75] Later in the century, when the French Revolution was interpreted as a preparation for the apocalypse, there would be further discussion of the regeneration of the Jews, a relaxation of traditional persecutions, and, in France, Napoleon would even reconvene the Sanhedrin.[76] The influence of typology on contemporary life could go to absurd lengths: Napoleon issued a coin which, on one face, showed himself, dressed in Roman robes, giving the tablets with the Ten Commandments to Moses.[77]

The situation of the Jews provides Hartley with matter for some of his most inventive use of abstracted typology, for he is convinced that the restoration of the Jews to their own land seemed to be predicted in the New Testament. He frames such questions as the following: "May not the two captivities of the *Jews*, and their two restorations, be types of the first and second death, and of the first and second resurrections?" The emphasis upon events mentioned in the book of Revelation is highly significant, for the book of Revelation was perhaps the most important single source of typological imagery and, particularly, of abstracted typology, in the eighteenth century. Hartley continues his interrogatories: "Does it not appear agreeable to the whole analogy both of the word and works of God, that the *Jews* are types both of each individual in particular, on one hand, and of the whole world in general, on the other?"[78] This is sweeping prediction at its apogee. Here we must remember that the interpreters of Revelation had, for

---

[75] *Ibid.*, 2, 366–394, esp. 371, 374–375.

[76] See, for example, Henri Grégoire, *Essai sur la régénération* . . . *des juifs* (1789), trans. Eng. 1791. Cf. Richard H. Popkin, "La Peyrere, the Abbé Grégoire, and the Jewish Question in the Eighteenth Century," *Studies in Eighteenth-Century Culture*, 4 (1975), 209–222.

[77] For a facsimile of this coin, see Ismar Elbogen, *History of the Jews after the Fall of the State of Jerusalem* (Cincinnati, 1926), facing p. 167.

[78] *Observations on Man*, 2, 374–375.

almost a century, habitually read their Scriptural texts as predictive structures to signal the imminence of the storm that would soon break over the heads of the world's sinful nations. "Let no one deceive himself or others," says Hartley with assurance. "The present circumstances of the world are extraordinary and critical, beyond what has ever yet happened."[79] Hartley is simply a secular manifestation of a rich exegetical tradition: virtually every commentator on the Book of Revelation from Joseph Mede to Moses Lowman had done the same, only in more detail and with a greater wealth of documentation.

The influence of the apocalypse, then, is the second major current in intellectual history that affected the course of prefigurative structures in late eighteenth- and early nineteenth-century literature. The types of the Old Testament apply, with few exceptions, to antitypes in the New. But the predictions of the Book of Revelation are different, for they transfer and transform traditional Biblical typology from the religious to the secular sphere. The types of the apocalypse can only refer to antitypes in history *since the writing of that book*. By the time of William Whiston's important *Essay on the Revelation of Saint John* (1706), the exegetes have universally agreed that Revelation is mainly a symbolical predictive narration, a typological narrative, or a series of types whose antitypes can be located in the events of secular history since St. John or which were yet to be fulfilled.[80] The numerology of Revelation is also serviceable to the exegetes, for it permits them to fix, with an appearance of certainty, the date of the Second Coming (for Whiston, it was to be 1716) and, in some cases, the country or countries most severely to be chastised. Moses Lowman, the most detailed historical exegete, intersperses his commentary with references to secular historians, both ancient and contemporary, for he is eager to establish what

---

[79] *Ibid.*, 2, 455.

[80] See Whiston, *An Essay upon the Revelation of Saint John, so far as concerns the Past and Present Times* (Cambridge, 1706), pp. 30, 213, 228–233, 256–257.

he called "a Plan of Prophecy, and Order of History."[81] Chronology is vital for the exegetes: some find that the Second Coming would occur around 1800, others favor the more symbolical year 2000.

Anglican exegetes are more reserved in their typological readings of Revelation than are members of the various Nonconformist sects, who are often committed millenarians and who are always enthusiastic in their predictions. But for Anglicans and Puritans alike, the interpretation of large portions of Revelation is historical. The ominous figural signs point directly to the antichrist and, indeed, whenever the beast from the sea or the many-headed monster comes up, we are in for a thorough pasting of paganism and popery.[82] "This Beast was a *Pagano-Christian Beast,* and a *persecuting one;* because he spake and acted like a *Dragon,* the *Type of Paganism and Persecution,*" writes one anonymous commentator (obviously a Nonconformist of some stripe) in 1693.[83] Benjamin Keach has no doubts whatsoever that Rome and the Roman Catholic Church are the true antitypes of the persecutions carried out by "*literal Babylon*"; he is unquestionably among the most inventive of typologists, as he had abundantly demonstrated in his *Tropologia* (1681).[84] Perhaps the most frequently cited of the seventeenth-century apocalyptical typologists, however, is not English at all. He is the French ecclesiastic Pierre Jurieu, whose strongly typological reading of the book of Revelation appeared, "Faithfully Englished," in

[81] Moses Lowman, *A Paraphrase and Notes on the Revelation of St. John* (London, 1737), pp. xii, xxiii, xxix–xxxiv.

[82] On seventeenth-century views of the Antichrist, see Christopher Hill, *Antichrist in Seventeenth-Century England* (London, 1971), *passim; The World Turned Upside Down: Radical Ideas during the English Revolution* (London, 1972), pp. 114–118; and *Change and Continuity in Seventeenth-Century England* (Cambridge, Mass., 1975), pp. 60, 70–71.

[83] *The Book of Revelation Paraphrased* (London, 1693), p. 290.

[84] See Keach, *Antichrist Stormed: or, Mystery Babylon the great Whore and great City, proved to be the present Church of Rome* (London, 1689), pp. 103–116. The alliance of popery and treason was hardly new, as John Miller demonstrates in his *Popery and Politics in England, 1660–1688* (Cambridge, 1973), pp. 67–90.

1687. Not only does Jurieu see much traditional typology in Revelation ("persons and actions *typical* of the good"), but he makes the helpful distinction of types of evil. "*Cain* was a *type* of the enemies of *Jesus Christ* coming of the seed of woman, he was a *type* of the seed of the Serpent; and his action against his brother was a *typical* sin, that representeth the persecution, which the Devil was to bring upon Jesus Christ and his Church."[85] Jurieu is more successful than any of his contemporaries in demonstrating that the types of Revelation foreshadowed contemporary European history and, since he focuses mainly on France as a particularly odious antitype, English writers in the 1790's would cite him frequently as one who has predicted the apocalyptic events of the French Revolution. With Jurieu as evidence, it is a relatively modest matter for contemporary theologians to conclude that the French Revolution itself is one of the antitypes forecast by the book of Revelation.

The Biblical prophecies, then, were widely regarded in a double sense: not only did exegetes and men of letters regard them as true in the theological sphere, but many prominent theologians and literary men thought that the prophecies, especially those in the book of Revelation, applied equally well to secular history, both past and present. Throughout the later eighteenth century, commentators on Revelation echoed the conclusions of Keach, Jurieu, Whiston, Lowman, and almost a score of other divines. The old seventeenth-century pastime of drawing parallels between Scriptural history and contemporary times which flourished, as John Wallace tells us, whenever times were bad, is succeeded, in the eighteenth century, by a new typological game.[86] When times were bad—which means when-

[85] Pierre Jurieu, *The Accomplishment of the Scripture Prophecies or the Approaching Deliverance of the Church* (London, 1687), Part 1, pp. 233–234. See also Part 2, pp. 245, 251–270. Jurieu deals with the typological relationship between ideas and language, between the sensible and the intelligible world (Part 2, p. 331).

[86] See John M. Wallace, "Dryden and History: A Problem in Allegorical Reading," *ELH*, 36 (1969), 279.

ever street violence, governmental corruption, war and famine, immorality and dissolution, rose above their normal levels—eighteenth-century clerical and secular writers were fond of pointing out that the present times shadowed forth the Apocalypse. This imagistic tendency was by no means confined to the decade immediately following the French Revolution: important occasions like the American Revolution, or important books like Gibbon's *Decline and Fall of the Roman Empire*, provided an opportunity for an occasional person to make the expected association.[87]

Typology flourishes in another area of eighteenth-century thought which is significant to the events of the 1790's: antiquarian mythology. In the last half of the eighteenth century, as we have seen, mythologists who focus on the mysteries of Eastern religions frequently suggest that ancient rites are in some way predictive of Christianity. Following Hartley, the syncretist Jacob Bryant, in a number of learned works, proposes that ancient Egyptian or Near Eastern religions and myths relate to the Hebrew and Christian Scriptures. Bryant is often extravagant, but, at his best, his notions of abstracted typology are splendidly broad, in a Blakean or Shelleyan sense. For example, in his study of the plagues of the Egyptians, Bryant presents an interpretation of the healing of Moses's leprous hand (Exod. 4: 6–7): "From hence I should judge, that these miraculous representations had a covert meaning: and that they did not relate to the Israelites only and their deliverance from bondage: but to the redemption of the whole world; and to the means by which it is to be effected."[88] It is a small step

[87] On the American Revolution, see Richard Price, *Observations on the Importance of the American Revolution* (London, 1784), pp. 5, 7, 27; on Gibbon's *Decline and Fall*, which provoked an outburst of theological refutations, see East Apthorp, *Letters on the Prevalence of Christianity before its Civil Establishment, with Observations on a late History of the Decline of the Roman Empire* (London, 1778), pp. 36–37. Apthorp rejects any suggestion that biblical prophecy might not be accurate.

[88] See *Observations upon the Plagues Inflicted upon the Egyptians* (London, 1794), p. 245. In general, pp. 193–306, on the divine appointment of Moses, is a broad defense of abstract typology.

from Bryant and George Stanley Faber, another student of pre-Christian religions, to the universal historiography of Condorcet, who stresses, again as Hartley had done, the typological basis of human language, actions, and history. Once man has learned, Condorcet argues, the philosophical bases of the past, it is a simple matter to predict the future:

If man can predict, almost with certainty, those appearances of which he understands the laws; if, even when the laws are unknown to him, experience of the past enables him to foresee, with considerable probability, future appearances; why should we suppose it a chimerical undertaking to delineate, with some degree of truth, the picture of the future destiny of mankind from the results of its history?[89]

The past becomes, for writers like Condorcet, a pattern of types whose antitypes are either to be seen in history since the types, or which are yet to happen.

The message that came down to commentators on the French Revolution, then, was clear: in theological terms, the events in France had been predicted by Old and New Testament prophecies; in secular terms, history was to be seen as a series of predictive structures. In each of these conceptualizations abstracted typology is at work. The interpreters of the French Revolution, whether secular or clerical, found in the cataclysmic events across the Channel a series of unmistakable signs. The prophecies of Revelation were being realized: a new age was about to commence.[90] Among the clergymen were such as Mark Wilks, who declared that "Jesus Christ was a Revolutionist," a shadowy type of those who were effecting present-day reformations; Richard Price, who thought that the events in France would lead to "the dominion of reason and con-

[89] *Outlines of a Historical View of the Progress of the Human Mind* (London, 1795), p. 316.

[90] Meyer H. Abrams, "English Romanticism: The Spirit of the Age," *Romanticism Reconsidered: Selected Papers from the English Institute*, ed. Northrop Frye (New York, 1963), pp. 26–72, esp. pp. 30–37, discusses the spirit of the 1790's in greater detail than I can do here.

science" in Great Britain; and Elhanan Winchester, who wrote a poem called the *Process and Empire of Christ* (1793) in pseudo-Miltonic blank verse stressing apocalyptic typologies and suggesting that Jesus prefigured modern innovators.[91] James Bicheno was more conventional, confining his predictions to the overthrow of the Pope, the end of despotism, the restoration of the Jews, and "the restoration of all things."[92] Bicheno was sometimes given to enthusiastic millenarianism: one of his later books, *The Probable Progress and Issue of the Commotions which have agitated Europe since the French Revolution* (1797), was a typological treatment of the 1790's, with the Book of Revelation serving as the typological text and the present as the antitype. And Bicheno's millenarianism was moderate compared to that of Joseph Priestley, who quoted liberally from the typological fancies of David Hartley's *Observations on Man*, and urged politicians to heed the signs of calamity.[93] Finally, to complete this catalogue of figural adventurers, I must mention Richard Brothers, the demented chiliastic visionary who, after hearing from God in a vision that destruction was imminent, made a special visit to the House of Commons to warn the legislators of doom. His whole work was an extended Pisgah-sight, his speech a quasi-biblical prefigurative-postfigurative garbling of the Book of Revelation. Brothers does not deserve to be neglected, but he demonstrates that the ultimate stage of abstracted

---

[91] See Mark Wilks, *The Origin & Stability of the French Revolution* ([London], 1791), p. 5; Richard Price, *A Discourse on the Love of Our Country* (London, 1789), pp. 49–50; and Elhanan Winchester, *The Process and Empire of Christ* (London, 1793), pp. 136–137. See also Winchester's *The Three Woe Trumpets*, 2nd ed. (London, 1793), pp. 33, 35, 43, for the argument that the French Revolution fulfilled the prophecies of Revelation.

[92] *The Signs of the Times: or the Overthrow of the Papal Tyranny in France, the Prelude of Destruction to Popery and Despotism; but of Peace to Mankind* (London, 1793), Sig. [π] 4ʳ. The restoration of the Jews was a popular notion: see Abbé Henri Grégoire, *An Essay on the Physical, Moral, and Political Reformation of the Jews* (London, 1791), p. 240.

[93] *The Present State of Europe compared with Ancient Prophecies* (London, 1794), pp. 18, 20–21, 27, 31–33, 35–44.

typology, as Swift had hinted a century before in *A Tale of a Tub*, is madness.[94]

## IX

The politicizing of abstracted typology was not carried on without dissent, although the dissenters were few and scattered. The most eminent of them was Edmund Burke, who mocked the prefigurative style of Richard Price and generally ridiculed typological millenarianism. He recognized with great clarity how easy it was for an inspired preacher to parallel a contemporary event with the Book of Revelation and then to assure a credulous audience that the same event was a precursor of the Millennium or the Fifth Monarchy.[95] Thomas Paine, like a few others, revived an earlier deism in arguing that the style of Hebrew prophetical poetry had been misunderstood (a view for which Lowth had provided a basis in fact) and twisted by modern expounders, by the "whimsical conceits of sectaries." To these distorters, "Every thing unintelligible was prophetical, and every thing insignificant was typical. A blunder would have served for a prophecy; and a dish-clout for a type."[96] Burke's contemptuous view of Price's typologizing was part of his direct conservative reaction to Price's sermon, *A Discourse on the Love of Our Country* (1789), the work which was the direct catalyst of *Reflections on the Revolution in France*. But Paine was himself a revolu-

[94] See Brothers' *Prophecy of all the remarkable and Wonderful Events which will come to pass in the present year* (London, n.d. [1794?]), *passim*, and *A Revealed Knowledge of the Prophecies and Times* (London, 1794), pp. 45, 47, 67, etc. On Brothers, see Morton D. Paley, "William Blake, the Prince of the Hebrews, and the Woman Clothed with the Sun," in *William Blake: Essays in honour of Sir Geoffrey Keynes*, ed. Morton D. Paley and Michael Phillips (Oxford, 1973), pp. 260–293. This predictive style has become a staple of Christian fundamentalism; cf. a curious octavo entitled *The Doom of Britain. A Divine Warning. The German Conquest of England Foretold in the Scriptures* (London, 1911), an anonymous effort whose author treats Revelation as a type of conquest by the Kaiser.

[95] See *Reflections on the Revolution in France* (London, 1790), pp. 96, 97–98, 107, 108.

[96] *The Age of Reason; being an investigation of time and fabulous theology* (Paris and London, 1794), p. 53.

tionary whose criticism of prefigurative fancies sprang from an effort to vindicate himself of the charge of atheism. Thus he presented himself as a theist who finds typology acceptable enough in poetical fictions but inappropriate when it becomes a basis for political thought or action. Paine's rejection of typological figuralism was similar to the criticism of Biblical prophecy by the English deists in the 1720's in one interesting way: once again, opposition to typology did nothing whatever to diminish its prevalence in religious discourses or, for that matter, in other imaginative literature. Paradoxically, criticism of this sort tended to *solidify* the position of prefigurative imagery. If it was permissible for the ancient Hebrew poets to employ typology because it was a traditional form of discourse for them, then could not contemporary writers do the same?

The typological design of the years 1789–1805, then, impressed several genres of literature and several styles within those genres. We see the strict, almost teleological millenarianism of self-anointed prophets like Brothers and Joanna Southcott, the prophetic apocalypticism of divines like Price, Wilks, and Winchester, with the antitype always near at hand, and, thanks to the skepticism of writers on both flanks of contemporary politics like Burke and Paine, we see too the evolution of what I shall call *natural typology*. The theological opponents of the eighteenth-century deists, Warburton, Hartley, and a decent-sized phalanx of other worthies, had urged that typology was inherently logical, inherent within the structure of the religious systems that preceded Christianity, and therefore all but canonical. In the 1790's, this developmental argument is resurrected by such poets and scholars interested in the origins of religions as Charles Dupuis, C.F.C. de Volney, and Blake. The Comte de Volney's *Ruines* (1791), translated into English during the 1790's, may be taken as representative:

> Now, if you take a retrospect of the whole history of the spirit of religion, you will find, that in its origin it had no other author [than] the sensations and wants of

man: that the idea of God had no other type, no other model, than that of physical powers, material existences, operating good or evil, by impressions of pleasure or pain on sensible beings. You will find that in the formation of every system this spirit of religion pursued the same track, and was uniform in its proceedings; that in all, that dogma never failed to represent, under the name God, the operations of nature, and the passions and prejudices of men.[97]

The basis of typology is natural and, indeed, universal: de Volney indicates that there is a basis for prefigurative structures in *all* religions and in *all* cultures. The discovery that typology is a structural component of the way men build systems of religious belief may explain the casualness with which Romantic poets employ it.

Blake, as we know, was well acquainted with biblical and abstracted typology, both literary and iconographical. Swedenborg and Mosheim, whom he read closely, use typological expositions in a standard theological way; Jacob Bryant and Jacob Boehme, by whom Blake was profoundly influenced, are among the most proficient typological innovators since Nicholas de Lyra.[98] He was acquainted with traditions of visual typology in eighteenth-century illustration and illumination, and, to a limited extent, introduced typological scenes (highly telescoped, as they must always be in any visual art less ambitious than a large altarpiece) into his own engravings.[99] Yet his presentations of typology in his

[97] See C.F.C. de Volney, *The Ruins, or a Survey of the Revolutions of Empires* (London, [1795]), p. 296. De Volney regularly employs typology to demonstrate how primitive tribes applied euhemerism.

[98] See, for example, Ruthven Tood, *Tracks in the Snow: Studies in English Science and Art* (London, 1946), pp. 29–55 ("William Blake and the Eighteenth-Century Mythologists"); and Desirée Hirst, *Hidden Riches: Traditional Symbolism from the Renaissance to Blake* (London, 1964), esp. chs. IV, VII, VIII, and IX, for the mystical background with which typology has often been associated. One of Hirst's conspicuous oversights is the *Imitatio Christi* tradition, obviously important for Blake.

[99] Joseph A. Wittreich, Jr., *Angel of Apocalypse: Blake's Idea of Milton* (Madison, 1975), pp. 109–113, indicates some of Blake's acquaintance with typological iconography.

poems are seldom accompanied by the external ritual of signs that had been popular earlier in the eighteenth century, and even as recently as the 1770's in Christopher Smart's poetry. He mentions *types* infrequently, but so pervasive is his effort to explain the hidden meanings of the Biblical myths that he introduces the traditional typological characters of the Old Testament—Adam, Moses, David— on many occasions with clear prefigurative import. In his *Description of a Vision of the Last Judgment* (1808), for example, the kneeling figures of Adam and Eve, Abraham and Moses are types of the Throne of Christ, as is everything else in this design.[100] The typological structures of *The Everlasting Gospel* (1818) appear throughout, in every question and every answer indicating that Jesus was the fulfillment of earlier prophecies.

One of the rare occasions when Blake actually mentions typology, in the "To the Public" before *Jerusalem,* is complicated, practically Miltonic in its promise of didactic accomplishments:

> Therefore I print; nor vain my types shall be:
> Heaven, Earth & Hell henceforth shall live
> in harmony.[101]

Blake's "types" are, of course, his works, which he images forth as prefigurations of the eternal, universal harmony which is the ultimate goal of *Jerusalem.* Everything in this world is, or should be, "some Mental pursuit for the Building up of Jerusalem," the heavenly Jerusalem toward which everything in the poem seems to lead. Blake's message "To the Christians" (Pl. 77), a more specialized subgroup within the "Public" he first addressed, is an excellent instance of natural typology: "I know of no other Christianity and of no other Gospel than the liberty both of body & mind to exercise the Divine Arts of Imagination, Imagination, the real & eternal World *of which this Vege-*

100 *The Complete Writings of William Blake,* ed. Geoffrey Keynes (Oxford, 1966), p. 443.
101 *Ibid.,* p. 621.

*table Universe is but a faint shadow*, & in which we shall
live in our Eternal or Imaginative Bodies when these Vegetable Mortal bodies are no more."[102] This notion emanates
originally from Boehme, but the belief that quotidian
things in some unexplained way foreshadow an eternity is
traditionally part of meditative Christianity. More inventive
is the cry of Los, later in *Jerusalem*:

> "But General Forms have their vitality in
> Particulars, & every
> "Particular is a Man, a Divine Member of the
> Divine Jesus."[103]

The sweeping generality of Blake's typological equation
testifies to the central position prefigurative structures
occupy in his poetry. However, despite the importance of
typology for Blake, his is most often a silent typology, a
figural system based on a vast but still largely unstudied
tradition which until recent years has attracted little attention and even less scrutiny.

   The aspect of the figural system which appealed most to
English Romantic poets is natural typology, or typology
abstracted from theological concerns to natural phenomena
and normal aspects of human behavior. Natural typology,
as we have seen, often associates the secular and the
theological spheres in an obscure manner; such a style is
popular with mystical writers like Boehme. An early example of this tendency would be the following stanza from
Christopher Smart's *Song to David* (1763):

> O DAVID, scholar of the Lord!
> Such is thy science, whence reward
>    And infinite degree;
> O strength, O sweetness, lasting ripe!
> God's harp thy symbol, and thy type
>    The lion and the bee![104]

102 *Ibid.*, pp. 716–717 (italics added).
103 *Ibid., p.* 738 (Pl. 91. 30–31).
104 *A Song to David* (London, 1763), p. 10 (St. xxxviii).

The typological qualities of many animals—including the lion and the bee, as it happens—have been noted in commentaries to the editions of Wolfgang Frantze's *Historia Animalium*, but they have no known prefigurative association with David.[105] The natural typologist, however, need not observe an established or traditional symbolism. As he does frequently in *A Song to David* and *Jubilate Agno*, Smart simply makes an enthusiastic association and assigns to it a predictive basis. He thinks that he recognized a similarity between certain characteristics of bees and lions and those of the historical David, from which follows his conclusion that these creatures in some unstated way *foreshadow* David. The explanation of the relationship is less important, I think, than the existence of such predictive structures in eighteenth- and nineteenth-century literature. For, thanks to the labors of Warburton, Hartley, and others, who had suggested that there was a prefigurative basis to human thought and speech, it was now possible for the authors of poetry and prose fiction to embody such structures in their works without a second thought about their theological accuracy.

The notion of typological places, a form of natural typology, continues to develop during the later eighteenth century, and becomes relatively common in Romantic landscape poetry. This concept appears to derive from seventeenth-century Puritan treatments of Egypt, Babylon, wanderings in the desert, various biblical captivities, and other scenes related specifically to *places* as types of the Puritans' contemporary persecutions. And, later in the nineteenth century, Ruskin would make similarly sympathetic readings of history and would interpret the destinies of Venice and Tyre as types for nineteenth-century England. Wordsworth, who frequently refers to types in the theological sense, is especially sensitive to the possibilities of abstracted typology in landscape poetry, as in his famous description of the Simplon Pass:

[105] See above, Note 26.

Brook and Road
Were fellow-travellers in this gloomy Pass,
And with them did we journey several hours
At a slow step. The immeasurable height
Of Woods decaying, never to be decayed,
The stationery blasts of waterfalls,
And in the narrow rent, at every turn,
Winds thwarting winds, bewildered and forlorn,
The torrents shooting from the clear blue sky,
The rocks that muttered close upon our ears,
Black drizzling crags that spake by the wayside
As if a voice were in them, the sick sight
And giddy prospect of the raving stream,
The unfettered clouds and region of the heavens,
Tumult and peace, the darkness and the light—
Were all the workings of one mind, the features
Of the same face, blossoms upon one tree,
Characters of the great Apocalypse,
The types and symbols of Eternity,
Of first, and last, and midst, and without end.[106]

Symbolic landscape is a venerable poetic technique: Wordsworth can scarcely be said to operate within a new tradition. Landscape, however, though frequently endowed with symbolic values, is seldom explicitly typological, as it is here. The motion of the passage is manifestly typological, from a torrent of circumstantial details to unity and the unanimity of great eternal facts ("*one* mind . . . the *same* face . . . *one* tree"), from tumult to peace, darkness to light, type to antitype. Wordsworth's "types," even more significantly, are also "Characters," predictive structures drawn from natural phenomena. His types, then, are ready-made, and lie open to the reader of the great book of nature. Their purpose, as if part of a great physico-theological scheme, is to foreshadow the glories of that book's author, God the Father.

Since abstracted typology often involves the blending

[106] *The Prelude*, VI, 621–640.

of themes, theological and secular, Christian and pagan, it may be well for us to consider one further example in the earlier nineteenth century, Shelley. Like Wordsworth, Shelley often writes with a heightened awareness of mysterious meanings in natural existence. In *Mont Blanc* (1816), for instance, he meditates, "The wilderness has a mysterious tongue / Which teaches awful doubt, or faith so mild . . ." and suggests that, while this voice is not understood by all, "the wise, and great, and good" may interpret it.[107] From his reading of Milton and seventeenth-century mystics, Shelley extracted the notion of types as shadows; thus he often alludes to shadowy forms or intellectual concepts as suggesting larger, more fully developed entities in the future.[108] *Mont Blanc*, however, lacks the typological perfections of the passage from *The Prelude* quoted above. Shelley glimpses the shadows of a greater meaning and nothing more: *Mont Blanc* may hint at an apocalyptic revelation, but Shelley's prophecy lacks the assurance of Wordsworth's.

Typological figuration, as Hans Frei has recently suggested, declines in popularity around the turn of the nineteenth century because "it strained credulity beyond the breaking point by the suggestion that sayings and events of one day referred predictively to specific persons and events hundreds of years later."[109] One symptom of this decline is a change from pure to abstracted typology. Another is the gradual insinuation of pagan myth into typological situations or narratives. Typology and pagan myth have profound seventeenth-century associations (we need mention only Alexander Ross), and in this context we must note again how popular seventeenth-century mysticism was with English Romantic writers. Where Shelley fails to un-

[107] *Mont Blanc*, ll. 76–83.

[108] Particularly useful for Shelley's use of typological shadowing is Susan L. Hawk, "Shelley's Shadows: Studies in Analogy," unpub. doct. diss., Yale Univ., 1971.

[109] *The Eclipse of Biblical Narrative: A Study in Eighteenth and Nineteenth Century Hermeneutics* (New Haven, 1974), p. 6; see more generally, pp. 1–16.

cover typological qualities in natural landscape, he evokes
them successfully through his amalgamation of pagan and
Christian myths in *Prometheus Unbound* (1818). The signs
that surround Shelley's presentation of the pinioned Titan
are typological signals. At first, Prometheus appears as a
type, almost paradoxically, without an antitype. As the
Chorus observes in Act I, "And the future is dark, and the
present is spread / Like a pillow of thorns for thy slumber-
less head."[110] The typological sign, the pillow of thorns, is
present and there *is* a future, although at the moment it
promises nothing. The signs multiply. Panthea reports
shortly afterwards that she has seen "A woeful sight: a
youth / With patient looks nailed to a crucifix."[111] Prometheus becomes an "emblem" (I. 594) of those who suffer for
the wrongs of men, and the Titan himself recognizes his
role in a pagan drama of expiation and salvation:

> Thou subtle tyrant [i.e., Jupiter]! Peace is in the grave.
> The grave hides all things beautiful and good:
> I am a God and cannot find it there,
> Nor would I seek it: for, though dread revenge,
> This is defeat, fierce king, not victory.
> The sights with which thou torturest gird my soul
> With new endurance, till the hour arrives
> When they shall be no types of things which are.
>
> (I. 638–645)

The more Christlike Prometheus becomes, the more numerous are the signs of typological affirmation that surround
him. Toward the end of Act I, the Chorus of Spirits enun-
ciates the refrain of prefigurative promise: ". . . the
prophecy / Which begins and ends in thee!" (I. 690–691,
706–707, 799–800). The types of *Prometheus Unbound* are
crowded together on the canvas of Act I, a situation which
is fitting indeed for a predictive drama combining pagan

---

[110] *Prometheus Unbound*, I. 562–563.

[111] I. 584–585. Prometheus as the Crucified Christ was an enduring
Renaissance emblem. See Stuart Curran, *Shelley's Annus Mirabilis:
The Maturing of an Epic Vision* (San Marino, Calif., 1975), pp. 53–58.

and Christian elements. For the first act serves as an icono-graphical prefiguration of the achievements of Acts III and IV—the dethronement of Jupiter and the jubilant cosmic dance of the finale. The dialogue between The Earth and The Moon suggests the accomplishment of the prophecies. The key speech of Earth concludes:

> And the abyss shouts from her depth laid bare,
> Heaven, hast thou secrets? Man unveils me; I have none.
>
> (IV. 422–423)

The removal of the veil is complete, just as an antitype ex-plains and removes the mystery of its type.

The intricate backgrounds to Shelley's mythmaking, both Christian and pagan, western and oriental, reveal the rich typological vein available to the creative artists of the later eighteenth and early nineteenth centuries. Shelley relies not only on syncretic mythologists like Jacob Bryant and George Stanley Faber, but on a host of other scholars and commentators the fruits of whose researches had been un-available to Swift, Pope, and Johnson.[112] Indeed, the seven-teenth-century students of euhemerism and the pagan or-igins of Christianity like Isaac Vossius, Samuel Bochart, and Athanasius Kircher, whose writings were never trans-lated out of the Latin, are to a large extent subsumed and continued by this later generation of scholars in a language open to all readers. Thus the typology of Shelley's *Prome-theus* is extraordinarily complex, embodying the mysterious lore of the professional mythologists and much of the fa-miliar prefiguration of Old Testament exegesis. Robert Lowth, speaking half a century earlier of Old Testament typologizing, exemplifies the vein that runs to the more biblical sort of abstracted typology: "Hence that truly

---

[112] Curran, *op. cit.*, pp. 33–94, 212–230, thoroughly documents Shel-ley's reading of Bryant's *A New System, or An Analysis of Ancient Mythology* (London, 1774–1776) (a work which much influenced Coleridge, whose annotated copy survives), Faber's *The Origin of Pagan Idolatry ascertained from Historical Testimony and Circum-stantial Evidence* (London, 1816), and dozens of other available sources.

Divine Spirit, which has not disdained to employ poetry as the interpreter of its sacred will, has also in a manner appropriated to its own use this kind of allegory, as peculiarly adapted to the publication of future events, and to the typifying of the most sacred mysteries."[113] If Shelley's Prometheus resembles the typologically resonant heroes of late eighteenth-century biblical epic, then, we should not be surprised at the similarity. The central characters of the biblical epics by Klopstock, Bodmer, Richard Cumberland, and even Bishop Vida help to promote the popularity of abstracted typology in the Romantic era.[114] What Wordsworth and Shelley accomplish in verse, novelists from Sarah Fielding to William Godwin had already accomplished in popular prose. The continuation of these pre- and post-figurative processes in later nineteenth- and twentieth-century literature must await further examination.

## X

As I have suggested in the foregoing pages, the shape of the prefigurative style in the later eighteenth and early nineteenth centuries is closely linked with the language of

[113] See *Lectures on the Sacred Poetry of the Hebrews*, trans. G. Gregory, 2 vols. (London, 1787), I, 238 and I, 234–249, *passim*, Lowth's important chapter "Of the Mystical Allegory."

[114] Klopstock, *The Messiah*, trans. Joseph Collyer, 2nd ed., 2 vols. (London, 1766) is laden with typological import, much of it original with its author. See II, 101, 174, 212, 263. Collyer also translated Bodmer's *Noah: Noah, Attempted from the German of Mr. Bodmer*, 2 vols. (London, 1767), in which see esp. II, 191–255. Both translations are in prose. Richard Cumberland's *Calvary; or The Death of Christ. A Poem in Eight Books* (London, 1792) presents a complex Jesus who, like Shelley's Prometheus, is surrounded by iconographical detail from various mythologies. An especially fine passage is the one in which the resurrected Jesus addresses the souls of the patriarchs and welcomes them to eternal life: the antitype holds a conversation with the types (see pp. 266–267, ap. VIII. 170–201). Moses responds with a stirring recollection of all his typological actions (pp. 282–285; VIII. 568–650). It would appear that typology so caught the fancy of many writers that they embroidered upon it freely. Vida's *Christiad*, translated several times in the later eighteenth century, is also prefigurative in an inventive manner; see *The Christiad: An Heroic Poem; in Six Books*, trans. Edward Granam (London, 1771), pp. 35–36, 131–172.

signs, with the semantic enclaves of character and fable, with the visual, and with that most human desire to predict the future. It has been plausibly argued that typological patterns of thought exist in all societies and in all centuries. If we limit our quest to mere predictiveness, this may indeed be so. But the language of types in this period works through a recognizable code—a type always has an antitype, an antitype always presupposes a type somewhere in its past. The prefigurative style, when we find it, will have an extra-verbal quality about it, for types are, after all, signs. Here, for example, is the kind of typological text contemporary readers could have enjoyed:

> Nature *labours* with its utmost Diligence upon this corrupted dead Earth, that it might generate Heavenly Forms and Species or Kinds; but it *generates only* dead, dark, and hard Fruits, which are no more than a mere Shadow or Type of the Heavenly.

Or, if they continued in the same work:

> Further, if you will consider the heavenly Divine Pomp, State, and *Glory*, and conceive how it is, and what Manner of Sprouting, Branching, Delight, and Joy there is in it, view this World diligently, and *consider* what Manner of Fruit, Sprouts, and Branches, grow out of the *Salitter* of the Earth, from Trees, Plants, Herbs, Roots, Flowers, Oils, Wine, Corn, and whatever else there is that your *Heart* can find out; *all* is a *Type* of the heavenly Pomp.[115]

True, this is a seventeenth-century translation of Jacob Boehme's *Aurora* (trans. English 1620), but I am quoting from the eighteenth-century edition ascribed to William Law, from the very copy which belonged to Coleridge.[116]

[115] "Aurora: The Day-Spring, or, Dawning of the Day in the East," in *The Works of Jacob Behmen; the Teutonic Theosopher*, ed. G. Ward and T. Langcake, 4 vols. (London, 1764–1781), 1, pt. 1, 42–43.

[116] Coleridge's annotated copy, now in the British Museum, has the shelfmark C.126.k.1.

Boehme's comment is one example of the many typological interpretations of the seventeenth century which retained popularity and influence in the next century and a half. To an acquaintance with Boehme we may ascribe, in part, the typology of natural existence that we find in Smart, Blake, Wordsworth, and Shelley.

The prefigurative style will involve specifically contemporary achievements, as we may see in Richard Glover's "Poem on Sir Isaac Newton" (1728). Newton's scientific accomplishments, Glover proclaims, surpass anything the ancients could do. But he does not put his message in terms of *praise*; he expresses Newton's glory as the consummation of a type in the person of an antitype. The poet addresses Nature:

> Thee the wise
> Of ancient fame, immortal PLATO's self,
> The Stagyrite, and Syracusian sage,
> From bleak obscurity's abyss to raise,
> (Drooping and mourning o'er thy wondrous works)
> With vain inquiry sought. Like meteors these
> In their dark age bright sons of wisdom shone:
> But at thy NEWTON all their laurels fade,
> They shrink from all the honours of their names.
> So glimm'ring stars contract their feeble rays,
> When the swift lustre of AURORA's face
> Flows o'er the skies, and wraps the heav'ns in light.[117]

The abstracted typology here has all the usual chaperones: a *type* (Plato, Aristotle, the other ancients), an *antitype* (Newton), and the traditional and necessary *extra-verbal signs* (the meteors, which are prophetic signs; the dawn = the Sun = Newton, with a sideways glance at Christ). Pope, perhaps, put it more neatly: "Nature, and Nature's

---

[117] Glover's poem is prefixed to Henry Pemberton, *A View of Sir Isaac Newton's Philosophy* (London, 1728). See Sigs. [a]3$^{r-v}$. Cf. Marjorie Hope Nicolson, *Newton Demands the Muse: Newton's "Opticks" and the Eighteenth-Century Poets* (Princeton, 1946), pp. 13–14.

Laws lay hid in Night. / God said, *Let Newton be!* and All was *Light*."[118] From type to antitype in two lines: it is hard to better that.

And the prefigurative style, finally, will involve a blending of Christian and pagan, as in the typological character, or in the christianizing of fabulistic plot structures in the novel. The allegorical essays in *The Rambler*, to take a prominent case, which we have long taken as evidence for Johnson's adherence to Renaissance traditions, may be something quite different. In one of them, Johnson falls asleep, and dreams that he walks through a landscape which, to our eyes, appears unbelievably emblematic and prefigurative, complete with images of a Dantesque wood and an Edenic vale. The dreamer is saved from a melancholy doom by the figure of Religion, who assures him that good behavior, as it were an *imitatio Christi*, will bring him to eternal happiness:

> To such a one the lowliest self-abasement is but a deep-laid foundation for the most elevated hopes; since they who faithfully examine and acknowledge what they are, shall be enabled under my conduct to become what they desire. *The christian and the heroe are inseparable*; and to the aspirings of unassuming trust, and filial confidence, are set no bounds.[119]

The Christian and the hero—Christ and Hercules or, indeed, Everyman—the prefigurative qualities of two entire classes of images are here blended into one. Are not the foreshadowing and emulation of Christian heroism what typology is all about?

[118] "Epitaph. Intended for Sir Isaac Newton, In Westminster Abbey" (c. 1730).

[119] *The Works of Samuel Johnson* (New Haven, 1954–), 3, 241 (*Rambler*, No. 44; italics added).

## FROM FATHER TO SON:
## THE EVOLUTION OF TYPOLOGY IN
## PURITAN NEW ENGLAND

DURING the last decade the study of typology in colonial America has clearly come of age, its maturity marked by the 1972 publication of the important collection of essays, *Typology and Early American Literature*. Although these essays and other significant studies have provided a deeper understanding of the role of typology in the theology and intellectual history of early New England, they have clearly recognized the long and complex history of typology in biblical exegesis, beginning in the work of the authors of the New Testament themselves. As Thomas M. Davis observed in his survey of the backgrounds of Puritan typology, "it is the relative importance allotted to typology which marks the line between Patristic and Protestant allegory."[1] In addition, these scholars pay tribute to the richness of English literature in the seventeenth century and to the central place that typology held in the theological and political disputes of the Puritan movement. In particular, the debates on the key issues of church-state relations and the questions of separatism and congregationalism frequently made use of typology in expressing the continuity between contemporary affairs and biblical precedents.[2]

What makes the function of typology in early American thought and writing unusual, if not unique, is however, that the special experiences of the New England Puritans seem to have provided a remarkable continuous analogy of

[1] Thomas M. Davis, "The Traditions of Puritan Typology," in *Typology and Early American Literature*, ed. Sacvan Bercovitch (Amherst, 1972), p. 44.

[2] See, for example, "The Separatist Background of Roger Williams' Argument for Religious Toleration," in *Typology and Early American Literature*, pp. 107–137.

biblical events. Thus, in the imaginations of seventeenth-century American preachers and writers, typological interpretations of Scripture provided a basis for shaping a powerful cultural vision. Most important for literary studies, such investigations have revealed the imaginative power and the rich verbal complexities of Puritan writing which had long remained unrecognized. Through our awareness of the figural mode of thought in early American writing, we have now begun to recognize the epic grandeur of Cotton Mather's *Magnalia Christi Americana* and the verbal subtleties of Edward Taylor's private poetry.[3]

Perhaps the most important aspect of the early American mind that the study of typology has illuminated is the fundamental tension in Puritan thought between two irreconcilable ways of understanding man's relationship to God, ways underlying two quite different methods of applying biblical types to modern history. Although the officially stated version of Puritan hermeneutics insisted upon the strict and literal interpretation of the Old Testament, American Puritan ministers from John Cotton to Jonathan Edwards were inclined to interpret modern historical events as fulfillments of the scriptural prophesies. Thus, typology was neither a static nor an inflexible system of thought. Over the course of the seventeenth century in New England there occurred significant shifts in the emphasis of certain scriptural types and in the use of such types in historiography and religious writing.[4]

[3] The important studies to which I refer, besides the Bercovitch collection, are Ursula Brumm, *American Thought and Religious Typology* (New Brunswick, N.J., 1970); and Bercovitch, "Horologicals to Chronometricals: The Rhetoric of the Jeremiad," *Literary Monographs* (Madison, Wisconsin, 1970), 1–126; "Typology in Puritan New England: The Williams-Cotton Controversy Reassessed," *American Quarterly*, 19 (1967), 166–191; "The Historiography of Johnson's *Wonder-Working Providences*," *Essex Institute Historical Collection*, 104 (1968), 138–161; and "New England Epic: Cotton Mather's *Magnalia Christi Americana*," *English Literary History*, 33 (1966), 337–350. See also Bercovitch's annotated bibliography of typology and early American literature in *Typology and Early American Literature*, pp. 243–337.

[4] For commentary on the two schools of typological interpretation, see especially Bercovitch, "The Williams-Cotton Controversy," and

It is now clear that behind each of these modes of application there existed separate perceptions of the role of the Puritans in human history and of the immediate relationship of the individual to God. But important questions still remain to be answered. How may we account for the changes in application of typology in seventeenth-century New England? Why did certain types predominate in Puritan writing during particular periods? We can seek answers to such questions by examining the changes that occurred in a rather brief space of time—from the late 1660's to the late 1680's—against the background of some of the important developments in the society during those years, especially the passing of the theocracy from the first-generation founders to the second and third generations. We shall discover that social factors played a significant part in reshaping the vision of the Puritan mission and in expressing that vision through biblical exegesis.

The one metaphor in early American Puritan writing which held the greatest imaginative power in the minds of the first-generation founders was the idea that they were leaders of a holy quest into the wilderness.[5] In such works as Edward Johnson's *Wonder-Working Providence* and Puritan sermons from John Cotton to Samuel Danforth, the controlling image was the dream that God had commis-

---

"Horologicals to Chronologicals"; and Mason I. Lowance, "Cotton Mather's *Magnalia* and the Metaphors of Biblical History," *Typology and Early American Literature*, pp. 139–160.

[5] In *The Mathers: Three Generations of Puritan Intellectuals* (New York, 1971), Robert Middlekauf has argued that the vision of the sacred mission was created by the second and third generations rather than by the founders. Though Middlekauf is correct in finding the idea of the errand to be more fully articulated by the later generations, his assertions about the founders are not borne out by the works of such first-generation ministers and magistrates as John Cotton and John Winthrop; see, for example, Cotton's *God's Promise to His Plantations* (London, 1630) in *Old South Leaflets* (Boston, 1874–1876), III, no. 53, p. 15, and Winthrop's *A Model of Christian Charity* (London, 1630), in *Puritan Political Ideas, 1558–1794*, ed. Edmund S. Morgan (New York, 1965), p. 87. Cf. Bercovitch, "Horologicals to Chronometricals," in particular pp. 3–26.

sioned this small band of colonists to fulfill the special mission of creating a new Jerusalem in a barbarous land. The Puritan founders perceived the story of the exodus of the Jews from Egypt in search of the promised land as the "type" or prefiguring of their own journey: they were the saints, the newly chosen people of God, and their "city upon a hill" would be the sacred ground where the pure worship of God would be preserved throughout the final days of the antichrist's rule in the world. It is in such typological terms that the first-generation settlers conceived of themselves, and these are the metaphors which helped them to interpret their trials and successes.

During the second half of the seventeenth century New England society underwent a series of crucial events: specifically, the establishment of the Half-Way Covenant, the Indian Wars, fires and plagues, the revocation of the charter, and the witchcraft delusion. These events deeply affected the second- and third-generation Puritans. They feared that the errand begun by their fathers was being destroyed by acts of Divine Providence; they needed an explanation of the reasons for God's wrath and a means for regaining God's favor. Diaries, biographies, and autobiographies reveal that the members of the second and third generations possessed deep fears about themselves.

The writings of the later generations reveal that they too were venturing upon an errand into the wilderness—a journey into the terrible wilderness of their own inner selves to overcome severe feelings of inadequacy and insecurity in order to survive in their rapidly changing world. This errand of the second generation was all the more difficult because it was not an external quest across the Atlantic to a new land or westward into the frontier. The years from 1665 to 1685 were a critical period of personal and corporate searching—a quest involving a separation from the past, an initiation in the fires of self-doubt, and a return to the faith of the fathers. The quest was completed for the people of the second generation only when they found in their religion a new meaning and power that enabled them to make sense of their special cultural situation. The private writings tell us of the inner struggles men endured; it was the sermon that provided the outlet for public expression of the deepest tensions of the society and the sermon literature that records the inner quest of the second generation.

As part of the process of development of the Puritan sermon from the 1660's to the 1690's, there occurred a significant shift in typological emphasis from the Old Testament image of the angry and wrathful God the Father to the New Testament image of the gentle, loving, and protective Christ. The transition from the first image to the second occurred as the second generation came into power. Through their sermons the ministers helped the society move from the sense of disorientation and alienation which marked the years of separation from the fathers (1665–1675) through the transition years of frustration and social malaise (1670–1682) to the final years of assurance and confidence (1680–1695). The metaphors and themes of men like Increase Mather and John Wilson, whose writings dominated the early 1670's, express the bitterness of the aging first generation and voice the sense of inadequacy and of inevitable failure among the young people. By the late 1680's and 1690's the new message of assurance and the language of exuberance—even rapture, as in the writings of Cotton Mather—demonstrate the intensity of the new vision of cultural and spiritual identity of the second generation's mature years.

The ministers who dominated the presses and pulpits of New England from about 1665 to 1679 devoted much of their creative energy and literary art to creating a myth about their society. In spite of full churches and growing prosperity, they envisioned the society as one in decay: a society which was losing the strength and zeal of the founders, was rapidly being passed to a weak and degenerate generation, was threatened on all sides by the forces of evil and from above by an angry God, and was therefore likely to be doomed to destruction. To give these themes a compelling imaginative power, the ministers searched the Scriptures for striking imagery and for typological parallels between the Old Testament Hebrews and the Puritans.[6]

Throughout the 1660's and 1670's, whenever the ministers lamented the sickness and decay in the religion of the second- and third-generation Puritans, they stressed the parallels between the trials of the apostate Hebrews and the probable fate of the degenerate Puritans. In 1669 the Reverend Thomas Walley assumed that his congregation would apply the biblical type of Israel to its own situation as he recounted the story of the Hebrews, who possessed good health, the prophets, and sacred ordinances, and were guided by God's favor when they went into the wilderness —only to arrive at Canaan diseased and languishing in corruption. Worst of all, the Hebrews were unable to find a cure for their sickness: *"Sometimes a People may be sick, and though they have the most proper and suitable Means of Health, yet no Means may be effectual for their Recovery."*[7] Walley further demonstrated that the Hebrews did not seek a cure because, like the people of New England, they were not even aware of their sickness. The process of spiritual decline is so imperceptible, he argued, that sometimes even the minister, the prophet-physician, cannot discover the secret cancer which devours the people from within: "Because oft times the Diseases of Kingdoms, Countries, and Churches are so occult and hid, that the wisest of Physicians cannot find them out" (p. 6). In such cases, "it comes to pass that a people perish, or continue sick, because they do not find out the reason of their sickness"; and before the people are aware of it, "the Disease is old, and deeply rooted, grown Malignant" (p. 6).

Another minister believed that he found the source of New England's disease in the conflict between the genera-

---

[6] For an examination of these shifts in Puritan society and the sermons of which the developments in typology are a part, see my *Power and the Pulpit in Puritan New England* (Princeton, 1975).

[7] Thomas Walley, *Balm in Gilead to Heal Sions Wounds* (Cambridge, Mass., 1669, reprinted 1673), p. 5.

tions. The Reverend Samuel Arnold recognized that the dissatisfaction and confusion of the younger generation was becoming a serious problem for the churches. In *David Serving His Generation* (1674) he used typological parallels to try to instill in the young people some pride in the role of dutiful sons that their elders wished them to assume. Confidently, Arnold declared that "Every Generation hath . . . some special Service to do for God," and he found the contrast between David and Solomon an appropriate metaphor for the relationship between the founders and their sons: "Some are to lay the Foundation for God and others to build thereupon; *David's* work was to settle the *Ark* in *Zion* under Curtains, and *Solomon's* to build a Temple."[8] But although he set out to embolden the rising generation, the more Arnold explained the role of second-generation Solomons in New England, the more it became clear that their labors were distinctly subordinate to those of the first-generation Davids: "*Our generation is our Master's Family*, God is the Father and Master of the *great Family* in Heaven and Earth," and as for the role of this generation, "we serve . . . God . . . as the Steward of a *great man* in serving his *Master's Family* according to his will, serves his Master" (p. 4). To be sure, the first generation had also served their master, but as founders; the role of their offspring would be confined to temple-keeping.

Increase Mather was the minister who most forcefully expounded this message of the decline and probable doom of the rising generations, and who took the most liberties in his biblical exegesis in exploring the parallels between New England and Israel. Although himself a member of the second generation, in the 1670's Mather became the most powerful and prolific spokesman of the bitterness of the aged patriarchs as he sought fitting language for arousing the fears and guilt of the members of the younger generations. In sermons and tracts throughout the decade Mather set forth his favorite analogue for New England:

[8] Samuel Arnold, *David Serving His Generation* (Cambridge, Mass., 1674), p. 3.

Yea, it is a sad Truth, that Religion hath seldom been up-
held in the power of it, for above one or two Generations
together. . . . [History] maketh it very manifest that that
most corrupt Generation were the grand-Children of
those that were first embodied as a peculiar People, when
the Lord . . . did build up the Children of Israel . . . the
*third Generation* among that People proved degenerate
and apostate.⁹

By interpreting external events like the Indian Wars of
1674–1675 in the light of typological readings of Scripture,
Mather managed to bring the whole weight of current
events and biblical history upon the hearts of the guilty.

In *The Day of Trouble Is Near*, which he preached in
1673 and published in the following year during the King
Philip's War, Mather began with an account of the religious
decline of the second-generation Israelites and the resulting
wrath of God. He then showed that the present "inward
spiritual troubles, Soul troubles" indicated the approach of
apocalyptic destruction: *"There is a day of trouble coming
upon all the World* and such trouble too, as the like hath
not been, for I am persuaded that Scripture is yet to be
fulfilled."¹⁰ As he was frequently inclined to do, Mather
went beyond his fellow ministers in applying his types to
New England as he compared the emotions the Hebrews
must have felt as they awaited God's wrath with the
rampant fears of Indian attacks that were spreading across
the colony. He used this fear itself as proof of impending
disaster: "Secret dismal Fears upon the Spirits of men are
sometimes a sign that a day of trouble is near" (p. 9). And
comparing himself to the prophets of the Old Testament,
Mather proposed that the very fact that he had been
moved to speak of such a calamity was evidence that God
was about to remove his protective wall which had en-
circled the garden of New England: *"When God stirs up*

⁹ Increase Mather, *A Discourse Concerning the Danger of Apostasy*
(Boston, 1679), pp. 57–58.
¹⁰ Increase Mather, *The Day of Trouble Is Near* (Cambridge, Mass.,
1674), p. 20.

*the Spirits of his Messengers to sound the Trumpet, and to cry an Alarm against his people; that's a sign that the day of trouble is near"* (p. 10).

A master at reinforcing the meaning of current social events with biblical types, Mather shifted back and forth from New England to biblical history to find certain signs of the end of the world in the record of seventeenth-century history: the antichrist appeared in the restoration of the English monarch; famines and plagues had ravaged both America and Europe; and symbolic earthquakes had occurred in the "statequakes" of political turmoil. While his more optimistic brethren were "sleeping and dreaming of nothing but worldly Prosperity at such times as this," Mather declared, "O take heed" because the signs of heaven foretell the coming of "miserable Dearths and Scarcity," of "War among the Nations," and of "Lamentable Deaths and destruction."[11]

Often Mather found an execution sermon to be a fitting occasion to preach upon the theme of the obedience of children to parents. In 1674 he used the hanging of two servants who had murdered their master as an opportunity to warn *"especially such as are of* the Rising Generation"[12] of the fate of the rebellious. In *The Wicked Man's Portion* he stressed that the most heinous aspect of the crime was not murder so much as the rebellion of a servant against his master. With the condemned men on the scaffold behind him, he told the young people in his audience that the sin of disobedience constituted a crime as serious as murder, and as worthy of capital punishment. Although the Massachusetts law prescribing death for disobedient children was never enforced, Mather used the confessions of the murderers that they had once been guilty of such disobedience as proof that disobedient children do not escape their proper fate: "So when children shall rebel

[11] Increase Mather, *Heaven's Alarm to the World* (Boston, 1681), pp. 2, 11, and 8–9.
[12] Increase Mather, *The Wicked Man's Portion* (Boston, 1675), sig. A2.

against their Parents, their wickedness is excessively great.
And such Children do usually die *before their Time"* ( p. 9).

Turning to the Scriptures, Mather recalled the stories of
Absalom, who was destroyed for his rebellion against his
father, and of the sons of Eli, who were slain by God for
failing to follow their father's counsel. These scriptural
episodes of "those proud and profane young men . . . [who]
died before their Time" should serve as reminders to those
brash young men of the second generation who were so
bold as to ignore the advice of their fathers: "Doth thy
Father give thee good counsel? but wilt thou not harden
to him? This is a sign, that *the Lord will slay thee*. . . .This
cometh of not harkening to the voice of a Father" (p. 11).
Mather found that the biblical story of Absalom carried a
fitting message for willful children:

> Absalom, He was a rebellious Child, and what came of
> him? was he not hanged at last? and three darts thrust
> through his heart while he was yet alive. . . . *Thus shall
> it be done to the son that rebels against his Father*, Thus
> shall it be done to the child that riseth up against his
> Parents. . . . *The eye that mocketh his Father and de-
> spiseth to obey his Mother, the ravens of the valley shall
> pick it out and the young eagles eat it.* (pp. 9 and 18)

Mather concluded that those who had not learned from
scriptural example should heed God's most recent warning against the increasing discontent and impatience of the
young men of New England: "Therefore, no marvel that
such an awful Providence doth come to rebuke and humble
us, that servants have conspired together to Kill their Master. . . . If ever *New-England* be destroyed, this very sin
of disobedience . . . will be the ruin of this Land" (p. 17). Increase Mather was not the only master who chastised New
England's young, but he must have recognized that he had
a particular talent for choosing imagery and biblical types
which aroused fear in young hearts.

In the early 1670's Mather's portrayal of the relationship
between man and God did not yet include the possibility of

man's actively struggling to overcome evil and win the favor of his divine Father. The idea that Christ has atoned for man's sins and acts as mediator with the Father was not a consideration in Mather's early works. However, in the late 1670's the people began to long for a sign that their period of trial might be ending, and they began to look to their ministers for a new message of hope and some assurance that God's favor might be restored to New England. At first Mather resisted this changing mood, and evidence of his resistance is ample in his post-war sermon of 1676. In the face of the people's rejoicing over the end of King Philip's War, Mather's sermon was *An Earnest Exhortation to the Inhabitants of New-England to Hearken to the Voice of God in his late and present Dispensations As ever they desire to escape another Judgment seven times greater than any thing which as yet hath been.*

In this sermon he tried to counter those who had taken solace in the end of the war as a sign of the return of God's favor to New England. He warned that just as God said to Jerusalem, "Be instructed lest my Soul depart from thee and thou become desolate, a Land not inhabited," God used the recent losses of war to speak to New England: "Be thou instructed that I depart from thee, and thou become desolate."[13] For other examples of the subsequent ordeals that awaited the people, Mather turned to the Scriptures: the book of Revelation warns New England that *"Famine and Pestilence* are not far off. We have seen the Lord come riding among us upon his *Red horse"* (p. 2). He found in the Book of Kings scorn for those young soldiers who celebrated their recent victory: "let the young men now arise and play before us, it may be it will be bitterness in the latter end" (p. 11). And he chastised *"the haughty Daughters of Zion"* in their "whorish Fashions" who are "fulfilling the third chapter of Isaiah" (p. 7). The young people of the second generation had waited for some sign of God's favor and had tried to view their victory in King Philip's War as

---

[13] Increase Mather, *An Earnest Exhortation* (Boston, 1676), p. 1.

such a sign. But Mather was still convinced of their apostasy, and in response to their rejoicing he used typology effectively to reinforce one of his shrillest statements of impending doom.

In the late 1670's, however, the people of New England were becoming increasingly dissatisfied with the message of doom and decay that methods of biblical exegesis such as Increase Mather's had provided. It was a sign of the changing times that it took Mather and his fellow ministers five years to convince the General Court that a colony-wide day of fast, penance, and covenant renewal was in order. When in 1679 such a day was finally declared, Mather preached a sermon on the need for a renewal of the original covenant of the fathers in which he made it quite evident that at the heart of the disagreement over the fast day there was a controversy over the ways of scriptural interpretation. Mather noted that "there are [those critics] who have opposed the Doctrine of the *Church-covenant,* not only as to *Renewals* thereof, but they strike at the thing itself, denying it to be an Ordinance of Christ . . . [saying] we find nothing in the New Testament concerning a *Church Covenant.*"[14] Such renewed emphasis upon the supremacy of the New Testament over the Old would have significant implications for Puritan hermeneutics. Mather had to admit slim Gospel evidence, but he insisted that the denial of the covenant on such grounds was based upon narrow literalism and upon a limited understanding of the spirit of biblical exegesis which allows the rituals of the Old Testament to have continued meaning even under the New Dispensation. But Mather must have felt his position weakening as he came under increasing attacks even from his own congregation.

In another sermon of 1679, *A Call from Heaven to the Present and Succeeding Generations,* Mather opened by acknowledging the complaints of some clever young men who had turned his reading of the Scriptures against him.

---

[14] Increase Mather, *Renewal of Covenant the Great Duty Incumbent on Decaying or Distressed Churches* (Boston, 1677), sig. A2–A3.

In order to take issue with his assertions that the former age in New England was better than the present and the future, they had argued that biblical history reveals the past age to be the "iron age," and that the promised golden age of the millennium still lies ahead.[15] Mather admitted the validity of this interpretation and even cited the words of the preacher in Ecclesiastes who declared that it is "vanity" to complain that *the former days were better than these.*" But he still scorned these rebellious "Professors of this Age" who "have more of Light and Notion, but less of love and Zeal and Power than did appear in the Martyrs and blessed *Puritans*" (sig. A2r).

In spite of his continued resistance, the people and many of Mather's fellow ministers were beginning to reexamine the method of finding spiritual antitypes in modern historical events. In 1683 Samuel Mather, Increase's brother and an eminent Dublin minister, published his lengthy scholarly treatise, *The Types or Figures of the Old Testament*, in which he reasserted the conservative model for Puritan hermeneutics. Insisting upon the definition of a type as limited to *"some outward or sensible thing ordained of God under the old Testament to represent and hold forth something of Christ in the new,"* Samuel Mather urged his readers "to persevere in their Christian Profession, and not to fall off to *Judaism*, from the Gospel to the Law."[16] Samuel feared that the Puritans had begun to forget "the Excellency of the *Gospel* above the *Law*, the Excellency of *Christ* above *Moses*" (p. 1). Although his brother Increase may have been stunned by this book, which almost seemed to be a direct reprimand to those, like himself, who had gone to extremes to give meaning to modern history, there were many ministers in New England who gratefully welcomed the counter-movement which Samuel's work

15 Increase Mather, *A Call from Heaven to the Present and Succeeding Generations* (Boston, 1679), sig. A2.

16 Samuel Mather, *The Types or Figures of the Old Testament* (London, 1683), reprint of the 1705 edition with an introduction by Mason I. Lowance (New York, 1969), p. 52.

signaled as the only hope for providing a Gospel message of assurance to the rising generation.

One such minister was the Reverend William Hubbard (1621–1704), whose eighty-three years permitted him to witness the maturity of three generations of New England Puritans. Hubbard was never certain that there had actually been a decline of religion in New England in the 1670's, and he tended to distrust the mythologizing of New England history and the prophecies of doom, particularly those of Increase Mather. Hubbard's opposition to Increase Mather is well known. As preacher at Ipswich, Hubbard occupied one of the most enviable positions for a minister in New England, for Ipswich possessed more talent and intelligence than almost any other town. In 1676 he published his own *History of the Indian Wars*, an objective account of events to balance the spiritualized rendering in Increase Mather's *Brief History of the War with the Indians*. Hubbard's later *General History of New England*, commissioned by the General Court and completed in 1682, was never published because of Mather's opposition.[17] Hubbard was a shrewd man who brought to the pulpit of the 1670's a rational voice and an intellectual skepticism unmatched by his peers. Accordingly, his departures from conventional preaching and from traditional doctrine were subtle enough to avoid the condemnation of his fellow ministers. Thus, even in those sermons that at first appear to be standard jeremiads, there are important rhetorical differences which seem to have been designed to counter the myth of decline and doom.

In *The Happiness of a People* (1676) he began traditionally with an eloquent description of the planting and growth of the New England settlement:

> The time was not long since, that we in New England might have said with Job, "the eye that saw us, whether of friends or foes, was ready to bless us, or envy our

[17] On Hubbard's conflicts with Mather, see Perry Miller, *The New England Mind: From Colony to Province* (Boston, reprinted 1966), pp. 135–136 and 140–141.

prosperity." . . . When God first brought this vine out of another land where it might be much overshadowed, he cast out the heathen, and planted it; he caused it to take deep root, and it was ready to fill the land, the hills began to be covered with the shadow of it, its boughs began to look like goodly cedars: it might have been said in some sense that we sent out boughs to the Seas and our branches to the rivers.[18]

But later in the sermon Hubbard expressed his bewilderment that a people who had had such an auspicious beginning now complained that the best days of the colony had passed: "But now we may take up the Lamentation following: 'Why are our hedges broken down, and the wild boar out of the wood doth waste it, and the wild beast out of the field doth devour it?" (p. 49). He was not ready to conclude that a decay of religion had already occurred or that the rising generation was the cause of God's displeasure. Indeed, he was convinced that "there [are] many hopeful buds springing up among the rising Generation" (p. 52). Thus Hubbard shunned the rhetoric of decay and doom, and he avoided drawing typological parallels between fallen Israel and New England. Instead, he sought ways to use the power of metaphor to expose and calm the fears of his people. By the time he published his *Benefit of a Well-Ordered Conversation* in 1682, his efforts to provide new metaphors for new religious problems had been recognized. In their preface to the sermon, John Allin and Joshua Moodey praised Hubbard as an eloquent preacher who could compose "Words in season [which] are as Apples of Gold in Pictures of Silver" and whose *"fitness of words (well tuning them) is the grace of them, and puts wheels to the Chariots to carry them to the mind."*[19]

In this sermon Hubbard tried to lift the spirits of his people by clarifying how the new dispensation of Christ had

18 William Hubbard, *The Happiness of a People* (Boston, 1676), p. 49.
19 William Hubbard, *The Benefit of a Well-Ordered Conversation* (Boston, 1684), sig. A3.

modified the meaning of the Old Testament for New England and how Christ's redemptive act had affected the lives of every Christian. Hubbard warned against the misuse of Old Testament types for making false, too-specific prophecies about New England, and he argued that the most important lesson to be learned from biblical history is that men tend to bring their own troubles upon themselves by their failure to use their God-given reason:

> If we cast an eye upon all the following Histories of the Church in succeeding Ages, we shall find that much of those sufferings which have fallen upon the Generation of the just, might either have been prevented or much abated if they had governed their affairs by a suitable measure of Wisdom in their concerns with themselves or others. (p. 47)

Hubbard asserted that Christ has given his believers every reason to look forward joyfully to eternal happiness rather than backward to the wrath and damnation threatened under the Old Covenant, and therefore that Christians need not repeat the errors of the Hebrews.

If the Puritans felt obliged to compare themselves with the Hebrews, Hubbard encouraged them to keep in mind the possibilities for contrast as well as parallels between the two peoples: "It was a joyful time with *Israel* when they encamped in the *Wilderness* at *Elim*, where were . . . twelve wells of water." But Hubbard emphasized that now with Christ "there are wells of Salvation now under the Gospel in every station" (p. 80). To those who had feared that evil invaders would break down New England's wall of protection, Hubbard offered assurance: "*We have a strong City, Salvation will God appoint for Walls and Bulwarks*: mountains of Brass and Gates of Iron are not so strong as the promise of God" (pp. 86–87). Against the menacing storms of political struggle with England, he was also certain that New England would be protected: "The Storm may be sharp, yet it will be short. If Christ be in the Ship, all that are embarked shall be saved" (p. 91). He declared with certainty: "The Ship of Christ's Church may be tossed, yet it shall be preserved," and "The Church may sing her triumphant Song in all her troubles" (pp. 91 and 86).

Finally, Hubbard turned to the members of the rising generation, whom he believed to be willing but to "know not how to perform" (p. 110). In a remarkable departure from convention, he encouraged the young to seek their own individual and personal relationships with God in whatever form seemed best for them, and he urged them not to worry if their spiritual strivings did not conform to some pattern designed by the society. A man who at the age of seventy-three married his second wife, much to the displeasure of his parish, Hubbard stressed sincerity before God rather than conformity before men: "Let every one say for himself in his own particular . . . '*I and my Family will serve the Lord*'" (p. 110). Because of his appeal for assurance and individualism and his faith in the power of human reason, Hubbard was to be followed in the 1680's and 1690's by many younger ministers as they sought to accommodate the message of Puritanism and the method of biblical exegesis to the new generations.

In the years between 1680 and 1685 Increase Mather also struggled to reexamine his exegetical principles and to redefine his position in relation to some of the important issues of his time. Some modern historians have accused Mather of opportunism in shifting his position on such issues as church membership during this period. However, three sermons published in the early 1680's—two in 1680 and one in 1684—show that the change in his vision of the nature of God's church in New England and the character of man's relationship to God was difficult and gradual. For example, in *Returning to God* (1680), there emerges an important difference in the way Mather handled typological parallels. Although he still had recourse to the Old Testament for types of the situation in New England, he no longer went to his earlier extremes in finding relationships between these types and the second and third generations. He now presented these figures only as scriptural examples, as "lessons," not prophecies, for New England. He said that the calamities that fell upon the Hebrews need not fall upon the colonists so long as they would show their willingness to return to God.[20]

The most striking demonstrations of the changes in Mather's message and language appeared in two works published in 1686. Both revealed his endorsement of the return to the use of Old Testament types in order to illuminate the events in the New Testament rather than those of New England history, and they indicated his acceptance of the figure of Christ as the image of the deity that would dominate New England Puritanism for the next decade. The title alone, *The Greatest Sinners Exhorted and Encouraged to Come to Christ and that Now without Delaying,* disclosed Mather's new emphasis upon New Testament salvation. He left no question about his new position: "The Law *must be preached, inasmuch as thereby is the* Knowledge of Sin *without which men will never be duly Sensible of their need of* Christ. *But it is the* Gospel (*and not the Law*) *which is* the world of Faith."[21] Instead of choosing his text from Isaiah or Jeremiah, he found his meaning in Christ's words in John 6: 37: "And him that come to me, I will in no wise cast him out." He focused upon Christ the savior instead of upon a patriarchal God the Father to be feared.

In 1686 he published a collection of sermons on the nature of Christ, *The Mystery of Christ Opened and Applied,* a work frequently compared with Edward Taylor's *Christographia.* After a "Preface" in which Mather reprimanded his fellow preachers for leaving the people in ignorance and confusion about the meaning of the New Dispensation and Christ's life, he attempted to rectify some misunderstand-

[20] Increase Mather, *Returning to God the Great Concernment of A Covenant People* (Boston, 1680), p. 2. See also *The Divine Right of Infant Baptism* (Boston, 1680), and *The Doctrine of Divine Providence Opened and Applied* (Boston, 1684).

[21] Increase Mather, *The Greatest Sinners Exhorted and Encouraged to Come to Christ and that Now Without Delaying* (Boston, 1686), "To the Reader," p. 1.

ings about Christ. His opening sermon bore the comforting title, "There is a Covenant of Redemption." Here Mather again defined the important difference between Old and New Testament times. The words of the wrathful Father and the Laws of the Old Testament do not apply to Christians in the same way that they applied to the Hebrews: "JESUS is better than *Moses*. The *New*-Testament than the *Old*. . . . It is better being a Christian than a Jew."[22] Although the Old Testament Law still "cryeth and says, This is a poor guilty sinner, let him be *condemned* for ever," Mather assured his audience that "the blood of Christ cries *louder* and says, All his sins are satisfied for, and therefore let him be *pardoned*, and his soul live for ever" (p. 151). Under the new dispensation the mediation of Christ had become the believer's protection against the anger of the Father. When, therefore, the Christian arrived in heaven, he would be greeted and defended by his mediator and redeemer: "By Him we have *Access unto the Father*. Jesus the *Son of* GOD does as it were take the believing soul by the hand, and leadeth him into the *Presence*-Chamber. He opens the door for him, and presents him before the *Father of Glory*, and says 'Behold O Father, Here is a soul that I died for' " (p. 151). Thus, with Christ now established as the leader of the New World, and with the members of the churches of New England assured of their salvation in Christ, Increase Mather became convinced that the sacrifice of the Son of God had reconciled the children of the rising generations with the Father: "God the Father has received full Satisfaction in the Obedience of His Son, Jesus Christ" (p. 157).

During the 1680's the figure of God the Father became less threatening, and his actions appeared more explicable and benevolent. One minister explained that in all he does "God is a rational Agent aiming at a special mark . . . [and thus] we may understand much of the loving kindness of

22 Increase Mather, *The Mystery of Christ Opened and Applyed* (Boston, 1686), p. 117.

the Lord." [23] The difficulties God had sent his people were no longer interpreted as proof of God's departure but as evidence of His special favor: "Crosses and troubles of themselves [are not] an Argument of God's hatred, but rather a token of his love, and a witness of our Adoption."[24] As the image of God the Father became more benign and abstract, the figure of Christ gained in splendor. In rich and ornate imagery the preachers presented Christ as the hero who had interceded with the Father to win a Covenant of Redemption for his people in New England. The ministers explained that in the past there had been "a controversy" between the people and God and "no possibility on our part to pacify the Anger of God," but "Christ interposed himself as our Mediator . . . to Reconcile and make peace between God and us."[25]

With the image of the fearful deity supplanted by the figure of the merciful and gracious Son, the New England churches began to lose their character as places to be avoided by sinners and feared by children. Now the ministers sought to have the people think of religion as a refuge from fears and trials. As Samuel Willard said, when "there is little peace to be expected in or from the world . . . happy [are] those Souls who are got into this Rock."[26] John Higginson declared that in his church Christ gives His people "a Sovereign Cordial to preserve their hearts from the malignities and venome and poison of all the troubles of the world."[27] Those who were rooted securely in the church of Christ could expect "Peace in general [by which] we are to understand Prosperity, and Happiness, consisting in the absence of all Evil and presence all of good."[28] Not

[23] James Allin, *Serious Advice to Deliver One from Sickness* (Boston, 1679), pp. 6–7.
[24] Richard Standfast, *A Little Handful of Cordial Comforts for a Fainting Soul* (Boston, 1690), p. 32.
[25] John Higginson, *Our Dying Savior's Legacy of Peace* (Boston, 1686), p. 11.
[26] Samuel Willard, "To the Reader," in John Higginson, *Our Dying Savior's Legacy of Peace* (Boston, 1686).
[27] Higginson, *Dying Savior*, p. 2.
[28] *Ibid.*, p. 3.

only did Christ protect his people against the threatening external enemies, but his peace calmed the inner forces as well; for those who abode with him "the Conscience is pacified, the heart quieted, the will Satisfied, the Affections well pleased, and the whole soul at rest in *God*."[29]

Without question the real virtuoso of the new themes and language of the sermons of the last decades of the century was the vigorous young minister Cotton Mather (1663–1728). In the sermons he preached between 1686 and 1695, Mather was indefatigable in offering encouragement to his people. Despite all the trials New England endured during those years, Mather was unshakable in his conviction that God's people in America were destined for glory on earth and in heaven. Cotton Mather firmly believed that he had been sent on a special mission by God to lead his own and his father's generations out of their years of confusion and doubt and into a new time that would see the coming of Christ and the establishment of the New Jerusalem in America.

The sermons of Mather's early years were charged with millenarian optimism as he tried to dazzle his listeners with a vision of promised glory for New England. In his interpretation of the typological analogue, the people of New England had never been the cause of the colony's hardships. The forces of evil outside the garden had jealously attempted to wreck God's plan. But in spite of the efforts of all New England's enemies, the people had triumphed: "The Vine which God here *Planted*" had taken "*deep root, and filled the land, so that it sent its Boughs unto the* Atlantic *Sea* Eastward, *and its Branches unto the* Connecticut *River* Westward, *and the Hills were covered with the Shadow thereof*."[30] Thus Mather confidently told his people: "We shall soon Enjoy *Halcyon Days* with all the *Vultures* of Hell *Trodden under our Feet*."[31] In the early

---

[29] *Ibid.*, p. 10.

[30] Cotton Mather, *The Wonders of the Invisible World* (Boston, 1693), pp. 13–14.

[31] *Ibid.*, p. 14.

years of the colony the ministers had frequently expressed the hope that New England might one day become the scene of Christ's triumphant descent to His New Jerusalem. But it was the chiliastic Cotton Mather who so clearly and emphatically expressed the belief that the glorious day was at hand and that New England was certain to be the site of the New Jerusalem: the coming of the Lord was not "a Metaphor," young Mather declared, it was "the Next Thing that is to be Look'd for."[32] The themes and language of Mather's early writings were designed to infuse all New Englanders with religious certainty and a new national pride.

Cotton Mather looked back upon the difficult years of New England's "decline" as a time when "all Debauchery was coming in among us like a mighty Flood. . . . We were in a *Sea of Fire* miserably scorched and scalded, and yet it was *mingled with Ice* . . . there was no getting out."[33] In those perilous days the people were right to fear God's departure and to cry out, "*Return we beseech thee O God!*" (*WW*, p. 43). But he was certain that the period of trials had passed for God's people: "And now behold He is *Returned* [to us]" (*WW*, p. 43). He promised his congregation that "a Day" was soon to be expected when "*the Son of Man shall appear . . .* [when] *The Lord shall consume that wicked one with the breath of his mouth, . . . with the brightness of his coming* (*WW*, pp. 3–4). When Governor Andros was overthrown and the Glorious Revolution had ended the reign of England's popish James II, Mather took these events as signs of "*the Dawnings of that day*" (*WW*, p. 4).

In this exuberant tone of millennial hope Mather introduced the members of the established second generation and the young people of his own third generation to a new theme of national salvation. In the preface to one of his

[32] Cotton Mather, quoted in Perry Miller, *From Colony to Province*, p. 188.

[33] Cotton Mather, *The Wonderful Works of God Commemorated* (Boston, 1690), p. 43.

sermons that he dedicated "To my Country," he declared, "Our *Good God* will not *ever* . . . Remove the People which is now enriching this part of the New World, for *Another Nation* to succeed in the room thereof."[34] Whenever Cotton Mather compared America to the other countries of the world, he always found that "there is no Land in the Universe more free from the debauching and the debasing Vices of Ungodliness" than his own.[35] Only New England "enjoys these Dews of Heaven when the rest of the world is dry,"[36] for the people on this "little spot of Ground . . . *have known* [Christ's love] above all the Families of the earth."[37]

Because the change in Increase Mather's thought at first appears strikingly rapid and complete, it has raised questions about his intellectual integrity. However, the process of development of his religious message—which became obvious about 1678 and culminated in 1685 and 1686—must be viewed in the larger context of the general shift in the meaning of Puritan theology and the form of biblical interpretation practiced in New England. Such developments had begun to receive expression in the works of some ministers as early as the late 1660's. Increase Mather strongly resisted the trend of the new theology for nearly a decade before he began to recognize the necessity for striking new chords in the hearts of the people.

Similarly, the spiritual transformation which occurred with the second generation was not so sudden nor so political as it may seem. The religious zeal and political confidence evident in the revolt against Governor Andros in Massachusetts in 1689 were rooted in, and nourished by, a new spiritual assurance which the ministers had preached throughout the decade. With the shift in the role of the second generation from enforced passivity toward active leadership, the meaning of the Puritan sermon had also

[34] Cotton Mather, *The Serviceable Man* (Boston, 1690), p. 2 of preface.
[35] Cotton Mather, *Wonders of the Invisible World*, p. 11.
[36] Cotton Mather, *The Call of the Gospel* (Boston, 1686), p. 24.
[37] *Ibid.*

changed. Gradually, the ministers ceased their lament of the lethargy of the rising generation and their exhortations to weep and mourn over New England's decline. For the ministers and people alike, the Old Testament types of Israel and the image of an angry God now had their greatest imaginative powers as they figured forth the smiling face of Christ and the promise of national salvation.

Significantly, the writers of the revolution found that the traditional verbal patterns—the imagery, religious metaphors, and biblical types—continued to hold vital meaning for Americans well into the eighteenth century. For example, the idea of slavery to England was personified into a demonic figure described in the imagery the Puritans had used to depict Satan. Some writers employed simple biblical types to characterize the patriots as Joshua and Moses and King George as the Whore of Babylon; others presented elaborate exegesis of biblical narratives as lessons and prophecies for America. Reflecting upon such an interpretation, John Adams noted in his diary that "America is Joseph; the King's Lords and Commons, Joseph's father and brethren. Our father sold into Egypt."[38] Even Thomas Paine made extensive use of biblical typology throughout *Common Sense*, opening with a long explication of the story of the Midianites as proof that "the Almighty hath here entered his protest against monarchical government."[39] By refurbishing this richly symbolic language, the Revolutionary War writers discovered a crudely formed national mythology rooted in Puritan eschatology and expressive of the persistent hold of typology upon the American imagination.

[38] *The Works of John Adams*, ed. C. F. Adams (Boston, 1850–1856), 2, 197.
[39] *Basic Writings of Thomas Paine*, ed. Richard Huett (New York, 1942), p. 14.

## TYPOLOGY AND MILLENNIAL ESCHATOLOGY
## IN EARLY NEW ENGLAND

THE subject of this chapter is millennial eschatology in eighteenth-century American writing—primarily the role of typology in defining that millennial vision. The most prominent spokesman of Calvinist millennialism in eighteenth-century America was Jonathan Edwards, and much of what Edwards said concerning the millennium lies buried in the language of biblical typology, through which he interpreted Scripture and by which he understood God's revealed will in both the book of nature and the Old and New Testaments. It is the thesis of this essay that American millennial writers of the seventeenth and eighteenth centuries reflect the tensions present in the transformation of typology from a literal and historical exegesis of Scripture to an allegorical symbolism, but that they restore to typology the authority of prophecy.

Although primary loyalties were to colony and empire in 1750, America was about to become a new nation, and the images of emerging nationalism prominent in the literature indicate how strongly a governing conception of civil union was challenging earlier Puritan visions of theocracy and religious uniformity. The ministers reflect the insecurity of this transformation by recalling the glories of the past while they deplore the degeneracy of the present. The millennial writers, however—especially the New-Light Calvinists of the Great Awakening—were able to insure continuity in their visions of history by establishing their future expectations in the language of the biblical past. On the one hand, they gave precision and specificity to arguments concerning the millennium by anchoring their visionary constructions in scriptural typology and the language of biblical prophecy. On the other, some ministers were able to develop new ways of understanding the future by restoring prophetic value to typological figures that they found not only in Scripture but also in nature. Moreover, the prophetic correspondences were developed by a wide variety of writers.

For example, the librarian and jurist James Winthrop developed a series of exegetical treatises that attempted to bring contemporary history into relation with ancient revelation. In the spring of 1794, he wrote *An Attempt to Translate the Prophetic Part of the Apocalypse of St. John*, which established a traditional exegetical foundation for his later writings on the millennium. In 1795, he produced *A Systematic Arrangement of Several Scripture Prophecies Relating to Antichrist, with their Application to the Course of History*, in which he clearly showed a direct association between the ancient nations specifically mentioned in biblical prophecy and the new nations more recently created in the American and French Revolutions. Finally, in 1803, he published *An Attempt to Arrange, in the Order of Time, Those Scripture Prophecies yet Remaining to be Fulfilled*, in which Scripture prophecies were applied to contemporary history from 1792 to the end of human time.

Similarly, Thomas Bray developed a biblical argument justifying the American experience in *A Dissertation on the Sixth Vial* (Hartford, 1780), in whose brief introduction he says, "The Grand Scene is chiefly the vast Roman Empire; within the limits of which, and its appendages, the principal great and interesting scenes and changes of the church of Christ would be exhibited down to the time of the Millennium." The Roman Empire, in turn, is more specifically defined to include America:

By the appendages of the Roman Empire, I intend those acquisitions in any part of the world, to all, or either of those kingdoms, of which the empire was made up at the

time of the vision. This takes in America, which is un-
doubtedly comprehended in these prophecies. This is one
of the grand divisions of the earth, where great and interesting scenes, respecting the church of God, have already opened, and no doubt, still greater ones yet to
follow. . . . America is plainly comprehended, and has a
grand part, in some of the greatest and most interesting
scenes. (vii, n.)

Although there were contemporary movements in Europe
and in England attempting to prove a connection between
ancient prophecy and modern historical developments,
American millennialism enjoyed a special opportunity to
associate "signs of the times" with the revelations of Scripture. This opportunity was not lost on New England writers
of the Great Awakening and the pre-Revolutionary era.

I should offer one caveat preliminary to the remarks that
follow. It will appear to some that my treatment of millennialism leads inevitably to Alan Heimert's conclusion concerning the influence of the Great Awakening on the American Revolution—that somehow the enthusiasm released
through Calvinism in the 1730's and 1740's played a causal
role in determining the events of the 1760's and 1770's.
Though I admire certain aspects of Heimert's treatment of
the Awakening, it is not my intention to support his conclusions, nor would I consciously endorse the assertions of
Bernard Bailyn, Heimert's ideological rival and exponent
of the notion that a fear of conspiracy against the colonies
was a primary cause of the outbreak of hostilities, and that
the colonists became convinced that the British government
was determined to destroy liberty both at home and abroad.
However, it is possible to examine certain patterns in eighteenth-century American thought that stress millennial
utopianism and to perceive in those patterns a convenient
ideology for the revolutionary psychology—all without concluding that the American Revolution necessarily grew out
of the Great Awakening and the psychological climate the
Awakening generated.

I

As recently as April, 1974, "causal ideology" as an approach to this period was discredited by two demographic and statistical social historians, Thomas Archdeacon of the University of Wisconsin and Maris Vinovskis of the University of Michigan. Their arguments were directed primarily against Bernard Bailyn, but the conclusions they drew argue against our assuming that either the ministers' sermons or the radical pamphlets had much to do with causing the outbreak of revolutionary hostilities. "Historians have long been engaged in a debate over the relative importance of political ideas and of socio-economic conditions in propelling the American colonists to revolt against the English mother country . . . and the proponents of ideological interpretations and those of social or economic explanations have alternately enjoyed periods of dominance in the historical discipline."[1] But historians have not successfully demonstrated that either ministers or rationalist pamphleteers overshadowed social and economic causes; rather as Alan Heimert has done, they have illuminated certain ideological patterns that reflected (more than they controlled) the emerging revolutionary ethos. One of these patterns was millennial typology as the eighteenth-century American ministers understood it.

Even as New England society was being transformed from a Puritan theocracy to political republicanism, the ministers' writings and sermons—all widely distributed from pulpit and press—developed a millennial utopianism that is rooted in traditional Scripture promises. By employing typology, a special kind of prophetic system emphasizing the value of Old Testament figures as adumbrations of Christ and his kingdom, they restored to exegesis the authority of prophecy at a time when many theologians were busy looking for allegorical symbols throughout the

1 Maris Vinovskis and Thomas Archdeacon, "Some Versions of the Causes of Revolution in America," unpublished paper delivered at the April, 1974, meeting of the Organization of American Historians, Denver, Colorado, manuscript page 3.

Bible. In so doing, the millennial thinkers stressed the historical and literal veracity of Scripture, extending the tradition begun by the Puritans in England and reinforced by John Cotton, Thomas Shepard, and the Mathers in New England. Moreover, they provided the early American imagination with a symbolic mythology and a prophetic force that allowed writers to predict future events through a process of historical analogies.[2]

The tradition of typological and prophetic language extending from scriptural figures to more recent images, like Freneau's graphic description of the millennium in *The Rising Glory of America*, was critically important to early America since it provided a foundation for arguments about the nature of America's destiny. For seventeenth- and eighteenth-century American Puritans, who placed faith in the truth of Scripture and whose beliefs about the future depended on their understanding of God's dispensations in the past, the revelations of the Bible were interpreted both *figuratively* and *literally*, with early emphasis on the restricted boundaries of biblical description and the rules governing typological exegesis. They saw in the Bible a *linear* teleology, with God leading his chosen people from Babylon to Jerusalem through the perils of earthly existence. However, through an evolving awareness of the cyclical patterns in human history and through a perception of themselves as the New English Israel, instituted to continue God's providential design, the later Calvinists like Joseph Bellamy and Jonathan Edwards developed a *spiraling* vision of the future and of post-Reformation history. More important, they saw in America not only the progressive fulfillment of scriptural promises, but a conclusion to God's plan and a locus for the building of the earthly Jerusalem,

[2] The tradition of exegesis in which the authority of Scripture governs the movement of typology from historical prophecy to static metaphor would include John Cotton, Thomas Shepard, Samuel, Increase, and Cotton Mather (though Cotton less than his predecessors), Thomas Bray, and the nineteenth-century adventist leader named William Miller. See also Robert E. Shalhope, "Toward a Republican Synthesis: The Emergence of an Understanding of Republicanism in American History," *William and Mary Quarterly*, 3rd series, 29 (1972), 49–80.

the "New heaven and new earth" prophesied by Isaiah. For these "New Lights," as the Edwards party was called, history would culminate in the establishment of the millennial kingdom of God so that the distinctions between heaven and earth would ultimately disappear. Throughout the two centuries from 1650 to 1850, the image of America as a millennial paradise was used by writers to assure Americans that they were about to inherit the earth. Secular and religious writers alike shared the mythology of the Bible, and the prophetic declarations of Daniel, Ezekiel, and Revelation gave some specific details of the coming events. Much less well-known were those images of the future provided by typology as it was employed by the writers of pre-Revolutionary America.[3]

The prophetic writers of old had been able to develop a beatific vision of the millennium by transmitting the contents of revelatory visions, and the commentators of the early church reinforced this eschatology by viewing the Scriptures as a progressive series of inspired dispensations, all of which would culminate in fulfillment at the end of human time. Recent studies provide grounds for linking this tradition of interpretation to exegetical customs prominent in England during the late Middle Ages and Renaissance.[4] By extending the Puritan emphasis on a typological exegesis

[3] For a discussion of typology as an exegetical system, see G.W.H. Lampe and K. J. Woolcombe, *Essays on Typology*, Studies in Biblical Theology Series (Naperville, Illinois, n.d.); Thomas M. Davis, "The Traditions of Puritan Typology," in Sacvan Bercovitch, ed., *Typology and Early American Literature* (Amherst, 1972), pp. 11–47; and Mason I. Lowance, "Samuel Mather and New England Typology," introduction for Samuel Mather, *The Figures or Types of the Old Testament* (London, 1705; New York, 1969), pp. v–xxvi. [See also the notes to the essays by Froehlich, Roche, Lewalski, and Zwicker.–Ed.]

[4] The biblical prophecies of the millennium are varied, but a few central passages are repeated without end by early American writers. They are: Isa. 65: 17–25; Dan. 12: 12–13; Rev. 20: 1–3, 7; and Ps. 90: 4, which reads, "For a thousand years in thy sight, are but as yesterday when it is past, and as a watch in the night." The passage from Psalms is particularly important for early American chiliasm, since the writers were able to argue a historical scheme commencing over four thousand years before Christ and culminating sometime in the early nineteenth century. See Marjorie Reeves. *The Influence of Prophecy in the Later Middle Ages* (Oxford, 1969), pp. 295–305.

of Scripture and history, one by which the authority of the past could be employed to understand the process of the future, American millennial writers posited convincing conclusions about the nature of America's destiny, and, as Archdeacon and Vinovskis have demonstrated, there is statistical evidence to support at least the dissemination of these ideas from the pulpits of New England in 1750. Even while the eschatological forces of typology and prophecy were gradually transformed from the conservative, historical, and linear teleology prominent in the early seventeenth-century commentaries to the more allegorical and Platonic imagery found in the eighteenth century, most advocates of the American millennium rooted their conclusions firmly in Scripture-oriented exegesis that allowed little variation from a designated scriptural pattern. Even so secular a writer as Philip Freneau employed biblical eschatology to describe the coming fulfillment of America's promise:

> And when a train of rolling years are past,
> (So sung the exiled seer in Patmos isle)
> A new Jerusalem, sent down from heaven,
> Shall grace our happy earth,—perhaps this land,
> Whose ample bosom shall receive, though late,
> Myriads of saints, with their immortal king,
> To live and reign on earth a thousand years,
> Thence called *Millennium*. Paradise anew
> Shall flourish, by no second Adam lost,
> No dangerous tree with deadly fruit shall grow,
> No tempting serpent to allure the soul
> From native innocence.—A *Canaan* here,
> Another *Canaan* shall excel the old,
> And from a fairer Pisgah's top be seen.
> No thistle here, nor thorn, nor briar shall spring,
> Earth's curse before: the lion and the lamb
> In mutual friendship linked, shall browse the shrub
> And timorous deer with softened tygers stray
> O'er mead, or lofty hill, or grassy plain;
> Another Jordan's stream shall glide along,

And Siloah's brook in circling eddies flow:
Groves shall adorn their verdant banks, on which
The happy people, free from toils and death,
Shall find secure repose. No fierce disease,
No fevers, slow consumption, ghastly plague,
(Fate's ancient ministers) [shall] again proclaim
Perpetual war with man: fair fruits shall bloom,
Fair to the eye, and sweeter to the taste;
Nature's loud storms be hushed, and seas no more
Rage hostile to mankind—and, worse than all,
The fiercer passions of the human breast
Shall kindle up to deeds of death no more,
But all subside in universal peace.
Such days the world,
And such **AMERICA** at last shall have
When ages, yet to come, have run their round,
And future years of bliss alone remain.[5]

The images of the last days drafted by these harbingers of the millennium were generally conservative in their development of scriptural patterns, and they employed some traditional methods of typological exegesis by which a type or figure would anticipate a future event in a linear and historical continuum. Although contemporary pressures on the language to abandon a literal reading of Scripture for a figurative and allegorical interpretation were increasingly strong, the millennial visions developed out of very narrow scriptural contexts, and some echoed earlier assessments of the end of the world. If the piety of New England was truly declining as ministerial hermeneutics turned toward the jeremiad, then the imagery of eschatology held even more firmly to those traditional patterns of exegesis by which commentators had understood the last days from the time of the primitive church. Put another way, "if the figure most often repeated in the sermons of the late seventeenth-

5 Philip Freneau and Hugh Henry Brackenridge, "The Rising Glory of America," as edited by Fred Lewis Pattee, *The Poems of Philip Freneau* (New York, 1963), 1, 83–84.

century was the departing of the father, usually symbolized by the abandonment of New England by God the Father, the most prominent figure during the eighteenth century was the eschatological symbol of the millennium, usually figured by anticipation of the return of the son."[6] These mythopoeic and archetypal symbols were employed successfully by the early writers to produce a systematic vision of the future of New England that was based on the patterns discernible in her biblical and historical past.

At the same time, the Great Awakening and Jonathan Edwards produced a revitalized typology optimistically transformed to explore the prophetic figures of the natural world. Though rooting their conclusions in scriptural parallels, the Calvinists argued an eschatology derived from prophetic images found in nature and current events, so that the millennial expectation became less a fear of the judgment than an awareness of God's transforming power over men's hearts. During the mid-eighteenth century, and just before the American Revolution, the force of the prophetic arguments was intense and provided reassertions of America's future in the writings of Edwards and his disciples, Joseph Bellamy, Timothy Dwight, and David Austin.[7] This late emphasis on typology and the millennium continued into the nineteenth century, where it may be found in the adventist treatises of William Miller and in the writings of Joseph Smith and the Mormons.

## II

Although a comprehensive survey of interpretations surrounding the millennium would be much too broad for the

[6] Emory Elliott, *Power and The Pulpit in Puritan New England* (Princeton, 1975), p. 105. See also Robert Scholes, *Structuralism in Literature* (New Haven, 1973), particularly ch. 1, "Structuralism as a Method," and ch. 4, "The Mythographers: Propp and Levi-Strauss"; and Richard Noland, *Psychological Approaches to Literature* (forthcoming).

[7] The symbolic value of the American Revolution was not lost on those advocates of the millennium who saw in America an opportunity to promote the new nation as a divinely sanctioned society. See Sacvan Bercovitch, "The Image of America: from Hermeneutics to Symbolism," *Bucknell Review*, 20 (Fall, 1972), 7.

scope of this essay, certain fundamental patterns are important to an understanding of millennial typology. From the time of the early church, there has been a controversy over whether the thousand years would be a "literal" *and* historical experience, or a "spiritual" one signifying the end of the world. Generally, the literalists held that Christ would personally come to earth to reign during the millennium and that the saints could look forward to a rebuilding of the temple and city of Jerusalem, the reinhabitation of the land of Israel by the Jews, following their conversion, and to the investiture of all the risen elect with a kingly pre-eminence over the remnant nations of the world. This chiliasm was shared by Joseph Mede and Increase Mather, both of whom looked forward to a Judgment that was to precede the millennium of Christ's personal glory. This tradition persisted throughout the eighteenth century and reappeared in the adventist prophecies of the Millerites in the 1840's.

Opposed to this position is the "spiritual" or "allegorical" view, which held that the millennium would consist of a spiritual transformation of the world, during which Christ was to reign in spirit but not in person. Like the literalists, the spiritualists viewed the happy paradise as being a future state, but they argued that man's estate would become so blessed that a perfect society of gathered saints could constitute the visible church of Christ on earth even before the Second Coming and Judgment. Both groups embraced advocates of the utopian view of America as a future paradise, a theological idea that bore secular fruit in the edenic, pastoral visions of the United States so popular in the early nineteenth century. They also supplied a host of metaphors that reappear in the mythology of America's wilderness from the time of the earliest settlements to the Civil War.[8] For example, Thomas Bray, a literalist who

8 Among modern studies occupied with the themes of wilderness and pastoral, usually without reference to scriptural foundations, we may include Perry Miller, *Errand into the Wilderness* (Cambridge, 1956); R.W.B. Lewis, *The American Adam, Innocence and Tradition in the Nineteenth Century* (Chicago, 1955); and Henry Nash Smith, *The Virgin Land, the American West as Symbol and Myth* (Cambridge, 1950); and Leo Marx, *The Machine in the Garden* (New York, 1964).

argued the personal return of Christ in his exegesis of *Revelation*, implored his readers:

> Let your faith and hope, O believer, be strong in the divine promises; they shall be all accomplished in their season. Although the daughter of Zion may be covered with a cloud, and be in a wilderness state, yet the Lord himself is her *Light*, and her *God her Glory; and Salvation will be Appointed for Walls and Bulwarks*. The time is coming when Jehovah will dry up the rivers of her persecuting enemies, and make the *Depths of the Sea Away for the Ransomed to Pass Over*; Thereafter, the *Ransomed* of the *Lord* shall *Return, and Come With Singing unto Zion, and Everlasting joy shall* be upon their Heads.[9]

Samuel Sherwood, Bray's contemporary, actually observed in his own time the fulfillment of scriptural promises by citing current events and the growth of the church in the American wilderness:

> . . . her degree of peace and quiet rest has been greater than she has ever known since she has had existence and being. When that God, to whom the earth belongs, and the fulness thereof, brought his church into this wilderness, as on eagle's wings, by his king, protecting providence, he gave this good land to her, to be her own lot and inheritance forever. He planted her as a pleasant and choice vine; and drove out the Heathen before her. He has tenderly nourished and cherished her in her infant state, and protected and preserved her amidst innumerable dangers . . . God has, in this American quarter of the globe, provided for the woman and her seed, a fixed and lasting settlement and habitation, and bestowed it upon her, to be her own property forever. . . . He was not conducting them from a land of liberty, peace, and tranquility, into a state of bondage, persecution, and distress; but

[9] Thomas Bray, *A Dissertation on the Sixth Vial* (Hartford, 1780), pp. 103–104.

on the contrary, he wrought out a very glorious deliverance for them, and set them free from the cruel hand of tyranny and oppression, by executing his judgments in a most terrible and awful manner, on the Egyptians, their enemies, and was, by his kind providence, leading them to the good land of Canaan, which he gave them for an everlasting inheritance.[10]

The thousand-year period during which the forces of evil will be bound and the righteous saints will enjoy abundance and plenty, peace, and tranquility became so dominant an image in sermons and literature of the eighteenth century that commentators saw in contemporary events "signs of the times" which indicated the beginning of the grand and prosperous period.[11]

It is also important to clarify the two schools of thought denominated "premillennialism" and "postmillennialism." Put simply, the premillennial interpretation held that Christ's Second Coming would occur before the millennium could begin, whereas the postmillennial view held that Christ would come at the end of the thousand years of peace and prosperity.[12] Obviously, there is a close relationship between the literal and premillennial, the spiritual and postmillennial, but the association is not so clear as it might seem. The tensions between attempts to maintain a literal veracity in prophetic interpretation and the tendency to endow biblical figures with allegorical and metaphorical

---

[10] Samuel Sherwood, *The Church's Flight into the Wilderness* (New York, 1776), pp. 22–46.

[11] In 1794, David Austin brought together under one cover several millennial documents that argued the perfection of society as a sign of the coming millennium. He included Jonathan Edwards, *The Millennium, or, The Thousand Years of Prosperity, promised to the Church of God in the Old Testament and in the New, shortly to commence and to be Carried to Perfection under the Auspices of Him, who, in the Vision, was Presented to St. John*; and Joseph Bellamy, *Prophecy of the Millennium*, which had originally been published in Boston in 1758. See Austin, *The Millennium* (Elizabethtown, N.J., 1794).

[12] James Davidson, "Searching for the Millennium: Problems for the 1790's and 1970's," *New England Quarterly*, 5 (1972), 242.

value were present in both pre- and postmillennialism throughout the seventeenth and eighteenth centuries. A conservative tradition including John Cotton, Thomas Shepard, Increase, Samuel, and Cotton Mather, Thomas Bray, Samuel Langdon, Abraham Cummings and even William Miller attempted to hold together a view of Scripture and history that leaned heavily on biblical typology for "proof" and resulted in a premillennial eschatology. Meanwhile, Jonathan Edwards and his postmillennial followers were also Calvinists who argued from a strong scriptural foundation, but they succeeded in transforming typology by renewing the prophetic authority lost in the static imagery of the jeremiad. A consequence of their success was the resurrection of typology as a prophetic language, one that could describe their vision of a glorious society soon to be built on earth.

It is the language of the scriptural allusions to the millennium that allowed commentators the paradoxical freedom to recreate the vision of the thousand years provided by Daniel and St. John, while restricting the boundaries of the vision to those scanty references contained in the Bible. Although the millennium was revealed in only a handful of prophetic scriptural verses, it has been one of the most broadly interpreted visions in the Judaeo-Christian tradition. Thus when the Puritans of the first two centuries in New England turned to their Bibles for assurance of the future fulfillment of those promises they regarded to be their right and legacy, they drew heavily upon typology to give their arguments the kind of literal authenticity that a typological adumbration would supply.

As recent scholarship has observed, the typological systems developed by New England writers from 1630 to 1650 were necessary precedents for their understanding of America's historic role in establishing the kingdom and planting the seeds of the New Jerusalem.[13] But the typology

[13] For discussions of typology among the first-generation writers see Jesper Rosenmeier, "With My Owne Eyes: William Bradford's *Of Plimouth Plantation*," and Richard Reinitz, "The Separatist Background

of the millennium and the rich imagery associated with it in early American writing have often been overlooked because millennialism, like typology, is an inexact prophetic system that needs constant clarification. Millennial symbols provided a host of interpretations for current events from the early New England Puritans to the Civil War, affirming that the pressure on language to explain historical movements arises not only out of the changes brought by the events themselves, but also out of the necessity for each generation to reconcile traditional scriptural mythology with contemporary developments in the interpretation of God's revealed will. For example, premillennial writing, with its emphasis on the Judgment, developed visions of the future with proofs derived from selected scripture prophecy. *The Day of Doom* by Michael Wigglesworth is such a narrative vision, with imagery drawn primarily from Daniel and Revelation. But Jonathan Edwards and his postmillennial disciples argued a historiography from the Scriptural types that placed the millennium before the judgment and put the Calvinists in the position of providing American theology with a radical justification for early nationalism, as Alan Heimert has demonstrated.[14] If the premillennial-

---

of Roger Williams' Argument for Religious Toleration," both in Bercovitch, *Typology and Early American Literature*. See also essays relating to the Cotton-Williams controversy: Sacvan Bercovitch, "Typology in Puritan New England: the Williams-Cotton Controversy Reassessed," *American Quarterly*, 19 (1967), 166–191; Jesper Rosenmeier, "The Image of Christ: the Typology of John Cotton" (Dissertation, Harvard University, 1965), and "The Teacher and the Witness: John Cotton and Roger Williams," *William and Mary Quarterly*, 3rd Ser., 25 (1968), 403–431; and "New England's Perfection: The Image of Adam and the Image of Christ in the Antinomian Crisis, 1634–1638," *William and Mary Quarterly*, 3rd ser., 27 (1970), 435–459.

[14] Alan Heimert, *Religion and the American Mind from the Great Awakening to the Revolution* (Cambridge, 1968), pp. 62–63. Heimert notes that "Edwards' achievement in placing the millennium on this side of the apocalypse was to provide Calvinism with a formula in which the good society would and could be attained solely through natural causes. But the aspect of creation involved in the Work of Redemption was, for Edwards, the supernatural realm—that portion of the universe which was above and beyond nature, consisting in

ism of the Mathers stressed the decline of contemporary
piety and the imminence of the judgment, Edwards argued
that the beauty and perfection revealed through nature
*and* Scripture to a regenerated perception was a prophetic
synecdoche of the future redemption of the world. Edwards and the New Lights, Jesper Rosenmeier reminds us,

> regarded man's life after rebirth as a vessel to be used
> by the Spirit. . . . The conviction that their present lives
> prophesied future fulfillments was the deepest impulse
> of the New Light movement. New Lights read their
> Bibles to understand what future realities God had
> revealed in the words and lives of His chosen peoples.
> And they used sermons, histories, poetry, autobiography
> and biography not to lament the present order as much
> as to propel their audiences towards the realization of
> the New Jerusalem.[15]

The Great Awakening aroused millennial spiritualism, and
Edwards' party showed that paradise could be realized in
America by a transformation of society and a restoration
of the human soul. Moreover, they justified their conclusions with scriptural arguments that extended the historical
boundaries of the typological system into the modern
world even while they explored the contemporary scene
for signs that the cycles of millennial revolution were about
to commence.

---

man's union and communion with God, or divine communications
and influences of God's spirit. The earthly kingdom of the Calvinist
Messiah was not of the natural, material world, but within men. It
consisted not in things external, but in happiness and the dominion
of virtue in the minds and hearts of mankind. The Work of Redemption was one with the regeneration of humanity; it depended on no
awful display of Divine power, no shattering of the physical creation,
but on the gradual restoration of the influences of the Holy Spirit
which had been withdrawn at the Fall." Obviously, the restoration
of typology was one of these influences.

15 Jesper Rosenmeier, "Jonathan Edwards and the Great Awakening," unpublished manuscript, pp. 10–11.

### III

The changes in typological reasoning during the seventeenth century resulted in a conservative restriction of the types to scriptural boundaries, although some liberal exegetes extended the figures to modern times through analogy and allegorical correspondence. The decline in piety so painfully evident in the jeremiads of the end of the century led writers to practice caution in their association of New England with Old Israel; the eschatological imagery of the early settlers had lost the prophetic force it had once enjoyed. But earlier, when John Cotton chose 2 Samuel 7: 10, as the text for *God's Promise to His Plantations*, he had been exploring the analogy between the departure of Winthrop's Puritans in April, 1630, and the movement of Old Israel out of Egyptian bondage into the Land of Canaan. "Moreover, I will appoint a place for my people Israel," the Scripture reads, "and I will plant them, that they may dwell in a place of their own, and move no more." As the individual soul is provided the grace to escape bondage in sin, so the nation Israel was to move from Egyptian bondage to a land of milk and honey. This "type" was not only a literal event; it was also a prefiguration of that eternal moment when Christ would lead his people out of bondage into eternal freedom. In the spiraling and progressive dispensations revealed to man about the future of God's saints, the New England Puritans figured prominently as a reincarnation of those primitive, prophetic, typological Israelites. And as they fulfilled the promises of Scripture in Cotton's exegesis, so they were also prophetic themselves of the dawning of a new day, one in which the saints would be gathered by Christ in a glorious moment when all peoples would speak the "language of Canaan."

Recent scholarship is filled with assessments of the role of this prophetic force in New England historiography. The Mathers are particularly prominent subjects in attempts to demonstrate the strong tradition of biblical metaphor that extends into the eighteenth century. Perry Miller observed that "the two Mathers were . . . possessed by the rule of the true apocalyptic spirit; they marched into the Age of Reason loudly crying that the end of the world was at hand."[16] Sacvan Bercovitch has shown how Cotton Mather fused a vision of his personal destiny with the future promise of New England, so that his desperate efforts to turn the city on a hill from Babylon into Jerusalem must be understood as part of the larger process of his personal millennial eschatology.[17] Emory Elliott argues that "Cotton Mather firmly believed that he had been sent on a special mission by God to lead his own and his father's generations out of their years of confusion and doubt and into a new time which would see the coming of Christ and the establishment of the New Jerusalem in America."[18] Moreover, many of the original documents produced by Increase and Cotton Mather reveal changes in their attitudes toward Scripture and its efficacy to support their views of the last days. Increase Mather explored the typical significance of Samson and David in *Meditations on the Glory of Jesus Christ*, concluding that their exemplary virtues had been fulfilled and abrogated by Christ's earthly ministry; he also argued the importance of typology as a prophetic system in *The Mystery of Israel's Salvation*, which treated the future of the Jewish nation at the time of the millennium.[19] "It is evident," he wrote, "that the salvation of Israel will be wonderful, if we compare it with those former deliverances which in the days of old have been vouchsafed unto the Tribes of Israel. It is indeed true, that God hath in former times bestowed more eminent and wonderful salvations

[16] Perry Miller, *The New England Mind: from Colony to Province* (Cambridge, Mass., 1967), pp. 185–188.

[17] Sacvan Bercovitch, "Images of Myself: Cotton Mather in His Writings 1683–1700," in Everett Emerson, ed., *Major Writers of Early American Literature* (Madison, 1972), pp. 93–151, and *From Horologicals to Chronometricals* in *Literary Monographs* (Madison, 1970), pp. 1–126.

[18] Elliott, p. 189. [See also Elliott's essay in this volume.—Ed.]

[19] Increase Mather, *Meditations on the Glory of Jesus Christ* (Boston, 1705) and *The Mystery of Israel's Salvation* (Boston, 1699).

upon the Israelitish Nation than upon any Nation in the world . . . but because their deliverance was a TYPE of this, therefore this will be the more eminent and wonderful, for the TYPE must needs come short of the ANTITYPE."[20] Similarly, Cotton Mather anticipated the imminent return of Christ and a literal fulfillment of the scriptural promises:

> Good News for the *Israel* of God, and particularly for His *New English Israel*. The Devil was never more let *loose* than in our Days; and it proves the *Thousand Years* is not very *far off. Shortly*, didst thou say, Dearest Lord! O Gladsome word! I may Sigh over *this* Wilderness, as *Moses* did over *his. We are consumed by thine Anger*, yet if God have a Purpose to make here a *Seat for any of Those Glorious Things, which are spoken of Thee, O Thou City of God*; then even thou, *O New-England*, are within a very little while of Better Dayes than ever yet have Dawn'd upon thee. *Our Lord Jesus Christ shall have the uttermost parts* of the Earth for His Possession, the last shall be the *first*, and the *Sun of Righteousness* come to shine *Brightest*, in Climates which it rose *Latest* upon.[21]

The historical metaphors adopted by the Mathers were primarily scriptural, arising out of their concern to identify for New England the peculiar providential role established for the saints in the first dispensation, which was revealed to a regenerate understanding through a proper interpreta-

---

[20] Increase Mather, *The Mystery of Israel's Salvation* (Boston, 1699), p. ix. Elliott shows how Mather, not when treating the millennium but when developing frightening images of the judgment, relied less on typology and used Scripture for metaphorical examples: "Although [Increase Mather] still went to the Old Testament for types of the situation in New England, he no longer pressed an obvious relationship between these types and the second generation. In *Returning to God*, he presented these figures only as scriptural examples, as "lessons," not prophecies for New England. He said that calamities that fell upon the Hebrews need not fall upon the colonists, if they would show their willingness to return to God" ("Generations in Crisis," 137).

[21] Cotton Mather, *Wonders of the Invisible World* (Boston, 1692) as quoted by Bercovitch, "Images of Myself," *Major Writers of Early American Literature*, p. 109.

tion of the biblical types and prophetic figures. The tensions present in the typology of Cotton Mather indicate the pressures on him to accommodate his traditional reading of Scripture to the revelations of God in the natural world, and the image-patterns of his writing associated with the New Jerusalem reinforce the central idea through which he explained how, in the cyclical process of history, New England might assume a role analogous to that of Old Israel in prophecy. One crucial passage from the *Biblia Americana* is particularly revealing of Mather's efforts to hold these forces in balance:

> *To Earthly Creatures this world is their own countrey, & their Father's house.* Tho' there are many places which they know little of, yett in general, they know what ye *World* is, and what its enjoyments are. Here they are at home, & with their *Kindred*; with people disposed like themselves. *Heaven* is a countrey more unknown to them, than *Canaan* was to *Abraham*. It is God that can discover the countrey unto us, & the way to it, as He led *Abraham*, into *Canaan*. Abraham's action is in the Scripture, made a Figure of a Christian's life in this world; who is but a *Pilgrim* and *Stranger* here. . . . Tho' the Patriarchs did certainly beleeve, that their posterity should inherit the *earthly Canaan*, yett they have understood *Better Things* contained in this promise, even an *Heavenly Countrey*, which they expected as their *Inheritance.*[22]

Mather here extends the biblical type into modern times not only by declaring its emblematic significance but also by showing how its typological promises are still to be fulfilled. Thus the prophetic value of the Old Testament figures was sustained even while commentators employed them as "meer metaphors and moral examples."

[22] Cotton Mather, *Biblia Americana*, II (n.p., n.d.). This unpaginated 6-volume folio manuscript Bible translation and commentary is housed by the Massachusetts Historical Society, Boston. I am grateful to Director Stephen Riley for permission to quote from it.

In the early years of the colony some ministers, like John Cotton, had expressed the hope that New England might one day become the scene of Christ's triumphant kingdom. But it was Cotton Mather's chiliasm that "clearly and emphatically expressed the belief that the glorious day was at hand and that New England was certain to be the site of the New Jerusalem: the coming of the Lord was not a 'metaphor,' he declared, 'it was the next thing to be looked for.' "23

IV

The primary concerns of the Mathers were to establish that the millennium had been prefigured in Scripture and to prove that it was about to take place by examining such signs of the times as the conversion of the Jews, an aspect of the millennial promise regarded as a crucial prerequisite by which the advent of the last things might be identified. But their chiliasm depended on assumptions provided earlier by Thomas Shepard and Samuel Mather. Because the Sabbath was considered by some to be a "type" of the millennial rest, and because all commentators freely used the concept of a day as a thousand years, the typology of the Sabbath figured centrally in arguments about the time of the approaching end.

Thomas Shepard carefully presented the case for the abrogation of Old Testament types of Christ's incarnation in *Theses Sabbaticae* (1649). He then proceeded to show how the types might still have efficacy in the scheme of world history, despite their abrogation by the coming of the flesh. The *Theses* provide exhaustive arguments for the

23 Elliott, pp. 189–90. Another obvious source of this chiliastic emphasis in the late seventeenth and early eighteenth centuries was Samuel Sewall's *Phaenomena quaedam Apocalyptica . . . or, Some Few Lines Towards a Description of the New Heaven, as it Makes to Those who Stand Upon the New Earth* (Boston, 1697). In his opening argument, Sewall declares: "The New Jerusalem will not straiten, and enfeeble; but wonderfully dilate, and invigorate Christianity in the several Quarters of the World, in Asia, in Africa, in Europe, and in America." The geographical argument was a prominent proof of America's destiny as the site for earthly kingdom.

conclusion of ceremonial, legal, and judicial types, but they also present a logically persuasive statement endorsing the moral authority inherent in the biblical figures, because they possess eternal and perpetual equity.

Although the distinction between moral perpetuity and exegetical typology in the figures of the Old Testament was not original to Shepard, his *Theses Sabbaticae* is the classic Puritan defense of the use of types in perpetuating the New England way. Shepard showed how the types are actually of two kinds, the "*typus fictus . . .* or *arbitrarius* (which is all one with a similitude)," and the "*typus destinatus . . .* purposely ordained to shadow out Christ."[24] The example Shepard elected to contrast the two kinds of types showed how the true types may only be observed under the Covenant of Grace:

> The Covenant of Works, by which Adam was to live, is directly contrary to the Covenant of Grace by Faith in Christ, (Rom. xi. 6) by which we are to live. Christ is revealed only in the Covenant of Grace, and therefore could not be so revealed in the Covenant of Works directly contrary thereunto. Adam therefore was not capable of any types then to reveal Christ unto him; of whom the first Covenant cannot speak, and of whom Adam stood in no need . . . hence, it follows, that he stood in no need of Christ or any revelation of him by the types; no, not to confirm him in that covenant.[25]

The central theme of the *Theses Sabbaticae* involves Shepard's effort to establish legitimate limits for typology under the Covenant of Grace, and his arguments seek to restore the significance of the Sabbath as it had been ordained by God in the Decalogue. Shepard did not deny that the types were originally instituted to shadow forth events and persons fulfilled in the earthly ministry of Christ; however, he refused to accept the view adopted by

24 Thomas Shepard, *Theses Sabbaticae*, ed. Thomas Albro, 2 vols. (Hartford, 1850), 1, pp. 163–164.
25 Shepard, 1, pp. 169–170.

his contemporaries who argued that the abrogation of the typical Sabbath in Christ was a termination of its efficacy for Christian history. He was careful to clarify the distinction between the Old and New Testament dispensations, and then distinguished equally carefully the moral value of the Sabbath from its typological significance:

> If therefore the Sabbath was given to Adam in innocency before all types, nay, before the least promise of Christ, whom such types must shadow forth, then it cannot be in its first and native institution typical and ceremonial, but moral; and therefore in its first and original institution of which we speak, it did not typify either our rest in Christ from sin in this life, or our rest with God in heaven in another life, or any other imagined rest which man's wit can easily invent and invest the Sabbath with. (2, 171)

Even if the Sabbath were considered typologically, Shepard argued, so that its ceremonial nature would have been abrogated in Christ's incarnation, its moral value was derived from its eternal institution in the providential scheme:

> But the question is . . . whether it be not therefore of perpetual and universal obligation, binding all Nations and persons in all ages, in their Hearts, Lives, Manners, to the observance thereof, as a part of that Holiness we owe to God, and which God required of all men according to the rules of moral equity; or, on the contrary, whether it be not rather a typicall, ceremoniall, figurative, and temporary precept, binding onely some persons, or that one nation of the Jews for some time, from obedience of which law, Christians (in respect of any law of God) are now exempted. (1, 35)

Shepard's answer to this question was that the Sabbath carries the whole authority of moral equity for Christians in all times, and his objective in the *Theses* was to solve once and for all the problem of justifying the institution in a society whose few ceremonies were being challenged by the

Antinomians as instituted extensions of the Old Testament types. The core of his arguments for the moral equity of the Sabbath consisted of his distinctions among the kinds of laws given under the Old Dispensation. Disclaiming a typical significance for the Sabbath in modern times, he emphasized strongly the moral equity inherent in the institution:

> *Thesis 38*: There were three sorts of laws which are commonly, known, and which were most eminently appearing among the Jews: 1. Moral. 2. Ceremoniall. 3. Judiciall.

> *Thesis 39*: The moral respected their manners as they were men, and are therefore called moral. The ceremonial respected them as a church, and as such a kind of church. The judicial as a commonwealth, and as that particular commonwealth. Moral laws were to govern them as a human society, ceremonial as a sacred society, judical as a civil society. (1, 51)

Shepard then indicated how the moral law was derived from the law of nature, and because it was divinely instituted, it had a perpetual value for Christian history and society that is eternal and continuous:

> *Thesis 40*: The moral law, contained in the decalogue, is nothing else but the law of nature revived, or a second edition and impression of that primitive and perfect law of nature, which in the state of innocency was engraven upon man's heart, but now again written upon tables of stone, by the finger of God. (1, 151)

The law of nature and the moral obligations of that law are to be obeyed because they were instituted to have eternal and perpetual value. The Sabbath belongs to both the moral *and* the ceremonial systems, and is therefore preserved under the continued efficacy of natural cycles.[26]

[26] The obligations of the Massachusetts Bay theocracy were then explained wholly in moral terms: "Now this law, thus revived and reprinted, is the decalogue, because most natural and suitable to hu-

Shepard's doctrine drew the Old and New Dispensations close together, minimizing their differences. He understood that the Sabbath may be an "accidental" or an "affixed" type, but this desgination is unimportant in comparison to its eternal, moral signification. If the Sabbath held ceremonial importance for the Jews of the Old Testament and its typological value was abrogated by Christ's incarnation, it was even more richly endowed with a moral equity that is perpetual and universal, complementary to the typological scheme. Since the first Sabbath was given before there was any real promise of Christ, that is, before the Fall, then "in its first and native institution, the Sabbath is not typicall and Ceremoniall but morall onely" (2, 165). Although the cermonies were "types and shadows of things to come and therefore being to cease when the body was come," because of its *natural* institution, the Sabbath continued to have value for the New English Israel.

Shepard's continuous efforts to distinguish between the *typus fictus* and the *typus destinatus* represented a conservative victory for exegesis, because it established clearly the boundaries of typology in the early theocracy. If the Sabbath was instituted before sin and could be typical only by accidental assignment, then its efficacy for New England had to be reasoned from a scriptural premise other than the typological system. But Shepard preserved the integrity of typology and also gave the Sabbath a perpetual, figurative prominence by relieving typology of the burden of providing moral and spiritual authority for sabbatical justification. The Old Testament types seemed to be securely in place, and the Sabbath continued to be celebrated, sanctified by God, and not abrogated or concluded by Christ.

---

man nature, when it was made most perfect; therefore, it is universal and perpetual; the substance also of this law being love to God and man, holiness towards God, and righteousness toward man. . . . Hence also this law must needs be moral, universal, and perpetual . . . the things commanded in this law are therefore commanded because they are good, and are therefore moral, unless any shall think that it is not good in itself to love God or man, to be holy or righteous" (1, 151–153).

Shepard's resolution of the sabbatical controversy was important because it extended morally, figuratively, and metaphorically, the value of the Old Testament into modern times. His argument was supported by others. Samuel Mather taught that the Sabbath had both moral and prophetic value, and he declared it to be typical:

> The general Notion of a Sabbath is a *time of Rest*. They had *three sorts of Sabbaths*: their *weekly Sabbath*, every seventh day; their *yearly Sabbath*, every seventh year; and their *great sabbatical Year*, reckoning seven times seven years, which was their *Jubilee*, every *fiftieth year*. In every one of which was something of a Shadow of things to come, the Apostle is express, *these things are a Shadow of Things to Come*.
> *Quest*. Wherein?
> *Answ.* 1. *Their weekly Sabbath on the seventh Day of the week*; this was partly *Moral* and *Perpetual*, considered as a seventh part of weekly time, sanctified and set apart by God from common use, for Man to rest from the Works of his weekly Calling, in imitation of God, and in remembrance of the great work of the Creation of the World. But tho' the Sabbath be *partly Moral*, and it must needs be so, seeing it is one of the *Ten Commandments*, . . . therefore *Adam* in his innocent and sinless Estate needed a Sabbath; and God sanctified this Day before the Fall of Man. . . .[27]

Unlike Shepard, Mather sought to establish both the moral and the typological significance of the sabbatical scheme, and to identify its figurative significance for the millennial kingdom:

> Yet the *Jewish* Sabbath was in *some Respects Ceremonial* and therefore it is abrogated, and the Christian Sabbath substituted instead thereof; and therefore the Holy Ghost

[27] Samuel Mather, *The Figures or Types of the Old Testament, Opened and Explained* (London, 1705), pp. 444–445.

here . . . reckons the Jewish Sabbaths in the same rank with the *New Moons* and yearly Festivals amongst the Shadows of good things to come; for it had some typical Respects and Uses, some ceremonial Rites and Observations annexed to it. (p. 445)

Among those "typical" uses Mather cited *"the Commemoration of their typical Redemption and Deliverance out of Egypt"* (p. 445). More important, he went on to argue that the Sabbath was indeed a "type" of rest, prefiguring the rest of Jesus in the grave and the eternal rest designed to be the reward of the saints: "As there was in the Jewish Sabbath a Commemoration of that typical Redemption out of *Egypt*, so secondly, it was a *typical Prefiguration of the Rest of the Body of Jesus Christ in the Grave that whole Day* . . ." (p. 446). The Christian Sabbath is established in the place of the abrogated Jewish Sabbath, and the cyclical pattern of prefiguration and fulfillment continues throughout history: "From all which you may see the Morality of the Sabbath considered as in general, together with the shadowy Nature of the Jewish Sabbath of the seventh Day, having these typical Respects and Relations annexed to it; and so therein you see the Grounds for the Abrogation of it, and of the Substitution of the Christian Sabbath instead thereof" (p. 446).

This was an important achievement. Millennial theology was a prominent prophetic force during the early stages of the colonial migrations and settlement, and it had enjoyed importance until the last three decades of the seventeenth century. In the rivalry between conservative and liberal typological commentators late in the century, however, the question of the Sabbath as a figure of the millennial rest became a critical focus that would later supply writers with a systematic, scriptural argument for the time and nature of the millennium. Typology and prophecy were obvious keys for understanding the relevance of the past for the present, and when applied to the cycles of history they also unlocked the secret mysteries of the future.

## V

One of the New Lights who assumed the typological justification for the sabbatical millennium was Joseph Bellamy, a follower of Jonathan Edwards in Bethlehem, Connecticut, who published some *Sermons on the Millennium* in 1758. Bellamy began cautiously by explaining the precise role of the types in prefiguring the events of the New Testament:

> Hitherto God had supported his People's Hopes chiefly with Promises, with verbal predictions; but from the Days of Moses to the Days of Solomon King of Israel, to assist his People's Faith, God did, besides repeated promises of the same Thing, by a great Variety of wonderful works shadow forth the glorious day; and at the same time shew, that he had sufficient Wisdom to accomplish the greatest designs. . . .[28]

Almost immediately, however, Bellamy extended the typological system to provide an argument for the time of the coming millennium:

> But when shall the Son of David reign? and the Church have Rest? When shall the cause of Truth and Righteousness thus prevail? Perhaps the very Time was designed to be shadowed forth in the Law of Moses, in the Institution of their holy days. The *Seventh Day*, said God, "The Seventh Day shall be a Sabbath of Rest, the Seventh Month shall be full of Holy Days, and the seventh Year shall be a Year of Rest;" So, perhaps, after *Six Thousand* years are spent in Labour and Sorrow by the Church of God, the Seventh-Thousandth shall be a Season of spiritual Rest and Joy, an Holy Sabbath to the Lord. And as God the Creator was *Six Days* in forming a confused Chaos into a beautiful world, and rested the *Seventh*; so God the Redeemer, after *Six Thousand* Years Labour in the Work of a New Creation, may rest on the *Seventh*,

[28] Joseph Bellamy, *Sermons on Several Subjects: The Millennium* (Boston, 1758), pp. 48–49.

and then Proclaim a General Liberty to an Enslaved
World. . . . And as surely as the Jews were delivered
out of the babylonish Captivity, and Babylon itself
destroyed; even so surely shall all these Things be accomplished in their Time. And mystical Babylon shall
"sink as a Mill-stone into the sea." (pp. 50–52)

In the long discussion that follows, David becomes a figure
of Christ's kingship in the millennial vision, and his kingdom in Jerusalem prefigures the New Jerusalem. Biblical
figures were extended into modern times prophetically and
typologically, and the sabbatical pattern liberated by
Thomas Shepard and christianized by Samuel Mather provided Bellamy and Edwards a foundation for numerological predictions about the time of the fulfillment of
millennial promises.[29]

For the Calvinists, the millennium seemed imminent, and
most broke with Samuel Hopkins over what they considered to be his Federalist-inspired postponement of the
millennium to the end of the nineteenth century.[30] But for
Abraham Cummings, a post-Revolutionary premillennial-
ist, the millennium was very near, and the prophetic image
of the sabbatical rest offered typological proof:

[29] Joseph Bellamy was by no means the only eighteenth-century
millennial commentator to give prominence to the role of typology.
Aaron Burr, president of Princeton, argued that the regenerate only
could understand the types, and that the elect, eventually, "shall
clearly see how the *Glorious Grace of the Gospel* was revealed under
all the *Types and Shadows of the Law.*" Meanwhile, however, when
God converses with his people, he retains a veil of mystery, "for the
internal Glories of his Ministration which were delivered in *Types
and Figures of Good Things to Come* were rendered obscure and
dark," by the carnal perceptions of fallen men, "by the *blindness and
Prejudices of their Carnal Hearts.*" Aaron Burr, *A Sermon Preached
Before the Synod of New York* (New York, 1756), pp. 8–11. See also
George Duffield, *A Sermon, Preached in the Third Presbyterian
Church in the City of Philadelphia* [Thursday, December 11, 1783]
(Philadelphia, 1784); Isaac Backus, *The Testimony of the Two Wit-
nesses, Explained and Improved* (Providence, 1786), pp. 42–43; and
Samuel Hopkins, *A Treatise on the Millennium* (Boston, 1793).
[30] Heimert, p. 114.

Under the old dispensation, the Jews had a Millennium in prospect as well as we. They were in constant expectation of a glorious time, in which holiness and happiness should be general, if not universal; but they considered that glorious time only as the continuation of their own dispensation, and expected that the nations would embrace their religion and their kind of government, that all flesh would worship at their temple, from one *New Moon* to another, and from one *Seventh Day Sabbath* to Another. They expected as a nation to have a portion of this promised glory with the rest of mankind. And in general it appears, that both the righteous and the wicked among them had the same leading sentiments on this subject. The nature of our dispensation was doubtless as well known to the Apostles when Christ arose as to any of the pious Jews; and yet they ask, Lord, wilt thou at this time restore again the kingdom of Israel? Of the like nature are the views and expectations of Christians in general as this day. THE MILLENNIUM IS AT HAND, SAY WE, TO MAKE OUR POSTERITY HAPPY, AND ALL NATIONS HAPPY, UNDER THE IMPERFECT GOVERNMENT OF MERE MEN, BY THEIR EMBRACING THE EXTERNALS AS WELL AS THE INTERNALS OF OUR RELIGION: THE MILLENNIUM WILL BE A GLORIOUS CONTINUANCE OF OUR OWN DISPENSATION.[31]

Though Cummings disagreed with Edwards by specifying the personal appearance of Christ in a premillennial dispensation, he argued the cyclical institution of types and figures in the progressive revelations of history:

Now, since it is allowed that our gospel glory typifies the millennium and that the destruction of the Jewish world typifies the destruction of the Christian world; with equal propriety we may consider the first coming of Christ as a type or representation of his second coming; . . . the

[31] Abraham Cummings, *A Dissertation on the Introduction and Glory of the Millennium* (Boston, 1797), p. 31.

first coming of Christ to destroy the Jewish world and introduce our dispensation; and the second coming of Christ to destroy the Christian world and introduce the millennium, the former being a type of the latter. We have seen in what order the type has been fulfilled; what doubt then can remain of the completion of the antitype in the same order. (p. 33)

What doubt, indeed. Typology was providing the millennial advocates scriptural foundations for their numerological predictions, and the cyclical patterns of history advanced by Cotton Mather were no longer metaphorical representations of an earlier dispensation proved by analogy. Rather, the prophetic emphases of typical adumbration and antitypical fulfillment were restored to show how America would be the setting for a grand millennial conclusion. Nor was the typology of the Sabbath unique in its restored efficacy. If the jeremiads had employed biblical figures to indicate how the magistrates and leaders of New England should return to the moral examples they exhibited, mid-eighteenth-century preachers were convinced that the leaders of Massachusetts Bay could prefigure Christ's leadership of his elect, as Joseph Bellamy used David to adumbrate Christ's millennial kingship. In 1758, Thomas Frink preached the election sermon in Massachusetts and set out a doctrine of the types as a foundation for his own interpretation of the role of modern magistrates.

The controversy over the role of biblical leaders as examples for the New English Israel goes back to John Cotton and Roger Williams. Frink's sermon is especially important because he argues wholly from typology and prophecy, and because he represents so. well those Calvinists of the Great Awakening who used typology to predict the coming of the millennium. Characteristically, Frink established a direct relationship between New England and Old Israel:

'Tis to be observed, that under the Old Testament, the most considerable Persons and Transactions were mentioned were typical, and Prefigured the State of things under the Messias. . . . And from whence we may conclude, that there is a Resemblance or Correspondence between many of the Transactions mentioned in the Old Testament, and those which should come to pass under the New; and consequently, that the Prophets when they spake of some Events near their own Times, probably had more distant views, which might reach even to the latter Ages of the world.[32]

Moreover, Frink's assumption of Samuel Mather's argument that the types were reinstituted in New England, although originally fulfilled in Christ's incarnation, gave the language of this sermon a renewed prophetic force. "And indeed my Text and Context have never yet been fulfilled," he continued, "since the coming of Christ, in their most sublime sense, nor shall be, untill the Millennial State advances, when the Kingdoms of this world shall become the Kingdoms of our Lord and of his Christ" (pp. 7–8).

This extension of typology liberated the system from the confining boundaries of Scripture and developed a new series of instituted prefigurations of the Second Coming. In a section generally overlooked by modern students of the election sermon, Frink justified the use of biblical typology in the interpretation of contemporary historical events, showing how historical cycles of adumbration and fulfillment are repeated:

This *sense* is very evident in a great many Prophecies of the Old Testament. It is called a *Secondary Sense*, not as if it were less principally intended by the Prophets, but rather with Respect to the Time, because it is the last and ultimate completion of their Predictions: Which is also called the *mystical* or *figurative* sense, by which is meant a more remote, but a natural and necessary signification, which is a Type or Figure of the Other. All types or

[32] Thomas Frink, *A King Reigning in Righteousness* (Boston, 1758), p. 6.

258

figures being to have a respect to the things figured; if we consider them as figures, we speak at the same time of that which they represent; so that which is said, has necessarily two proper and natural senses; one that agrees to the figure, and another to the thing figured: sometimes the Figure is more evidently spoken of than the Thing figured, but sometimes also such Words are purposely chosen, as agree better to the Thing figured than the Figure, to shew that what is said is but a Figure, and ought not to be rested in. The Old Testament is a Figure of the New, and all those things which befell the Jews, were figures of whatever should happen to Jesus Christ, and his Disciplines.[33]

Frink has distinguished the two senses of Scripture, and has assigned the label "mystical" to typology. "They are capable of two senses, that of the Figure and that of the thing Figured," he reasoned, and he concluded with the distinction that "the words themselves shew that the Design of the writer was to represent by a Figure something more sublime" (p. 21). That "something more sublime" is the kingdom of Christ, both earthly and heavenly. "And therefore I consider this Prophecy as typical of that happy state of the Church and the world in the latter days," he continued, and his sense of the broadened typological correspondences outside the boundaries of Scripture led immediately to an argument for the coming of the kingdom. "The Reign of Antichrist began in *Bonifice* the Third, but *Hezekiah* was a Type of Christ in one of the last and glorious displays of His Regal Power and Office, when He shall thoroughly cleanse the Christian church from all antiChristian Idolatries and Impurities" (p. 24). The church

---

[33] Frink, p. 20. See A. W. Plumstead, *The Wall and the Garden: Massachusetts Election Sermons from 1670 to 1775* (Minneapolis, 1968), introduction. Plumstead has not included Frink's sermon in this collection because he does not consider it to be as significant as others artistically, but he does view it as a philosophical statement of typology's importance to New England.

of the visible kingdom of Christ is therefore prefigured in the Old and New Testaments, and will be fulfilled in the course of human events by Divine intervention:

> If we look into the *Prophecies* of the Old Testament, we shall find they speak of the vast extent of Christ's visible Kingdom on Earth, and seeing those Prophecies have never yet been accomplished, we must conclude that there is a Time yet to come, before the Consummation of all Things, wherein our Saviour will once more display the glorious Banner of his *Cross*, and like a mighty man of war, march on conquering and to conquer, 'till he has compleated his Victory over all the Powers of the Earth, and brought all the world into a State of Subjection and Obedience to him and His Gospel; when the Kingdoms of the World shall become the Kingdoms of the Lord and of his Christ. (pp. 29–30)

Prophetic typology becomes Frink's system for proving the future realization of scriptural promises of the millennium, and he restates the progressive, cyclical historiography so prominent in the writings of Jonathan Edwards:

> It is very evident, and I suppose universally agreed, that Jerusalem the Metropolis of Judea, was a Type of the Christian visible Church (as the Temple and Sacrifices of other Ceremonial Services thereof, were a Type of the Pure Gospel service and Worship) and *David* under this Figure, celebrates the beauty and glory of the Gospel-church in the latter days. . . . (p. 31)

The temple worship of the Old Testament becomes typical of the whole Christian church in the kingdom of God, of which the history of New England is a part. The "Millennial State of the Gospel Church, represented under the figure of the City of Jerusalem and the Temple," is attended by a total reformation of the society of Christian believers, and Hezekiah is a "most lively emblem of what shall be done in the latter times, when the Christian Church shall be restored to its pure State & Worship, according to the Gospel" (pp. 38–39).

Hezekiah is, therefore, both a prefigurative type and a moral example. Frink's exegesis established him as an emblematic example for all rulers who would regard their tenure as part of the progressive reformation of society leading to the final emergence of Christ's kingdom. "The Reformation begun and brought to Perfection by *Hezekiah*, an eminent Type of Christ, in this glorious display of his regal power does most graphically set forth in Figure this wonderful Reformation of the Church and of the World in the latter days" (p. 38). All secular history, particularly that of the Roman Empire before Constantine, is denoted "anti-Christian," and the purification of the church that was begun with Luther and Calvin is thought to have been carried to New England under the continued history of the work of Redemption.

The significance of Frink's use of typology to interpret the events of world history lies in his working out a scheme of divine history based on the eschatological value of the Old Testament dispensation. His eschatology is based entirely on scriptural revelation and the fulfillment of scriptural promises in world history after Christ's incarnation, but he has rejected the conception of a "type" as a figure of specific events or persons having its conclusion in the coming of the flesh. Frink used Hezekiah not only as a moral example all magistrates should endeavor to follow, but as a typical prefiguration of Christ's millennial purification of the world. He saw the role of the New England magistrates as obedience to the example of Hezekiah, an original type in the tradition of Reformation rulers through which Christ will eventually usher in his kingdom. Frink's emphases on the prefigurative value of Hezekiah's figure indicate how strong the tradition of typological exegesis had remained in the conservative setting of Massachusetts Bay.

The millennial harbingers continued to explore the prophetic types for evidence of God's imminent return, and in the 1840's, when Emerson had virtually concluded the association of typology with historical prefiguration by declaring a type and a symbol to be synonymous, William Miller grounded his whole adventist prophecy in a typological scheme exhaustively argued from Scripture. Millennial schemes were common to periods of revival enthusiasm. There were those during the 1830's and 1840's who prophesied the imminent return of Christ and the commencement of the earthly kingdom. The Millerites predicted the commencement of the millennium in 1843 and not only argued from Old Testament prophecy and the Book of Revelation, but also incorporated the typical figures commonly used by Shepard, Mather, and the early Puritans.[34]

## VI

If the typical efficacy of the Sabbath as a figure of the millennium was extended into modern times, and if the moral authority of the Old Testament types was employed as an example for the magistrates of New England, the renewed prophetic power endowed typology by Jonathan Edwards gave it an even greater scope. Moreover, Edwards' declaration that the millennium would occur on earth before the Second Coming and Judgment nurtured utopian enthusiasm during the Great Awakening and foreshadowed a society of God's saints out of which the millennium would emerge. This progressive and evolutionary view of prophetic fulfillment was fully developed in Edwards' theology, making him the most prominent exponent of millennial utopianism in America before the Revolution. His writings on the millennium and his many attempts to construct a synthetic typological doctrine were centered on a transformation of the typological figures themselves to give

[34] Though the Millerites were a radical group of advent enthusiasts during the 1830's and 1840's, the role given to typology in proving Miller's argument was in fact more significant than that accorded Scripture prophecy. The prophecies were treated in *Evidence from Scripture History of the Second Coming of Christ, about the Year 1843, exhibited in a Course of Lectures* (Troy, N.Y., 1836), but Miller's own numerological proof was deduced from his commitment to the typology of the Sabbath in *A Lecture on the Typical Sabbaths and Great Jubilee* (Boston: Joshua Himes, 1842).

meaning to the events of contemporary history. For Edwards the types were instituted to be organic and vital; they became richer images than the static metaphors of the jeremiad tradition, exceeding the extension of typical efficacy into modern cycles of history because they were not just reflections of God's grand design but harmonious prophecies of the world's redemption.

Edwards extended typology beyond the boundaries of the two Testaments by minimizing the distinction between the figure and the thing figured.[35] However, he always retained an eschatological sense of a future fulfillment of the promises made through *natural and scriptural revelation*. Although orthodox typology applied to this historical scheme established between the Old and New Testament dispensations, for Edwards it also embraced correspondences between external representations and the spiritual ideas they shadow forth. Typology was for Edwards "a denial of the possibility that the universe is devoid of meaning . . . it served the classic purpose of giving coherence and unity to history. Just as the events and personages of the Old Testament foreshadowed the Redeemer, so too did all that transpired in Edwards' own day strike him as being prophetic of the coming Kingdom."[36] Edwards perceived a progressive "harmony between the methods of God's Providences in the natural and religious worlds, in that as when day succeeds the night, and the one comes on, and the other gradually ceases, those lesser lights that served to give light in the absence of the sun gradually vanish as the sun approaches. . . ."[37] Edwards was not allegorizing the types into static metaphors or emblems; rather, he was re-

[35] A treatment of Edwards' epistemology and reading of the book of nature lies beyond the scope of this essay. But for some discussion, see Roland Delattre, *Beauty and Sensibility in the Thought of Jonathan Edwards: an Essay in Aesthetics and Theological Ethics* (New Haven and London, 1968); and my own essay, "The *Images or Shadows of Divine Things* in the Thought of Jonathan Edwards," in Bercovitch, *Typology and Early American Literature*, pp. 209–249.

[36] Alan Heimert, *Religion and the American Mind*, p. 68.

[37] Jonathan Edwards, "Miscellany Number 638," as quoted by Perry Miller, *Images or Shadows of Divine Things* (New Haven, 1948), pp. 52–53n.

vitalizing them by using typology as a renewed prophetic
language for God's promises revealed in nature.

Unfortunately, some of his most illuminating passages on
the subject of typology remain in manuscript. In Miscellany
119, for example, he observed:

> The things of the ceremonial law are not only things
> whereby God designedly shadowed forth spiritual things;
> but with an eye to such a representation were all the
> transactions of the life of Christ ordered. And very much
> of the wisdom of God in the creation appears, in his so
> ordering things natural, that they livelily represent things
> divine and spiritual, [such as] sun, fountain, vine; as also,
> much of the wisdom of God is in his Providence, in that
> the state of mankind is so ordered, that there are in-
> numerable things in human affairs that are lively pictures
> of the things of the gospel, such as shield, tower, and
> marriage, family.[38]

Edwards' ultimate aim throughout his unpublished writing
on typology was "to show how there is a medium between
those that cry down all types, and those that are for turning
all into nothing but allegory and not having it to be true to
history. . . ."[39] His reasoning about the distinctions between
typology and allegory was always clear, and he restored to
typology its original historical and prophetic meaning while
applying earlier dispensations to contemporary and future
ones. He gave a cautious warning in his "Notebook on the

[38] I am indebted to Professor Thomas Shafer of the McCormick
Theological Seminary, Chicago, for allowing me to use his personal
transcriptions of these miscellaneous entries, which will appear in his
edition of Edwards' miscellaneous notebooks for the Yale edition
of the *Works of Jonathan Edwards*.

[39] This observation Edwards made in his manuscript "Notebook on
the Types," a small gathering of observations about typology that
contains some of his most succinct statements of theory. It is largely
unknown, but is being edited for the Yale edition by Professor
Wallace Anderson of the Ohio State University, and should be published soon as part of the volume on prophetic miscellanies. The
manuscript of "Types" is part of the Andover Collection, never before
published.

Types," that "persons ought to be exceeding careful in interpreting of types, that they don't give way to a wild fancy; not to fix an interpretation unless warranted by some hint in the New Testament of its being the true interpretation, or a lively figure and representation contained or warranted by an analogy to other types that we interpret on sure ground."[40] However, he regarded typology to be a "certain sort of language, as it were, in which God is wont to speak to us."[41]

Consistently with his published declarations about the natural universe being typical and prophetic of God's future redemption of the world, he concluded the "Types" notebook by observing:

> To say that we must not say that such things are types of those and these things unless the Scripture has expressly taught us that they are so, is as unreasonable as to say that we are not to interpret any prophecies of Scripture or apply them to those and these events, except we find them interpreted to our hand, and must interpret no more of the prophecies of David, etc. For by the Scripture it is plain that innumerable other things are types that are not interpreted in Scripture (all the ordinances of the law are all shadows of good things to come), in like manner as it is plain by Scripture that those and these passages that are not actually interpreted are yet predictions of future events.[42]

Several clear declarations of typological doctrine illuminate Edwards' theory of God's revelation in cycles of historical dispensation. His writings frequently offer conclusions about the coming millennium, and they also abound in typological proofs of its imminent fulfillment that show how the biblical figures were revitalized to strengthen the case for the coming kingdom.

Two published documents are central to Edwards' millennial prophecies: the *History of the Work of Redemption,*

40 "Types" typescript, p. 4.  41 *Ibid.*, p. 8.
42 *Ibid.*, p. 10.

a series of sermons first preached in 1739 but not published until after his death, and *An Humble Attempt to Promote Explicit Agreement and Visible Union Among God's People*, which gave the Awakening a prophetic role in calling for civil as well as religious union. Edwards declared: "*Union* is one of the most *amiable* things that pertains to human society; yea, it is one of the most beautiful and happy things on earth, which indeed makes earth most like heaven"; and thus he suggested not only the image of God's perfection that would be reflected in a perfect civil union, but also prophesied the harmonious earthly kingdom that is to be an image of heavenly beauty.

This kind of millennial emphasis was exceedingly strong throughout Edwards' writing. For example, in *Some Thoughts Concerning the Present Revival of Religion in New England* (1742), we find:

> It is not unlikely that this work of God's spirit . . . is the dawning or at least a prelude of that glorious work of God, so often foretold in Scripture . . . and there are many things which make it probable that this work will begin in America. . . . And if we may suppose that this glorious work of God shall begin in any part of America, I think if we consider the circumstances of the settlement of New England, it must needs appear the most likely of all the American colonies.[43]

In the same year that he had preached the History of Redemption sermons, 1739, he stated in his *Personal Narrative* that the relation he perceived between the present and the future could be determined by analyzing prophetic images in Scripture:

> My heart has been much on the advancement of Christ's Kingdom in the world. The histories of the past advancement of Christ's Kingdom have been sweet to me. When

[43] Jonathan Edwards, "Paradise in America," ed. Michael McGiffert, *Puritanism and the American Experience* (Reading, Mass., 1969), pp. 160–163.

I have read the histories of past ages, the pleasantest thing in all my reading has been, to read of the kingdom of Christ being promoted. And when I have expected, in my reading, to come to any such thing, I have rejoiced in the prospect, all the way as I read. And my mind has been much entertained and delighted with the Scripture promises and prophecies, which related to the future glorious advancement of Christ's Kingdom upon earth.[44]

It should not be surprising, then, that Jonathan Edwards' central spiritual and intellectual endeavor became the discovering of those harmonious correspondences prophesied in Scripture and, in his resurrection of typological patterns, that he should apply the types and antitypes to the natural world. The close relationship he understood to exist between Scripture, history, and nature is clearly seen in the well-known letter he wrote to the Trustees of the College of New Jersey (later Princeton University) when they offered him its presidency:

I have had it on my mind and heart (which a long ago began, not with any view to publication), a great work, which I call a *History of the Work of Redemption*—a body of divinity in an entire new method, being thrown into the form of a history . . . wherein every divine doctrine will appear to the greatest advantage, in the brightest light, in the most striking manner, shewing the admirable contextual harmony of the whole. . . . I have also for my profit and entertainment, done much towards another great work, which I call the *Harmony of the Old and New Testaments*, in three parts. The first, considering the Prophecies of the Messiah, his redemption and kingdom . . . showing the universal, precise, and admirable correspondence between predictions and events. The second part, considering the Types of the Old Testament shewing the evidence of their being intended as representa-

44 Jonathan Edwards, *Personal Narrative*, in *Selections from Jonathan Edwards*, ed. Clarence H. Faust and Thomas H. Johnson (New York, 1962), p. 68.

tions of the great things of the gospel of Christ; and the agreement of type and antitype. The third and great part, considering the Harmony of the Old and New Testament, as to Doctrine and precept.[45]

Edwards' assumption of the Princeton presidency prevented his completing this ambitious work.[46] But at his death, a few months later, he did leave us the redemption sermons and some manuscript fragments of the "Harmonies" in addition to the manuscripts called "Prophecies of the Messiah" and "Fulfillment of the Prophecies of the Messiah," all of which corroborate with detail those exegetical principles advanced in the *Types of the Messiah* and the posthumously published *History of the Work of Redemption*. The vision of the last days provided by the *History* is yet more important, since it may be explicated by those assertions in the typology and prophecy manuscripts. Although his son, Jonathan Edwards, Jr., and his friend, John Erskine, had a substantial hand in reshaping some of the sermons to complete the book, finally published in 1774, the views are those of Edwards and may be checked by opinions he offered elsewhere on the same subject.

Following the example of the "late expositor" Moses Lowman, whose *Paraphrase and Notes on the Revelation of St. John* had been to Edwards' eschatology what John Locke's

45 Jonathan Edwards, *The Works of Jonathan Edwards* (Worcester, Mass., 1820), 1, pp. 569–570. See also C. C. Goen, "Jonathan Edwards: A New Departure in Eschatology," *Church History*, 27 (March, 1959), 32.

46 Of Edwards' work on the *Harmony*, Jesper Rosenmeier remarks: "Had Edwards lived to complete the Harmony, he would have made the most exhaustive compendium of Biblical metaphors yet undertaken in America. His purpose, however, went far beyond working out the precise meanings and correspondences between Old Testament prefigurations and their New Testament fulfillments. Rather, Edwards was interested in the harmony and beauty of the relationships, for he was convinced that it would continue to grow in the future, and that whoever understood the present divine communications might gain a view of the harmony that would be manifest in the New Jerusalem. So dynamic did Edwards consider the process of redemption to be that he perceived not only the Bible but Nature as a prophetic part of the gyre of salvation" (unpublished manuscript, p. 17).

*Essay Concerning Human Understanding* had been to his epistemology, Edwards asserted that the fifth vial (of the seven prophesied in Revelation which would destroy Satan's kingdom), had already been unleashed.[47] This interpretation, incorporated into the redemption sermons, placed the work of redemption very far along in its progressive course. The prophecy was proved by a scheme of typological adumbration and antitypical fulfillment. In the events of the last days, Edwards saw an extension of the prophetic fulfillment that has been progressive and continuous from the Creation. In the figure of David, for example, he perceived a foreshadowing of Christ and His Kingdom:

> David, as he was the ancestor of Christ, so he was the greatest personal type of Christ of all under the Old Testament. The types of Christ were of three sorts: instituted, providential, and personal. The ordinance of sacrificing was the greatest of the *instituted* types; the redemption out of Egypt was the greatest of the *providential*; and David the greatest of the *personal* ones. Hence Christ is often called David in the prophecies of Scripture.[48]

Another typological correspondence Edwards developed fully is that of the Holy City. The traditional conception of Jerusalem as a prefiguration of the Heavenly City is repeated in the *History*, but it is not merely a literal reincarnation, as some earlier millennial typologists had suggested. Rather, it is both a *literal and a spiritual* city, a "type" of God's spiritual kingdom, which was to be established after the defeat of Satan at the end of human time.

[47] I am indebted to Mr. Christopher Jedrey for a close comparison of Lowman's *Paraphrase* and Edwards' *Redemption*, which he prepared as a course paper in 1972. Although Lowman's study is not concerned with typological figuralism, it is very concerned with the interpretation of symbols and figures that appear in the Book of Revelation as they apply to literal events of the future. See Moses Lowman, *A Paraphrase and Notes of the Revelation of St. John*, 2nd ed. (London, 1745).

[48] Jonathan Edwards, *A History of the Work of Redemption*, in *Works*, ed. Sereno Dwight (Hartford, 1820), Vol. III, p. 227.

That the Jerusalem of the Old Testament was prophetic of this spiritual state in Edwards' vision is made quite clear:

> This city of Jerusalem is therefore called the *holy city*; and it was the greatest type of the Church of Christ in all the Old Testament. It was redeemed by David, the Captain of the Hosts of Israel, out of the hands of the Jebusites, to be God's city, the holy place of his rest forever, where he would dwell. So Christ, the Captain of his people's salvation, redeems his church out of the hands of devils, to be his holy and beloved city. And therefore how often does the Scripture, when speaking of Christ's redemption of his church, call it by the names of Zion and Jerusalem? This was the city that God had appointed to be the place of the first gathering and erection of the Christian church after Christ's resurrection, of that remarkable effusion of the spirit of God on the apostles and primitive Christians, and the place whence the gospel was to sound forth into all the world; the place of the first Christian church, that was to be, as it were, the mother of all other churches through the world.[49]

Edwards' perception of the church as a progressive historical movement leading to the gathering of the saints in Christ was supported by his reading of the biblical types. Just as Jerusalem signified typologically the Holy City and the center of Christ's spiritual kingdom on earth in the continuum of human time, so it would also signify the coming of the church kingdom that will be established for eternity at the end of human time.

Throughout the *History of the Work of Redemption*, these typological associations abound. Edwards envisions the setting up of Christ's kingdom as a succession of great events, each revealed in the prophecies of Scripture and each having a spiritual significance for his own time. The *History*, moreover, contains a vivid description of the arrival of millennial peace and the coming of the kingdom. This conclusive interpretation of the prophecies and the

49 *Ibid.*, III, p. 233.

types is dramatically conceived and beautifully preached; the conviction with which Edwards approached his own last days is resonant throughout the climactic scenes depicting the arrival of God's glory. The gathered church of God's elect saints is brought forward to enjoy forever the beauty of redeemed creation in a period of perfect peace. "Then shall the whole church be perfectly and forever delivered from this present evil world," Edwards says, and the sense of religious community that has characterized the Puritan vision of God's holy city from primitive times to the present echoes throughout his vision of the end:

. . . now they shall all be gathered together, never to be separated any more. And not only shall all the members of the church now be gathered together, but all shall be gathered unto their Head, into his immediate glorious presence, never to be separated from him any more.[50]

Similarly, in Miscellany 262, Edwards developed a millennialism that clearly suggests the fusion of civil and religious forces in the fulfillment of God's glory:

Millennium: 'Tis probable that the world shall be more like Heaven in the millennium in this respect: that contemplation and spiritual enjoyments, and those things that more directly concern the mind and religion, will be more the saint's ordinary business than now. There will be so many contrivances and inventions to facilitate and expedite their necessary secular business that they shall have more time for more noble exercise, and that they will have better contrivances for assisting one another through the whole earth by more expedite, easy, and safe communication between distant regions than now. The invention of the mariner's compass is a thing discovered by God to the world to that end. And how exceedingly has that one thing enlarged and facilitated communication. And who can doubt that yet God will make it more perfect, so that there need not be such a tedious voyage

50 *Ibid.*, III, p. 417.

in order to hear from the other hemisphere? And so the country about the poles need no longer be hid to us, but the whole earth may be as one community, one body in Christ.[51]

Thus the millennial vision and progressive eschatology were joined in a comprehensive image of a future paradise in which human relations, scientific invention, and earthly achievement would be developed under the guidance of divine Providence. The vision was progressive and utopian. The proof of its revealed promise was governed, however, by the truths Edwards received from Scripture and nature, and from the typological associations he perceived between the two.

For Edwards, the prophetic language of the Bible, this "language of Canaan," which John Cotton knew the saints would all speak at the final resurrection, was instituted at the beginning of time in the building of the natural world in God's image, so that all Creation resonates with prophetic images of God's ultimate glory and his redemption of the saints. Similarly, the incarnation was more than the arrival of the Word as flesh; the antitype is eternal, not temporal, so that Christ's fulfillment of the prophetic figures, like the figures themselves, operates throughout human time, from *alpha* to *omega*. In a little-known passage from the *Miscellanies* that confirms this view, Edwards says:

479. WORK OF REDEMPTION: TYPES. Things even before the fall were types of things pertaining to the gospel redemption. The old creation, I believe, was a type of the new. God's causing light to shine out of darkness, is a type of his causing such spiritual light and glory by Jesus Christ to succeed, and to arise out of, the dreadful darkness of sin and misery. His bringing the world into such beautiful form from out of a chaos without form and

[51] Jonathan Edwards, Miscellany 262, as quoted by Douglas Ellwood; *The Philosophical Writings of Jonathan Edwards* (New York, 1961), p. 74.

void, typifies his bringing the spiritual world to such divine excellency and beauty after the confusion, deformity, and ruin of sin.[52]

If the millennial writers of the first and second generations had restricted their arguments to specific scriptural promises or to the allegorical metaphors derived from them, and if those millennial seers during the eighteenth century had also viewed the historical process as a fulfillment of specific passages in the Bible, seeking "signs of the times" that would corroborate their predictions, Edwards also found scriptural authority for his vision of the millennium, but he transformed the typological system by extending it to embrace the natural and historical universe. And the "typology" of nature set forth in Edwards' numerous writings on the subject becomes more than an academic extension of the biblical figures into modern time. It is an original epistemology by which Edwards and his successors learned to read the vast and complex Book of Nature, in which they found prophetic figures of the imminent millennium and the kingdom of Christ. Like John Cotton, they envisioned a time when all the saints would understand and speak this prophetic language of Canaan, by which God's revealed will had been dispensed to regenerate perceivers through a glass, darkly. And they looked forward with joy to that time when the veil would be lifted, and all the prophecies and types would be fulfilled in a time of peace and harmony. It is the vitality of this millennial vision, recalling the conviction with which the first New England Puritans had interpreted their Bibles, that gives Edwards' typological argument an organic life that would later inspire Emerson's reading of nature and Whitman's millennial vision of America's promise.

[52] Jonathan Edwards' miscellaneous notebooks. Again, I am grateful to Thomas Shafer for the use of these entries that treat typology.

## Alephs, Zahirs, and the
## Triumph of Ambiguity:
## Typology in Nineteenth-Century
## American Literature

> The writers on heresy, the heresiologists, will no doubt remember him; he added to the concept of the Son, which seemed exhausted, the complexities of calamity and evil.
>
> Jorge Luis Borges, "The Three Versions of Judas"

### I

Something happened to religious typology on its way to, and during the course of, the nineteenth century in America.[1] In the hands of the major writers it became abused, diffuse, and even amusing. It moved from the mark of True Belief among the New England Puritans to the butt of iconoclastic joking by the time of Emily Dickinson and Mark Twain. The conceit of medieval allegory turned into ambiguity. The will-to-metaphor mystique of Puritan piety became de-christianized, dis-edened, disinherited, dysfunctional. In the hands of America's major writers, the point of it all got lost.

We remind ourselves disinterestedly that the settlers of early America brought two allegorical systems with them, both of them carrying the tag "typology." Both were biblically sanctioned and had on them the sweet exegetical glaze of the Church Fathers, from Philo and Origen to Calvin and William Ames. Both achieved the status of exegesis in the new world as proof of the continuity of the theology

---

[1] I wish to dedicate this chapter to Professor Sacvan Bercovitch, whose various studies of the Puritan imagination, especially of typology, have inspired me and whose help with the ideas of this essay I greatly appreciate.

from the old. Like other metaphoric systems that helped to form early American culture, both encouraged considerable innovation, because they were splendid abstractions, and so were alive in the imagination; the tradition, even at the outset, was a handful of sterile ideas but a fertile structure. Both were overwritten versions of the platonic, epic in scale and utopian in tone, frivolous in method and provincial in effect, but for American writers structurally sound because appealing to something in the imagination.

Orthodox typologizing (what Stephen Manning calls "the *classic* tradition of typology") formed types/foreshadows/ prophecies out of the Old Testament to satisfy the need of Christians to make Jesus (the antitype/the light/the fulfillment) divine, and therefore central to human history, even "the meridian of time." This equation came to the colonies not in the form of a set of ideas but as a structure built on the formula $a > B$ *if* $B = a$, which could be superimposed on human events. It worked for them, I believe, after the manner of Borges' Aleph, a point that contains all other points:

> The only place on earth where all places are—seen from every angle, each standing clear, without any confusion or blending. . . . If all places in the universe are in the Aleph, then all stars, all lamps, all sources of light are in it, too. . . . In that single gigantic instant I saw millions of acts both delightful and awful; not one of them amazed me more than the awful fact that all of them occupied the same point in space, without overlapping or transparency. What my eyes beheld was simultaneous. . . . One hell of an observatory! . . . [It is] the pure and boundless godhead; it is also said that it takes the shape of a man pointing to both heaven and earth, in order to show that the lower world is the map and mirror of the higher. ("The Aleph")

Christ the Antitype, the touchstone/focus/end of previous time, is the Aleph of the medieval mind (and then the Puritan mind). *Through* him, the Hebraic past gains significance; *for* him, it had the shape it did; *in* him, it is alive because fulfilled, though dead because finished. Because of Christ, human history is ordered, simultaneous, and dynamic, if obsolete. Christ—"one hell of an observatory" on the past—is the beginning and end of history.

In America, orthodox typologizing sent ministers, and a few others, to their pens to connect actual biblical facts imaginatively to Christ. As English and continental writers had discovered in the course of the Renaissance, the structure was extremely easy to use. Thomas Shepard makes Joshua's inheritance of Canaan a type of Christ's kingdom of heaven and Isaiah's remnant a type of Christ's Church. John Davenport makes the bowing before kings and queens in Isaiah a type to the antitype of the humility of Christ's followers. Samuel Sewall makes the giving of the earth to Adam a type to the antitype of the conquest of souls by Christ. Samuel Mather makes Samson the perfect foreshadow of Christ, in looks, actions, motives, and even death. Cotton Mather, in his *Just Commemorations*, makes the form of death mentioned in the Psalms "a Type of our Saviour speaking in the Psalm." Edward Taylor makes "Joseph's glorious shine a Type of thee," "Joshua's [sun] but a Beam / Of thy bright Sun," and "all the shine that Samson wore is thine, / Thine in the Type." Christ serves the purpose of an antitype in the hand of almost everyone who cared about the relation of the divine to human history. The process was an easy one: like Borges' character, one could stand at Christ's point in time and, with any device of language available, read the past for its relevance to one's piety. This structure allowed the illusion of coherence in Jewish and Christian thought and the self-satisfaction of the primacy of Christian over Jew. The Aleph is Puritan piety itself.

Because classic typology was for the American ideologues a structure rather than a dogma, as it was for their English brethren, innovation began just as soon as the American sense of mission took hold. Stripped of authoritative interpretation, classic typology in New England became a device of doctrinal convenience. Perhaps no one believed it very much as a set of ideas anyway, for into the structure the settlers of the first several generations consistently inserted new material, initiating typology's service to American culture. Its truth for them lay in the fact that it worked in many different ways. These changing boundaries of thought in the colonies were part of the rise of individualism, the dissolution of hierarchy, and the defiance of authority. The typological structure applied, in the early-American mind, wherever there was a situation involving partial and total fulfillment. In time the structure of types turned faith in Christ into national and personal egocentrism.

Thus, John Cotton proclaimed the Bay Colony "the antitypical fulfillment of all biblical types" and yet also the "prefiguration of the Second Coming." He wanted the relationship between New England saints in a wilderness and the children of Israel in a wilderness to reproduce (as in a cyclical process) Christ's relationship to the children of Israel. William Bradford saw the separatists imitating Christ in re-enacting Old Testament events and therefore as a realized antitype to the conventional biblical types. For him, through some correspondence with Christ, that which is fallen gains life. Samuel Sewall saw an excuse to impose a typal allegory on historical events, making New England the antitype to all religious history that had preceded it, selective of those events which served and foreshadowed the colonization. Such hermeneutics as his encouraged an early nationalism. Cotton Mather followed suit in defining types in terms of "the histories of all ages, coming in with punctual and surprising fulfillments of the divine prophecies, as far as they have been hitherto fulfilled." America was for him the antitype because it would "bring a blessing upon all nations of the earth." Roger Williams wrote of the Jews "as the type of the . . . [American] Kingdom of Christ Jesus." He believed that the "full and final deliverance and restoration of the Church may be applied to us." Urian Oakes saw America antitypally as "a candle in the candlestick that giveth light to the whole house."

Thomas Shepard spoke of justification as a form of antitype giving force to the specific acts of one's sanctification. The Covenant of Grace itself fits the structure. Similarly, Thomas Hooker turned one's election into an antitype facilitating all the acts, the types, that make up one's piety. Edward Taylor tried a number of variations on the Aleph: he made himself dirt for Christ as Rose of Sharon, a hungry man for Christ the broken bread, a babe to Christ the Father, a bride to Christ the Bridegroom.[2] Jonathan Edwards' antitype in the scheme of human psychology was the will or individual inclination; all else was determined by, fulfilled in, cancelled out by, the will. All of these were versions of the Aleph, the variety encouraged by the structure.

More liberal (or "spiritual") typologizing (what Perry Miller called "the vogue of *plebeian* typology") was an allegorical structure which also served to justify certain beliefs and one that was eventually far more attractive to the first American generations. It extended the historical order of classic typologizing to the cosmos; a teleological order becomes a moral order within the same structure. The plebeian method made types out of specific worldly facts and objects after a more inductive/subjective/metaphorical manner (whether natural or arbitrary) by holding to an antitype, the divine, to which they pointed and by means of which they took on value. "To spiritualize the common actions of life and make a religious improvement of worldly affairs," wrote Cotton Mather in his *Agricola* (1727), "is an holy and happy art." It had the same structure as the more orthodox method, but functioned rather

---

[2] For a discussion of the typological innovations of Edward Taylor, see my essay " 'The World Slickt Up in Types': Edward Taylor as a Version of Emerson," in *Typology and Early American Literature*, ed. Sacvan Bercovitch (Amherst, 1972). The essays in Bercovitch's collection make the best definition of typology for students of American literature, yet overlook the structural side of the issue and so do not account for the continuance of typology in American literature into the nineteenth century.

after the manner of Borges' complementary Zahir—the Absolute as a momentary God, the ephemeral given universality, essence hidden in experience:

> Every coin in the world is a symbol for all the coins that forever glitter in history and in fable; . . . [the Zahir is] a species of infinite Tiger. . . . The Zahir is the shadow of the Rose and the rending of the Veil. . . . There is no deed, however so humble, which does not implicate universal history and the infinite concatenation of causes and effects. . . . The visible world is implicit, in its entirety, in each manifestation. . . . Perhaps behind the Zahir I shall find God. ("The Zahir")

Classic allegorizing begins with the fact of Christ and hunts for points in the past to which he can be anchored and which might serve as imaginative prophetic parallels for the sanctified minutiae of his life and person: biblical proof-texting elevated to an eschatology. Plebeian allegorizing, on the other hand, begins with a fact of one's life or a feature of nature and locates the divine behind it after the formula $a = B$ if $B > a$: metaphor elevated to cosmic symbolism. The Zahir leads one beyond itself as synecdoche to significance/the Christ/all, *made* a vehicle by the tenor. The former kind of type is distinguished by time but the latter, by and large, by a use of space. Both impose the orderliness of one's piety on multiplicity/possibility/infinity.

Plebeian types—making allegories out of anything personal, anything individual—are everywhere in early American writings. The binding of typology to actual historical events was an exciting hermeneutic adventure in the sixteenth and seventeenth centuries, but it was fast becoming redundant and, by the time of the New England Puritan apologists, with very few exceptions, fairly stale. The platonizing of typology (the spiritual represented by the physical, the physical enlivened by the spiritual) was, on the other hand, a liberty taken by most writers in the later period, from Lord Herbert to Edwards to the Romantics and Transcendentalists, not for the sake of liberty but to reclaim nature for divine purposes. It was a different realism.

Thus, Anne Bradstreet moved from the worldly to the divine in her plebeian typologizing: "How excellent is He that dwells on high, / Whose power and beauty by His works we know?" Similarly, Samuel Sewall came to hold that "all the universal verities . . . [are] under pleasant types and tropes decided." So also Cotton Mather fancifully allegorized types outside their biblical contexts and applied them to New England issues; the Ark is his Boston congregation, making it representative of ideal Christianity. And by analogy with biblical types (an important esthetic innovation on his part), Edwards spiritualized the natural universe: "The wisdom of God in the creation appears in his so ordering things natural, that they livelily represent things divine and spiritual. . . . Natural things were ordered for types of spiritual things. . . . The type is only the representation or shadow of the thing, but the antitype is the very substance and is the true thing."

Where classic reasoning moved from the antitype to the type, plebeian reasoning proceeded from type to antitype— an existential difference—thereby refreshing the structure considerably. The movement from Christ out to the specifics of human experience had its severe limitations. The movement from experience to the divine was, however, virtually limitless, if also a serious threat to the doctrines sustained by classical typologizing.

Within the context of American culture, much of the success of plebeian typologizing from the seventeenth century to the nineteenth—figures instituted in nature in a variety of ways, depending on the subject matter that needed to be fitted into the structure—can be laid almost certainly to Cotton Mather and Edwards. Just as materialistic as the many New England plebeian typologizers before them but more articulate in their optimistic natural-science conjectures, they superimposed the type-to-antitype structure on world and universe with imaginative effort, forcing the metaphoric convention of tenor and vehicle to have, well into the nineteenth century, a dominantly religious bearing, even as the convention lost its religious importance. "This is God's manner," Edwards wrote in his *Miscellanies*, "to make inferior things shadows of the superior and most excellent; outward things shadows of spiritual. . . ." "The presence of a higher, namely, of the spiritual element," Emerson wrote in *Nature*, "is essential to [nature's] perfection." The type here is a looser, more subjective allegory, far more respectful of personal experience than the orthodox method but permissive of gross conjectures far beyond the Christ-bound/Old Testament-bound classic typologizing.

The plebeian types—"the shadow of the Rose and the rending of the Veil"—must be distinguished, however, from the simple platonic. It is more than the easy harmony of things with the eternal archetype, but signifies that, in typological fashion, the things, even in their independence, proceed *from* the archetype. The vehicle precedes yet proceeds from the tenor: the only known is made a spiritual medium by the power of the believed.

There is, for American literature, a difference, too, in the idea that the antitype, though an unknown/unseen, has Yankee insistence, even a hovering dominance over the known—almost meaning, with William Carlos Williams, too, "No meaning but in things" though with the important added feature of a self-interested Maker. It is a religious difference, I believe, an *American* religious difference.

I rehearse these commonplaces of colonial hermeneutics only to underscore my argument that typological allegorizing came down to the nineteenth century in structural form and therefore encouraged lively innovation. Because it was a structure of thought, writers could vary the content with need. As a system of ideas, typology died with the Edwardsians and millennialists, for the most part, long before the end of the nineteenth century, but a typologizing possibility remained because fixed as construct in the minds of the first generations, even as the doctrines and passions that made them possible died out or changed drastically. As a structure, a construction, it is at the heart of much nineteenth-century literature. The continuing temptation to write *by analogy with typology*, sharing the quality of types and antitypes, shows the power of it as a structure.

Even when no longer vibrating to a strictly theological terminology, typology is therefore one of the features that sustained Puritanism in America long after it ceased to be socially or even religiously viable. The structure is still here. The transformation was a gradual and not a radical one that American culture was undergoing. It cohered structurally, even at the expense of most of its idealistic energies and practices.

One trouble with following the flow of typology into the nineteenth century, however, is with the word itself. As I have suggested, it lost its religion. By the nineteenth century the dogmatic sense of typological terms became unbearable, and typology became an instrument of a measure of secularization. In the secularizing process, the religious images were drained of their specifically religious content. Religion was remade poetically. After Cotton Mather and Edwards, "type" and "typology" by and large meant something else, so there is no use watching the evolution of those terms,[3] especially after Wordsworth, who referred to his imagery rather loosely as "types and symbols of eternity." By "type" he meant merely example or model or, more technically, synecdoche. Throughout the nineteenth century, the terms "symbol," "emblem," "type," "allegory," and "figure" were, through carelessness, often interchangeable and therefore largely negligible. The variety of concepts about metaphor does not correspond to the variety of terms.

[3] The trouble with Ursula Brumm's thorough, pioneering discussion in *American Thought and Religious Typology* (New Brunswick, N.J., 1970), the only full-length discussion of the evolution of typology from the seventeenth to the nineteenth century, is with terms. Professor Brumm follows the term "type" through American literary history as opposed to following the concept or structure of typology itself. When she gets to the nineteenth century, therefore, her argument begins to go wrong, and by the sections on the twentieth century, it is almost completely erroneous.

Emerson (as in his essay "Imagination") calls almost everything a type that moves and points to something beyond itself:

> Whilst common sense looks at things or visible nature as real and final facts, poetry, or the imagination which dictates it, is a second sight, looking through these, and using them as types or words for thoughts which they signify.

Similarly, Thoreau (as in *Walden*) understands a type to be a mere example:

> Next Spanish hides, with the tails still preserving their twist and the angle of elevation they had when the oxen that wore them were careering over the pampas of the Spanish Main,—a type of all obstinacy, and evincing how almost hopeless and incurable are all constitutional vices.[4]

Also careless in using the term, Hawthorne has his Reverend Mr. Hooper (from "The Minister's Black Veil") use the term to mean soteriological symbol:

> Know then, this veil is a type and a symbol, and I am bound to wear it ever, both in light and darkness, in solitude and before the gaze of multitudes, and as with strangers, so with my familiar friends.

Melville uses the term variously, as one among many describing his symbolic purposes in *Moby-Dick*: "[The meeting of the ships] may involve at once a type, a parallel and a prophecy." And in *The Confidence Man*: "Here reigned the dashing and all-fusing spirit of the West, whose type is the Mississippi itself." Whitman makes the same term (as in his poem "To a Locomotive in Winter") mean

---

[4] Among his uses of the terms in *Walden*, Thoreau gets "type" and "antitype" confused: "I am particularly attracted by the arching and sheaf-like top of the wool-grass; it brings back the summer to our winter memories, and is among the forms which art loves to copy, and which, in the vegetable kingdom, have the same relation to types already in the mind of man that astronomy has."

KELLER

ideal representative or emblem, almost totally blurring its
origin:

Thy train of cars behind, obedient, merrily following,
Through gale or calm, now swift, now slack, yet
steadily careering;
Type of the modern—emblem of motion and power—
pulse of the continent,
For once come serve the Muse and merge in verse,
even as here I see thee,
With storm and buffeting gusts of wind and falling
snow,
By day thy warning ringing bell to sound its notes,
By night thy silent signal lamps to swing.

So we see that the terms were expropriated for use in the
later period, but the original meaning was by and large
gone out of them. What was left was a tension between the
new meanings and the residue of (or allusion to) the old.
We sense, then, the value of religious frames of reference
for secular/esthetic terms in nineteenth-century America.
The secular retains a moral/spiritual tone.

II

What is more important is what happened to the typology construct itself. And what we see is by and large a
liberalizing effect: the construct demanded constant renewal. American Romanticism differs notably from the
movement in Europe by virtue of the kinds of innovations
of typology. We cannot know what caused the nineteenth-
century American imagination to find merit and satisfaction
in the archaic technique of typologizing. We only know that
it turns up in curious and significant places.[5] Without

5 In his *Symbolism and American Literature* (Chicago, 1953), Charles
Feidelson, Jr., misread a select group of nineteenth-century American
writers as early *symbolistes*, in part because he disregarded the workings of the Puritan typological construct in them. He saw their symbolism—whether Hawthorne's scarlet letter or Whitman's India or
Melville's Pacific—as consisting of objects alive in their own right,
objects resonating with their own time and space, and overlooked the
large variety of antitypes in which the writers kept their faith and

the various uses of it as a structure, the history of American literature in the nineteenth century would be substantially different.

Observe the case of the success of the classic form in the hands of some of the canonized writers. Christ takes on a variety of attractive forms, creating new media and bringing much more of human experience into an esthetic focus. Emerson, for example, did not invent the Over-Soul, "a power / That works its will on age and hour." It was ready-made for him by the typological construct. It is his anti-type.[6] Though often platonized into a near-fuzziness, it is just as religious and just as strong as the Puritan antitype in Jesus. "It is one soul which animates all men." The things of the world "take their shape and sun-color / From him [the World-Soul] that sends the dream." In the form of Emerson's Sphinx, it "melted into purple cloud, . . . silvered in the moon, . . . spired into a yellow flame, . . . flowered in blossoms red, . . . flowed into a foaming wave." The inscrutable God makes the world scrutable: "Genius detects . . . through all genera the steadfast [anti]type." The Holy Spirit from Unitarianism (what is left of the Trinity by mid-century) is given Yankee connections with *things*. Given a voice and the consciousness of a benevolent Übermensch, Emerson's antitype sings thus:

> I wrote the past in characters
> Of rock and fire the scroll,
> The building in the coral sea,
> The planting of the coal.

---

which are the reference points on which their symbols are often contingent. He missed the classic typology in each (even when parodied) and so moved these writers in an existential direction away from their New England bearings.

6 The immense bibliography on the metaphorical character of Emerson's thinking and writing provides little insight into his need of the typological. It is a fairly new point to make about him. I wish to emphasize, however, that we do not need to think that Emerson *believed* in the assumptions behind typology, for it was *already* the frame of his mind. Typology was not what he thought about but the way he thought about things in general.

> And thefts from satellites and rings
> And broken stars I drew,
> And out of spent and aged things
> I formed the world anew. ("Song of Nature")

Except for the deliberately anti-institutional language and the anthropocentric emphasis, Emerson's Over-Soul is just as antitypal as the Puritan's meridianized Christ:

> The Supreme Critic on the errors of the past and the present, and the only prophet of that which must be, is that great nature in which we rest as the earth lies in the soft arms of the atmosphere; that Unity, that Over-Soul, within which every man's particular being is contained and made one with all other; that common heart of which all sincere conversation is the worship, to which all right action is submission; that over-powering reality which confutes our tricks and talents, and constrains every one to pass for what he is, and to speak from his character and not from his tongue, and which evermore tends to pass into our thought and hand and become wisdom and virtue and power and beauty. We live in succession, in division, in parts, in particles. Meantime within man is the soul of the whole; the wise silence; the universal beauty, to which every part and particle is equally related; the eternal ONE. And this deep power in which we exist and whose beatitude is all accessible to us, is not only self-sufficing and perfect in every hour, but the act of seeing and the thing seen, the seer and the spectacle, the subject and the object, are one. We see the world piece by piece, as the sun, the moon, the animal, the tree; but the whole, of which these are the shining parts, is the soul. . . . From within or from behind, a light shines through us upon things and makes us aware that we are nothing, the light is all. ("The Over-Soul")

Though Emerson often works, à la Wordsworth and plebeian types, from specifics (his "each") to the universal/divine (his "all"), his method is also the manner of the classic type: God is the focus and the fulfillment bestowing contingent worth on all things. Things are not merely synecdoches (and here is the difference from the easy platonizing of the period) but *made* synecdoches by the force of the strong outpouring of desire from a god-figure on things; not vehicles determining the effect of a tenor but the tenor taking any apt thing of the world (as with metaphysical conceits) and turning it (often, through play on words) into a vehicle through connection or correspondence with It. Being, as with Edwards, precedes, dictates, enspirits, and qualifies beings.

Emerson's identification of the Over-Soul with the self turns the self into (in typological terms) the Jesus of the Transcendentalists. Self-reliance is God-reliance, Emerson tautologized, because each individual is a type to the divine antitype, yet at the same time, when God-infused, is himself an antitype to the world without, giving Nature its nature. The iron string of the immanent antitype activates (under certain Emersonian conditions) all facts. As Brahma, a man has senses (the new antitype) that give reality to all else (the types). Without him they cannot (to him) exist. He *wills*, if he has the inbuilt Will, their significance for him. The reason that beauty is in the eye of the Emersonian beholder is because, as antitype, he makes the quality of the beheld possible; he is *their* maker. Man-Thinking, still another Emerson name for the antitype, brings the facts of the world to his feet. The inevitable circles of Emerson's supra-politics radiate outward to the types of creation from the phenomenal antitype: "Throw a stone into the stream, and the circles that propagate themselves are the beautiful type of all influence." Representative men *create* the world because Emerson has the antitypal position for them to work out of, giving life to all else, the types. Self-reliance, Emerson's catch-all, makes all things rely on the self/Over-Soul/Christ: "A ray of relation passes from every other being to him."

From a structuralist point of view, the distinctions are insignificant between the antitype of Winthrop's city upon

a hill, Sewall's fulfilled America, Cotton's phenomenaliz-
ing Christ, Taylor's attention-giving love-Jesus, Mather's
heroic New England, Edwards' will, and Emerson's imperial self. They all get their worlds going, whether temporally as with orthodox types or spatially as with many of
the plebeian innovations, by conceiving of a Christ who is
the means and the end of all else in their purview.

The influence of Swedenborg, Kant, Coleridge, and
Carlyle on Emerson's anthropology pales, I believe, before
the dominance of the Puritan typological construct in his
fondest positions. The Emerson world is never wholly
secular or autonomous, never *symboliste*, but contingent
(in type-antitype order) on the divine or the divine sur-
rogate, the over-souled self. His effort was, as self-ap-
pointed minister to the needs of the world's types, to stim-
ulate the antitype, a man, to his largest benevolent function.

Since Emerson, this imperial self appears in Thoreau,
Whitman, and many others.[7] Typology is, if carefully used,
a helpful way of distinguishing this aggressive party of
canonized nineteenth-century writers from the disaffected
party—Poe, Hawthorne, Melville, Dickinson, and Twain.
It helped to make social reformers out of conservatively
self-obsessed individualists. The others did not have that
advantage.

Even as he dissociated himself from all religious systems,
Thoreau also succumbed to the pressure to typologize. But

---

[7] See Quentin Anderson's attractive and troubled book, *The Imperial Self: An Essay in American Literary and Cultural History* (New
York, 1971), which identifies the self-reliant consciousness in these
writers as the world's imposing, activating source, but which fails to
identify the Imperial Self in these writers as a religious allusion, a
version of the Puritan antitypal Jesus, an inherited/inherent structure
making some of their innovations possible. For Anderson we have in
these writers an arrogance which is among the sources of America's
social alienation and disorder. Another view (mine, "Emerson and
the Anti-Imperialist Self," *Emerson: New Appraisals: A Symposium*
[Hartford, Conn., 1973]) finds the self in these same writers a powerful
counterforce to American imperialism. Substituting self for Christ in
the typological structure made their nineteenth-century leftism possible. Without it they could not have put literature so easily to the
service of social reform.

with an entertaining difference. Thoreau's Thoreau, an antitypal hero of near-mythic proportions, replaces Emerson's theoretical Over-Soul and over-self. The radical solitary, with his idiosyncratic extremeness and absolutist moral abilities, made his uniqueness inclusive, an antitype actuating typicalities. The types of Thoreau's experience are incarnated in a fantastic, antitypal distinctiveness named for himself. The activity of being oneself in this manner is, in his works, a supreme authority: the Congregational-Unitarian Jesus (man-God in the form of a spirit-personality) is generated in the person who can incorporate the world in himself and then bestow metaphorical ability upon natural facts. Grace abounds, through his presence, to his world and bounds back again to engrace *him*.

The unity of personality makes order out of chaos. Interiorizing God transforms facts. Types ("hieroglyphic[s] of man's life") become the antitype ("ecstas[y] begotten of the breezes") acting itself out. The spirit (a "new sense of things") demands loving the natural (the "forms and phases of the life in nature universally dispersed") into an influence on it, transvaluing the inward and the outward. The objects of nature are organic to (and derive from) the subjective antitype, the whole.

> It is something to be able to paint a particular picture, or to carve a statue, and so to make a few objects beautiful; but it is far more glorious to carve and paint the very atmosphere and medium through which we look, which morally we can do. To affect the quality of the day, that is the highest of arts. Every man is tasked to make his life, even in its details, worthy of the contemplation of his most elevated and critical hour. ("Where I Lived, and What I Lived For," from *Walden*)

In Thoreau's hands, the antitype becomes a quirkily antinomian redeemer of not only the types/the world but also of himself.[8]

[8] In his essay on the emergence of typology in nineteenth-century American literature, "From Edwards to Emerson to Thoreau: A Re-

The Whitman ego is still another antitype with very
much the same structure, conceived from a similar motive,
though with quite a different result. Emerson is, of course,
Whitman's link to Puritan hermeneutics, but Whitman is
still at quite a remove. Other sources of his rhapsodic, anti-
type-like egotism should be considered, such as his experience of the Bible itself, Quaker enthusiasm, Jeffersonian
manifest-destinarianism, Hegelian utopianism, and phreno-
logical personalism. Still, his typological frame of mind
parallels the form taken by mid-nineteenth-century nationalism, millenarianism, and frontier individualism. The role
that Whitman takes in his poetry is that which Puritanism
had desired to build, through innovations on the antitype,
in the American mind. In his more personalistic poems,
Whitman is a type ("I celebrate myself, and sing myself")
who has inflated himself to the position of an antitype
("Walt Whitman, a kosmos, of Manhattan the son"), who
puts his real self and its world to the service of an ideal
self and whose voice is a real man's voice speaking with the
volume, great warmth, and sublimity of the divine. The
ideal actuates the real. In this role, Whitman has stretched
himself to the size of Emerson's universe, one side of him
at the concrete, personal extreme (as type) and his other
side at the divine, universal extreme (as antitype)—both in
one person, himself. He is (understandable, I believe, only
in typological terms) both body *and* universe. The distance

valuation," *American Transcendental Quarterly*, no. 18 (Spring 1973),
Mason I. Lowance, Jr., makes the point that the Transcendentalists
perhaps had the mystical ability to fuse type and antitype: " 'Types'
were no longer needed as prefigurations of 'antitypes.' Rather, the
type and antitype were present together in the eternal mystical moment that transcended all time in a 'sweet' and beautiful experience
of union." The main service of Lowance's essay, the strongest of the
few accurate pieces on nineteenth-century typologizing, is its argument,
particularly with regard to Thoreau, that much of the identity of the
Transcendentalist movement came from its Puritan typological inheritance. A valuable contribution to this argument is William H.
Schurr's review essay, "Typology and Historical Criticism of the
American Renaissance," *Emerson Society Quarterly*, no. 74, Old Series
(First Quarter, 1974), 57–63.

and connection—antitype to type to antitype—is a metaphor for oneself, and a hope for all mankind. The abundance of the universe lies between, in the structure, and so is at one with oneself:

> I speak the pass-word primeval, I give the sign of
> democracy,
> By God! I will accept nothing which all cannot have
> their counterpart of on the same terms.

> Through me many long dumb voices,
> Voices of the interminable generations of prisoners and
> slaves,
> Voices of the diseas'd and despairing and of thieves
> and dwarfs,
> Voices of cycles of preparation and accretion,
> And of the threads that connect the stars, and of
> wombs and of the father-stuff,
> And of the rights of them the others are down upon,
> Of the deform'd, trivial, flat, foolish, despised,
> Fog in the air, beetles rolling balls of dung.

> Through me forbidden voices,
> Voices of sexes and lusts, voices veil'd and I remove
> the veil,
> Voices indecent by me clarified and transfigur'd.
>           ("Song of Myself," 24)

Through the antitype (the cosmic Whitman), the types (the abundance) have coherence, direction, personality, and a single voice. By means of the typological structure, Whitman is the new American Christ. "O to struggle against great odds. . . . To be indeed a God." The mythical Whitman he creates would not have been as possible without typology.

Further, when Whitman describes himself as Poet, he speaks as antitype: "To him enter the essences of the real things," he writes in his 1855 Preface to *Leaves of Grass*, "and past and present events, . . . the enormous diversity." He is the redeemer who would create a new kind of consciousness in us so we might all be "antitypal," giving the world fulfillment by our love. Imposed desire exists on the level of types ("dumb beautiful ministers"), and benevolent, narcissistic assimilation on the level of the antitype, which is the bestowing and absorbing poet/person, "the knot of contrariety." He is, to use Whitman's own metaphors from the 1855 Preface, a great ocean into which all rivers flow after he has fed them with rain, a sun sending out light to be reflected back to him, a phallus exciting others and interacting with them. Whitman as the Brooklyn ferry is an effective Aleph, incorporating "all things at all hours of the day" (the types, in this instance) into "the soul" (the antitype):

> The impalpable sustenance of me from all things at all hours of the day,
> The simple, compact, well-join'd scheme, myself disintegrated, every one disintegrated yet part of the scheme,
> The similitudes of the past and those of the future,
> The glories strung like beads on my smallest sights and hearings, on the walk in the street and the passage over the river,
> The current rushing so swiftly and swimming with me far away,
> The others that are to follow me, the ties between me and them,
> The certainty of others, the life, love, sight, hearing of others.
> . . . . . . . . . . . . . . . . . . .
> You furnish your parts toward eternity,
> Great or small, you furnish your parts toward the soul.
> ("Crossing Brooklyn Ferry")

Whitman is nineteenth-century American literature's most spectacular typologist, though I think he would never have thought of his schemes along medieval lines. He is most certainly the millennialist Cotton Mather called for in his various lives, for he made himself an exemplary prophet (much like an Old Testament seer of the Messianic/utopian) typing out a fulfilled, antitypal America of the future, "confront[ing]," as he wrote in *Democratic Vistas* (1871), "the voiceless but ever erect and active, pervading, underlying will and typic aspiration of the land, in spirit kindred to itself." This America-bound/spirit-bound hope of Whitman's is an innovation within the typological structure of New England millennialism, proclaiming (1) that American history and American lives have their value only in the (typal) process of achieving a fulfilled land ("One common indivisible destiny for All"), and (2) that the fulfilled (antitypal) land, even as hoped for and in process, blesses the spiritualized, democratic abundance with purpose/unity/godhood. The millennialism[9] is itself a process that is very much like Mather's linking of the heroic American past, by way of Christ, to a glorious American future: the types (*all* the facts of American life) point to and are fulfilled in the poet-messiah who blesses them with value and direction and proclaims them and himself further types of a Messianic age ("the *true* America") to come:

> I see in you, certain to come, the promise of thousands
>    of years, till now deferr'd,
> Promis'd to be fulfill'd, our common kind, the race.

> The new society at last, proportionate to Nature,
> In man of you, more than your mountain peaks or
>    stalwart trees imperial,
> In woman more, far more, than all your gold or vines,
>    or even vital air.

[9] It has become a commonplace among students of typology to assign to typology the source of the idea of manifest destiny in the American imagination. But this is difficult to prove. Perhaps the same structure which made New England the antitypal Israel also made American imperialism religious, but this excludes other creative forces than the hermeneutic one. Perhaps typology assisted many writers to make of America a messiah among nations, but it seems safer to hold, until a fully documented discussion can prove otherwise, that not all the nationalist impulses had a source in Puritan typology.

Fresh come, to a new world indeed, yet long prepared,
I see the genius of the modern, child of the real and
    ideal
Clearing the ground for broad humanity, the true
    America, heir of the past so grand,
To build a grander future.

("Song of the Redwood-Tree")

Other appearances of such types in the period are only somewhat less spectacular. Poe's representation of the structure (explored in *Eureka*) is the primordial atom, out of which all creation flies and back to which all creation returns, as antitype to type to antitype. It is, as Poe describes it in "The Fall of the House of Usher," "an inherent positive quality, poured forth upon all objects of the moral and physical universe in one unceasing radiation of gloom." Poe was fairly remote from the pressures of Puritan esthetics and so could not sense the New England justification of the contingent independence of types distant from an antitype but could imagine the world begraced (in the decadence, dissolution, drugged thought, and death as movements toward the divine) only as it seeks, fated, its antitype. The pull of cosmic unity (through madness, disease, overwhelming sensuousness) mocks individuality where puritanized typology justified, even encouraged, it. Yet, curiously, Poe's very static universe is dynamic only in the type-antitype interchange. By virtue of the attracting relationship, it is, for him, a living heart. Because it is fated and because it cannot produce types after the manner of the Judaeo-Christian desire of worldly abundance, Poe's schema is not an entirely convincing typology, but a handful of plebeian types.

As with the classic type in these writers, the plebeian is also a nineteenth-century inheritance. Quanta suggest The Great Quantum in almost everyone's work in the nineteenth century in so obvious a fashion as to require little discussion, except perhaps for the need to show how the form encouraged innovation and helped to father the large body of transcendentalized nature writings of the period from Bryant to Whitman and on to Frost. For the nineteenth-century writer as for the seventeenth-century Puritan, the universe is miraculous and therefore metaphorically alive. Puritan esthetics had been, from the outset, a science of dynamics: a constant watch for God's hand in the world. This watching, at best simplistic but also colorful and stimulating, made both phenomena and the phenomenal providential, as it was to do with America's later writers.

Thus, Emerson's lower forms "predict" the higher ones and are signifiers of the Signified by virtue of the contingency. "Particular natural facts," he is sure, "are symbols of particular spiritual facts," and "Nature is the symbol of spirit." His synecdoches are not mere symbols but organic parts of the overwhelming whole. "The soul of man," he writes in *Representative Men*, "must be the type of our scheme, just as the body of man is the type after which a dwelling house is built." Similarly, Thoreau's walking is a cosmic pilgrim's progress, the ideal walk giving direction and purpose to the real one: "We would fain take that walk, never yet taken by us through this actual world," he wrote in his essay, "Walking," "which is perfectly symbolical of the path which we love to travel in the interior and ideal world. . . ." Similarly, Whitman's homosexuality is a plebeian type to his idea of cosmic unity in much that he wrote, the experiences spiritualized by divine attention on them. "Think of spiritual results," he wrote in a late poem, "Think of the Soul," "Sure as the earth swims through the heavens, does every one of its objects pass into spiritual results."

What is surprising in these plebeian innovations is that, for the most part, they do not go beyond the typological construct while proving the writers' major ideas, but validate it for a new age. The "heresies" affirm the belief.

What *is* new is each writer's own skepticism, reservations, ambiguity. There never was the possibility that typology could dominate any one of these major writers very completely. Emersonian Compensation balances good with evil, evil with good, success with tragedy, war with peace, man with thing, making complex and diffuse the typological simplicities of an earlier age of faith. "All things are double," Emerson admits in contradistinction to his own monism, "one against another." His antitypic Over-Soul cannot hold them and becomes in the end a tragic, because never realizable, ideal. Thoreau discovered at Walden Pond, to give another example of factors that were working against the typological, that life is achievable only in process, undercutting typology as a fixed schema. An antitype on the go cannot affect its types convincingly; the Oriental in him has changed the neat Christian types in his thinking into ungraspable, unknowable flux. Whitman, very much like these others, allows his self to equivocate, polish its self-doubts, and nourish multiform inconsistencies, until we suspect (against his best art and wishes) that he, as antitype, is perhaps merely an inflated ego. The god-mask falls as soon as we touch (at his own insistence) his body. Whitman is grand, perhaps, because he is lonely and loves everything, and not because, Christ-like, he can encompass all things. Autobiography betrays the ideal.

Far stronger objections to typologizing come from Hawthorne, Melville, and Twain, however, for they are by and large disaffected with what are to them the arrogant assumptions and unquestioned demands of the structure to which the other party fits its typological needs. To their minds, the antitype has become the means of a literary fascism. In Hawthorne the antitype is therefore turned into the evil in the heart, a principle stimulating (yet ultimately also negating) all typal actions. "The heart, the heart,—" he wrote in his sketch "Earth's Holocaust," "there was the little yet boundless sphere wherein existed the original wrong of which the crime and misery of this outward world were merely types." In Melville the antitype appears as a tragically self- and world-destructive ship's captain, a confidence man, a chronometrical principle separated from all earthly types. His antitype/archetype, the whale, is merely (but awfully) a whitewashed malevolence, mingled beauty and horror. For the most part, Melville's antitypes have a tragic or even grotesque effect, are parodies of the varieties of fascism in the writings of the conventional typologizers of the period. For Melville, the antitype is always inscrutable; then the world is unavailable for types related to it. Specifics are cancelled as indicators of another world. Without the typological structure, purposefulness is lost. In Twain the negation is pushed even further: the antitype takes the form of a horrifying Satan, a malevolence reducing all types to an illusion. His ambivalence toward his messianic Connecticut Yankee mixes hostility and affection. The antitypal principle of damnation motivates/ruins the entire human race. No antitype can survive such ambivalence except as fool's illusion and arrogance.

The Emerson-Thoreau-Whitman frontier of types (a world of infinite, inspirited possibilities) evolves into the other party's bitter paradoxes. This disaffected party of writers is less sure of the tenor, less sure of the spirit that makes the types go, less sure of an antitype giving direction and purpose. For them (to use Melville's analogy in *Pierre*) the chronometrical is *not* the horologicals. Typology has, for the most part, gone sour. It is an icon to be blasted, a butt of jokes, a whipping-post, an object of fairly violent anger, a mistake.

Like the attack on the American dream in twentieth-century American literature, typology inspired much iconoclastic writing.[10] Hawthorne's Mr. Smooth-it-away is Emerson's antitype turned deceiver. Ethan Brand's antitype, the Unforgivable Sin, drives him to suicide. Young Goodman Brown's antitypal principle of evil scars his life. The Great Carbuncle, Peter Goldthwaite's treasure, and Owen Warland's butterfly are antitypes reduced to illusory

---

[10] With a tremendous pun, Cooper's psalmodist David in *The Last of the Mohicans* (1826) parodies Puritan typologizing: "Never before have I beheld a beast which verified the true Scripture war-horse like this. . . . It would seem that the stock of the horse of Israel has descended to our own time; would it not, friend?"

symbols. Melville's antitypal Ahab is Whitman's passer-to-more-than-India as fascist leader. His whale is the antitype as unknowable, his messianic Captain Delany as naif, his Billy Budd (at the outset an intended antitypal figure) a disrupter of realities and therefore criminal. And in Twain, damnation is the organizing principle of an unfathomable world, an antitype gone cynical. Moral conscience, formerly the organizing agent, is the villain. In all these writers, the parodies are tragedies. The antitype is monstrous—and empty.

Plebeian typologizing, on the other hand, continued as a structure with a life of its own in nineteenth-century American literature—as synecdoche, metonymy, symbol, objective correlative, imagistic image, and other self-extending forms—in part, I would like to suggest, because of the survival of some measure of belief in some kind of holy spirit that holds all things together in revealing relationships, in part because of the sheer momentum of an interwined moralistic-hermeneutic tradition, and in part because of an increasing trust in subjective experience as spiritual indicator. Mather's "extraordinary things wherein the existence and agency of the invisible world is more sensibly demonstrated" and Edwards' "whole viewed in various lights" or "consent between the beauty of the skies, trees, fields, flowers, etc., and spiritual excellencies" were adjusted only slightly in the plebeian structure of metaphor in nineteenth-century writing. Analogy became the nineteenth century's relic of religion; it is about all that is left of a once-magical, harmonious universe, the surviving supposition of half-believers.

I find little distinctive about nineteenth-century American plebeian typologizing, however, from that of other literatures, except, perhaps, for the religious emphasis, its preponderance, and the fact that it became strongly democratized: all things suggested the *all* of things. And perhaps these are the effects of the seventeenth century.

The structure of the plebeian type, it seems necessary to reiterate, continued into the nineteenth century as innovations: a relationship encouraging new matter drawn from one's needs. The structure was not a symbol itself, or a set of symbols, which the writers used to replace earlier religion,[11] but a form which kept the *form* of earlier thinking alive without much extending the earlier ideas into a new age. The difference is a matter of some importance, helping us to explain how, in the nineteenth century, Puritanism could be dead as a coherent system of beliefs, yet explaining how a Puritan mode of thinking could persist in the major writers, no matter how liberalized. Plebeian typologizing—as structured by the Bible, medieval exegetes, the Puritans, and especially Mather and Edwards in a long mind-ordering tradition to the point of making it *mythic*— became to the nineteenth century (to use Borges' example once more) *any* shadow of *any* rose. *Because* it had become the structure of American thinking, it was used as widely and wildly as it was. The structure set a person free. Puritanism thus liberated the liberators from Puritanism.

But I was pointing out how there were also American writers in the nineteenth century on the offensive against this myth, in whichever form, classic or plebeian. Quite a number of weapons were wielded by the Disaffected Party of writers, but ambiguity was by all odds the voice to which these writers most effectively resorted to bring the typological constructs down. And I believe it won out. The scheme of literary history that I make here, giving the Disaffected Party of Hawthorne, Melville, Twain, and Emily Dickinson the final triumph over the positions of Emerson, Thoreau, and Whitman, may, like F. O. Matthiessen's *American Renaissance*, not give the whole story. Yet while the influence of Emerson and Whitman on the politics, the social sciences, the educational theory, and the arts in America has been more pervasive, the teleology of the other writers appears now to have been considerably more modern. Changed by such writers as Kafka, Nabokov, Borges, and others, we can now recognize their triumph.

With Hawthorne, Melville, and Emily Dickinson we have, over against the true belief of the typologizers of the

---

[11] A mistake, I feel, in the argument of Charles Feidelson, Jr., *op. cit.*, pp. 162–212.

period, the beginning of a literature of humility—and largely because of the services of ambiguity.

Hawthorne, for one, would not have been able to use typology in Puritan fashion, for it presumes knowledge of the transcendent/omnipotent antitype, God. His tendency, when he uses metaphorical terms like "type" and "allegory," is often to qualify them with the subjunctive or conjectural. In "The Vision of the Fountain," we have: "Dreamy as the scene was, might it not be the type of . . ." and in "Egotism, or the Bosom Serpent," we have: "It was the general opinion . . . that the Brazen Serpent . . . was really the type of. . . ."

Ambiguity in these writers—and many others of this period of increasing uncertainty about the settled assumptions that made typology possible—does not represent polarized imagination or conceptual antithesis but, instead, an ability to synthesize and suspend that the typologizer did not have. American ambiguity is not a desperately divided state of mind or tormented perspective, not mere conflict, but balance without resolution, without coherence —a condition that would undercut any proposed antitype. Such ambiguity does not so much show a dual point of view or simple perception of inherent paradox—which could, after a fashion, be inserted into the typological construct —as it does a tentativeness—which, I believe, could not. Ambiguity is an attempt to realize an ineffable complexity, and it represents a struggle with materials but without victory, certainly conditional. The ambiguist, unlike the typologizer, is a confessed loser: alternatives become juxtaposed without offering a choice; all is shown, nothing wins; something is many things, *anything*. Melville's poem "Art" makes an effective definition:

> In placid hours well-pleased we dream
> Of many a brave unbodied scheme.
> But form to lend, pulsed life create,
> What unlike things must meet and mate:
> A flame to melt—a wind to freeze;

Sad patience—joyous energies;
Humility—yet pride and scorn;
Instinct and study; love and hate;
Audacity—reverence. These must mate,
And fuse with Jacob's mystic heart,
To wrestle with the angel—Art.

Ambiguity as we find it in these writers of the Disaffected Party is a form of irrationalism. Their effort is not to emphasize confusion, flux, or the unfinishedness of the Creation, but our condition of unknowing, thereby frustrating our customary intellectual desire for logical resolution, like that which types attempt to satisfy. The result is stasis, self-consciousness, humility. They recognize reversal, ambiguity, anomaly, complexity, the impossibility of naming, identifying, knowing, and therefore the pervasiveness of the Fall; yet at the same time they recognize the richness, depth, and fullness of things (albeit unknowable, untouchable) and therefore the grace inherent in existence. A neo-Puritanism—Hawthorne's, Melville's, Emily Dickinson's—is the result. *Nothing is sure, everything is possible.* Not always knowing the truth, these writers fabricate it in forms that include, humbly, the possibilities. The uncertainty principle is their answer to typology. They become the realists we tend to call them by *not* understanding the structure and substance of things. The suspension is creative. The Fortunate Fall in their hands is a creative misunderstanding. A universe that is provisional makes any structural arrangement imposed on it, as typology had been, totally artificial, even foolish.

The simultaneity of contrarieties—that is, ambiguity as a rich condition of unknowing—was for these writers an apposite order, replacing simplicities like those of typology. Doubt is faith. Uncertainty is a certainty, insecurity a security. Forever is made up of nows. The real is fictitious, fiction real. The light is dark enough. Success lies within failure.

This persistent dualism in these writers wards off tragedy as I feel neither of the structures of typology could. It works against the consecutive and for "naturalness," for the settled, determined state of things, for lush, fractured, meaningless, observed reality. By ambiguity these writers emphasize their contingency. Ambiguity is a statement of faith for them.

Thus, we have among nineteenth-century American writers those (Emerson, Thoreau, and Whitman have been our present examples) who lost faith in Puritan ideology but retained the Puritan typological structure of ideas by means of innovation—*because* it was a structure. And we have those (Hawthorne, Melville, Emily Dickinson, and Twain) who maintained closer ties with Puritan ideas (however much to their personal and artistic detriment at times) but only by dismantling seventeenth-century structures that had come down to them, among them the typological. To some extent, both heresies are, ironically, affirmations.

## III

I would like to make a special case of Emily Dickinson, if only for emphasis of my points. Because I find in her some of the most faithful remnants of Puritan esthetics of any nineteenth-century writer, some of the strongest resistance to Puritan controls, and some of the subtlest transformations of major Puritan assumptions of her age, I would suggest that in her poetry one may find the late nineteenth-century's best example of what became of religious typology.[12]

[12] I confess that another set of nineteenth-century writers—the less esteemed—might show the survival of typology in a different light. Writers closer to religious institutions (like, say, Channing, Whittier, Brownson, Jones Very, and Beecher) also kept the forms of the faith. I do not emphasize what they might have retained of the tradition because, although they might have kept the earlier content very much in mind, we in the twentieth century have not kept *them* very much in mind. A contemporary of Emily Dickinson's, Harriet Beecher Stowe, for example, gets typology right. See her poem "A Day in the Pamfili Doria":

> And this strange and ancient city,
> In that reign of His truth and love,
> Shall *be* what it *seems* in the twilight,
> The type of that City above.

Typological terminology turns up in Emily Dickinson's poems, to be sure, but most of the medieval/religious sense has gone out of it. It means little that she uses it.

> Further in Summer than the Birds
> Pathetic from the Grass
> A minor Nation celebrates
> It's unobtrusive Mass.
>
> No Ordinance be seen
> So gradual the Grace
> A pensive Custom it becomes
> Enlarging Loneliness.
>
> Antiquest felt at Noon
> When August burning low
> Arise this spectral Canticle
> Repose to typify. . . . (no. 1068)

Here "typify" makes a religious allusion that fits the devotional imagery of the poem, but its intent is Wordsworthian: the crickets suggest the idea of repose.

In two other cases, Emily Dickinson uses the terms somewhat more traditionally, although the intent is still a little vague. Here we have her definition of "types":

> The Things that never can come back, are several—
> Childhood—some forms of Hope—the Dead—
> Though Joys—like Men—may sometimes make a
>     Journey—
> And still abide—
> We do not mourn for Traveler, or Sailor,
> Their Routes are fair—
> But think enlarged of all that they will tell us
> Returning here—
> "Here!" There are typic "Heres"—
> Foretold Locations—
> The Spirit does not stand—
> Himself—at whatsoever Fathom
> His Native Land. (no. 1515)

And here her definition of "antitype":

> The murmuring of Bees, has ceased
> But murmuring of some[thing]
> Posterior, prophetic,
> Has simultaneous come.
> The lower metres of the Year
> When Nature's laugh is done[,]
> The revelations of the Book
> Whose Genesis was June.
> Appropriate Creatures to her change
> The [anti]Typic Mother sends
> As Accent fades to interval
> With separating Friends[,]
> Till what we speculate, has been
> and thoughts we will not show
> More intimate with us become
> Than Persons, that we know. (no. 1115)

The terms themselves do not interest her much; the method is largely lost on her. As with the bulk of writings in the late nineteenth century, the terminology of typology in Emily Dickinson cannot be depended on to yield a Puritan sense.

Quite a number of things present themselves tentatively in her poetry as antitypes, but none of them is very convincing. For her, Jesus does not have either control over historical events nor the ability to order the world spatially. He is reduced to the sentimental role of friend ("Jesus! thy second face / Mind thee in Paradise / Of our's"), indifferent lover ("Jesus—it's your little John! / Don't you know me?"), lost savior ("And 'Jesus'! Where is *Jesus* gone? . . . Perhaps he doesn't know the House"), and undependable redeemer ("Say, Jesus Christ of Nazareth— / Hast thou no Arm for Me?"). Christ is available to Emily Dickinson for analogy but not for typology:

> A piercing Comfort it affords
> In passing Calvary—

To note the fashions—of the Cross—
And how they're mostly worn—
Still fascinated to presume
That Some—are like My Own— (no. 561)

God is a reference point for her life and for nature but lacks the main feature of an antitype—a clearly absolute magnanimity and inclusiveness.

I think, they call it "God"—
Renowned to ease Extremity—
When Formula, had failed—

And shape my Hands—
Petition's way,
Tho' ignorant of a word
That Ordination—utters—

My Business, with the Cloud,
If any Power behind it, be,
No subject to Despair—
It care, in some remoter way,
For so minute affair
As Misery—
Itself, too great, for interrupting—more— (no. 293)

Her "If any Power behind it be" suggests her need more than her faith, which no antitype could satisfy. She could confront God only as the object of her skepticism. "Faith *is* doubt!" she exclaimed in an 1874 letter. What antitype could survive such ambiguity? "Grant me, Oh Lord, a sunny mind— / Thy windy will to bear!"

In a poem above we have still another possible antitype, nature, "The Typic Mother." But try as she might to transcendentalize the world, Emily Dickinson cannot keep her mind on the Iron String on which all things are strung, as types to antitype, in Emerson, Thoreau, and Whitman. It is difficult for her to personify into some antitypal force-that - through - all - the - green - fuses - of - the - world - might-drive-the-flower those characteristics of nature of which her experience teaches her, simply because it includes not only an abundance of possible types ("The spreading wide my narrow Hands / To gather Paradise") but also illusion, ellipsis, elusiveness, and delusion ("Nature is what we know — / Yet impotent Our Wisdom is / To her Simplicity"). The antitype, no matter how open, cannot be a riddle. "Can I expound the skies? / How still the Riddle lies!"

Still another place in Emily Dickinson where one might attempt to find a sufficient antitype to convince him that the classic structure still functions in the late nineteenth century in some innovation is in the role of a superior sensibility to which she elevates herself, making a self somewhat parallel to Whitman's. All the types in the world might be seen as turned into possibilities by the influence of her strong, antitypal personality—a personality that is just the weight of God, that selects its own society, that "unto itself / Is an imperial friend." She seems never to have thought through thoroughly enough, however, the metaphysics of sentience (Edwards and Emerson, her more accessible esthetic forebears, had made the senses the criterion of the sensed) to make of her delight a center bringing both herself and her world alive. She could not/ would not elevate her knowns to an Unknown which was both cause and effect of things. Puritan meiosis in her prevented such security:

> Why—do they shut Me out of Heaven?
> Did I sing—too loud?
> But—I can say a little "Minor"
> Timid as a Bird! (no. 248)

Her solipsism is not strong enough to impose a will on the world to make it yield, narcissistically, a pattern of herself. The typological structure implies a relationship, and she cannot relate.

The Bible pervades her poetry just as much as it does the writings of the most orthodox of the period, and among the wide variety of uses to which she puts Scripture (from private consolation to crude parody) some typologizing can be found. Her application of the method is generally extremely personal, however, undercutting the historical and platonic in the Christian tradition of types. In a poem of 1862, for example, she can argue that an intimate friendship of hers is true because related typologically to Christ's "new Marriage" with the elect hereafter:

There came a Day at Summer's full,
Entirely for me—
I thought that such were for the Saints,
Where Resurrections—be—

The Sun, as common, went abroad,
The flowers, accustomed, blew,
As if no soul the solstice passed
That maketh all things new—

The time was scarce profaned, by speech—
The symbol of a word
Was needless, as at Sacrament,
The Wardrobe—of our Lord—

Each was to each The Sealed Church,
Permitted to commune this—time—
Lest we too awkward show
At Supper of the Lamb. . . .

Sufficient troth, that we shall rise—
Deposed—at length, the Grave—
To that new Marriage,
Justified—through Calvaries of Love— (no. 322)

It is difficult to believe that Emily Dickinson thinks of this, however, as any more than simple biblical analogy. More often she feels that because her life is significantly anomalous and unique, she cannot gain typal significance from Christ the Antitype:

Our Lord—indeed—made Compound Witness—
And yet—
There's newer—nearer Crucifixion
That That — (no. 553)

Her own sufferings are her own sufferings. No metaphorical connections with Christ can stop the pain.

In her most conventional use of typological icons from the Bible, a poem of about 1860, she refreshes Augustus Toplady's popular "Rock of ages, cleft for me" by personalizing and parodying the conventional images of Christ that had come down from the Middle Ages:

A *Wounded* Deer—leaps highest—
I've heard the Hunter tell—
'Tis but the Extasy of *death*—
And then the Brake is still!

The *Smitten* Rock that gushes!
The *trampled* Steel that springs!
A Cheek is always redder
Just where the Hectic stings!

Mirth is the Mail of Anguish—
In which it Cautious Arm,
Lest anybody spy the blood
And "you're hurt" exclaim!   (no. 165)[13]

Her "Extasy of death," the gushing rock and springing steel, and the reddened cheek are trite and excessive by 1860 standards, certainly by her own standards; she is parodying the typological method by which Christians took significance into their lives in an earlier age. She does not believe the typal Moses-Jesus parallel to apply to her: the crucified Christ ends up "highest" but *her* defense against anguish is to laugh. She scoffs at the typological solution and has one, more playful, of her own.

Typologizing was largely impossible to Emily Dickinson because most of her biblical analogies are undercut by doubt:

Ararat's a Legend—now—
And no one credits Noah— (no. 403)

[13] The italics are in the original. I am indebted to Professors George P. Landow and Barton L. St. Armand of Brown University for pointing up this example. [See below, p. 339.—Ed.]

in soberer moments—
No Moses there can be    (no. 597)

That after Horror—that 'twas *us*—
That passed the mouldering Pier—
Just as the Granite Crumb let go—
Our Savior, by a Hair—
A second more, had dropped too deep
For Fisherman to plumb—  (no. 286)

Though she treasured the Bible in her own way, she by and large thought it "an antique Volume— / Written by faded Men / At the suggestion of Holy Spectres—" (no. 1545).

There is, however, one other interest in typology that Emily Dickinson shows, and it has to do with hermeneutics itself rather than the Bible. In a letter of 1851, she introduces an intriguing innovation—that a word *as a word* is a type of, not the antitypal thing represented by the word, but the maker of the word:

> I cant write but a word, dear Austin, because its already noon and Vinnie is waiting to go to the office for me, and yet a *single word* may be of comfort to you as you go travelling on. It should be a word big and warm and full of sweet affection if I could make it so—Oh it should fill that room, that small and lonely chamber with a thousand kindly things and precious ministrations—I wonder if it *will*, for know that if it *does* not, it is bad and disobedient and a most unworthy type of its affectionate mistress.

There is a typological poetics hinted at here: the words made by a poet lead to her personally, vindicating her existence, having no worth in themselves after they are fulfilled in the antitype, their maker, yet serving her worth even as they lose their own. A word is projected as a living synecdoche/foreshadow of the "mistress"/Master, who is the archetype of the private poet: wordy, disinterested, self-sufficient, shy of production yet dependent on the negligible. The word has purpose only in its abrogation in the idiosyncratic egotism of an absurd imperial self. Emily Dickinson's words/poems are subsumed in her elect person. But this possibility for an inventive poetics of typology goes undeveloped by her, hardly sensed at all. Her philosophy of words—her self-conscious epistemologicality—is varied and confused and only by accidental turns classically typological.

In Emily Dickinson one might expect orthodox typology to have had a final, glorious appearance. But Puritanism could not elevate the sacred, nor Transcendentalism the secular, to an antitype in her mind, even though she tried her hand at such in these few of her poems, as if she was sometimes tempted by the old/new orthodoxies. But she seemed to have sensed for the most part that both made tyrannies out of superstitions. The antitype was largely missing from her poetry because it was *immaterial* for her to have an antitype. Like many, Emily Dickinson found out the inaccuracy of the structure. Like Hawthorne and Melville, she preferred uncertainty. Over against the argument of the persistence of Puritanism in this woman, we have the absence of orthodox typologizing as an effective argument that she was of sufficiently different mind.

What was left of the typological for her and others in the late nineteenth century to use, as I have mentioned above, was the plebeian, what she called "The Glimmering Frontier that / skirts the Acres of Perhaps." The structure had to be *projected*, from plebeian materials and from one's own interesting and fallible experience—an easier, less innovative, yet more dangerous, method of believing.

> A science—so the Savans say,
> "Comparative Anatomy"—
> By which a single bone—
> Is made a secret to unfold
> Of some rare tenant of the mold,
> Else perished in the stone—

So to the eye prospective led,
This meekest flower of the mead
Upon a winter's day,
Stands representative in gold
Of Rose and Lily, manifold,
And countless Butterfly! (no. 100)

The "representative" flower (perhaps herself) stands, after the Emersonian manner of each and all, as typal synecdoche of the whole of nature. The plebeian method thus justifies/rationalizes/enlivens one's own small world. Awe over a little is Emily Dickinson's personal idiosyncratic adaptation of plebeian typologizing.

In a poem of 1862, she defines plebeian typology for us after a nineteenth-century New England fashion: the type is homely and arbitrary; the antitype is remote and spiritual; the language chosen for the type makes it possible to delight in the superiority of the antitype; and the result is that the means for exploring and explaining the antitype are more fascinating than the antitype itself.

... Least Village has it's Blacksmith
Whose Anvil's even ring
Stands symbol for the finer Forge
That soundless tugs—within—
Refining these impatient Ores
With Hammer, and with Blaze
Until the Designated Light
Repudiate the Forge— (no. 365)

A catalog of the plebeian types in Emily Dickinson's poetry might run to the thousands, though presenting the annoying difficulty of requiring one to distinguish between types, simple Wordsworthian platonizing, and simple vehicles of regular metaphors. The difficulty reveals that she did not think typological distinctions worth making.

Her poetry teaches us that the descent of plebeian typology from Cotton Mather and Edwards to Emily Dickinson and the late nineteenth century is marked by increasing mistrust in the old symbolical arrangements. The Puritan antitypes dislodged, the types become more and more private, ambiguous, eccentric, playful. The vehicle cannot find its tenor. The signs do not divine.

This is not to suggest that Emily Dickinson was blind to the methodology of types, only (as suggested in the following lines from a poem of 1864) that she could not see the practice without some irony, complexity, ambiguity:

> . . . The Finite—furnished
> With the Infinite—
> Convex—and Concave Witness—
> Back—toward Time—
> And forward—
> Toward the God of Him— (no. 906)

"Furnished / With," indeed! The antitype has become an invention, a projection, a mere convexity made by a mere concavity.

The honest duplicity with which Emily Dickinson faced her Puritan background—using but abusing its forms, often amusingly—is an example of how belief often remained possible in the period only in the guise of ambiguity. At least this was the case with Emily Dickinson.[14] She could deal with "The mingled side / Of [God's] Divinity" by means of what she called her "Compound Vision," her "Compound Witness," her ability to "see Comparatively," that is, by ambiguity rather than by means of any pious structure handed her by tradition like that of the typological. We have it from her herself that, given the world's opportunities and confusion and given man's condition of unknowing, "Opposites—entice." This was a religious-esthetic principle with her. Her concept of ambiguity was

---

[14] In his biography of her, *This Was a Poet* (New York, 1938), p. 200, George F. Whicher says of Emily Dickinson that "her long struggle to face down frustration gave her a curious doubleness of vision, as though her two eyes did not make one in sight but, bird-like, were focussed in opposite directions. . . ."

religious simply because religion did not have the sharp edges and distinct shadows for her that it had for those who could use the typological structures with some conviction. Faith and doubt were grasped in a single act of vision. The substance of religion was to be enjoyed, as it was by Hawthorne and Melville to a similar extent, on heretical grounds.

Opposites entice, she held, because both faith and the imagination work ambiguously, oxymoronically: *Nothing is sure, everything is possible.* Hope and hopelessness intermix: "So bubble brooks in deserts / On Ears that dying lie." The absolute diffracts: God is simultaneously "Burglar! [*and*] Banker." Life persists amid flux and change: "How much can come / And much can go / And yet abide the world." Emotions, a sure thing, deceive us: Grief is "A piercing Comfort"; "A woe of Ecstasy"; a "perfect—paralyzing Bliss." Life may be at various times for her a "lonesome Glory," a "mute Pomp," "sordid excellence," an "Honor honorless." Existence, the unknown, is, in the perfect ambiguity/oxymoron for both her faith and her art, "a magic prison."

These enticing opposites throughout her writing come from defective vision, not insight. Any structured piety must be dismantled because, as she puts it in a poem of 1862, we cannot see "The Thing so towering high" and so must be content with tentative things ("This Morning's finer Verdict—"). We are thereby spared "The Anguish" of trying for all and failing. The duplicity of things is still a matter of hope, however: "The waking in a Gnat's embrace — / Our Giants further on—" (no. 534). This is what she has in place of any structured belief like that of the typological, an Uncertainty Principle. Like Hawthorne and Melville, she became a realist by *not* understanding things. The suspension is, after a very Puritan manner, creative.

She seems always to have sensed that human life is ambiguous at its core—and (here was her Christian optimism) that that was its *advantage*. She detected life to be an oxymoronic situation in which contrarieties occur simultaneously, where contingency persists amid paradise, where nothing is sure but much is possibly possible. Her definition of "a Life . . . Below" is:

'Tis this—invites—appalls—endows—
Flits—glimmers—proves—dissolves—
Returns—suggests—convicts—enchants—
Then—flings in Paradise— (no. 673)

The motive of her poetry appears for the most part to be modification of the sure (" 'Tis a Baffling Earth") and documentation of the possible (what she calls "the Acres of Perhaps"). Her antinomies are those of a woman doing battle without victory—with faith, however, in the possible. This is her reconstruction of Puritan piety as ambiguity.

# MOSES STRIKING THE ROCK: TYPOLOGICAL SYMBOLISM IN VICTORIAN POETRY

ALTHOUGH it is a commonplace that we have lost the intimate knowledge of the Bible which characterized literate people of the last century, we have yet to perceive the full implications of our loss. In the Victorian period—to go back no further—any person who could read, whether or not a believer, was likely to recognize scriptural allusions. Equally important, he was also likely to recognize allusions to typological interpretations of the Scriptures. When we modern readers fail to make such once common recognitions, we deprive many Victorian works of a large part of their context. Having thus impoverished them, we then find ourselves in a situation comparable to that of the reader trying to understand a poem in a foreign language after someone has gone through his dictionary deleting important words. Ignorant of typology, we under-read and misread many Victorian works, and the danger is that the greater the work, the more our ignorance will distort and inevitably reduce it.

The writings of John Ruskin, the great Victorian critic of art and society, well exemplify major works which have thus fallen victim to modern inabilities to supply a once obvious context. Figural symbolism and the habits of mind derived from it provide a major, if little noticed, source of unity in his thought, informing both his interpretations of art and his theories of beauty, imagination, and ideal art.[1] Drawing upon his knowledge of Evangelical typology,

---

[1] For a detailed explication of the effect of typological symbolism upon his thought and writings, see my *Aesthetic and Critical Theories of John Ruskin* (Princeton, 1971), especially pp. 329–356. The emphasis in this earlier work is upon how Ruskin moves, in the manner of

Ruskin explicates Giotto and Tintoretto, and, sounding like any Victorian preacher, he uses typological interpretations of the Levitical sacrifice to argue that men of the nineteenth century should lavish money upon their houses of worship. Figuralism, in fact, permeates Ruskin's thought, appearing in the most unexpected places—not only in his readings of individual paintings and buildings but also in his discussions of geology, history, and aesthetics. The emphasis of typology on the reality of both type and antitype—of signifier and signified—left a particularly heavy impress upon his thought. For example, such an emphasis lies at the heart of Ruskin's theory of typical beauty, which asserts that men instinctively enjoy certain visual qualities, such as proportion and balance, because they are the material embodiment of divine qualities. Ever a polemical author, he uses this conception of beauty, as he does many of his other aesthetic theories, as a means of avoiding a crude didacticism; and he can do so because he believes that typical beauty, like types of Christ, exists simultaneously on two levels or in two different contexts: the aesthetic surface of nature (or of a painting) has its own reality, but, Ruskin emphasized, this reality is completed only by reference to God. Since he believed that the perception of beauty is thus intrinsically a religious and moral act, the art which records or creates it necessarily possesses great value. This simultaneous emphasis upon two poles of meaning, or two levels of existence, appears again in Ruskin's notions of an ideal art which combines a realistic style with complex symbolic intentions as a way of reconciling fact and imagination, materialism and idealism.

Students of the Pre-Raphaelites have long realized that Ruskin had a major influence upon the program of these painters and poets. Few have realized, however, that Holman Hunt and his associates read, not the first volume of

---

many nineteenth-century exegetes, from typology to allegory (see pp. 370–457).

*Modern Painters*, which emphasized truth to nature, but the second volume, which contained Ruskin's theories of beauty and imagination.[2] As Holman Hunt several times points out in *Pre-Raphaelitism and the Pre-Raphaelite Brotherhood*, he gained inspiration from the critic's description of the way Tintoretto used typology to reconcile the demands of a realistic technique with the need for spiritual truths.[3] If Hunt is correct, then we must make a major reassessment of the Pre-Raphaelites and their significance in the history of art. Certainly, Hunt appears to be supported by the large number of Pre-Raphaelite paintings and poems which employ this form of symbolism—Millais' *Christ in the House of His Parents*; Rossetti's paintings of the Virgin Mary and the poems which accompany them; his *Passover in the Holy Family* and its companion poem; the Llandalf triptych; Holman Hunt's own *Scapegoat, Finding of the Saviour in the Temple, The Shadow of Death, Triumph of the Innocents*, and *Christ Among the Doctors*; Collins' *Pedlar*; and poems by Collinson and Christina Rossetti.

Sounding strikingly like Hunt and Ruskin, Elizabeth Barrett Browning also founds a theory of the arts upon typology. In the seventh book of *Aurora Leigh* (1856), her heroine thus asserts that one must emphasize both

> Natural things
> And spiritual,—who separates those two
> In art, in morals, or the social drift,
> Tears up the bond of nature and brings death,
> Paints futile pictures, writes unreal verse.

2 Although Herbert Sussman's "Hunt, Ruskin, and *The Scapegoat*," *Victorian Studies*, 12 (1968), 83–90, points out that Hunt had read the second volume of *Modern Painters* and that the artist was interested in symbolism, it does not recognize that typology is a central issue.

3 See my essay "William Holman Hunt's 'The Shadow of Death,'" *Bulletin of the John Rylands Library*, 55 (1972), 197–239 for a documented discussion of typological symbolism in Hunt's painting. In a work now in progress I plan to examine in detail the role of figural symbolism in Pre-Raphaelite painting and poetry.

Combining scriptural allusion, Platonism, and standard Augustinian explanations of symbolism, she argues that without the spiritual,

> The natural's impossible,—no form,
> No motion: without sensuous, spiritual
> Is inappreciable,—no beauty or power:
> And in this twofold sphere the twofold man
> (For still the artist is intensely a man)
> Holds firmly by the natural, to reach
> The spiritual beyond it,—*fixes still*
> *The type with mortal vision, to pierce through,*
> *With eyes immortal, to the antetype*
> Some call the ideal, better called the real,
> And certain to be called so presently
> When things shall have their names. (my emphasis)

As we might expect from a poet who advances such an artistic program, Mrs. Browning makes use of typological symbolism in her own works, and she is also drawn to figuralism's connection of two times, the second of which fulfills and completes the first. Thus, "The Lost Bower," one of many Victorian paradises lost, explains that the speaker's inability to rediscover an idyllic forest retreat prefigures all the losses which come about with adulthood and immersion in everyday existence. In contrast, "Italy and the World" borrows the notion of prefiguration for an overtly political poem, as, like Swinburne, she presents the Risorgimento in religious terms.

I may also point out in passing that the poetry of Gerard Manley Hopkins, which frequently makes use of figural symbolism, seems to have intentions strangely similar to those of Hunt, Ruskin, and Mrs. Browning.[4] The persistent inability of critics to perceive how deeply Hopkins is rooted

---

[4] Hopkins, for instance, alludes to the sacrifice of first fruits (and probably the levitical sacrifice as well) in "Barnfloor and Winepress"; to the "old drouth" and "new song" in "He hath abolished the old drouth"; to the latter rain in "Thou are indeed just, Lord"; and to a very complex series of figural images in "New Readings."

in his Victorian environment nowhere appears more clearly than in their failure to perceive the genesis of his most characteristic poems in typology. Like Ruskin—here almost certainly a major influence—the poet continually seeks a means of combining a rich, complex aesthetic surface with a carefully articulated symbolism. It is not so much that "The Windhover" and similar poems exemplify Ruskin's theocentric aesthetic theories deriving from typology, though of course they do, but rather that his entire conception of inscape and its relation to the structure of a poem seems to develop from a mind accustomed to seeking types and figures of Christ. A poem such as "The Windhover" elaborately presents the sensuous, visible details of a really existing thing—here the hawk—and then makes us realize the elaborate Christian significance of each detail, as (like a type) the image of the bird is "completed" only by reference to Christ. Once again the effect of typology is to create an experimental art which demands that the audience meditate upon both literal and symbolic senses.

A rather different, if equally important influence of figuralism appears in Tennyson's *In Memoriam*. Here it is typology's linking of times and events, rather than its equal emphasis upon signifier and signified, which is important. Organizing his poem in terms of plays upon the word "type," the poet closes the elegy with the now calm assurance that Hallam

> was a noble type
> Appearing ere the times were ripe,
> That friend of mine who lives in God,
>
> That god, which ever lives and loves,
> One God, one law, one element,
> And one far-off divine event,
> To which the whole creation moves.

As John D. Rosenberg has commented of these lines, "Hallam is at once the noble type of evolution's crowning race and forerunner of 'the Christ that is to be.' . . . With the

'one far-off divine event' we confront Tennyson's final
effort at uniting evolutionary science and Christian faith.
For that event holds out the promise both of the Kingdom
of Heaven, when all shall 'live in God,' and the Kingdom
of Earth, when all shall have evolved into gods."⁵ Rephras-
ing Professor Rosenberg's point, we can observe that
Tennyson has resolved the crisis of faith precipitated by
Hallam's death by assuming that his friend is doubly a type,
one which foreshadows both the second appearance of
Christ and also that of the higher race of men. In making
this characteristically Victorian—that is, characteristically
idiosyncratic—use of typology, Tennyson "solves" the problem raised earlier in the poem by his other uses of the word
"type" where it means "biological species." The central sections 54 through 56, which dramatize his groping for consolation, show how his doubts raised increasingly appalling
spectres. He thus begins section 54 with trust that when
God's plan is understood, all will see that not one life is
"cast as rubbish to the void," but even as he tries to assert
this hopeful view, his doubts wear away his confidence.
Retreating, he tries in the next section to find consolation
in the fact that though nature may be careless of the
individual life, she is nonetheless "careful of the type." In
response to this last desperate hope, that nature preserves
the species if not the individual, section 56 immediately
replies:

> "So careful of the type?" but no.
> From scarped cliff and quarried stone
> She cries, "A thousand types are gone:
> I care for nothing, all shall go."

Thus, his friend's death, which first made the poet experience the emotional reality of loss, soon forced him to realize
the possibility that not only man the individual but also
man the species could die out. But, as the final lines of
the poem make clear, Tennyson can accept this once terrify-
ing possibility—that man the "type" may disappear from

⁵ "The Two Kingdoms of *In Memoriam*," *Journal of English and
Germanic Philology*, 58 (1959), 240.

the earth—precisely because he believes that Hallam, the original cause of his investigations, is a dual type. In other words, Tennyson can accept the possibility that man will become extinct, because he believes that such extinction would occur only when God was ready to replace man with a higher, more spiritual descendant. At the close of the poem, then, theological type replaces biological type, or rather encompasses it, because faith reveals that God's eternal plan includes purposeful biological development.

Robert Browning makes a surprisingly similar use of typology in *The Ring and the Book*, where Pompilia is also seen as a type of both Christ and the highest in human nature. Wondering at the ignorant girl's magnificence of spirit, the Pope observes how she could

> rise from law to law,
> The old to the new, promoted at one cry
> O' the trump of God to the new service, not
> To longer bear, but henceforth fight, be found
> Sublime in new impatience with the foe!
> Endure man and obey God: plant firm foot
> On neck of man, tread man into the hell
> Meet for him, and obey God the more! (1050–1057)

Throughout the poem Browning has made use of typological commonplaces, particularly in the sections devoted to Guido (4. 718–728, 1411, 2043), Archangelis (8. 632–650, 690–718), and of course the Pope himself (10. 300–302, 803). In the Pope's description of Pompilia's nature Browning shows that she both rose to a higher form of the human, acting fully as a Christian, and served as a type for Christ who will finally tread Satan into hell. Browning several times has his speakers allude to the typological significance of the passage in Genesis where God tells the serpent: "And I will put enmity between thee and the woman, and between thy seed and her seed; it shall bruise thy head, and thou shalt bruise his heel" (3. 15). According to the conventional figural reading of this passage, Christ was the seed who would bruise the serpent's head, and he in turn would be bruised—crucified—in thus conquering evil. Characteristically, Browning places the same text in the mouth of more than one speaker: whereas the Pope uses it to define Pompilia's nature, the priest Giuseppe Caponsacchi does so to emphasize the satanic element in her husband (6. 676–678).

The chief difference in terms of figural imagery between Tennyson's presentation of Hallam and Browning's presentation of Pompilia is that in *The Ring and the Book* Browning not so confidently assumes that his heroine is necessarily a type of a coming higher humanity. This use of typology to describe a higher form of the human race does, however, appear earlier in his poetry. *Paracelsus*, for example, proclaims:

> All tended to mankind,
> And, man produced, all has its end thus far:
> But in completed man begins anew
> A tendency to God. Prognostics told
> Man's near approach; so in man's self arise
> August anticipations, symbols, types
> Of a dim splendour ever on before
> In that eternal circle life pursues.   (5. 770–777)

Both Browning and Tennyson, in other words, find typological symbolism capable of describing—and sacralizing —their conceptions of human evolution.

For Victorian writers typology can thus provide a means of talking about the future of man in a particularly reassuring manner. At the same time, this form of symbolic thought can provide a way of reconciling surface and symbol, fact and imagination, realism and an elaborate iconography. Nonetheless, although figuralism had some major and often fascinating influences upon English thought of the past century, its most widespread effect was rather more humble— to provide an important source of poetic imagery.

As a means of indicating the contribution that typology made to Victorian iconography, I propose in the following pages to examine the poetic appearances of a single commonplace type, that of Moses striking the rock. When the children of Israel were desperate with thirst during their desert wanderings, the Lord instructed Moses: "Behold, I will stand before thee there on the rock in Horeb; and thou shalt smite the rock, and there shall come water out of it, that the people may drink" (Exodus 17: 6). According to Henry Melvill, one of the most popular Victorian preachers, "it is generally allowed that this rock in Horeb was typical of Christ; and that the circumstances of the rock yielding no water, until smitten by the rod of Moses, represented the important truth, that the Mediator must receive the blows of the law, before He could be the source of salvation to a parched and perishing world. It is to this that St. Paul refers, when he says of the Jews, 'They did all drink of the same spiritual drink; for they drank of that spiritual rock that followed them, and that rock was Christ'" (1 Corinthians 10: 4).[6]

Turning to almost any popular nineteenth-century hymnal or collection of religious verse, we are certain to find numerous examples of this type. Thus, *The Book of Praise* (1886) compiled by Roundell Palmer, first Earl of Selborne, contains four uses of the image. The author draws heavily upon writers of the late eighteenth-century Evangelical revival as well as the earlier Watts, and the fact that as late as 1886 he chooses to print these earlier works, and selects those which employ typology, might suggest how important this mode of thought was to worshipers in England and America. Isaac Watts' "Go, worship at Immanuel's feet" (1709) exemplifies one manner of incorporating typology into verse structure. Asking a series of questions which define the nature of Christ, the hymn inquires if he is a fountain, fire, door, temple, and so on. The tenth stanza thus asks:

> Is He a Rock? How firm he proves!
> The Rock of Ages never moves:
> Yet the sweet streams, that from Him flow,
> Attend us all the desert through.[7]

[6] "The Death of Moses," *Sermons*, 2 vols. (London, 1836), 2, 163–164. For a brief reference to matters of typological interpretation in nineteenth-century England, see my "Postscript" following this chapter.

[7] *The Book of Praise: A Treasury of Sacred Poetry* (New York, 1886), p. 378.

Since the structure of this hymn is cumulative, heaping up more and more qualities of the Saviour, it never concentrates long on any particular analogy. Although this poetic structure prevents any satisfying aesthetic development of the initial idea, it compensates somewhat by making its main point effectively—that Christ is many things simultaneously to man, and that a listing of the various facts serves well to remind us how complex, how hard for the human to encompass, he is.

Other works in *The Book of Praise* develop this type differently. William Williams begins the brief "Guide me, O Thou great Jehovah!" (1774) by emphasizing that he and all men are pilgrims in a "barren land." Here, as so frequently in Evangelical hymns, the image of man as a pilgrim in the desert of life brings to mind Moses guiding the children of God; and Moses leads one's thoughts to the type of the stricken rock:

> Open now the crystal Fountain,
>   Whence the healing streams do flow;
> Let the fiery cloudy pillar
>   Lead me all my journey through.   (p. 243)

Similarly, in the course of John Newton's "When Israel, by Divine command" (1779) we learn our resemblance to those who accompanied Moses out of Egyptian bondage. Newton begins by focusing upon the wanderings of Israel:

> When Israel, by Divine command,
>   The pathless desert trod,
> They found, though 't was a barren land,
>   A sure resource in God.
>
> A cloudy pillar marked their road,
>   And screened them from the heat;
> From the hard rocks their water flowed,
>   And manna was their meat.

The hymn then points out that "Like them, we pass a desert too," and then goes on to enforce the type, for "We drink a wondrous stream from Heaven, / 'Tis water, wine, and blood" (pp. 141–142). This last line makes the Old Testament passage serve as a type of several aspects of the Christian dispensation, for it figures forth the crucifixion, the salvation purchased by it, the sacrament of communion, and possibly also the miraculous changing of water into wine, which is itself a type of communion. Rather than assembling a series of discrete symbols, as does Watts' "Go, worship at Immanuel's feet," this hymn conflates various antitypes, all of which fulfill the Old Testament narrative differently. The effect is to emphasize the complexity and richness of the Gospel scheme by demonstrating how many of its strands come together at any one time. The type of the stricken rock therefore becomes a powerful meditative image, a window into the miraculous world of salvation.

Augustus Montague Toplady's "Rock of Ages" (1776), perhaps the most famous application of this type in a hymn, conflates the rock in Horeb with that rock in which God placed Moses to protect him from the immanence of his glory.[8] Exodus 33: 22–33 relates that after Moses asked to see the face of God, the Lord told him that no man could survive such a sight, but that "I will put thee in a clift of the rock, and will cover thee with mine hand while I pass by: And I will take away mine hand, and thou shalt see my back parts: but my face shall not be seen." Toplady's hymn opens with the image of the Rock of Ages which has been cleft—and crucified—for the speaker:

> Rock of Ages, cleft for me,
> Let me hide myself in Thee!
> Let the water and the blood,
> From Thy riven side which flowed,
> Be of sin the double cure,
> Cleanse me from its guilt and power.   (p. 160)

The poem develops this initial image by emphasizing that the worshiper remains helpless without Christ's aid, after

8 I am grateful to Professor Karlfried Froehlich of the Princeton Theological Seminary for pointing out this second allusion to me.

which it ends with a repetition of the two opening lines. The extent to which this kind of hymn was immediately understood to use the commonplace type appears in an illustration the Dalziel brothers engraved more than a century after the hymn's composition, apparently for a volume of Felicia Hemans' poems. The wood engraving, which depicts Moses striking the water from the rock, bears the caption "Rock of Ages cleft for me"—words which immediately establish the Old Testament event in a Christian context.[9] Illustrations of Moses bringing water forth from the rock in Horeb seem to have been fairly popular in the nineteenth century, perhaps suggesting the importance this type held for the average believer. Giulo and Polidoro painted this scene as part of the series in the Vatican Logge, and Nicholas Poussin painted it three times, once explicitly as a type, but on the whole it does not seem to have been a very common theme in earlier religious art.[10] On the other hand, chapbook Bibles depicted this scene with crude woodcuts, and the Dalziel brothers alone made more than a half a dozen versions of it.[11]

The nineteenth-century popularity of this figure of Christ

[9] This illustration is contained in the large volumes, apparently assembled to provide a running record of the firm's work, which are now in the Print Room of the British Museum (C247 c12; 1913–4–15–205 [389]). This particular wood engraving appears in a volume for 1882–83, but I have not yet located the edition of Mrs. Hemans' poems for which it seems to have been cut.

[10] The picture in the Logge is reproduced in S. J. Freedberg, *Painting of the High Renaissance in Rome and Florence*, 2 vols. (Cambridge, Mass., 1961), 2, 368. For Poussin's depictions of the subject and his concern with typology, see Anthony Blunt, *Nicholas Poussin*, 2 vols. (New York, 1967), 1, 179–181; 2, Plates 116, 198, and 258.

[11] According to Robert Collinson, *The Story of Street Literature: Forerunner of the Popular Press* (ABC-Clio: Santa Barbara-Oxford, 1973), p. 116. *The New Pictorial Bible* "included two small and indifferently printed woodcuts on each page, below each of which it gave the Biblical reference, accompanied by the actual text." It devoted six woodcuts to the Creation and another twenty-three to the remainder of the Old Testament, and among these last were several events conventionally read as types: Moses striking the rock, Abraham and Isaac, Joseph cast into the pit, Samson pulling down the temple, and David killing Goliath.

appears in its continuing use as a source of poetic imagery.
Thus, Horatius Bonar (1808–90), who makes frequent use
of typological symbolism, ends "The Cross" with the
recognition that

> Here the living water welleth,
> Here the rock, now smitten, telleth
> Of salvation freely given.
> This is the fount of love and pity,
> This is the pathway to the City;
> This the very gate of Heaven.[12]

The previous four stanzas have emphasized the calm and
peace which the cross represents for the true believer, and,
using a Tennysonian poetic structure, Bonar has them build
toward a moment of vision or recognition. Appropriately,
the type provides the core of this rhetorical and spiritual
climax, to which the last three lines add the idea that the
stricken rock, which prefigures the crucified Christ, is thus
source of the new dispensation's "love and pity," the way to
heaven, and, finally, our entrance into it.

Although these poems thus appear richer and more interesting once we recognize their use of typological
imagery, clearly nothing we have seen has proved to
possess any major poetic value. Few of these poems in fact
release very much of the intrinsic imaginative power of
typological thought. Since each type is a synecdoche for the
entire Gospel scheme, it possesses the property of being
able to generate the entire vision of time, causality, and
salvation contained in that scheme. A typological image
always has the potential to thrust the reader into another
context, demonstrating in the process how everything and
every man exist simultaneously in two realms of meaning.

12 *The Illustrated Book of Sacred Poems*, ed. Robert H. Baynes
(London, Paris, and New York [1867]), p. 91. Bonar, who makes an
extensive use of typological symbolism in his poetry, uses the same
image in "The Desert Rock," *The Song of the New Creation* (New
York, 1872), pp. 57–59 and, more obliquely, in "The Rod," *Hymns
of Faith and Hope* (New York, 1857), pp. 122–126.

In contrast to these rather pedestrian employments of this image, Gerard Manley Hopkins' "Soliloquy of One of the Spies left in the Wilderness," which dates from about 1864, makes a particularly skillful use of it. The opening stanza forcefully presents the rebelliousness of a man who prefers the safety of Egyptian slavery to the dangers of the prophet's rule in the desert:

> Who is the Moses? who made him, we say,
> To be a judge and ruler over us?
> He slew the Egyptian yesterday. To-day
> In hot sands perilous
> He hides our corpses dropping by the way
> Wherein he makes us stray.

After two more stanzas which emphasize how much the speaker loathes both the discomforts of the journey and the manna which sustains him, he exclaims,

> Sicken'd and thicken'd by the glare and sand
> Who would drink water from a stony rock?

The reader, of course, is tempted to reply that in such a situation anyone would. Hopkins' use of this typological image —like that of the manna—effortlessly allows him to produce one of the important effects of the dramatic monologue, the creation of an ironic disparity between what the speaker intends to state and that additional meaning the reader perceives. The commonplace type creates this essential disparity by setting the speaker simultaneously within two parallel contexts, which we may variously define as literal and figural, historical and metahistorical, or even Old Testament and New. Thus, on the literal level, the poem attempts to portray the rebelliousness and self-justifications of one of the Jews who preferred Egypt to the dangers of freedom with Moses. By the time the penultimate stanza presents his relishing the pleasures of slavery above the pains of liberty, we have also understood how much human weakness can do to corrupt itself:

Give us the tale of bricks as heretofore;
To plash with cool feet the clay juicy soil.
Who tread the grapes are splay'd with stripes of gore,
    And they who crush the oil
Are spatter'd. We desire the yoke we bore,
    The easy burden of yore.

Groping for excuses, for easy pleasures, the rebellious spy descends to a porcine or reptilean wallowing in cool Nile mud. On this level, then, the poem is analogous to those paintings by Holman Hunt, such as *The Miracle of Sacred Fire*, which attempt an archeological reconstruction of scriptural or religious subjects. On this most basic level, it is also obvious that the speaker comes rather quickly to represent all men, or that element in human nature which prefers enslavement, degradation, and ease to more bracing enterprises.

But the presence of the typological image of the stricken rock abruptly, economically, forcefully adds another dimension to the poem, for its presence suddenly makes us aware that the speaker exists in the Christian as well as the Judaic universe; or, perhaps more accurately, that he exists as part of the Gospel scheme of salvation as well as in his own purely human right. He represents, in other words, the sinner who refuses the atonement so dearly bought by the crucifixion. He is the one for whom the rock is stricken in vain—the person who prefers the slavery of sin, the bondage of materiality, the imprisonment within time to the gifts offered by divine grace.

The appearance of the type establishes an entire additional set of spiritual meanings for all the details of the poem, and it also helps explain details that might otherwise remain enigmatic. For example, at first we readers do not understand why Hopkins used an upper-case "H" when he wrote "He [Moses] feeds me with *His* manna every day" (my italics), if the speaker refers, as he clearly does, to the prophet. When we come upon the type of the stricken rock, however, we then recognize that the speaker takes his place in the Gospel scheme, referring unknowingly to Christ. It could be argued, of course, that the initial recognition occurs six lines earlier, where the speaker mentions the gift of manna, since manna was often interpreted figurally. (It seems, however, that the poet's use of the food that miraculously sustained the tribes of Israel in the wilderness does not, like the smitten rock, at first demand interpretation as a type. After we perceive that the rock functions typologically, we then make the same recognition about the manna. But the important point here is that the manna does not possess the drama—because it does not possess the movement—of the poem's central type.) The type functions as a sign, an indication of the way we should react intellectually and emotionally to the words which surround its appearance.[13] In this way, Hopkins uses typological symbolism much as Holman Hunt does in *The Shadow of Death, The Scapegoat,* and *The Triumph of the Innocents,* to add another dimension of meaning which spiritually redeems the physical, the material, making it richer and more relevant. It should also be noted that the presence of the type has another effect, since it turns the reader back to the details of narrative and psychology. Because everything in the poem has gained new relevance from the presence of the symbol of Christ, that image demands close attention to the literal level in order that nothing be missed of the speaker's manner and habit of thinking. In emphasizing the symbolic implications of the narrative, the typological image paradoxically also emphasizes the literal elements as well. This effect, we should notice, is parallel to that of Pre-Raphaelite painting, where the presence of complex symbolic statements forces us back to the visual elements of the picture, thus insuring that we fully perceive the aesthetic surface.

[13] This emphasis upon the central importance of this type to the poet suggests that Hopkins may have begun "Soliloquy" with it; and the evidence of his 1864 diaries would seem to confirm this supposition, since he changed every line of the stanza in which it appeared except "Who would drink water from a stony rock?" See *Journals and Papers of Gerard Manley Hopkins,* eds. H. House and G. Storey (London, 1959), p. 29.

A second, perhaps less strictly orthodox type occurs when poets use the image of Moses striking the desert rock to prefigure, not the Old Law bringing forth the New by means of the crucifixion, but rather Christ himself bringing forth tears of repentance from the stony heart of the individual worshiper. It is this second version of the type which appears, for instance, in Book 6 of *The Excursion*. Ellen, whose lover has betrayed her, tells her mother that God's grace gave her strength to bear her pain, waking her at last from her deadened state:

> There was a stony region in my heart;
> But He, at whose command the parchèd rock
> Was smitten, and poured forth a quenching stream,
> Hath softened that obduracy, and made
> Unlooked-for gladness in the desert place,
> To save the perishing.          (6. 918–23)

John Ruskin employs the same type in his poem "The Broken Chain," when (probably imitating Wordsworth, then his favorite poet) he describes a character as a man who

> looked like one whom power or pain
> Had hardened, or had hewn, to rock
> That could not melt nor rend again,
> Unless the staff of God might shock,
> And burst the sacred waves to birth,
> That deck with bloom the Desert's dearth—
> That dearth that knows nor breeze, nor balm.[14]

Two points are striking about both Ruskin's and Wordsworth's employment of this type. In the first place, they both omit mention of Moses, assuming that the reader recognizes that since Moses prefigures Christ, it is therefore legitimate to describe Moses' literal action as if it were being performed by Christ himself. Second, although the omission of Moses requires a close knowledge of Scripture —or at least of the most popular passages in Scripture—it

---

14 *Works*, eds. E. T. Cook and Alexander Wedderburn, 39 vols. (London, 1903–12), 2, 174.

also serves to make the image fit more easily into the narrative context. Indeed, we do not have to realize that this is
a type, in order to read the passage with some basic understanding of what the author intends. Nonetheless, a recognition that both authors cite a commonplace type much en-
riches the significance and emotional impact of the image:
by perceiving that Ellen received God's grace and that it
will be necessary for Ruskin's hero to do so, the reader recognizes the essentially Christian basis of both men's moral
psychology. It might also be pointed out that for evangeli-
calism, such typological imagery economically demonstrates the essentially Christian conception of sympathetic
imagination shared by Romantic theory and evangelical
theology.

It is therefore not surprising that this image recurs frequently in Victorian poetry. It appears, for instance, in John
Keble's "Sixth Sunday after Trinity," which attempts to
comfort "bitter thoughts, of conscience born" by showing
their essential role in forgiveness and salvation. Employing
as an epigraph David's confession of sin to Nathan and the
prophet's assurance of divine mercy, the poem makes this
Old Testament episode itself function as a type of confession of guilt and Christ's subsequent forgiveness. Explaining how "Israel's crowned mourner felt / The dull hard
stone within him melt," the poem relates that when God
saw "the mighty grief," he quickly eased the repentant,
fearful sinner's pain. David's confession makes the angels
in heaven who have turned from his music welcome "the
broken heart to love's embrace." At this juncture Keble en-
forces his point by making use of another type, a technique
which demonstrates how interwoven are the acts and meanings of scriptural history:

> The rock is smitten, and to future years
> Springs ever fresh the tide of holy tears
> And holy music, whispering peace
> Till time and sin together cease.

This use of one type, here the smitten rock, to comment
upon another, David's confession and forgiveness, shows

how many layers of meaning the Victorian poet could employ, because he had an audience that was both capable of following his use of figuralism and delighted to discover commonplace types in new contexts.

Keble's "Easter Eve," which also uses other types, such as that of Joseph cast into the pit, again draws on the image of the stricken rock. After explicating the significance of the atonement, the speaker expresses his longing to be with God:

> But stay, presumptuous—CHRIST with thee abides
>   In the rock's dreary sides:
> He from the stone will wring celestial dew
> If but the prisoner's heart be faithful found and true.
>
> When tears are spent, and thou art left alone
>   With ghosts of blessings gone,
> Think thou art taken from the cross, and laid
>   In JESUS' burial shade;
> Take Moses' rod, the rod of prayer, and call
>   Out of the rocky wall
> The font of holy blood; and lift on high
> Thy grovelling soul that feels so desolate and dry.

During the course of this passage Keble shifts emphasis from the actions of Christ which affect the worshiper to those of the worshiper himself. This movement is appropriate to the entire poem, since it begins with the fact of the crucifixion and then proceeds to instruct us how we can secure the gifts it purchased. The movement, we observe, leads the poet to ring intricate changes on the basic figure. In the first place, Keble apparently conflates two uses of the type, so that the rock simultaneously figures both the worshiper's heart and the crucified body of Christ. When we are told, "Christ with thee abides," we wonder perhaps who then is going to strike the rock, thus bringing forth the waters of life. Keble clarifies this point by making a variant, yet quite orthodox, application of the basic type: "Moses' rod," it turns out, is "the rod of prayer," and *we* must be the ones to produce the waters that will flow, simultaneously, from both Christ and our own hearts. The words "Christ with thee abides" tell us both that he has elected to share our human nature and that he is always there to comfort us. There may also be another element of variation upon the basic type here: whereas in Exodus God tells Moses to strike the rock, in Numbers 20: 8-12 He instructs him to speak to the rock. But carried away by his anger at the people, Moses strikes the rock instead, bringing forth water but also a rebuke from the Lord. This second episode with the rock was intended to demonstrate, say some exegetes, that once Christ was crucified, prayer was enough to bring salvation. It is difficult to tell if Keble confuses the two types or follows some alternate tradition.

Christina Rossetti's "Good Friday" (1862), which makes a similarly complex use of the basic type, is a far better poem, both because it achieves the force of brevity and because its play upon the basic type generates the structure of the poem: here the figure of the stricken rock is not merely a forceful image employed by the poet but rather a conceit which contains the germ of the entire sixteen lines of the poem. Her initial opposition of stone and sheep sets the conceit in motion:

> Am I a stone and not a sheep,
> That I can stand, O Christ, beneath Thy cross,
> To number drop by drop Thy blood's slow loss.
>     And yet not weep?

The opening line establishes the contrasts which provide the axis of the poem—she finds herself a stone, one who does not react deeply enough, humanly enough, to the reality of Christ's sacrifice, and yet she wants to make herself one of the shepherd's flock, one of those whom he will save. The next two stanzas emphasize the other people and even things that grieved: Mary and the other women, Peter, the thief, even the sun and moon. After confessing at the end of the third stanza that "I, only I," remain a stone, she turns to God in lines which brilliantly resolve the spiritual—and poetic—problem produced by her initial contrast:

Yet give not o'er,
But seek Thy sheep, true Shepherd of the flock
Greater than Moses, turn and look once more,
And smite a rock.

The entire poem moves toward this last action and culminates in it. She manages a brevity, force, and wit not found in Keble's more diffuse poems, and unlike him she can purposefully blend her symbols without risking confusion. Most important, her poem, like Hopkins', employs the typological image as an essential part of its structure. It is clearly the core of the poem, its generating conceit, and when we arrive at the carefully prepared type, it detonates, releasing us into a new universe and a new law—greater than that of Moses.

Yet another use of this figure of the stricken rock appears in section 131 of *In Memoriam*, which closes the main portion of the poem:

O living will that shalt endure
When all that seems shall suffer shock,
Rise in the spiritual rock,
Flow through our deeds and make them pure,

That we may lift from out of dust
A voice as unto him that hears
A cry above the conquered years
To one that with us works, and trust,

With faith that comes of self-control,
The truths that never can be proved
Until we close with all we loved,
And all we flow from, soul in soul.

The image of the stricken rock works with that complexity we have come to expect from Tennyson. First of all, the "living will," which Tennyson himself glossed as man's free will, is also the will of God.[15] To appreciate the full mean-

15 Professor Rosenberg quotes the poet's remarks and comments upon them in "The Two Kingdoms of *In Memoriam*," p. 238. He also argues that "The progression from death to life is again implicit in

ing of the type, then, we must perceive that the living will is that of the speaker, Christ, and Hallam, or at least an embodiment, like him, of the highest element in mankind. After the shock the poet haş suffered, he now confidently expects the "living will" (which here essentially replaces grace or merges with it) to rise in his heart, in his life, guiding him out of the desert of this life to union with Hallam. At the same time, it is also Christ himself who is to rise in the spiritual rock, providing salvation. And, finally, it is also Hallam who is to be the guide. Hallam, who becomes analogous to both Beatrice and Christ in the course of *In Memoriam*, here also gains a resemblance to Moses. That mystical union of God, Hallam, and the poet which takes place in section 95 of the poem is here recapitulated in the lines which close it.[16]

Once the image of Moses striking the rock becomes a poetic commonplace, it begins to appear in what we may term a secularized form. Poetry can employ types in at least four different ways: first of all, hymns and devotional verse can simply remind the audience of the existence of types, providing standard interpretations of them and perhaps juxtaposing several to enforce points of doctrine. Here the poet does little more than assist the preacher to educate people to read the Bible in terms of types and figures of Christ. Second, at a level of somewhat greater complexity, the writer applies types to his own spiritual situation in verse of personal devotion. Of course, the dividing line between this and the first use of types is often difficult to lo-

---

the reference to the 'spiritual rock' from which Moses struck water in the desert and which Paul called the rock that 'was Christ'—the same rock from which man partakes of the baptismal waters of rebirth and on which Tennyson bases his faith that we shall *'close* with all we loved . . . soul in soul' " (*ibid.*). Professor Rosenberg here refers to the Pauline interpretation of the stricken rock as a type of baptism, a reading of the image which does not seem to work as well in this case as the interpretation I have suggested.

[16] This type, I should add, also well prepares for the epilogue's concluding emphasis upon Hallam's role as prefiguration of both Christ and the higher race of men.

cate, particularly in the case of minor poetry, but the distinguishing characteristic of the mode is its personal, even idiosyncratic, application and development of this form of symbolism. A third use of typological imagery occurs when the poet applies it to a fictional narrative. Such transference of biblical symbolism—which God himself had supposedly placed in the Scriptures—to secular fiction requires the poet to make a rather bold leap. Nonetheless, the resulting poetry still uses typological imagery to convey straightforward, orthodox Christian doctrine. Thus, when Wordsworth and Ruskin refer to the rock in Horeb they still intend it to convey an essentially Christian point about the way God vivifies the human heart. In contrast, Robert Calder Campbell, Emily Dickinson, and Robert Browning exemplify various secularized forms of this type, precisely because they employ it to create poetic emphasis rather than to communicate ideas about salvation and grace.

For instance, Campbell's untitled love sonnet in *The Germ* (1850), the short-lived publication of the Pre-Raphaelite Brotherhood, uses the commonplace type as the basis of a witty conceit. The linked images of manna and smitten rock define the positions of speaker and listener, lover and beloved, rather than conveying Christian doctrine. The sonnet opens with a description of the lovers at play, and a gamesome, light tone characterizes this not very inspired poetic effort. The speaker tells his beloved that when she pulls

> Pink scented apples from the garden trees
> To fling at me, I catch them, on my knees,
> Like those who gather'd manna.

This whimsical introduction of the miraculous food in the wilderness prepares here, as it does so often in hymns and devotional verse, for the associated type of the smitten rock. Pointing out that when he is with her he can speak his love, the poet confesses

> but when thou'rt gone
> I have no speech,—no magic that beguiles,
> The stream of utterance from the harden'd rock.

In the manner of many love poets, Campbell sets his beloved at the center of his imaginative world, thus displacing God, for her presence produced the desired vitalization of the heart—her presence, her grace replaces God's. Of course, the tone is light here, and this playful poem makes no attempt to be either blasphemously ardent or critical of the original text.

To what extent does this obviously secular poem require us to perceive the existence both of biblical allusion and typological symbolism? To begin with, it seems clear that unless we recognize the allusions to the Old Testament we cannot follow the poem very well; although on the other hand, the image of the manna seems rather strained if we do not perceive a figural significance, it still remains intelligible. Nonetheless, the reference to the miraculous food in the desert makes far more poetic sense when we recognize that it functions to prepare for the rock in Horeb. This second image, which provides the poetic climax for the sonnet, demands that we understand the allusion to a commonplace type—because the line "The stream of utterance from the harden'd rock" refers, not to the Old Testament passage, but to Christian interpretations of it as a figure of Christ: that is, not to the literal water that came forth from the rock but to its typological interpretation as the effect of grace upon the heart.

Glancing briefly across the Atlantic, we can observe Emily Dickinson's far less light-hearted use of the image in a poem that obviously owes much to Protestant hymnody:

A *Wounded* Deer—leaps highest—
I've heard the Hunter tell—
'Tis but the Ecstasy of *death*—
And then the Brake is still!

The *Smitten* Rock that gushes!
The *trampled* Steel that springs!
A Cheek is always redder
Just where the Hectic stings!

Mirth is the Mail of Anguish—
In which it Cautious Arm,
Lest anybody spy the blood
And "you're hurt" exclaim!     (c. 1860)

Like many hymns of old and New England, this poem proceeds by assembling a list of analogies, and to some extent the poet's italicizing serves to make the parallels she perceives clearer and more convincing. After the opening image of the stricken deer's leap, the poem provides three similar examples of the way a force impinging upon objects, whether animate or inanimate, produces a powerful—she proposes the most powerful—reaction. The last stanza then effects a turn, indeed a resolution, by offering the "solution" that mirth can protect us from such troublesome capacity for pain.

What role in the poem, then, does the line "The *Smitten Rock* that gushes!" have, and how essential is it for us to perceive its commonplace typological significance — whether as prefiguration of the crucifixion or the action of grace upon the heart? To begin with, unless we recognize the allusion this line makes little sense, for it does not seem to refer to drilling wells or any such enterprise. In fact, only by recognizing the original importance of the image as a type of Christ do we allow it full impact. Although it was originally an image of major Christian significance, Dickinson has here emptied it of its christological meaning, using it only for powerful emphasis. Nonetheless, in what is an apparent paradox, unless we recognize the original Christian import of the symbol, it will not function in its new role.[17]

[17] I am grateful to my friend and colleague, Professor Barton Levi St. Armand, for pointing out this example to me. One may also note that since the deer hunt is also an old allegorical image of both the Crucifixion and Christ's hunting down the sinner to save him, Dickinson may also be using the opening lines in the way she does the type to create a sharper emphasis. For the deer hunt, see Howard M. Helsinger, "Images on the Beatus page of some Medieval Psalters," *Art Bulletin*, 53 (1971), 161–176.

Browning, who at several points in his poetry makes extensive use of figural imagery, provides another secular version of this stock image. In "One Word More," the poem which dedicates *Men and Women* (1855) to Elizabeth Barrett Browning, the poet explicitly makes Moses a symbol for himself and all artists—as had Donne and Milton before him.[18] Complaining that the artist sorrows because of the way the "earth"—here largely the poet's audience—lessens and even negates the heavenly gift of poetry, Browning tells his fellow poet:

> He who smites the rock and spreads the water,
> Bidding drink and live a crowd beneath him,
> Even he, the minute makes immortal,
> Proves, perchance, but mortal in the minute,
> Desecrates, belike, the deed in doing.
> While he smites, how can he but remember,
> So he smote before, in such a peril,
> When they stood and mocked—"Shall smiting help us?"
> When they drank and sneered—"A stroke is easy!"
> When they wiped their mouths and went their journey,
> Throwing him for thanks—"But drought was pleasant."
> Thus old memories mar the actual triumph. . . .
> For he bears an ancient wrong about him,
> Sees and knows again those phalanxed faces,
> Hears, yet one time more, the 'customed prelude—
> "How shouldst thou, of all men, smite, and save us?"
> Guesses what is like to prove the sequel—
> "Egypt's flesh-pots—nay, the drought was better."

Clearly, this purely personal application of the old figure places its major emphasis upon the beleaguered, unappreciated Moses, since his actions and position in relation to the Jews receive more attention than does the water he

[18] During the course of the 1974 Princeton conference on typological symbolism, Professor Barbara K. Lewalski kindly pointed out to me that Milton makes Moses a type for the Christian poet in the opening lines of *Paradise Lost*, and that Donne does the same thing in the closing lines of *The First Anniversary*.

brought forth from the rock. Nonetheless, this use of the commonplace (which, incidentally, is very probably the direct source of Hopkins' more orthodox employment of the type)[19] receives additional impact if we recognize its figural sense. The poet, in other words, sees himself, like Moses and Christ, bringing the water of life—of truth, feeling, and spiritual strength—to the hostile crowd. Of course, this image works fairly effectively even if we do not perceive a figural dimension, a dimension which here serves largely to provide emphasis. Indeed, we find it difficult to demonstrate that the poet intended us to find a typological significance, although one somewhat ambiguous bit of evidence might be cited in favor of such a thesis: The line "Even he, the minute makes immortal" can be taken to indicate that in bringing forth water from the rock, Moses becomes "immortal" for a brief instant because he then (and only then) partakes of the type. Moses himself would not be seen as immortal in performing this act if it refers only to himself and not to the Gospel scheme. Nonetheless, we are reduced, finally, to accepting merely a probability: Browning draws extensively upon typology for the complex imagery of *Paracelsus, Saul*,[20] and *The Ring and the Book*; he here uses an image commonly taken as a type of Christ; therefore he probably made conscious use of the figural level of the image of the stricken rock.

Our brief examination of typological symbolism in Victorian poetry suggests what a wide range of different effects it had. A great deal of work needs to be done, particularly

19 Hopkins quotes other poems from Browning's *Men and Women* in his *Journals* about this time, thus demonstrating that he was familiar with the volume. Of course any study such as this one which emphasizes the role of the commonplace image or rhetorical *topos* in literary tradition tends to cast doubt on the notion that any one particular antecedent example by itself influenced a poet. I assume that after reading "One Word More" Hopkins, already well aware of the traditional type, was prompted to use it in a more purely Christian sense than did Browning.

20 See Ward Hellstrom's excellent "Time and Type in Browning's *Saul*," *ELH*, 33 (1966), 370–389.

on the iconography of popular secular and religious poetry, but we can already draw some tentative conclusions. First of all, figuralism furnished a large fund of intrinsically powerful stock images for the literature of the last century. Second, both secular and religious poetry drew upon this fund of types and shadows of Christ in such a way as to suggest that many authors who were not conventional believers in Christianity, much less evangelicals or high churchmen, also made use of it. Third, the rather anachronistic notions of time and existence implicit in typological symbolism were capable, on occasion, of producing an entire worldview, an entire imaginative universe. Finally, this kind of symbolism was used in ways which varied from thus generating an imaginative world to providing mere points of emphasis. We still need to examine in detail the many other standard types which appear in Victorian writing in order to determine the degree to which they diverge from those of an earlier literature, such as that of the sevententh century. The degree to which both popular and elite culture in the last century understood the poetry of Milton, Herbert, Marvell, and others still needs to be determined, as does the influence of all Puritan writings upon the use of typology in Victorian literature. In short, typological symbolism seems to have played an important, if little noticed, role in Victorian literature, and we have to inform ourselves far more about its nature and influence.

## Postscript

Evangelicals, both within and without the Church of England, were largely responsible for the widespread English revival of interest in typological interpretations of the Bible. Although members of the high church party also practiced typological exegetics, it was the evangelical Anglicans, the Methodists, Baptists, and similar sects who taught English men and women to read the Bible for types of Christ. In fact, since some members of the high church were at one time evangelicals, I suspect that it is not always necessary, or even possible, to distinguish between the effects upon Bible reading of the two parties opposed in so many other matters. By the last decades of the eighteenth century, sermons, tracts, biblical commentaries, and hymns all taught the individual worshiper how to perceive types and shadows of Christ throughout the Old Testament and within the life of Christ Himself. One reason for the popularity of this manner of interpretation among the evangelical sects was their need to relate all portions of Scripture —including the most apparently irrelevant—to the Christian dispensation. Distrustful of what Bishop J. C. Ryle, a leading writer of tracts, termed the "rubbish of patristic traditions," the evangelicals tended to cut themselves off from the ecclesiastical past. Their anti-historical views, combined with a non-canonical belief in verbal inspiration, created potentially severe problems for readers of Scripture. What, for example, was the Manchester cotton-spinner to make of the elaborate directions for animal sacrifice in Leviticus? What was the little boy in the local chapel to make of Christ's circumcision? Since the evangelicals urged that every word of Scripture—even in its English translation—was the literal word of God, they could not simply pass by these difficult sections. But since they would not accept an evolutionary conception of the Bible (at least not in the nineteenth-century Germanic manner), they could not make use of historical or anthropological explanation. Therefore, it was with a triumphant use of typology that the evangelical preacher revealed how God used the Levitical rites to anticipate the Gospel scheme. Typology once more played its hermeneutic role. Although moral exhortation provides the dominant theme for most nineteenth-century sermons, typological exegetics appear to have furnished the next most important subject—something we might suspect from the fact that Charles Simeon, the great Cambridge evangelical, devoted an entire volume of his sermon outlines to types and prophecies.

The result was that the individual worshiper, whether evangelical or High Anglican, American or English, learned to perceive an excitingly complex network spreading across scriptural events, making the most meaningless seem charged with Christian value and importance. From the practice of reading the Bible in terms of types and shadows of Christ came several important associated habits of mind. First, readers of Scripture learned to delight in complex unravelings of biblical history. Next, they learned to cultivate a love of paradox and enigma, something which appears in the writings of the various nineteenth-century sages, including Emerson, Thoreau, Carlyle, and Ruskin, all of whom were rooted in fundamentalist tradition—however far they eventually moved from it. Third, worshipers became indoctrinated with the notion that every fact, every event bears some meaning if we can only penetrate to it. Everything, in other words, can be an emblem if we can learn to see properly. Fourth, the student of Scripture perceived that all things existed simultaneously in two realms, the physical and the spritual. Fifth, delighting in elaborate exegeses of scriptural events, readers of the Bible frequently carried typological interpretation to such extremes that they unknowingly verged into allegory—something particularly ironic in light of the fact that they so deeply distrusted such interpretation, smacking as it did to evangelicals of a despised, dangerous tradition.

THEODORE ZIOLKOWSKI

## Some Features of
## Religious Figuralism in
## Twentieth-Century Literature

THE entry on "Typology" in Hastings' *Encyclopaedia of Religion and Ethics* concludes with the sobering observation that "typology has always flourished in times of ignorance and decay of learning"[1]—a caveat that may not strike quite the right note of confidence for a conference on religious figuralism in literature. But let us not despair. In the first place, the author of the article is addressing himself specifically to the issue of typology as a form of biblical hermeneutics, and it is undeniable that at various moments in history excesses in figural interpretation did in fact hamper the development of biblical scholarship and distract readers from any real understanding of the two Testaments in their integrity. In the second place, the author concedes in his last sentence that typological suggestions "are not without value and helpfulness if they are received gratefully, much as one might derive illuminating thoughts from the contemplation of a sacred picture, rather than as revelations possessing dogmatic authority." In other words, although typological or figural interpretation of the Bible has been discredited as a mode of exegesis, the technique can still claim a certain aesthetic validity. Yet, as we proceed, it would be well to bear in mind the caution that typological interpretation, employed mechanically or thoughtlessly, may well be as misleading for the literary critic as for the theologian. Let us attempt to avoid at least some of the inherent pitfalls by setting forth a few preliminary definitions and historical perspectives.

[1] J. R. Darbyshire, "Typology," in *Encyclopaedia of Religion and Ethics*, ed. James Hastings (New York, 1922), 12: 500–504.

*345*

There is little disagreement concerning the primary meaning of the synonymous terms "typology" and "figuralism," which can be understood in a specific or in a more general sense. Hastings' *Encyclopaedia* defines typology in the specific sense as "the science, or rather, only too often, the curious art of discovering and expounding in the records of persons and events in the Old Testament prophetical adumbrations of the Person of Christ or of the doctrines and practices of the Christian Church." Erich Auerbach's classic essay "Figura" represents the second, more general sense, which assumes a similar relationship between past and present without limiting it to the Bible: "Figural interpretation establishes a connection between two events or persons, the first of which signifies not only itself but also the second, while the second encompasses or fulfills the first."[2] In either sense, however, the faith of the exegete posits a mystical relationship between two historically discrete events. Thus a certain type in the Old Testament is said to find its corresponding antitype in the New Testament, as when Joseph's being sold by his brothers is fulfilled in Jesus' betrayal by Judas. Or, according to the term favored by the Latin exegetes, an incident in the New Testament is anticipated by a figure in the Old Testament, as Jesus carrying his cross up to Golgotha is prefigured by Isaac, who must help to cut and carry the wood upon which he is to be sacrificed. In all such cases Christian faith juxtaposes *umbra* and *veritas*, seeing, for instance, the "shadow" of the innocent shepherd Abel, slain by his brother, realized in the living "truth" of Jesus, the shepherd of men who is slain by his brothers. The essential relationship is characterized by the fact that both figures and types are felt by

[2] Auerbach's essay appeared originally in *Archivum Romanicum*, 22 (1938), 436–489; I refer here to the version in Auerbach's *Scenes from the Drama of European Literature: Six Essays*, trans. Ralph Manheim (New York, 1959), p. 53; cf. also A. C. Charity, *Events and Their Afterlife: The Dialectics of Christian Typology in the Bible and Dante* (Cambridge, 1966), pp. 1–3, which defines typology in both senses: Auerbach's "broad" sense and the more specifically biblical sense of Hastings' *Encyclopaedia*.

Christian faith to be real historical events or figures. It is this sense of historical reality that distinguishes figural or typological understanding from other forms of allegory, in which one pole of the relationship is generally an abstract notion.

Although typological or figural interpretation was not unknown to pagan and Jewish antiquity, the early Christian Church seized most eagerly upon the method since it enabled the exegetes to create instant history for their new religion by showing that Jesus and his teaching constituted fulfillments or antitypes of figures and types contained in the Old Testament. The prefiguring shadow of the Law had given way to the eternal truth embodied and fulfilled in the person of Jesus Christ. This characteristically Christian mode of interpretation, which reached three pinnacles of popularity and influence—in the Alexandrine period, again in the twelfth century, and finally in the seventeenth century—maintained its authority until it was finally undermined by eighteenth-century rationalism and wholly discredited by the scientific criticism of the nineteenth century. Yet strong traces of typological thinking can still be detected in the works of such post-Enlightenment writers as Hamann, Goethe, and Novalis, who emerged from the German pietist tradition.[3] And the figural mode was preserved by such American writers as Emerson, Hawthorne, and Melville, who received the Calvinist belief in typology by way of the Puritan theologians: Samuel and Cotton Mather, Edward Taylor, and Jonathan Edwards.[4]

From the catacombs to contemporary church décor, moreover, this mode of thought has had a profound effect upon Christian art and its iconography. From the statues of Synagoga and Ecclesia, which adorn the portals at

[3] Horst Meixner, *Romantischer Figuralismus: Kritische Studien zu Romanen von Arnim, Eichendorff und Hoffmann* (Frankfurt am Main, 1971). There is as yet no thorough study of typological thinking in the major German writers of the age of Goethe.

[4] Ursula Brumm, *American Thought and Religious Typology* (New Brunswick, N.J., 1970); *Typology and Early American Literature*, ed. Sacvan Bercovitch (Amherst, 1972).

Strassburg and Bamberg, to the mosaics, tapestries, and stained-glass windows within, the art of the great medieval cathedrals depended extensively upon the juxtaposition of type and antitype, *figura* and fulfillment. Such works as the English *Pictor in carmine* (c. 1200), whose verses record 508 types for 138 antitypes, or the late thirteenth-century South German *Biblia pauperum*, each of whose illustrations depicts an antitype flanked by two types, were widely used as models that catalyzed the imagination of medieval Christian artists and artisans.[5]

Although strict constructionists from St. Jerome to Martin Luther and Calvin always insisted that typological interpretation must be restricted to the relationship between the two biblical testaments, the mode of thought became so fashionable, indeed so ingrained, that it was frequently opened up to include extra-biblical types. Since Jesus was regarded as the fulfillment of all human history, his prefigurations could be sought in ancient history and even in classical myth. Thus the mysteries of Eleusis were seen to foreshadow the celebrations of the Christian Church, and Odysseus strapped to the mast of his ship was taken to prefigure Jesus on the cross.[6] During the past fifty years students of medieval literature have increasingly argued that evidences of typological thinking can be found in non-biblical works: that persons and events in the *Divine Comedy* or in Wolfram's *Parzival*, for instance, are prefigured by types supplied by the New Testament.[7] The extent to which typology may be expanded to embrace these possibilities and the extent to which such parallels were consciously exploited by medieval authors is still a matter of lively de-

[5] Hartmut Hoefer, *Typologie im Mittelalter: Zur Übertragbarkeit typologischer Interpretation auf weltliche Dichtung* (Göppingen, 1971), pp. 134–144.

[6] Cf. Friedrich Ohly, "Synagoge und Ecclesia: Typologisches in mittelalterlicher Dichtung," in *Miscellanea Mediaevalia*, ed. Paul Wilpert (Berlin, 1966), 4: 361–362.

[7] In addition to Auerbach, Charity, and Ohly, cf. especially Julius Schwietering, "Typologisches in mittelalterlicher Dichtung," in *Vom Werden des deutschen Geistes. Festgabe für Gustav Ehrismann*, ed. Paul Merker und Wolfgang Stammler (Berlin und Leipzig, 1925), pp. 40–55.

bate.[8] The controversy, however, brings us directly to the unique problems we encounter when we move beyond those writers, from the beginning down through the nineteenth century, whose beliefs were shaped principally by the Christian tradition. For a variety of reasons, the question of religious figuralism or typology must be redefined and restated when we reach the radically secularized writers of the twentieth century.

The first, and chronologically earliest, factor that distinguishes modern thinking about typology is the new understanding of the concept produced by the higher criticism of the nineteenth century. The principal, though by no means only, figure in this development was the German theologian David Friedrich Strauss, whose *Das Leben Jesu* (1835) was translated into English by George Eliot. Strauss, of course, was fully aware of figural interpretation; in fact, during his student years there was a revival of interest in typology as a serious hermeneutical method. Strauss' quest for the historical Jesus was revolutionary because he used typological methods as a critical tool *against* faith in any mystical connection between the two Testaments. Strauss knew that most of the deeds and miracles attributed to Jesus in the New Testament were explained by figural exegesis as fulfillments of types in the Old Testament. In his effort to strip away the legendary and mythic elements from the historical Jesus, Strauss reasoned that all these antitypal elements were literary conventions added to the Gospels by devout authors who were eager to make their savior conform to all the predictions of the prophets. Strauss' achievement, which wrecked his academic career but stimulated widespread discussion in nineteenth-century theological and intellectual circles, had an important result for the history of typological interpretation. Namely, he clearly distinguished the method from the phenomenon, the process from the product. Earlier exegetes, whether strict

8 Cf. esp. Hoefer, *op. cit.*, who concludes that the recent tendency to apply the term "typology" to secular writings does justice neither to those writings nor to typology itself.

*349*

constructionists or not, had assumed in their faith that figural exegesis was merely a means of uncovering parallels between the Old and New Testaments which, in fact, mystically existed. Strauss, in revolutionary contrast, denied any mystical connection between type and antitype: for him, figuralism was reduced to little more than a sophisticated literary device.[9] It was, to be sure, a device inspired by genuine faith, but a device nonetheless. After Strauss, it became impossible for any theologian seriously to insist on the mystical prefiguration of the New Testament in the Old.

In the second place, the new historicism of the nineteenth century, which denied any meaning or direction in history, shattered the salvation-oriented theory of history (*Heilsgeschichte*) that had justified typological thinking in its assumption that all history found its ultimate meaning in the person of Jesus Christ.

A third factor accounting for the twentieth-century revaluation of typology is the increasing sophistication in our understanding of myth. Ever since early Romanticism, writers and philosophers had been crying for a revival of myth, for what Friedrich Schlegel called "a new mythology."[10] And that rekindled interest, following the mythophobia of eighteenth-century rationalism, provided the impulse that led to the scientific study of myth. But it was only toward the end of the century, with the emergence of folklore, anthropology, mythology, and history of religion as areas of systematic study, that scholars became consciously aware

[9] In my study of *Fictional Transfigurations of Jesus* (Princeton, 1972), I have attempted to show how the techniques and consciousness isolated by Strauss were almost immediately appropriated by theologically sophisticated writers of the nineteenth century as a basis for Christian Socialist novels based typologically upon the Jesus theme.

[10] I am speaking, of course, of the scholarly study of myth and mythology—not of the so-called "return to myth" that had such a devastating effect upon the modern German consciousness. See my article "Der Hunger nach dem Mythos: Zur seelischen Gastronomie der Deutschen in den Zwanziger Jahren," in *Die sogenannten Zwanziger Jahre*, ed. Reinhold Grimm and Jost Hermand (Bad Homburg-Berlin-Zürich, 1970), pp. 169–201.

of the nature of myth and its workings. Strauss had already suggested that many of the "figural" or antitypal elements attributed to Jesus actually ought to be attributed to the myth-making impulse of the gospelists. Now, studies like James Frazer's *The Golden Bough* (1890), John M. Robertson's *Christianity and Mythology* (1900), or Arthur Drews' *The Christ-Myth* (1909) implied, or explicitly argued, that Jesus shared many elements or motifs with such non-Christian deities as Tammuz, Adonis, or Osiris. The effect of these investigations was gradually to reduce Jesus, at least for the non-devout, to a figure with no greater mythic validity than any other figure in myth, legend, or literature. As a character puts it in Hermann Hesse's *Demian* (1919): "Christ is not a person for me but a hero, a myth, an extraordinary shadow image in which humanity has painted itself on the wall of eternity." And the same sentiment is repeated by countless thinkers and artists of the twentieth century.

A final factor, which can hardly be overestimated, is the new *consciousness* of typological thinking that, in the first half of the twentieth century, begins to emerge in many disciplines. In *Totem and Taboo* (1913), and with specific reference to Frazer, Freud speaks of the "imitative" or "homeopathic" magic that inspires primitive peoples, as well as certain types of modern neurotics, to attempt to achieve certain desired results by "imitating" various ritual actions: e.g., fertility rites and rain dances.[11] (Needless to say, this kind of typological thinking has also determined most of the conventional liturgical practices of Christianity: e.g., the mass as a reenactment of the Last Supper.) In a similar vein, Ortega y Gasset describes in his essay "The Sunset of Revolutions" (1924) the "traditionalist" mode of thought that characterized early Graeco-Roman as well as medieval culture, in which "thought" means little but the ability to recognize among past models the particular

11 *Totem and Taboo*, trans. James Strachey (New York, 1950), especially ch. 3: "Animism, Magic and the Omnipotence of Thoughts."

course that is suitable for present behavior.[12] In his study *The Revolt of the Masses* (1930) Ortega elaborates this idea.[13] Opposing Spengler's statement that the Graeco-Roman peoples were incapable of grasping time and temporal sequences, Ortega argues that ancient man had a highly developed sense of time and history: but, blind to the future, he was anchored in the past. Like a torero who takes a step backward before he executes the stroke of death, ancient man always sought in the past a model into which he could slip as into a diving bell. Thomas Mann, in "Freud and the Future" (1936), cites Ortega in his discussion of the ancient mode of consciousness. "It was, as it were, open behind; it received much from the past and by repeating it gave it presentness again. . . . Thus this life was in a sense a reanimation, an archaizing attitude. But it is just this life as reanimation that is the life as myth. Alexander walked in the footsteps of Miltiades; the ancient biographers of Caesar were convinced, rightly or wrongly, that he took Alexander as his prototype. But such 'imitation' means far more than we mean by the word today. It was a mythical identification, peculiarly familiar to antiquity; but it is operative far into modern times, and at all times is psychically possible."[14]

Freud, Ortega, and Mann are merely three of the most familiar examples for the new awareness of typological thinking that emerged in non-theological contexts in the early twentieth century. But this increasingly widespread awareness helped to destroy the notion of an unconscious *imitatio* that faith attributed to genuine typology. Of course, the various literary scholars who began to turn their attention to typological questions in the twenties and thirties were stimulated by the general *Zeitgeist*. Julius

[12] "El ocaso de las revoluciones" in José Ortega y Gasset, *The Modern Theme*, trans. James Cleugh (New York, 1933), pp. 99–131.
[13] José Ortega y Gasset, *The Revolt of the Masses*, Authorized Translation (New York, 1932), especially ch. 7.
[14] Reprinted in *Essays of Three Decades*, trans. H. T. Lowe-Porter (New York, 1947), p. 424.

Schwietering's epoch-making article "Typologisches in mittelalterlicher Dichtung" (1925) suggested, probably for the first time, that Middle High German epics like *Parzival* make use of typological elements; Erich Auerbach's essay "Figura" (originally 1938) traced the etymology of the term and hinted at the extent of its impact in Dante; Herbert Grundmann (1927) pointed out typological influences in the works of Joachim da Fiore and also in medieval art;[15] and Friedrich Ohly emphasized the essentially typological structure of the Middle High German *Kaiserchronik* (1940).[16] These literary studies were, in part at least, the result of the new scholarly interest in typological thinking. At the same time, to the extent that they contributed to popularizing the notion of typology and making it explicit and conscious, they also constituted part of the cause. Whether or not Schwietering, Auerbach, and others were correct in their attribution of figural thinking to secular medieval authors is a matter to be settled by specialists in the period; but their work, right or wrong, clearly succeeded in heightening the modern literary consciousness so greatly that no reasonably sophisticated twentieth-century writer can any longer pretend to operate naively. To cite a single example: the criticism of his novel *The Sot-Weed Factor* (1960) stimulated John Barth's interest in the myth of the wandering hero. "From 1960 on I became enormously interested in this pattern and the great amount of learned commentary on it and decided that it would be a good skeleton for a large comic novel."[17] The novel that resulted from several years of note-taking on the hero-myth as described by Lord Raglan, Joseph Campbell, and other mythologists was *Giles Goat-Boy* (1966); and it should be

[15] Herbert Grundmann, *Studien über Joachim von Floris* (Leipzig and Berlin, 1927).

[16] Friedrich Ohly, *Sage und Legende in der Kaiserchronik: Untersuchungen über Quellen und Aufbau der Dichtung* (1940; reprinted Darmstadt, 1968).

[17] Phyllis Meras, "Interview with John Barth," *New York Times Book Review*, August 22, 1966, p. 22.

apparent that the author was working at an extraordinarily high degree of consciousness concerning the typological method of narrative that he employed, which exploits not only the theme of Jesus, but also those of Oedipus, Hamlet, and several other figures. Similarly, John Updike has said that *The Centaur* (1963) began "as an attempt to publicize this myth" of Chiron. "The mythology operated in a number of ways."[18] And Thomas Mann's correspondence with Karl Kerényi adequately demonstrates the great degree of consciousness with which he dealt with mythological and typological themes.[19] As Robert Scholes has observed about such modern writers, "the really perceptive writer is not merely conscious that he is using mythic materials; he is conscious that he is using them consciously."[20]

The four factors cited—the separation of the mode from the matter, historicism, the secularization of the potential material to include myth, and the heightened awareness of typology as a technique suitable for secular purposes—suggest that we can no longer speak with any real precision of religious figuralism in the conventional sense when we are dealing with writers of the twentieth century. If we take up the two parts of the phrase separately, we see that the term "religious" must be broadened in such a manner as to embrace myth as well as the conventional material of Christian typology. Upon the disappearance of the factor of faith, which provided the meaning for Christian typology from the beginning down into the nineteenth century, even the literary use of a Christian type or *figura* takes on a different and more essentially playful significance. The modern author who writes a novel based typologically on themes from the Bible, in short, is literally incapacitated by history and his own consciousness from writing out of the faith that was accessible even to the most sophisticated medieval authors. (Conversely, it is probably safe to assume

18 "Interview with John Updike," *The Paris Review*, 45 (1968), 103.
19 *Mythology and Humanism*, trans. Alexander Gelley (Ithaca, N.Y., 1975).
20 Robert Scholes, *The Fabulators* (New York, 1967), p. 171.

that any modern work that used typology seriously and naively would remain, almost by definition, sub-literary, like most Sunday-school readers.)

The secularization of the term "religious" also necessitates a modification of the term "figuralism." For centuries conventional Christian typology operated within a monolithic framework; as one scholar has put it, Christian typology is always "christocentric."[21] That is, the Christian typological exegete knows that his antitype is inevitably the person of Jesus himself or some person or institution (e.g., *ecclesia*) intimately associated with Jesus. Hence, he can ransack the Old Testament for the most far-fetched and random episodes or figures because the frame of reference remains constant: everything finds its fulfillment in Jesus. If, however, typology is expanded to include the possibility that other mythic figures prefigure the modern antitype, then the isolated motif no longer suffices to identify the theme.[22] To take a simple example: within a conventional Christian context, the motif of a leader surrounded by twelve followers suggests first and foremost Jesus and his twelve disciples. Within other contexts, however, the same motif could just as reasonably refer to Robin Hood and his yeomen, Charlemagne and his paladins, Arthur and the Knights of the Round Table, or a warlock and his coven. Similarly, the motif of a redemptive death, outside a narrowly Christian configuration, can be associated with any of various scapegoat-themes, just as the motif of death and resurrection could be attributed to Adonis, Attis, Osiris, Dionysus, and a host of other mythic deities. John Updike, speaking in *The Paris Review* of his use of mythic parallels in *The Centaur*, said that he was "moved, first, by the

21 Ohly, "Synagoge und Ecclesia," p. 358.
22 I am using the term "theme" here in the technical sense that has been increasingly widely accepted in international comparative literature: that is, to designate a pattern of action that a) consists of a specific configuration of motifs and b) is associated with a specific name from history, literature, or mythology. Cf. Manfred Beller, "Von der Stoffgeschichte zur Thematologie: Ein Beitrag zur komparatistischen Methodenlehre," *Arcadia*, 5 (1970), 1–38.

Chiron variant of the Hercules myth—one of the few classic instances of self-sacrifice, and the name oddly close to Christ." This is not to suggest, of course, that single instances of typological prefiguration may not occasionally occur in modern literature. But without an explicitly Christian context it is often difficult to be sure whether or not the analogy is intended or meaningful or even, if it is intended, whether it is serious or parodistic. Is Hemingway's Santiago (in *The Old Man and the Sea*) a Christ-figure simply because he collapses on the beach beneath his mast? Or Kafka's Josef K. (in *The Trial*) because he is killed with outstretched arms? If we are to speak confidently of "figuralism" in a modern literary work, we need to establish not merely a single motivic correspondence, but a pattern or configuration of motifs associated with a specific theme. Otherwise, in the absence of a clear context or intention, the critic runs the risk of reading his own ingenuity into the text.

This revised understanding of figuralism enables us to distinguish typological analysis from another contemporary form of analysis with which it is often confused: namely, myth criticism based upon Jungian archetypes and represented by such works as Maud Bodkin's *Archetypal Patterns in Poetry* or Northrop Frye's *Anatomy of Criticism*. According to Jung's simplest definition, archetypes are "the contents of the collective unconscious."[23] They exist, in other words, at a level of consciousness anterior to any discrimination into separately identifiable themes. For Maud Bodkin, therefore, both Orestes and Hamlet are variants of the same archetype of generational conflict. Useful as this sort of analysis may be from the psychoanalytical or anthropological or structuralist point of view, it obviously represents interests wholly different from those of typological analysis, which by its very definition depends upon the identification of a specific *figura* or *type* in history, or mythology, or literature, in contrast to a vague archetype

[23] Cf. *The Archetypes and the Collective Unconscious*, trans. R.F.C. Hull, 2nd ed. (Princeton, 1968), p. 4.

that has not yet emerged from the wells of the collective unconscious, where everything flows together. Myth criticism and figural analysis, in other words, may well be complementary, but methodologically they need to be distinguished with rigorous precision.

There seem to be two principal reasons why a twentieth-century writer, with his sophisticated awareness of typological thinking, would go to the trouble of creating a work that is extensively and consistently based on an existing prefigurative pattern. First, the prefigurative pattern can supply a form for the modern work. This is what T. S. Eliot had in mind, in his essay *"Ulysses,* Order, and Myth," when he argued that Joyce's "paralled use of the *Odyssey"* had the importance of a scientific discovery.[24] "In using myth, in manipulating a continuous parallel between contemporaneity and antiquity, Mr. Joyce is pursuing a method which others must pursue after him. . . . It is simply a way of controlling, of ordering, of giving a shape and a significance to the immense panorama of futility and anarchy which is contemporary history." This is not the place to discuss Eliot's correctness in attributing priority of invention to Joyce. As a matter of fact, the parallel use of the New Testament had already been widely explored by various European novelists with whose work Joyce was familiar.[25] What matters in the present context is Eliot's acknowledgment of the structural value of the typological method—a method he himself had recently employed in his own work, as he pointed out in his notes on *The Waste Land.* "Not only the title, but the plan and a good deal of the incidental symbolism of the poem were suggested by Miss Jessie L. Weston's book on the Grail Legend."

[24] Eliot's essay originally appeared in *Dial* (1923); reprinted in *Forms of Modern Fiction,* ed. William Van O'Connor (1948; reprinted Bloomington, 1959), pp. 120–124.
[25] See my *Fictional Transfigurations of Jesus,* esp. pp. 53–54. Joyce knew at least two famous novels based consistently and extensively on the prefigurative pattern of Jesus: Antonio Fogazzaro's *Il Santo* (1905) and Gerhart Hauptmann's *Der Narr in Christo Emanuel Quint* (1910).

A second reason for the use of prefigurative patterns seems to be that the pattern supplies, in addition to form, further dimensions of meaning that enhance the implications of the contemporary work. The theme of Parzival has been used seriously by Hermann Hesse (in *Demian*) and parodistically by Bernard Malamud (in *The Natural*) to lend a more general meaning to the quest motif that underlies their novels. The theme of Odysseus is most familiar, of course, from Joyce's novel, but it was adapted by a number of postwar German novelists to give a broader significance to the motif of the homecoming soldier.[26] In fact, Heinrich Böll has suggested that Homer's two epics prefigure all modern war novels and *Heimkehrerromane*, a notion advanced also by such critics as Hermann Pongs and Walter Jens.[27] In Hans Erich Nossack's remarkable novel *Nekyia: Bericht eines Überlebenden* (1947; *Nekyia: The Report of a Survivor*) Odysseus' journey to the underworld provides the pattern for a story set in a time and place resembling war-gutted Hamburg. Emil Barth's *Enkel des Odysseus* (1951; *The Grandson of Odysseus*), in contrast, presents a flier in Rommel's *Afrikakorps* whose aerial reconnaissance plane is shot down: when he is caught up in a sandstorm during his parachute fall, the temptation to succumb to oblivion is compared at great length and in considerable detail to Odysseus's adventure among the Lotus Eaters. The theme of Faust has been used by various modern writers to prefigure heroes characterized principally by their sinful lust for knowledge and experience: much less successfully by John Hersey in his college novel, *Too Far to Walk* (1966), than by Thomas Mann in his story of the demonic composer Adrian Leverkühn, *Doktor Faustus* (1947).

[26] See my study, "The Odysseus Theme in Recent German Fiction," *Comparative Literature*, 14 (1962), 225–241.

[27] "Bekenntnis zur Trümmerliteratur," in Heinrich Böll, *Erzählungen, Hörspiele, Aufsätze* (Kölin-Berlin, 1961), pp. 339–343. Hermann Pongs, *Im Umbruch der Zeit: Das Romanschaffen der Gegenwart*, 2nd ed. (Göttingen, 1956), p. 224; Walter Jens, *Moderne Literatur, Moderne Wirklichkeit* (Pfullingen, 1958), p. 18.

At the same time, however, the modern writer faces certain problems—largely as a result of his very consciousness —that do not present themselves in pre-twentieth-century works based on prefigurative patterns. And these problems, in turn, produce certain responses that characterize modern postfigurative works. I would like to consider three strategies that occur frequently enough in the twentieth-century novel to be considered representative: parody, incorporation of the type within the novel of the antitype, and the inverse relationship of consciousness to aesthetic organization.[28]

Among the themes that twentieth-century novelists have frequently chosen to lend form and meaning to their modern plots we can number—along with those of Parzival, Odysseus, and Faust—the theme of Jesus. During the past century, in fact, such "fictional transfigurations of Jesus" reflect with considerable accuracy both the shifting views of Jesus himself and the changing interests of society.[29] Thus the Christian Socialist Jesus of such turn-of-the-century novelists as Benito Pérez-Galdós (*Nazarín*, 1895) and Antonio Fogazzaro (*The Saint*, 1905) gives way, first, to the christomaniac Jesus of the psychiatrically oriented Gerhart Hauptmann (*The Fool in Christ Emanuel Quint*, 1910) and Nikos Kazantzakis (*The Greek Passion*, 1950), then to the "mythic" Jesus of Hermann Hesse (*Demian*, 1919) and Carlo Coccioli (*Manuel the Mexican*, 1956), and finally to the "Comrade Jesus" of such disaffected Marxists as Ignazio Silone (*Bread and Wine*, 1936) and Arthur Koestler (*Darkness at Noon*, 1940). But whereas the Christian Socialists were still quite sincere in their faith and whereas their novels were written within a Christian context to put across a Christian message, a growing secularization of the theme

[28] John J. White, *Mythology in the Modern Novel: A Study of Prefigurative Techniques* (Princeton, 1971) is the only major study that deals with problems of typology in modern literature; however, White does not approach the problem, as I have attempted to do, as a modification of conventional Christian typology.

[29] The following paragraph amounts to a summary of the conclusions of my *Fictional Transfigurations of Jesus*.

is apparent among succeeding generations. For Hauptmann and Kazantzakis, for instance, faith is a moot point: they are interested almost wholly in the psychological phenomenon of the man so obsessed with the notion that he is Jesus that he organizes the events of his life in such a way as to parallel, unmistakably, the events of the Gospels. Similarly, Hesse and Coccioli are fascinated by the extent to which the theme of Jesus is compatible with the theme, say, of Parzival or with Aztec mythology. For the Marxists, finally, Jesus has been wholly desanctified: Comrade Jesus is nothing but the model or *exemplum* of a good man.

The inevitable consequence of this process of secularization and detachment is parody, which occurs at the moment when form becomes absolute and the original meaning disappears. This is the form assumed by typology or religious figuralism in the works of such writers as Günter Grass or John Barth. The theme of Jesus, no longer inspired by any remnant of faith, is reduced simply to another plot that lends parodistic shape to the novel. Thus the hero of Grass' *Cat and Mouse* (1961) is the leader of a teenage gang in Nazi Germany: surrounded by his admiring "disciples," he performs miracles of swimming and masturbation, chants blasphemous hymns to the Virgin Mary, steals an Iron *Cross* to cover up his phallically protuding Adam's Apple, and finally fails in his redemptive act: after his death, he fails to be resurrected, much to the chagrin of his principal disciple and gospelist, Pilenz. Similarly, the faun-like hero of John Barth's *Giles Goat-Boy* (1966), called an "Enos Enoch with balls," lives a life modeled conspicuously after the life of Jesus: from the moment his mother *Virgin*ia is impregnated by the god-like computer that reigns over the world of the novel to his disappearance at the age of thirty-three and a third.

The stage of parody, which marks the exhaustion of any prefigurative theme, is by no means restricted to Jesus. The theme of Parzival is handled with equally great playfulness by Bernard Malamud in *The Natural*. Mikhail Bulgakov's treatment of the Faust theme in *The Master and Margarita*

(1967) is pure parody. Arthur Hoppe bases his political satire *Miss Lollipop and the Doom Machine* (1973) on the theme of St. George and the Dragon. Joyce's use of the Odysseus theme in *Ulysses*, of course, is more parodistically playful than thematically serious. In short, fiction employing religious figuralism or, more generally, prefigurative patterns, seems to be subject to the same impulse of twentieth-century art that impels Stravinsky to parody Mozart, that inspires Picasso to "imitate" Poussin, and that causes Thomas Mann's Adrian Leverkühn to argue that "all the methods and conventions of art today *are good for parody only*" (chap. 15).

If writers have to strain against parody because the prefiguring themes are so familiar as to have exhausted their meaning, at the same time—parodoxically—they are often confronted with audiences who have so totally lost touch with the cultural heritage that they do not recognize prefigurative patterns if they are present. For writers concerned with structure rather than substance this presents no problem. John Updike, for instance, argues that the mythic parallels should not be too obvious, implying that they exist principally for the needs of the writer and only secondarily for the delectation of unusually perceptive readers. Nevertheless, Updike adds a Mythological Index listing the figures that prefigure the characters of *The Centaur*. Similarly, T. S. Eliot finds it expedient to append to *The Waste Land* a number of notes in which he points out the sources and mythic analogies to readers who missed them. And it was with Joyce's blessing that Stuart Gilbert wrote his study of *Ulysses*, in which he made explicit for the first time the elaborate prefigurative structure at which Eliot had only hinted in his earlier essay. It is probably fair to say that modern postfigurative fiction has provided recent literary critics and scholars with an opportunity and challenge quite analogous to that encountered by the Alexandrine exegetes who first pored over the Bible in an effort to determine the typological relationships between the testaments.

Several contemporary writers, in full awareness of this dilemma yet unwilling to wait for a scholarly commentator to come along, have made the problem part of the solution: they have constructed their novels in such a manner as to incorporate the *type* within the fiction dealing with an *antitype*. In Emil Barth's *Enkel des Odysseus*, for instance, the central character, Nobisgat, is by profession a cultural historian who is at the moment writing an essay on the *Odyssey*, in which he presents Odysseus as "the first Western man" and as "the symbol of the awakening of a new consciousness." Odysseus, emerging from archaic mass consciousness, actively sought consciousness and hence fled the threat represented by the Lotus Eaters. Nobisgat, on the other hand, has reached the turning-point at which consciousness seeks to return into oblivion. Hence, as Nobisgat drifts down to earth in his parachute, the entire scene, deliberately contrasted with the Lotus-Eaters passage in the *Odyssey*, has been carefully prepared by the inclusion in the story of Nobisgat's theoretical reflections on Homer's epic. A similar device occurs in Alberto Moravia's novel *Il Disprezzo* (1954; *A Ghost at Noon*). Again, a contemporary action is contrasted with an episode from the *Odyssey* —this time the homecoming, involving the relationship between Odysseus, Penelope, and the suitors. The prefigurative parallels and ironic contrasts are made explicit, however, through the fiction that the central characters are film-makers discussing preliminary plans for a film of the *Odyssey*. In the course of their deliberations, three totally different interpretations of Homer's poem are advanced: the producer, Battista, wants to turn out a profitable film epic after the pattern of Hollywood biblical sagas; the director, Rheingold, reduces the entire action to a Freudian inversion of the ostensible plot; and Molteni, the scriptwriter, constantly compares the deterioration of his own marriage and the unfaithfulness of his wife with the homecoming of Odysseus and the faithfulness of Penelope.

Michel Butor varies and complicates this technique in his novel *L'Emploi du temps* (1956; *Passing Time*). The fact that the term "prefiguration" actually occurs in the text alerts us to the highly conscious use of the technique, which exploits two principal mythological themes. The commercial translator, Jacques Revel, must spend a year in the dreary English industrial town of Bleston. During the course of the year, like Theseus, he becomes entrapped in a labyrinth—not the labyrinth just of the city, but also of time and his own memory, from which he tries to extricate himself by writing a report of his sojourn. And he emerges from his experience in Bleston feeling that he has somehow assumed the guilt of Cain toward his fellow man. Without looking more closely at the plot, let us simply note that in each case the antitype, exemplified by Revel, is paralleled by the incorporation of its type: in the local museum Revel studies a series of tapestries depicting the adventures of Theseus, and in the local cathedral he sees a stained-glass window through which Cain's blood-stained hands seem to cast their light upon him. Like Nobisgat's reflections on the *Odyssey*, like Molteni's film, the tapestries and windows enable the author to bring the prefiguring type into the novel itself. In all three cases at least two reasons are clear. First, the incorporation of the type insures that the reader will not miss the point. (Emil Barth is clumsy to the point of condescension in his asides to the reader.) Second, in all three cases the modern action is *contrasted* with the prefiguring type; in order to bring out the full effect of the contrast the author permits his antitypal characters to reflect on the differences of time and circumstance.

We encounter precisely the same technique—incorporation of the type for the sake of clarity and contrast—in John Bowen's *A World Elsewhere* (1965). Here a young British Member of Parliament is sent to the island of Lemnos in order to persuade the former party leader— Gareth Payne, "the Honest Man," who retired in disgust following a scandal—to return to lead his party. This story is narrated with many parallels to the theme of Philoctetes, deserted by the Greeks on an island because of his stinking wound and now wooed by Neoptolemus because the Greeks need his magic bow at Troy. As it turns out, Gareth Payne is himself writing a fictionalized account of the Philoctetes legend; his own prose, along with his speculations on the myth and on the parallels between it and his own situation, are incorporated into the text, alternating with Bowen's narrative of the comtemporary action. The result is a fascinating reworking of the ancient theme, which is constantly present in the reader's mind through its incorporation; yet the fictional tension is maintained through Payne's reinterpretation of the theme and through our own curiosity concerning the outcome of the modern story.

Still another possibility occurs, finally, in Rhoda Lerman's recent novel, *Call Me Ishtar* (1973). In this work, which has been hailed as a major fictional achievement of women's liberation, it is the underlying conceit that the goddess Ishtar, in one of her cycles of metempsychosis, returns to earth and enters the body of a suburban housewife in Syracuse, New York. The author is concerned principally with unmasking the ancient mythic patterns that prefigure most of our daily lives—from sex and human relations to cookie-baking and everyday household chores. The point that needs to be stressed in our context, however, is the fact that Ishtar herself frequently interrupts her account of the modern action in order to recall, in a different type-face, episodes from her principal reincarnations in the past: as the Goddess of Death, as the Whore of Babylon, and so forth. So the reader, from whom presumably no detailed familiarity with the theme of Ishtar can be expected, is presented with all the information and motifs that are required in order to appreciate the latest incarnation of the goddess in Lerman's novel.

This brings us to a concluding generalization on the use of typology in modern literature. Jungian archetypes may presumably occur in literary works without the author's conscious intent. But if a prefigurative pattern, as we have defined it, occurs in a novel, poem, or play, then it is safe to assume that it has been put there consciously and intentionally. Occasionally the writer may use the prefigurative pattern purely as a catalyst for his fictional imagination, not caring whether or not it becomes apparent to the reader: this seems to have been the case with Joyce in *Ulysses*, and John Updike has implied much the same attitude in connection with *The Centaur*. In most cases, however, the pattern must be recognized if it is to be effective. This principle applies whether the intention is serious or parodistic. Now, there seem to be two chief ways whereby the writer can bring the typological analogy to the reader's attention: he can do it himself, or he can let his fictional characters do it. If he does it himself, then the principal means at his disposal is aesthetic organization: title, motto, chapter headings, names, plot structure, quotations, and so forth. If his characters draw the analogy, on the other hand, it is almost inevitably through their consciousness of a thematic analogy between their own lives and the prefiguring type: for it is not usually in their power to change their names or to arrange their own plots.

If we examine modern typological novels from this point of view, it turns out in almost every single case that the degree of consciousness among the characters varies in an inverse proportion with the degree of aesthetic organization. In the novels by Barth, Moravia, Butor, Bowen, and Lerman, for instance, in which the consciousness of the central characters is so high that they incorporate the type within the fiction itself, the number of motivic parallels between type and antitype is surprisingly low. But when the hero's consciousness of his roles is low, as it is often the case in parodistic works, the degree of aesthetic organization must be correspondingly high. In Malamud's *The Natural*, for instance, the hero exists at an intellectual level that is barely above the threshold of simple consciousness, and he has presumably never heard of the Holy Grail. Yet the reader is never in the least doubt concerning his role because the author supplies so much aesthetic organization. A hero with the telling name *Roy* comes charging out of the west with his invincible lance-like bat Wonderboy, with which he leads his baseball team, the Knights, to the World Series and heals the manager, Pop Fisher, of the affliction that has tormented him during the team's drought (a case of athlete's foot on his hands). No reader of the post-*Waste Land* generation could possibly miss the allusions that Malamud heaps up for our delectation and instruction.

The relationship between aesthetic organization and consciousness stands out clearly if we consider pairs of works that are based on the same prefigurative pattern. In Thomas Mann's *Doktor Faustus*, where the consciousness of the Faust analogy is exceedingly high both in Adrian Leverkühn and in his fictional biographer, Serenus Zeitblom, Thomas Mann *as author* needs to do very little: the degree of aesthetic organization is in fact quite low; there are astonishing few motivic parallels in the lengthy novel between the Faust theme and the life of Leverkühn. Yet we are kept constantly aware of the Faust theme by Leverkühn's own thoughts. By way of contrast, in John Hersey's college novel *Too Far to Walk* the characters are totally unaware of their Faustian roles. To bring the typological analogies to our attention, therefore, Hersey heaps up motif upon clumsy motif, beginning with the name of his hero, John Fist, and proceeding to a visit to the "hell" of the city dump.

Now, in actual practice most serious postfigurative fiction in the twentieth century has tended to establish its analogies through thematic consciousness rather than through extensive motivic organization, which seems to lead very quickly over the borderline into parody. As a result, although Hersey is under the impression that he is writing a serious novel, in fact the high degree of aesthetic organization causes his work to produce the effect of a parody. He simply did not understand properly the implications of his technique. The same relationship is evident if we contrast Joyce's *Ulysses* with Moravia's *Il Disprezzo. Ulysses*, of course, cannot be written off simply as a parody, yet few critics today would argue that the typological parallels have much thematic meaning for Joyce.[30] And certainly his characters have little awareness of their typological roles; the figuralism emerges because Joyce has constructed his novel with such an uncannily high degree of aesthetic organization, including details that scholars still continue to uncover after fifty years. In Moravia's novel, on the other hand, the low degree of aesthetic organization and the small number of motivic parallels is offset by the exceedingly high degree of consciousness among the main characters: not just Molteni, but also Battista and Rheingold are totally and articulately aware of the *Odyssey* and its relationship to the situation in which they find themselves.

If we recall, in conclusion, the cautionary words of Hastings' *Encyclopaedia*, there would seem to be some truth —though in a wholly different sense—to the assertion that "typology has always flourished in times of ignorance and decay of learning." John Updike, certainly, was speaking for many of his contemporaries when he observed in *The Paris Review* that "mine is a generation not raised on the Bible." Yet, as we have seen, resourceful writers have converted the problem itself into a solution, using the "decay of learning" as an occasion to expand the notion of religious figuralism to encompass extremely varied mythologies. As John Barth has observed, "To the objection that classical mythology, like the Bible, is no longer a staple of the average reader's education, and that, consequently, the old agonies of Oedipus or Antigone are without effect on contemporary sensibility, I reply, hum, I forget what, something about comedy and self-explanatory context."[31] Barth's "comedy" and "self-explanatory context" would seem to correspond precisely to the strategies that we have considered under parody and incorporation of the type within the fiction of the antitype.

[30] Cf. Harry Levin, *James Joyce: A Critical Introduction* (revised edition: Norfolk, Conn., 1960), pp. 74–75; and A. Walton Litz, *The Art of James Joyce* (New York, 1964), p. 21.
[31] John Barth, *Chimera* (New York, 1972), p. 199.

In addition, writers have compensated for the loss of faith, which inspired religious figuralism in its original and strict sense, by substituting consciousness. Even if typology has been discredited as a means of biblical exegesis, therefore, it has won a new standing as a legitimate technique of literary inquiry because the object of its analysis—the texts themselves—have changed. This appropriation of figuralism or typology is perfectly consistent with the history of hermeneutics, which shows that literary criticism, at least since the Renaissance, has regularly adapted its methods of textual analysis and exegesis from theology by a process of secularization. The techniques remain the same, but in a secular age literary texts replace Scripture as art comes to be regarded as a religion and the critic as its priest.

But to the extent that consciousness has replaced faith, the critic can no longer assume, as the exegete could do, that "salvation history" (*Heilsgeschichte*) accounts for the typological parallels between the literary antitype and its prefiguring type, whether in the Bible or elsewhere. Rather, it is in every case the writer himself who has created the analogies, consciously and for his own literary purposes. In the absence of *Heilsgeschichte* it remains for the critic to determine the purpose of the prefigurations: that is, to ascertain for what reasons of structure or meaning the writer has based his fiction consistently upon a prefigurative pattern. It is useful to approach such consciously structured texts with certain expectations as outlined above. If, for instance, the text displays a high degree of consciousness among its characters regarding the prefiguring theme, then we expect on the basis of experience that the aesthetic organization will be correspondingly loose and that the impact of the type will be primarily contextual rather than structural. If, on the other hand, the text displays a high degree of aesthetic organization, then we anticipate that the thematic meaning will be slight or, at least, not serious, and we begin to look for evidences of parody. It goes without saying, of course, that these observations on the twentieth-century novel apply, *mutatis mutandis*, to poetry and drama as well, although experience again suggests that poetry is more comfortable with archetypal images than with highly structured figures or types. The plays of Sartre, Cocteau, Tennessee Williams, Eugene O'Neill, the German expressionists, and many others, indicate that drama is an appropriate and grateful medium for typological themes.[32] Yet in all studies of this sort we should strive for the greatest terminological and methodological precision lest our typological understanding of myth deteriorate to nothing more than a new myth-understanding of typology.

[32] See, for example, Christoph Eykman, "Die Christus-Gestalt in der expressionistischen Dichtung," *Wirkendes Wort*, 23 (1973), 400–410.

## AFTERWORD

THE issues debated at the Council of Constance involved orthodoxy and heresy as well as life and death, all centering on the problem of how the Bible was to be interpreted. Neither side doubted that the Old Testament prefigured the New Testament, that the first Adam foreshadowed the second, Christ, in God's plan for our salvation. But when in Genesis we read about Adam in Eden, is Christ part of the "literal" sense or part of the "spiritual"? If the literal, does that sense refer to the "letter" of script? And is script Scripture? Or are they all one, with in particular the literal inclusive of the spiritual? The bursting forth of such questions at a crucial historical juncture shows how from early Christian times such terms as "literal" and spiritual"—"figure" and "type"—proved inevitable to hermeneutics and yet were themselves the continuing subject of interpretation.

The problem is not confined to Christianity. What Christians term the Old Testament (a name itself with typological implications)—or the Scriptures of the Jews—has its own problems of interpretations. How do we account for the status of the Israel of the prophets, now one thing and subsequently another? What relation do the institutions of judgeship and prophecy have to each other, or to the persons of various judges and prophets? Do we not read, "And there arose not a prophet since in Israel like unto Moses" (Deut. 34: 10)? And on what grounds other than an "allegorical" or "spiritual" reading was the Song of Songs admitted into the Hebrew Bible? The problems presented by the Wisdom Books, the Apocrypha, and the Pseudepigrapha, like the very question of canonicity, are matters of faith well enough. They are also matters of interpretation that themselves call for interpretation. Interpretation implies methods of exegesis, exegetes, and disagreement.

The central problem is universal to peoples with sacred scriptures, even as the terms of the problem vary from people to people and age to age. In this century the strict method may be imitated in a literature wholly secular, conscious, and parodic. Both sides at the Council of Constance would have been appalled by such blasphemy, but the developments in figuralism over the centuries have a history that connects Gerson with our contemporary novelists. Of course spiritual reading of unspiritual materials and figures seems a contradiction in terms. Yet the spiritual character of certain things in the Bible is not immediately apparent.

> Wherefore David arose and went, he and his men, and slew of the Philistines two hundred men; and David brought their foreskins, and they gave them in full [tally] to [Saul], that he might be the king's son in law. And Saul gave him Michal his daughter to wife. (1 Sam. 18: 27)

The ordeal Saul sets David to win Michal has many counterparts in literature. It derives its odor of sanctity from interpretation, however, rather than from evident fact. And in spite of this episode, David is one of the chief types of our lord and savior, Jesus Christ.

Questions of the kinds of truth available in Scriptures require interpretation, and interpretation involves connections between elements that do not always seem to all interpreters to justify connection. Some things cannot, it seems, be treated "literally" because they were parabolic, "spiritual" in the first place. These hermeneutic truisms are not confined to the Scriptures of the Jews and of the Christians. In the Buddhist Lotus Sutra, there is the parable of a man whose house catches fire. His children will not leave the burning building until he entices them out with promises of presents. So does the Buddha's teaching employ adapted truth, tantamount to presents for children, to deceive us into our enlightenment. As in the West, such good stories cannot be passed over unused by writers, and it may be worth looking at one of the poems by Izumi Shikibu (ca. 970–1030) treating that episode.

> Worldly thoughts alone
> Fill my flaming house of passion:
> Why not leave it, then,
> In death to soak my burning body
> In His universal rain?

Her poem is by no means idiosyncratic. Others use such figural images as the full moon for enlightenment and the empty sky for the Void (the doctrine of the insubstantiality of existence). Another example, by Emperor Fushimi (1265–1317) will prove that these matters are not purely Western.

> On the window frame
> The rain falls down in gentle drops,
> And as I listen
> I turn around against the wall
> The lamp that lights the depths of night.

This poem is written "On the topic, 'The Three Dogmas Are Not One Dogma, Nor Are They Three Separate Dogmas.' " The three dogmas are those of Tendai Buddhism (the Void, the Phenomenal, and the Mean) to elaborate on the insubstantiality of existence. We are given allegory rather than scriptural or figural detail.

Such examples could be greatly multiplied. A yet more telling one occurs in *The Tale of Genji* (ca. 1010). Many Japanese scholars believe that the life of its radiant but imperfect hero is based on an earlier work of hagiography. Among its many other Buddhist elements and symbols, there is a revealing passage on the art of prose fiction in "The Firefly" chapter. Genji uses a comparison between the Greater Vehicle (or Mahāyāna sutras) and the Lesser (or Hīnayāna).

"Even the Buddha, so awesome and so just in heart, employed differing methods and means to teach the Law. And can there be any doubt that for those of us who lack due wisdom the sutras have been left with many doubts over seeming contradictions? The truth of the third-period sutras has assistance from many aids to understanding in the Lesser Vehicle, but as we reach the end of the Buddha's teaching, we discover that the truth of the Greater Vehicle and the means of the Lesser have become single in their meaning, leaving as sole difference that between the enlightened and the ignorant. And just so, I think, in tales there is such a distinction between matters of human good and evil. If we interpret human affairs well, everything of any kind will surely be found to possess some significance."

In the two vehicles we have two scriptures. One resembles the Old Testament's Christian relation to the New in helping to establish the truth of the other and so issuing in a single final truth. Here we also have the need for interpretation; and here we have the idea that all is to our enlightenment (cf. Romans 15: 4 and the Nun's Priest's Tale B² 4631–32—the biblical passage refers to the Old Testament in Christian application). In the light of all this, it should not be surprising that Chinese Buddhists adapted the historical Confucius to their faith by claiming him as a Bodhisattva, or that Japanese Buddhists should have done much the same with the Shinto sun goddess, Amaterasu-ōmikami.

The Asian examples are meant to show what the essays in this book show, that scriptural elements and methods of interpretation easily become literary. Also we feel able to make certain discriminations. The last two lines of Fushimi's poem echo a verse by Po Chü-i, and that solely literary allusion is felt to be different from the religious. It is also true that poets could write of the moon, the rain, and the fires of passion without any religious import and with no figuralist method, even in adaptation. On the other hand, and again as in our literature, critics may sometimes dispute whether the moon is a fact or a figure, or both, or whether imagery of grasses and shrubs are figural for the doctrine of the possible Buddhahood of non-sentient things.

Not only does scriptural interpretation itself require interpretation; literary versions of spiritual meaningfulness also require critical care and alter as literary practice and religious experience change.

Plainly, for Buddhism as well as Christianity, figural methods are necessary for scriptural exegesis. The adaptations, the typologies, and the spiritual senses of Scripture all expand into polysemous richness, and often the gold seems to be beaten out at very great length into mere tinsel. Even when the interpreter of Scriptures and of literary usage modeled on scriptural interpretation stays within what are thought "strict" terms, polysemousness may take us from many directions to one goal, or from one goal out in many directions. As to the former, it would be difficult to say how many types of Christ and his ministry the Old Testament was thought to provide. Many individuals felt to be historically real and chosen by God—Noah, Abraham, Moses, David, etc.—foreshadow the Christ who renders them fulfilled and perfect. The New Testament itself was parabolically interpreted in ways requiring typological assumptions. In the parable of the prodigal son, the father was interpreted as God, the elder son as the Jews, the younger, prodigal son as Christians, the fatted calf as the sacrifice of Christ, and so on. We observe that the distinction between the sons is a typological one that provides the second major point to the glossing of the parable. Such interpretation may require that we read between the lines— in the original sense of the many great Vulgate Bibles containing glosses in small letters between the lines of Scripture. If to the pious, all that was written "aforetime" was written for our instruction (as Prince Genji believed to be true of reality itself), then all that is in the Bible may be thought to lead to the single Savior and his ministry.

Yet the same habit of mind may produce multiplicity. To take an example from George Landow, in Numbers 20: 8-11 and Exodus 17: 6, Moses strikes the rock with his rod at God's order and produces water for the thirsty, doubting "children of Israel." Of course this instance can be read as a type, shadow, or figure of the Christian sacrament of baptism. Yet it could also be read as the type of the spear thrust into Christ's side, which is to say of the salvation earned by his sacrifice. And as Landow also shows from the suggestion by Froehlich, the evangelical hymn, "Rock of ages, cleft for me / Let me hide myself in thee," can be read not merely in such ways but in a third fashion as a reference to Exodus 33: 22. Such variety appears in earlier poetry as well as in Victorian hymns, and it appears in art as well as literature. Manuscript illumination, stained glass, and cathedral architecture itself show how congenial such method was to medieval artists.

Figuralism of verbal or iconographical kinds does not exhaust the important features of this subject. Prophecy and eschatology may be bound up in typology. Or they may be bound up in some version of the Thomistic fourfold "spiritual" glosses of Scripture (literal, allegorical, moral, and anagogical), or in a triad more esteemed by Protestants, nature, grace, and glory. None of those terms has earned a universally agreed-on theological usage, much less a literary one. Where so much may be uncertain, it is particularly valuable to have access to the understandings of typology in a given age. We should not presume that all divines think alike on these matters, even now. One of the standard works on typology is Leonhard Goppelt's *Typos. Die typologische Deutung des Alten Testaments in Neuen* (Gütersloh, 1939; Darmstadt, 1966), although it has been severely questioned by Rudolf Bultmann, who distinguishes several forms of treating the Old Testament in the New.[1] These range from simple comparisons to examples ambiguous as to their kind of function. In any event, Bultmann argues that typology is distinguished as recurrence in cyclical time and prophecy as fulfillment in linear time. (Of course, such distinctions mean little or nothing for most writers before about 1700.) He also finds allegory and spiritualistic exegesis in the New Testament, and he shows that at times typology func-

[1] Bultmann, "Ursprung und Sinn der Typologie als hermeneutischer Methode," *Theologische Literaturzeitung*, 75–76 (1950–51), 205–212.

tions with such other procedures as prophecy, allegory, and spiritual exegesis. The book of Hebrews seems to be a special example of mixed procedures. Yet in these no more than in other matters does the world consist solely of Bultmannists. If the theologians argue because they regard typology in so many different guises, it will not be surprising to discover that it is not a single thing but a varied entity with a history. Our poets may therefore earn some sympathy if they do not always follow Aquinas or Bultmann. We who follow the poets must interpret them with understanding of ways of thought possible to them.

Such complexities and disputes would make a wise person flee the whole thing were it not so obviously central to interpreting Christian experience and therefore to much of our literature. Typology and figuralism exist, however they are defined, and the problem lies in their use. A partial solution can be obtained by approaching the use historically, and for that purpose the chapters of this book very much require being seen together rather than as individual essays. The reasons for historical change in typology and its literary use need be pursued no further at this point than one simple fact. In the course of time, the meaning of revelation has seemed to change, and so have the kinds of meanings of literature. Religion and literature do not, however, change in ways exactly common or at the same pace, and for both there will be some alternatives at the same historical moment.

Nonetheless, the chapters of this book show two things very clearly. The first principle may be termed the necessity of limited or conservative definition: Occam's razor. In the case of spiritual glosses, the conservative principle holds that literal or grammatical glosses are to be preferred when they make sense. In the case of typology, the conservative principle holds that we always bear in mind the exemplary meaning of the fulfillment of Old Testament type by New Testament antitype, with Old Testament person and New Testament Jesus being the normative example, and with both being considered real, historical. The second or liberal principle works contrarily, entailing the multiplicity of representation derived from the whole text or context of the religious, literary, historical, and artistic: polysemousness. The validation of either involves the first principle of hermeneutic method, caution. Our chapters have given us reason to think that we have at once a simpler kind of central method and yet a manifold spiritual meaning. If other cautions are observed, we may suspect both extremes of reductive literalism and free figuralism. We must remember the problems that "literal" represents. We must be able to discriminate literature with typological concerns from literature—often religious in nature—without them. We must recognize that, like all else in literature, typology can degenerate into mere ornament.

The ability to interpret typologically is essential to critics of our older literature. The ability to declare typology absent is a kind of proof of sound modern critical method. Along with these desirable extremes we can identify two over-simple emphases that grow from religious hermeneutics. There are dangers of a pre-Reformation kind in insisting on a continuous fourfold allegory and of a post-Reformation kind in insisting on a single sense. Since not even the Bible is continuously glossed in fourfold terms, we may suspect theories that claim as much for literary productions. The principle is one of compromise between Occam's razor and polysemousness, and the issue is that of doing so in discussion of specific literary works.

We who have participated in this book share a lively sense of the pitfalls in the way of typological interpretation of literature. Such dangers, or doubts, are entailed by any encompassing explanation. The importance and the danger of typological interpretation derive from its being at once a system and a symbolism. It would be particularly unfortunate if typological study were to become as predictable as vulgar Marxism. If that danger is not avoided by close attention to changing understandings of typology over the centuries, then we may well doubt the utility of the results. Certain other doubts appear to be less serious.

Some people may worry that a critic may get a poet wrong, or that a poet may have got typology wrong. And one of us acquainted with typological usage characteristic of a given age may doubt the respectability or the validity of usages at other times.

Some of these doubts can be allayed by straightforward lexicographical evidence. The commonest English nouns for the representations or symbols that this book is concerned with are "type," "figure," and "shadow." Inspection of the *Oxford English Dictionary* shows that of these three only "type" has as its primary meaning a symbol, with our kind of theological symbolism the basic example. The first instance quoted is taken from Robert Henryson, *The Moral Fabillis of Esope* (c. 1480—all dates referring to composition): "Suppose this be ane Fabill, / And overheillt with typis figurall." Here, well before the Reformation insisted on individual interpretation of the Bible, we have the seeming tautology of "typis figurall" for what is by no means "strict typology." Here is no David foreshadowing Christ, and in fact all that is meant is the parabolic character of fables. A later example from the *Works* of Samuel Hieron (1607) gives us what might be thought "strict typology": "The people of Israel were a tipe of Gods people; Canaan a tipe of heaven." It seems that exactness might come more easily after the Reformation than before.

Nearly two and three-quarters centuries later (1875), Henry Cardinal Manning showed similar "strict typology" in *The Internal Mission of the Holy Ghost*: "Ceremonial actions, and washings, and purifications, which were the types and shadows of things to come." A century before him, however (1795), John W. Fletcher wrote in his *Works* that marriage is "the most perfect type of our Lords union with his church." Here we have a typology that might seem wrong to some, a reversal of chronology and an absence of anything in the Old Testament as the symbol. It is of course retrospective typology, since to orthodox Christianity every marriage postdates Christ's love for his Church. But it is nonetheless a commonplace usage.

If such range in the basic word, "type," can be found between Henryson and Manning, then our calls for "strict
typology" should be heeded less—once we have acquired
a degree of knowledge of this symbolism—than should
caveats for careful discrimination. The same points can be
made by "figure" (as also "shadow" in the *OED*, 6. c.). The
first usage given is Chaucer's in *An A.B.C.* (ca. 1366):
"Ysaak was figure of his [Christ's] death certeyn." Perhaps
that is comfortingly "strict." On the other hand there is
quite a different pre-Reformation usage cited, that by
Bishop John Alcock in his *Mons Perfeccionis* (1496): "This
mount is in figure and sygnefyeth religyon." To this we
might say, "The bishop says 'figure' when he means 'allegory.' " But the point is that words may have different
meanings, and that interpreters must exercise as much care
with words like "type" or "figure" as with "nature" or "wit."
Bacon may seem looser still—or perhaps more abstract—
than Alcock in his essay "Of Counsel" (1607–12): "The
auncient tymes doe sett forth in Figure . . . the corporation
. . . of Councell with Kynges." Yet we may put beside
Bacon's a usage half a century later (1651), when Christopher Cartwright's *Certamen Religiosum* gives us a "figure"
familiar to us from George Landow's chapter: "The Rock
. . . was a Type and figure of Christ." As with "type," then,
so with "figure": both before and after the Reformation we
discover usages that may be thought "strict" or "loose."

Any such characterization depends on the expectations
of the modern characterizer. I do not think it amiss to accept the first *OED* definition of "type": "That by which
something is symbolized or figured; anything having a
symbolical signification; a symbol, emblem; *spec.* in *Theol.*
a person, object, or event of Old Testament history, prefiguring some person or thing revealed in the new dispensation; correl. to *antitype*." From both the definition and the
examples, we observe that "type" and "figure" may often be
translated "symbol," "metaphor," or "allegory." (*OED* on
"symbol," 2. a. and b., would enter into a full account.) We
might also say, following I. A. Richard's distinctions, that

a "type" is the *vehicle* of a symbol, allegory, etc., "that by which something is symbolized," just as the "antitype" is the *tenor* of the symbol, etc. Our copybook example of an antitype or tenor of a type must always be Christ. But the type need not be a person—it could be a rock. And Old Testament types need not refer to Christ, as is shown for example by the symbolic meaning of Jewish ceremonies, Aaron's bells and pomegranates, and the burning, unburnt bush. In short, the history of our language as represented by the *Oxford English Dictionary* shows that this half a millennium people have been using "type" and "figure" and "shadow" without restricting themselves to so-called strict usage. I think that this incontrovertible evidence, which might be greatly amplified, shows that two or three words have been used to characterize a number of kinds of symbolism.

The problem, or rather the reward, of moving from these shadowy types to truth entails making an opportunity, a resource, out of the presumed problem. Understanding the distinctions among kinds of spiritual reading can enable us to distinguish more finely among various figurative procedures in literature. It is quite evident that we *must* make various distinctions when words are used differently. Or rather, careful attention to usage can prepare us to make distinctions too easily overlooked among a wide variety of symbolic procedures. Any kind of literary study capable of sustaining such a claim need make no apology. Of course it must also be recognized that, as with so much else in literature, these distinctions are descriptive and become evaluative only in company with other considerations. Yet we shall have little chance of understanding either significance or value until we know descriptively what kind of signification is employed.

We need to bear in mind as well certain discriminations of a more historical character. Ziolkowski's chapter and the four or five preceding it present an implicit argument. At times, indeed, it is openly said that in some period after about 1700 literary versions of typological and other figural procedures often lost their religious bases. This conclusion may well seem so obvious as hardly to require elaboration. As so often, however, the convincing, detailed elucidation of the obvious enables us to approach a number of problems too easily passed by. For one thing, we must account for the existence of wholly orthodox typological practice by divines and poets in the nineteenth century, even after many earlier writers had "abstracted" typology of its religious character. Let us take a Victorian example not quoted by Landow, Cardinal Newman's "Praise to the Holiest in the height."

> O loving wisdom of our God!
> When all was sin and shame,
> A second Adam to the fight
> And to the rescue came.[2]

From this most basic of typologies we can make a major distinction in literary uses of typology on the basis of religious belief. Newman's belief in the two Adams and their typological connection distinguishes him from not a few writers before him and from most thereafter. Much depends on whether the writer is a believing Christian. Yet this basic distinction must be modified. Writers could continue to use variously conceived types and even typology after losing all or most of their religious faith if they could assume that a sufficient number of readers would at least understand them, regardless of the nature of those readers' own belief. Alternatively, believing Christians from at least Elizabeth I onward could use the method of typology without the full Christian reality by employing comparison and various forms of substitution. Dickinson's struck rock seems to offer yet another alternative: the non-typological use of a familiar type. We recall Hollander's worrying of this problem in medieval literature.

Discrimination is obviously necessary when such varied

---

[2] The second stanza. See also Newman's more successful, and more complex, poem, "The Call of David."

possibilities exist. It also requires differing kinds of evidence as well as effective methods of literary interpretation. More specifically, the preceding chapters show that typological usage varies on a historical scale, something as true of those ages of faith that we may arbitrarily conclude with the seventeenth century as of the ages of doubt and disbelief. There was no need during those earlier ages for the central features of religious belief and experience to be expressed in the same way. What a medieval poet might convey in terms of an untypological *imitatio Christi* might be conveyed by a Donne through retrospective typology in poems celebrating the symbolic virtue of certain of his contemporaries. The student of medieval literature should find it helpful to know about a later practice with its much more explicit historicity, just as the student of seventeenth-century poetry should be assisted by the understanding that christocentric thought need not require typology.

Karlfried Froehlich shows that the hermeneutic bases of typology deeply divided pre-Reformation theologians. All the more, anyone seeking in literature for a single typological entity has a mind that would insist that all flowers be roses. Such blinkering would seriously impoverish the rich variety of religious and literary experience that more variable conceptions allowed. And yet the evident fact of variability requires of typologically minded students of literature a greater rather than a lesser rigor. If not certain rules of evidence, then certain cautions are essential. As this book shows, the student must always keep in mind what "typology" means—for if "type" and "figure" mean many things, "typology" and "antitype" are not so wide. This is no less true—it is particularly true—when we deal with some of the headier kinds of seventeenth-century usage. In fact we must bear in mind that even consistent and heavy use of biblical materials and allusions—even when those involve figures often used as types—do not necessarily entail typology. Surprising though it may be for its subject, Abraham Cowley's aborted epic, *Davideis*, is not typological. Even when he traces in forecast the lineage from David to Jesus, he impressively avoids figuralism.

Cowley's practice illuminates other matters of importance. His non-typological treatment of David is all the less likely because his royalism made figural treatment of the king, David, and God altogether to be expected. In this, as in other literary matters, it is essential that we recognize that what is altogether likely or even natural is not necessary. Indeed, we might almost say that the *Davideis* ought to have been typological, because Cowley was writing at a time when typological writing had become especially fashionable, even in secular application. There is evidence in Butler's anger in *Hudibras*, in dates of publications, and in various writings of the time to show that the middle of the seventeenth century was uncommonly given to typology and other forms of "spiritual" apprehension. Such evidence entitles us to the presumption that a poem of that period entitled *Davideis*, or indeed by some other name, will use typology. In each instance, however, the burden of proof of the presumption is upon the interpreter, for it cannot be a proper axiom of historical scholarship that what is very likely to be actually is.

"The Troubles of David" was Cowley's subtitle for *Davideis*. That became the subject of Dryden's *Absalom and Achitophel*, an allegory for recent English history. Dryden of course took his story or parallel from 2 Samuel, but the *action* of the poem—the rise and quelling of a rebellion —is surprisingly difficult to gloss in typological detail. His yet more typological poem, *The Hind and the Panther*, is even less typological (and more tropological) in its meager action. And his first religious apologia, *Religio Laici*, is almost wholly devoid both of action and typology, although it begins with some figural details. Similarly, in spite of the fact that *Paradise Regained* uses typology as the basis of its major action, as Barbara K. Lewalski has shown so well, *Paradise Lost* is surprisingly free of typology in its main event. The *narrative* act of the fall of Adam does not in itself foreshadow the second Adam, Christ. That typology had been conveyed early in the poem but is not enacted in the actual narrative of those events—the losing of paradise—that Christians believed would require the second Adam to repair the ruin of the first. Of course some of the characters in *Absalom and Achitophel* are so rooted in typology and tropology that we fail to understand what Dryden is about if we miss such things, just as many of Milton's descriptions depend on typology for their true force. Both poets clearly have a typological habit of mind that deeply affects the intellectual character of their work. Still, we must understand that the habit could be given up for *Samson Agonistes* or *Religio Laici,* and that usage of general biblical as well as of specifically typological details varies sufficiently to require our making numerous kinds of distinctions.

Examples of other kinds of necessary discrimination are not difficult to find. Among medieval lyrics there is a number of poems with the refrain, *Quia amore langueo* (AV: "For I am sick of love") taken from the Song of Songs (e.g., 2: 5). It is not necessary that the declaration be thought that of Christ for his church, and, if it is so meant, there still remains the question whether that be taken as the "literal" allegorical meaning or whether it uses the type of Jehovah's love for Israel or of Solomon's love for a woman to shadow forth Christ's love for his church or the individual soul. In instances such as this, prior presumptions determine what is discovered.

There is also the interesting question of typology and generic practice. It should be clear that we may expect variation in a given period, but it also seems evident that we must be alert to differences in the practice within various genres, not only in a certain period but in the canon of an individual writer. We may recall Barbara Lewalski's distinctions in Donne's practice, which involve the particularly arresting fact that typology is all but absent from his devotional poems but present to a marked and radical degree in his panegyrics. Shakespeare uses typology most centrally in *The Merchant of Venice* to show, in the relation between Shylock and the action of the play centering on Portia, that the Old Law is fulfilled by the New.[3] Yet Shakespeare avoids typology in his non-dramatic literature. On the other hand, Dryden avoids typology in his plays and uses it in his non-dramatic poems, particularly in panegyrics and narratives. Much the same distinction may be made for Milton, at least in respect to his three greatest works. It very much seems that future study of the literary uses of typology will need to consider generic theory and literary history if the deeper significances of use are to be plumbed. Indeed, the result of such study should also tell us something about generic matters and literary history.

This volume seems to me to suggest certain additional propositions that have been skirted but not sufficiently emphasized in this Afterword. It cannot be stressed enough that differences exist among genres, writers, generations, and periods, although of course similarities also exist. The modernist is likely to err by underestimating the importance of typology for literature. The student of medieval or Renaissance literature is likely to err, not by expecting too much or too little, but by expecting that typological usages with which he or she is familiar define the uses that characterize other periods.

It also seems true, on the other hand, that a large distinction can be made between matters typological in the older literature and those in the modern. With whatever slow and complex development, the modern requires study in terms of a varied pattern of increasing "abstracting" of typology. That is, "strict" typological usage may continue to this day, but the course of development generally has been one of increasing dehistoricizing and desanctifying of typology into a form of comparison that is a secular ghost. No doubt it is the ghost of typology, but it is no more than a sometimes lively and mocking, if hollow, form of what once had been religious vitality. In earlier periods, the

[3] See Barbara K. Lewalski, "Biblical Allusion and Allegory in *The Merchant of Venice*," *Shakespeare Quarterly*, 12 (Summer, 1962), 327–343.

problem lies rather with the protean kinds of "spiritual" readings. These include the hermeneutic problem itself and the sisters of typology: allegory, symbol, tropology, prophecy, and eschatology. As Bultmann says, some of these may combine in given passages of the New Testament, and we have observed similar things in *Absalom and Achitophel*. In such instances, we must be aware of the multiplicity and seek to discriminate constituent parts that sometimes seem fused or open to quite different discriminations, as with *Quia amore langueo*.

It is quite clear, I think, that fruitful discrimination is possible among differing concepts and handling of types. As a last question to consider, I shall ask if it is not also possible to give a general characterization of the differing roles of typology in the thought and therefore the writing of several centuries? With attention to the chapters of this book and to other evidence, I believe the answer to be positive, but only if we assume that, like other gross characterizations, mine assumes numerous exceptions.

The strictest constructionist could not quarrel with a typological reading of the Jerusalem of the Jews as a type of the Christian heavenly Jerusalem, since that is sanctioned by the New Testament itself. Let us suppose that we have a story involving the Christian pilgrimage to Jerusalem over arduous ways and in dangers requiring that we put on the whole armor of God (Ephesians 6: 11, 13). The pilgrim discovers on the way a high hill, of which a Bishop Alcock might say: "This mount is in figure and syngnefyeth religion." After much effort, the pilgrim may descry Jerusalem, having arrived in Canaan, "a tipe of heaven," as Samuel Hieron put it. And if the writer of this story has chosen to comment on it, we may find at its end a charge like that by Henryson:

> Suppose this be ane Fabill,
> And overheillt with typis figurall.

We observe that "the whole armor of God" is perfectly scriptural without being in itself typological. We might wish to term it simply scriptural allusion, although of course it will appear on many occasions with types of various kinds. In the same example, the representation of a mount as religion emphasizes the didactic function of symbolism in what should be termed tropology or parable. The reader is being asked to adapt the fictional as it is informed by scriptural allusion to conduct of life. Such stories have something of the exemplum about them, and they need not be fictional in Thomas P. Roche's sense at all. David's friendship with Jonathan, his patience with Saul, his courage against Goliath, and his adultery with Bathsheba not only can be used, but often have been, as types and figures (in the senses of Henryson or Alcock) without necessarily being typological. Without typology, or along with it, they function parabolically or to give a moral. They are tropological, giving the *quid agas* application of Scripture discussed by Barbara K. Lewalski in her chapter. To declare as Hieron did that "The people of Israel were a tipe of Gods people: Canaan a tipe of heaven" is also to set forth a type. By comparison with the other examples just given, we can say with only seeming redundancy that *this* Canaan is a *typological* type. Unlike the instance from tropology, Hieron's examples use something in the Old Testament to foreshadow an antitype in the New Testament or in Christian hopes. In addition, the type and the antitype are alike taken to be real, historical, and their connection also entails history in God's providential plan linking two dispensations, two covenants. Fables are not real in their types, nor are they real things incorporated in a fiction, as is Tasso's Jerusalem. Fables do use fictions to symbolize a higher truth, but that truth may be abstract and the connection lacks historical direction. Similarly, in moral allegory or tropology directed to the reader, the historical connectedness and fulfillment are not present.

In these distinctions we may have a basis for gross discrimination between uses of types by the Middle Ages and by writers after the Reformation. It will be obvious to anyone that the Middle Ages knew, used, and appreciated typology, as so much of its art reveals, or as does Chaucer's statement that Isaac was a figure of Christ's death. We must also understand that parabolic and tropological thought well survived the Reformation. Paul J. Korshin has suggested the rise of popularity in the always popular Aesop during the seventeenth century and has related that phenomenon to others in the eighteenth century. (Tropology was becoming "abstracted" along with typology.) But the clearest example of traditional ideas about tropology, or moral allegory, known to me from post-Reformation sources is given by Dryden in "The Morall" affixed to *The Cock and the Fox* (1700), his translation or adaptation of The Nun's Priest's Tale. Dryden writes in part:

> The Truth is moral, though the Tale a Lie.
> Who spake in Parables, I dare not say;
> But sure, he knew it was a pleasing way,
> Sound sense, by plain Example, to convey.
> And in a Heathen Author we may find,
> That Pleasure with Instruction should be join'd:
> So take the Corn, and leave the Chaff behind.
>
> (815-21)

Here is the standard reference to Christ's parables, here the corn-chaff (or kernel-husk, nut-shell) distinction, and here also a reference to Horace as a grace-note. Centuries of readers would have recognized at once what Dryden was saying.

Yet when all allowances for multiplicity and continuance have been made, there seems to be a major shift in emphasis. It does seem likely that although writers before the Reformation thoroughly understood both typology and tropology, they believed that tropology—moral allegory—should play a more central role in their writings. Or, to put it differently, although post-Reformation writers were also thoroughly acquainted with tropology, to them typology was more important. Of course there could be many exceptions, the two could work perfectly well together, and in any given decade words such as "type," "figure," or "shadow" could be used for both procedures.

If this gross characterization holds, it must be susceptible to explanation. The change in balance seems to me to involve the crucial Protestant concern with hermeneutics, with the active attempt by all the faithful—lay as well as clerical—to interpret the Bible. As soon as exegesis of the Old Testament becomes an issue necessary to daily reading of Scripture, typology becomes of far greater importance than tropology. Of course Catholics as well as Protestants were exegetes, but by elevating Scripture to the Rule of Faith and by deposing Church tradition as its handmaiden, Protestants inevitably became a hermeneutically minded group. We must also follow Barbara K. Lewalski, I believe, in thinking that Protestant insistence on the "literal" sense made tropology (the third, or moral, of the fourfold senses) particularly suspect because particularly unnecessary to present verbal meaning. The moral sense of Scripture is precisely the least necessary to interpreting the Old Testament in a "literal" fashion. At best, tropology was an accessory, a derivative, of faith manifested in typology, among other things.

The Protestants did something else: they stumbled into discovery of a more modern idea of history. To them Christendom was not simply timeless, nor was it some kind of temporally vague contrast between the miserable now and blissful then which required an attitude of contempt for the world. The whole point of the Reformation was a historical one. Over the centuries the church had grown corrupt and needed reformation. To that end, Christianity had to return —at the peril of yielding to babylonish whoredoms—to the ages of primitive faith, to a *prisca veritas*. Paradox that it is, this return to an older purity implied a contrary temporal emphasis, the possibility for true improvement in time. The ideas of progress and historical change open to mankind were such unexpected children of the Reformation. It is no accident that within a century of Henry VIII's decisive act England was swept by a millenarian movement. The Roman antichrist had falsified God's providential plan, and hopes for "a more thorough, godly Reformation" implied expectations of Christ's return to his newly perfected but suffering English Church. Only on such grounds can we explain why hard-headed men like Oliver Cromwell should have wished to bring the long since banished Jews back to England: as the penultimate scene in history. Such strange, and to us unhistorical, presumptions led to something of even greater historical moment. The militant Protestants discovered that their age, the 1640's, was as real a historical period as the ages of Moses leading Israel from bondage, of Xenophon leading his retreat, or of Julius Caesar crossing the Rubicon. The excitement of a Milton in writing of such things testifies to a revolution in thought quite apart from that of a second reformation. With that revolutionary idea went an earlier one conceived of by the Marian exiles and reconceived by the Interregnum and by New England: a convenanted nation had its own special history under divine Providence. So important to historical presumptions was this experience that shortly afterward Dryden conceived both of the possibility of human progress and of a literary age. A few people before him had believed in the possibility of progress, but none to my knowledge had set forth what is one of our fundamental historical conceptions, a literary age or period.

Typology necessarily played a more important role than tropology to people thinking such things. Is typology not unique among symbolic systems in having a triple historical presumption: in the type, in the antitype, and in their connection? Protestants invented neither typology nor history, but they made the one more prominent and gave fresh definition to the other. In that effort to go backward to primitive truth and a primitive Bible, they ended by moving forward onto a modern stage. Like all who have much to boast of, they were often unaware of what they ought to repent of. For the historicizing emphasis on which they seized with such triumph led to important shifts in uses of types (again allowing for many exceptions) during the eighteenth century and after.

Such changes manifested the rise of a historicism. This slow alteration in our thought underlay the basic, gross shift in use of typology from traditional to recent uses. Although that shift is presently our major concern, something of the slowness also deserves stress. Long after the process of "abstracting" discussed by Paul J. Korshin had begun, a commentary on the Psalms was produced by George Horne (1730–92), Bishop of Norwich. Within four years of the appearance of Wordsworth and Coleridge's *Lyrical Ballads*, Horne's two-volume work appeared in its seventh edition. The title page of that 1802 edition reads in part as follows.

> A Commentary on the Book of Psalms. In which their literal or Historical Sense, as they relate to King David, and the People of Israel, is illustrated; And their Application to Messiah, to the Church, and to Individuals, as Members thereof, is Pointed Out: With a view to render the Psalter Pleasing and Profitable to all Orders and Degrees of Christians.

After reading that, we are not surprised to discover (1: liv) that the Psalms are historical or literal for Israel:

> But we are taught, by the writers of the New Testament, to consider this part of their [the Israelites'] history as one continued figure, or allegory. We are told, that there is another spiritual Israel of God; other children of Abraham, and heirs of promise; another circumcision; another Egypt, from the bondage of which we are redeemed; . . . another rock to supply them with living water; . . . another land of Canaan, and another Jerusalem, which they are to obtain, and to possess for ever. In the same light are to be viewed the various provocations and punishments, captivities and restorations of old Israel afterwards, concerning which it is likewise true, that they "happened unto them for ensamples," types, or figures, "and were written for our admonition" (1 Corinthians 10: 11).

Perfectly orthodox conceptions of typology of this kind were accessible to believers like Wordsworth and Coleridge as well as to freethinkers such as Shelley and Byron. In fact the same ideas about the Psalms have lasted on in numerous Bibles and liturgies printed in our century. This conservative undertow accompanied the rising tide of historicism.

The rise of historical consciousness was not sudden enough for a fully articulated historicism to appear before the nineteenth century. But earlier there had been significant signs of changing thought in the relativism on which Deism was founded. It seems no accident that late in Dryden's life Deism emerges as a named phenomenon, or that at about the same time England gained its first historically minded classical scholar worth serious consideration, Richard Bentley. Such events represent many others then occurring, although they do not seem as finally decisive as that which Theodore Ziolkowski represents in the person of David Friedrich Strauss. Yet the earlier events were steps on the same way. Emory Elliott shows throughout his chapter that momentous changes in what history seemed to mean could be contained, as it were, as long as a system like that of typological thought was flexible enough to interpret the changes with religious meaning. But in other countries as well as in America the time would come when for many people typology seemed less and less to contain—that is, fully to interpret—the changes people saw about them. Such alterations do not occur overnight, and even long afterward ways of thought may bear resemblance to older ways that no longer excite belief. It does seem quite clear that people were losing belief in the reality or historical character of type and antitype; or, what was still more deflating, that many believers came to grant so great a historicity to the type and the antitype that the historical *connection* that is the essence of typology was no longer credible. Some people whose ideas had changed in such fashion nonetheless found great interest in the symbolic system itself, even if an identifying connection between David and Jesus held no serious import for them.

It seems that developments in the use of types from the eighteenth century forward allowed for writers who continued to believe in and use for literature various kinds of type and typology. But we have also identified two other groups whose numbers were to grow at the expense of the adherents to the old ideas. There were those with so strong a historical conception of David and Jesus in modern terms that typology of the usual old kinds held little interest or credibility. And there were others to whom typology offered a kind of symbolic thought without any necessary Christian presumptions. To such writers, the types and figures were not truly typological in possessing the triple historical presumption spoken of earlier, but were rather symbols to be used after the *manner* of typology, as indeed many have been for centuries. From Lowance's chapter to Keller's in American literature and from Korshin's to Ziolkowski's in European, we see the emergence of these alternatives to dominance. As Ziolkowski remarks, by our time the result has become "parody, which occurs at the moment when form becomes absolute and the original meaning disappears . . . reduced simply to another plot that lends parodistic shape to the novel."

The question may arise why such writers bother at all. Not to rule out human curiosity, we may recall the lesson that T. S. Eliot read from Joyce's *Ulysses*. The seeming absence of significance in modern experience requires what he termed a myth, a valued coherence that might be taken from the classical past or some similarly valued source. Not all parody is as serious as Joyce's and, as *Ulysses* shows, not all parody relates to typology. Christian typology has continued to matter in various strange forms, however, precisely because it had been developed into one of the fullest, most comprehensive and supple symbolic systems devised by the human mind in its encounter with experience in time. Such a system could only seem inviting to writers in search of meaning, even if their versions lacked religious purpose or if they worked to parodic ends. Of course it must be added that typology continues to have validity to biblical interpreters and to other believers. But as the number of believers has dwindled, the number of the adapters has grown.

If this gross historical characterization has any use, it does not spare us the necessity of discriminating what we discover in various literary or other examples. We must as it were account for Landow between Korshin and Ziolkowski, or for Chaucer being typological and Dryden tropological when they choose. Like the multiple senses assignable to "type" and "figure," my rather too single gross characterization is simply a way of leading us to discriminated understanding. Typology and her sisters belong to a large family whose members often seem to step forth as identical twins or to bear the same name but have different identities. Some danger may yet remain that she and her sisters will go unnoticed by too many students of literature. After all, there has been a great decline in knowledge of the Bible and of Christian tradition. The peril in a volume such as ours is more likely to be the opposite one of substituting those sisters for that other set, the Muses. I believe that those preceding me in this book have escaped the danger with considerable grace.

One last danger may be emphasized. It would be a mistake comparable to those sometimes made by students of irony, philosophy, politics, and much else in literature to assume that the mere use of typology or of types in other senses determines high literary quality. John Milton is a great poet who uses typology in ways necessary to his poems, but those poems are not great simply because they incorporate typology. In all these matters, the enduring caveat must be some version of "Reader, beware." If that warning is attended to, we have much to discover, as these chapters show singly and together. And once we have entered all due caveats and have made the necessary distinctions, knowledge of typology and her sisters can greatly enhance our understanding. Knowledge of them and their ways is often required for full understanding of much of the greatest literature of the Christian world.

# INDEX

Names are included, as are usually works when quoted from. The Bible, its books, and its personages are to be assumed present *passim*. The table of contents sets forth the range of subjects. The authors of individual chapters are not entered here when they appear in the notes to their chapters. The copiousness of the notes serves bibliographical ends, adding to the general (by no means solely American) bibliography compiled by Sacvan Bercovitch for his collection, *Typology and Early American Literature* (Amherst, 1972).

Hughes, John, 135
Hull, R.F.C., 356
Hunt, Holman, 316–18, 318, 329, 330
Hunter, J. Paul, 118
Hunton, Samuel, 127
Hus, Johannes, 38, 43
Hutchinson, F. E., 90

Isidore of Sevile, 33
Izumi Shikibu, "Worldly thoughts alone," 372

Jackson, Arthur, 125
James II, 155, 156
Jauss, H. R., 12
Jedrey, Christopher, 269
Jens, Walter, 358
Jerome, St., 30, 348
Joachim da Fiore, 353
John of Burgundy, 28
John of Patmos, 108
Johnson, Edward, 206
Johnson, Samuel, 149, 152, 175, 199; Rambler no. 44, 203
Johnson, Samuel (of Great Torrington), 168
Johnson, Thomas H., 267
Jonson, Ben, 120
Jordan, Richard, 79–80, 99
Joyce, James, 357, 358, 361, 365, 366, 367, 393
Jung, Carl Gustav, 356, 364
Junius, Franciscus, 107
Jurieu, Pierre, 185–86

Kafka, Franz, 299, 356
Kallich, Martin, 149
Kantorowicz, Ernst H., 171
Kaske, Carol V., 18
Kaufman, U. Milo, 81, 118
Kazantzakis, Nikos, 359
Keach, Benjamin, 158, 185-86
Keble, John, 332–34, 335; "Easter Eve," 333–34; "Sixth Sunday after Trinity," 332
Keller, Karl, 393
Kerényi, Karl, 354
Keynes, Geoffrey, 193
King, Edward, 103
King, Henry, 132

Kinsley, James, 115
Kircher, Athanasius, 155
Klopp, Charles, 71
Klopstock, Friedrich Gottlieb, 200
Knox, Ronald A., 145
Koestler, Arthur, 359
Kolve, V. A., 73
Korshin, Paul J., 115, 388, 391, 393, 394
Krailsheimer, A. J., 50
Krouse, F. Michael, 103
Kyrle, Robert, 142, 143

La Bruyère, Jean de, 161
Lamont, William, 117
Lampe, G.W.H., 233
Landow, George P., 308, 374–75, 379, 381
Langland, William, 9
Langton, Stephen, 25
Legouis, Pierre, 115, 148, 149
Leigh, William, 127
Lerman, Rhoda, 364, 365
L'Estrange, Sir Roger, 176-79
Levin, Harry, 367
Levine, J. A., 141
Lewalski, Barbara Kiefer, 74, 115, 118, 125, 233, 340, 383–84, 385, 387, 389
Lewis, C. S., 12
Lewis, R.W.B., 237
Litz, A. Walton, 367
Locke, John, 128, 132, 268–69
Lord, George deF., 135
Lowance, Mason I., Jr., 150, 206, 289–90, 393
Lowe-Porter, H. T., 352
Lowman, Moses, 185, 186, 268–69
Lowth, Robert, 179, 199–200
Lubac, Henri de, 54–55
Lucan, Pharsalia, 16–18
Luther, Martin, 26–27, 42, 79, 97, 108, 109–10, 348

MacCallum, H. R., 81
Mack, Maynard, 152
Madsen, William, 79–80, 103, 115
Malamud, Bernard, 358, 360
Manheim, Ralph, 346
Manley, Frank, 88, 115
Mann, Thomas, 352, 354, 361

This book has been composed and printed by
Princeton University Press

Designed by Daniel Kunkel
Edited by Marjorie C. Sherwood

Typography: Baskerville
Paper: Warrens Olde Style
Binding by Maple Press

LIBRARY OF CONGRESS CATALOGING IN PUBLICATION DATA

Main entry under title:

Literary uses of typology.

Based on papers presented at a seminar sponsored by the Dept.
of English, Princeton University in April 1974.
1. Symbolism in literature—Congresses.
2. Typology (Theology)—Congresses. I. Miner, Earl Roy.
II. Princeton University. Dept. of English.
PN56.S9L5      809'.915      76-45904
ISBN 0-691-06327-3